MUIRHEAD LIBRARY OF PHILOSOPHY

An admirable statement of the aims of the Library of Philosophy was provided by the first editor, the late Professor J. H. Muirhead, in his description of the original programme printed in Erdmann's *History of Philosophy* under the date 1890. This was slightly modified in subsequent volumes to take the form of the following statement:

'The Muirhead Library of Philosophy was designed as a contribution to the History of Modern Philosophy under the heads: first of different Schools of Thought—Sensationalist, Realist, Idealist, Intuitivist; secondly of different Subjects—Psychology, Ethics, Aesthetics, Political Philosophy, Theology. While much had been done in England in tracing the course of evolution in nature, history, economics, morals and religion, little had been done in tracing the development of thought on these subjects. Yet "the evolution of opinion is part of the whole evolution".

'By the co-operation of different writers in carrying out this plan it was hoped that a thoroughness and completeness of treatment, otherwise unattainable, might be secured. It was believed also that from writers mainly British and American fuller consideration of English Philosophy than it had hitherto received might be looked for. In the earlier series of books containing, among other, Bosanquet's *History of Aesthetic*, Pfleiderer's *Rational Theology since Kant*, Albee's *History of English Utilitarianism*, Bonar's *Philosophy and Political Economy*, Brett's *History of Psychology*, Ritchie's *Natural Rights*, these objects were to a large extent effected.

'In the meantime original work of a high order was being produced both in England and America by such writers as Bradley, Stout, Bertrand Russell, Baldwin, Urban, Montague, and others, and a new interest in foreign works, German, French and Italian, which had either become classical or were attracting public attention, had developed. The scope of the Library thus became extended into something more international, and it is entering on the fifth decade of its existence in the hope that it may contribute to that mutual understanding between countries which is so pressing a need of the present time.'

The need which Professor Muirhead stressed is no less pressing today, and few will deny that philosophy has much to do with enabling us to meet it, although no one, least of all Muirhead himself, would regard that as the sole, or even the main, object of philosophy. As Professor Muirhead continues to lend the distinction of his name to the Library of Philosophy it seemed not inappropriate to allow him to recall us to these aims in his own words. The emphasis on the history of thought also seemed to me very timely; and the number of important works promised for the Library in the near future augur well for the continued fulfilment, in this and other ways, of the expectations of the original editor.

H. D. LEWIS

MUIRHEAD LIBRARY OF PHILOSOPHY

General Editor: H. D. Lewis

Professor of History and Philosophy of Religion in the University of London

Moral Sense. By JAMES BONAR.

Natural Rights. By D. G. RITCHIE. 3rd Edition. 5th Impression.

Nature, Mind and Modern Science. By E. HARRIS.

The Nature of Thought. By BRAND BLANSHARD. 2nd Impression.

On Selfhood and Godhood. By C. A. CAMPBELL.

Our Experience of God. By H. D. LEWIS.

Personality and Reality. By E. J. TURNER.

The Phenomenology of Mind. By G. W. F. HEGEL. Translated by SIR JAMES BAILLIE. Revised 2nd Edition. 3rd Impression.

Philosophical Papers. By G. E. MOORE.

Philosophy and Political Economy. By J. BONAR. 4th Impression.

Philosophy of Whitehead. By W. MAYS.

The Platonic Tradition in Anglo-Saxon Philosophy. By J. H. MUIRHEAD.

The Principal Upamsads. By RADHAKRISHNAN.

The Problems of Perception. By R. J. HIRST.

Reason and Goodness. By BRAND BLANSHARD.

Some Main Problems of Philosophy. By G. E. MOORE.

The Theological Frontier of Ethics. By W. G. MACLAGAN.

Time and Free Will. By HENRI BERGSON. Translated by F. G. POGSON. 6th Impression.

The Ways of Knowing: or The Methods of Philosophy. By W. P. MONTAGUE. 4th Impression.

The Muirhead Library of Philosophy

EDITED BY H. D. LEWIS

THE RELEVANCE OF WHITEHEAD

THE RELEVANCE OF WHITEHEAD

Philosophical Essays in Commemoration of the
Centenary of the Birth of Alfred North Whitehead

EDITED BY

IVOR LECLERC

x

LONDON: GEORGE ALLEN & UNWIN LTD
NEW YORK: THE MACMILLAN COMPANY

PRINTED IN GREAT BRITAIN
in 11 *on* 12 *point Imprint type*
BY UNWIN BROTHERS LIMITED
WOKING AND LONDON

EDITORIAL FOREWORD

ALFRED NORTH WHITEHEAD was born in Ramsgate, Kent, on February 15, 1861, and died in Cambridge, Mass., on December 30, 1947. In his long life he had two professional careers. First, and for the longer period, he was a scientist—a mathematician and physicist. Then, on the eve of his retirement as professor of applied mathematics in the University of London, at the age of 63, he commenced his second career, as professor of philosophy in Harvard University.

His writings on philosophy, more particularly on some philosophical aspects of science, began to appear when he was already in his middle fifties. It is a common, but erroneous, belief that Whitehead became interested in philosophical problems only late in life. In fact, his active interest in philosophy dates back to his undergraduate days in Cambridge.[1] In his writing prior to the explicitly philosophical papers, that is to say, prior to 1916, there is definite evidence of profound philosophical reflection. We find this in comments scattered throughout his more technical mathematical works, basic to which in any case was a preoccupation with the philosophy of mathematics, which culminated in *Principia Mathematica*. A wider philosophical interest is clear in the 1906 paper "On Mathematical Concepts of the Material World". Further, the earlier papers and addresses on educational topics are no disconnected and *ad hoc* reflections on educational matters. It can now be recognized that Whitehead's views on education, even at that time, had as their basis the organic philosophy which he was to work out in detail in his later period.

That the relatively late appearance of Whitehead's philosophical writing has tended to obscure his life-long preoccupation with philosophical problems, is not as such of much consequence. But it has fostered the belief, still widespread, that Whitehead's acquaintance with and understanding of philosophy was comparatively slight and superficial. On the basis of this assumption it has become easy to ignore or even to dismiss Whitehead's philosophical thought as that of a gifted amateur, who, moreover, wrote in a difficult style, apparently overburdened with neologisms. The

[1] Cf. "Autobiographical Notes" in *The Philosophy of Alfred North Whitehead*, Library of Living Philosophers, Vol. 3, edited by P. A. Schilpp, Northwestern University, 1941, p. 7.

effort required to labour through his works has frequently been felt to be incommensurate with the philosophical profit to be derived from them.

This attitude towards Whitehead's work has been the more readily accepted because his thought is at such variance with the dominant trends of the present day. It is Whitehead's view, determining his entire approach, "that the movement of historical, and philosophical, criticism of detached questions, which on the whole has dominated the last two centuries, has done its work, and requires to be supplemented by a more sustained effort of constructive thought".[2] At a time when, especially in the English-speaking countries, the emphasis on the analysis of detached questions has tended rather to be intensified, this has, not surprisingly, been unpopular.

With great philosophical perspicacity Whitehead realized that we are living at the end of the epoch of "the cosmology of the seventeenth century, whose chief authors were Galileo, Descartes, Newton, Locke".[3] He saw that developments in our time, especially in science, but not only in science, had ushered in a new epoch of thought. It was clear to Whitehead, who had a profound sense for the history of ideas, that advance in thought is no longer possible within the framework of the seventeenth-century cosmology, and that the fundamental need of our time is a reorganization of basic cosmological schemes of ideas.

Thought in science nowadays—physical, biological, sociological, and psychological—still proceeds largely within the framework of the old materialist-mechanist presuppositions, though with an admixture of new fundamental conceptions, for the most part only dimly and very partially recognized. Whitehead held that the primary task of philosophy in the immediate future must be concerned with the ultimate notions, with cosmological schemes. It is the particular function of philosophy to make explicit the schemes of ideas (established and newly emergent) which guide thought in the various specialist inquiries and in the various fields of applied sociology. This is the more urgent today as these are playing a crucial part in the reshaping of the present rapidly changing structure of human communities, institutional and organizational, political and economic, moral, social, and religious. If mankind is not to flounder helplessly under the pressure of increasingly urgent

[2] PR ix–x.   [3] PR ix.

problems, in immanent peril of the total disruption and break-down of civilization, the ultimate determining notions have to be brought to the surface for criticism and adjustment, and some kind of coherence and consistency effected.

Whitehead held that "the true method of philosophical construction is to frame a scheme of ideas, the best that one can, and unflinchingly to explore the interpretation of experience in terms of that scheme".[4] His entire philosophical endeavour was devoted to that end. The outcome has been a philosophy which, in the view of many, will take its permanent place among the great philosophical systems of the history of thought.

The comprehension and appreciation of Whitehead's work has been relatively slow; but gradually, throughout the last three decades, understanding of it has spread and deepened. No definite school has developed, however. Rather, Whitehead's philosophy has influenced the thought of an increasing number of scholars. This, I think, is as he would himself have preferred it.

It is fitting to the occasion of this centenary, and in accord with Whitehead's own forward-looking spirit, that the collection of essays here presented should exemplify the continuing influence and significance of Whitehead's thought. This volume is not devoted to an assessment of the present state of Whitehead scholarship; it does not attempt to be of the same kind as the Whitehead volume in the "Library of Living Philosophers". Nor must it be taken to be fully representative of the extent and nature of Whitehead's influence in present-day thought. For obvious reasons it would not have been possible to include all those philosophers in many different countries who have come under the influence of Whitehead's thought, nor indeed even all Whitehead scholars. Moreover, in practice it had to be a choice between a large number of short statements—which might have provided a more representative coverage—and a limited number of longer contributions. The latter alternative was given preference, in the hope that the result might freely reflect the relevance of Whitehead to the present philosophical scene.

Contributors were given a free hand in their choice of subject-matter and approach. It was left entirely to the individual writers to exemplify the relevance of Whitehead to their own thought and to the topic chosen by each.

4 PR x.

The fourteen contributions of this volume are prefaced by one essay of a different kind, one specifically devoted to a consideration of Whitehead and contemporary philosophy. The editor thought it appropriate that this paper be written by someone who had been in close personal contact with Whitehead.

IVOR LECLERC

ABBREVIATIONS

The following abbreviations of titles of the works of A. N. Whitehead have been used in footnote references:

AE   *The Aims of Education and Other Essays.* Williams and Norgate, 1929. The Macmillan Company, 1929.

AI   *Adventures of Ideas.* Cambridge University Press, 1933. The Macmillan Company, 1933.

CN   *The Concept of Nature.* Cambridge University Press, 1920.

FR   *The Function of Reason.* Princeton University Press, 1929.

Imm   "Immortality", in P. A. Schilpp (Ed.), *The Philosophy of Alfred North Whitehead*, Northwestern University, 1941.

MC   "On Mathematical Concepts of the Material World", in *A. N. Whitehead: An Anthology*, Ed. F. S. C. Northrop and Mason W. Gross. The Macmillan Company, 1953.

MG   "Mathematics and the Good", in P. A. Schilpp (Ed.), *The Philosophy of Alfred North Whitehead.* Northwestern University, 1941.

MT   *Modes of Thought.* The Macmillan Company, 1938. Cambridge University Press, 1938.

PM   *Principia Mathematica* (with Bertrand Russell). 3 Vols. Cambridge University Press, 1910–13, 2nd. ed. 1925–7.

PNK   *An Enquiry Concerning the Principles of Natural Knowledge.* Cambridge University Press, 1919, 2nd ed. 1925.

PR   *Process and Reality.* Cambridge University Press, 1929. The Macmillan Company, 1929; page references to this edition in square brackets.

PRel *The Principle of Relativity.* Cambridge University Press, 1922.

RM   *Religion in the Making.* Cambridge University Press, 1926. The Macmillan Company, 1926; page references to this edition in square brackets.

Symb *Symbolism, Its Meaning and Effect.* Cambridge University Press, 1928. The Macmillan Company, 1927; page references to this edition in square brackets.

SMW   *Science and the Modern World.* Cambridge University Press, 1926. The Macmillan Company, 1925; page references to this edition in square brackets.

CONTENTS

WHITEHEAD AND
CONTEMPORARY PHILOSOPHY

BY CHARLES HARTSHORNE

WHITEHEAD AND
CONTEMPORARY PHILOSOPHY

BY CHARLES HARTSHORNE

I

I begin with a somewhat personal statement.

There are two ways in which we may come to look favourably upon the views of a living philosopher. One way is to be exposed, at a tender age or state of development, to a philosophical teacher, master, authority, under conditions which protect the student from serious encounter with modes of thinking incompatible with the teacher's. The other way is to undergo the philosopher's influence only after, or along with, intimate reaction to fundamentally different philosophical attitudes, and after one has achieved some clarity as to one's own experience of reality and value. Or again, it is one thing to derive philosophic individuality largely from another person and a different thing to recognize a certain congruity between one's thinking, already firmly individualized, and his. Of course, there is no absolute difference here, but a considerable relative one. It happens that I was never in the usual sense a 'pupil' of Whitehead's; also that long before knowing anything of his work I had already reached some basic philosophical convictions, grounded upon explicit reasons in whose force I still today put some trust. And before (in 1925) becoming a colleague, and for a semester an assistant, of Whitehead, I had been exposed for nine years to the influence of many other philosophers, for four of those years to a powerful group of teachers at Harvard, and for two more to Edmund Husserl and several other distinguished European professors. Simultaneously with the exposure to Whitehead came the more detailed influence of Peirce, the study of whose manuscripts occupied most of my time during the same three years. The main effect of Whitehead was to reinforce and crystallize into a technical doctrine a vague sense already acquired that reality on its most concrete level is process not 'substance', creative becoming not mere being, and also to clarify another vague notion that what is usually meant by 'personal immortality' is probably beside the point, since the divine immortality, and our oneness (in some sense) with God, is the proper solution to the problem of the transitoriness of life. Whitehead's 'objective immortality' was a lucid explication of this notion. But the basic beliefs: that reality consists of feelings, that these are essentially 'social' (in Whitehead's language, cases of 'feeling of feeling'), that there must be a supreme, all-inclusive mind, which is somewhat misconceived both in most theologies and in historical pantheism, that the future is open and in process of determination, that there are new facts from moment to moment, and even new divine cognitions, that process is all-inclusive—so much I already thought I knew, thanks to influences, experiences, and reasonings too complex to touch upon here. And of course, similar ideas are either stated or, in some passages at least, implied by Peirce. But Whitehead was the only living thinker who seemed to have an adequate grasp of these matters, and also the only one in whom I could find the sort of systematic clarity and comprehensiveness that we admire in Leibniz. I still see no rival to him in our time, or in the nineteenth century, in this latter respect.

This estimate may seem excessive or even quaint to many. However, there are signs that Whitehead's influence is still substantial, and indeed is probably growing, perhaps fairly rapidly.

One sign of this increasing influence is the appearance of four books, within as many years, dealing with Whitehead's philosophy.[1] Of these, I find the work by Leclerc a useful and largely sound introduction; in the other three, especially Christian's book, I can

[1] Nathaniel Lawrence, *Whitehead's Philosophical Development; A Critical History of the Background of Process and Reality*, University of California Press, 1956.

Ivor Leclerc, *Whitehead's Metaphysics: An Introductory Exposition*, London: Allen & Unwin; New York: Macmillan, 1958.

William A. Christian, *An Interpretation of Whitehead's Metaphysics*, Yale University Press, 1959.

W. Mays, *The Philosophy of Whitehead*, London: Allen & Unwin; New York: Macmillan, 1959.

A fifth book, by Robert Palter, undoubtedly excellent, is about to appear. And I have seen a fine manuscript on the application of Whitehead's philosophy to aesthetics.

For constructive and searching criticism of the second and third of the above works see V. C. Chappell, "Whitehead's Metaphysics", *Review of Metaphysics*, Vol. 13 (1959), pp. 278–304. Personally, I think the criticisms of Leclerc are too drastic, and those of Christian not drastic enough; but the article deserves attention.

recognize certain merits. As Popper keeps telling us, the rational method in general is that of free criticism. Therefore, if Whitehead is important, he ought to be criticized. We should be looking for indications that he is, in this or that respect, mistaken. Also it is vicious to be so critical of criticisms of a favourite author that one would, if successful, protect him against exposure of his weaknesses. However, criticism of an author who dealt in a comprehensive way with the central scientific and philosophical issues of our time, with much technical knowledge and immense imaginative daring, must fulfil exacting requirements if it is to be of much value. Most of us are at a disadvantage here, and I suspect that this is not the least of the reasons why so many writers have been ignoring Whitehead of late. I confess that, on grounds well stated by Leclerc,[2] I have regarded the general approach taken by Lawrence in his book as rather unpromising, and have therefore not reckoned in detail with his criticism; though I presume Leclerc is right in thinking the job rather well done, assuming the type of approach.

The book by Christian is admirable in style, organization, and lucidity; moreover, in most respects I find that he grasps Whitehead's meanings well. However, he imputes to Whitehead a few conceptions which he admits are not obviously in the text, and which I believe were not intended, unless perhaps in moments of partial absent-mindedness on Whitehead's part. These concern chiefly the meaning of 'objective immortality', or the 'immanence' of actualities in subsequent actualities prehending them, and the sense in which God is conceived as infinite and perfect. I think we have here intelligent and beautifully argued (partial) misconstructions, an attribution to Whitehead of the author's own convictions (as I gather). Be that as it may, this is a fine and interesting book.

Also interesting, though in a rather different way, is the largely critical study by Mays. Here, despite some penetrating *aperçus*, especially concerning the relations of Whitehead's philosophy to mathematics, misinterpretation is almost pervasive; or else I do not know at all what Whitehead meant. The book is ingenious, and at some points illuminating; and for all I know, there is some justice in the author's objections to Whitehead's way of arguing from the physics which he knew—essentially that prior to Heisenberg and Schrödinger; for, as Whitehead admitted, he was

[2] "Whitehead's Philosophy", *Review of Metaphysics*, 11 (1957), pp. 68–93.

unable to keep up with the subject after he began his teaching at Harvard and plunged into intensive study of the history of philosophy. Certainly Mays is right to this extent, that if one interprets physics as does Bridgman (the chief authority cited), the way to Whitehead's metaphysics will not be altogether clear! But Mays' failure to grasp various important aspects of Whitehead's thought will, I am confident, be apparent to close students of his writings. Think of reading *Process and Reality*, including (apparently) Part V, and then writing,[3] "It is difficult to follow Whitehead when he says that 'the consequent nature of God is conscious', but it is questionable whether he means by this more than that we are consciously aware of the concrete world in perception." Only gross confusion or blatant dishonesty could have led Whitehead to try to express any such obvious truism by the ten pages or so of eloquent writing devoted to the Consequent Nature, not to mention various passages which implicitly say the same sort of thing. And no one so confused or dishonest could have written those majestic pages.

It would be more reasonable to say that Whitehead is the first great systematic philosopher who does mean it when he says that God is conscious, i.e. knows the world to be such and such (although it might have been otherwise) and knows that he knows this. It is the older theologians who seem not to mean what they say when they attribute 'knowledge' to deity. For knowing, being aware of, are relational properties or states, and Aquinas takes pains to tell us (and he is only saying more sharply what many had already said) that relations between the world and God are not relations for God. In other words, the world is perhaps known by God, but God does not know the world! Whitehead deliberately avoids this paradox by attributing relativity, intrinsic relatedness, to God. There are divine 'physical prehensions' of the world. Mays[4] mentions this, but takes it to mean something[5] it could not honestly mean in this philosophy. Yet only through such prehensions can deity, or anything else, be concrete or 'actual'. The Primordial Nature, Whitehead expressly and repeatedly tells us, is by itself a mere entity of reason, a mere abstraction from the divine actuality.[6]

The attempt of Mays to make a certain phase of theoretical physics the source and essence of Whitehead's philosophy is in

---

[3] W. Mays, *op. cit.*, p. 61.   [4] *Ibid.*, p. 65.   [5] *Ibid.*, pp. 64–5.
[6] PR 42 [46], 46 [50], 486 [522].

my opinion less correct than Leclerc's view that Whitehead is trying to solve certain traditional problems of metaphysics and epistemology, or than the suggestion of Lowe that 'sociological' phenomena, the broad distribution of societies in nature, constitute the more important source of his beliefs.[7] But as the two authors just mentioned fully realize, the matter is more complex than any single account of this sort. As Lowe has put it, "Whitehead is aware of almost everything". The philosopher himself once told his students that (I quote from memory), "as physics is the interpretation of our external perceptual experiences, so metaphysics is the interpretation of our religious experiences". Nor is it correct to say, as Mays in effect does,[8] that these religious experiences were taken to be essentially our reactions to order in nature, or to permanence as constituted merely by order. (See the surprising exegesis at the top of p. 63.) Any careful textual examination will show that the permanence which religion is thought to be most concerned with is "objectification by the physical prehensions of God" (to Mays evidently mere circumlocution for ordinary physical prehensions), since these are the only experiences free from 'negative prehensions', or from the 'abstractness' whereby the vividness of achieved values drops down and down, in 'physical memory', until in the end the values must be wholly lost, or fall as close to zero as you please, were it not for the divine 'love' which 'tenderly cherishes' them everlastingly.

Whitehead was a very honest writer. He may sometimes have got 'mixed up'—who doesn't?—but he always tried to say what he meant. When he said 'love', he did not mean something very different, such as the 'extensive scheme', with which[9] Mays apparently identifies the Whiteheadian God. Here, as at several other points, Mays has an ingenious thesis, valiantly carried through against considerable textual odds, concerning what Whitehead might have meant, had he been a very different sort of man and philosopher—for instance, intellectually more simple-minded and morally more complicated—than he was.

It would be less than fair not to add that Whitehead's exposition of his natural theology was sufficiently defective (a fact of which he was aware) to make it impossible to find a trouble-free interpretation of all that he said on this subject. One is forced to suppose him

7 *The Philosophy of Alfred North Whitehead*, ed. P. A. Schilpp, 1941, pp. 114 f.
8 W. Mays, *op. cit.*, pp. 64–5, 71.   9 *Ibid.*, p. 60.

mistaken, or at least ill-advised in his choice of words, in some passages. But Mays' interpretation of the doctrine of God is not only not trouble-free; it offers little but trouble. At least ten pages of his author become gibberish, and many others by implication needlessly puzzling. And Whitehead has been quoted (I forget by whom) as saying that the final chapter of *Process*, which includes the ten pages spoken of, was the best essay in his writings; an evaluation in which I incline to concur. Is it so paradoxical that it should also be true that there are some grave defects in the exposition? Where thousands of gifted minds have earnestly sought to arrive at a rational conception of deity, and according to Whitehead have not succeeded ("traditional theology is a scandalous failure"), is it to be expected that the feat could be accomplished for the first time, in a great systematic philosophy, without blunder or blemish? Whitehead said once that he felt that his thought about God was "very vague", but that others would be able to clarify the matter.

I will say in passing that I deem it a serious slip to have termed the *primordial* nature of God an 'actuality'. This taken literally is just what it cannot be, in the system in which every actuality is a unit-becoming in its concreteness. But it can be shown that there are reasons for the slip; that the confusion was rather natural.

Perhaps it has been unfair to take Mays' treatment of the theistic aspect as sample, since here he is at his weakest. But there is in his book a general trend toward over-simplification, both of Whitehead's views and of the problems he was trying to solve. To evaluate the criticisms, one must check carefully with *Process and Reality* and *Adventures of Ideas* (in all earlier works Whitehead was groping toward his philosophy; only in these works was he free to expound it). One must also remind oneself that an attempt to develop an explicit doctrine cannot be discredited by showing that if we fall back into some much vaguer notion, the definite difficulties of the more explicit view disappear. Of course they do, and so do its advantages.

When, for example, Mays says[10] that human experiences do not interact with 'molecules', because the latter are not concrete particular entities but abstract general conceptions useful in interpreting our concrete experiences, he is really declaring either for phenomenalism, or for something like naïve realism, without

10 W. Mays, *op. cit.*, pp. 225–8.

telling us how the difficulties of any more explicit development of these positions are to be dealt with. For instance, are cells not particular realities either? And where do we draw the line between actual particulars and mere concepts? Whitehead has his way of dealing with a host of problems; there may be a better way, but merely to remind us that, as Whitehead himself was very fond of emphasizing, the concepts of physics are highly abstract, can hardly suffice to show the needlessness of his doctrines. Whitehead had things to say early in his career about this very way of seeking to banish the problems of a scientific cosmology.

II

Although, as the books we have been discussing seem to evidence, there is increasing interest in the philosophy of Creativity (a better summary description, perhaps, than 'philosophy of organism'), it cannot be denied that this philosophy meets with great resistance in some quarters, especially outside the United States. Let us consider some of the reasons for this. We cannot undertake to cover all the important reasons.

(1) Positivism. The conviction that synthetic propositions can only be empirical, and that non-synthetic propositions can only be linguistic, seems to imply that either Whitehead was engaging in scientific guessing, unjustifiably extended beyond its observational base, or he was merely setting down some verbal stipulations, with some emotive, especially religious, associations.

(2) Dogmatic Pluralism. In spite of the great vogue of the dilemmatic argument just sketched against any such metaphysics as Whitehead's, certain views which seem at least as hard to defend against that argument pervade current philosophical writing, and constitute a principal obstacle to a genuine encounter with the philosophy of creativity. The Russellian reiteration of Hume's thesis that distinguishable events are 'separable', each event being devoid of internal relatedness or logical dependence upon any other, is extremely common; although if it is not metaphysical I wonder what would be. Is it analytic? Ayer says flatly, yes.[11] In that case, it appears that something besides language and its contingent rules is at stake in the analytic. According to Whitehead's own language, events 'prehend' certain other events, and this

[11] A. J. Ayer, *The Problem of Knowledge*, London and New York, 1956, p. 27.

implies that they depend logically upon these others. Moreover, since this concept of prehension is held to be of universal relevance, presupposed in all more special conceptions, a language in which it were really analytic that no event could depend logically upon any other would, for Whitehead, be incoherent.

(3) Dogmatic 'Naturalism' (Materialism). Another view which is quite as problematic, whether taken as empirical or as analytic, but which causes many philosophers to dismiss Whitehead practically unread, is the belief that the emergence of mind out of non-mind is almost axiomatic. Whitehead's dismissal of the concept 'matter', except as an abstract way of viewing sequences of 'experient occasions', or concrete units of 'feeling of feeling'—his 'panpsychism', to use a term which, for perhaps sufficiently good reasons, he avoided—is felt by some to furnish almost ground enough for rejecting his entire system. They *know* (I have talked to them) that atoms and electrons do not feel, or in any way consist of feelings of any sort. Or at least, they know that this *might* be the case and that Whitehead can have no sound reason for applying the psychical terms universally. I have also talked to some scientists about this, and I find them less sure that a view like Whitehead's is mistaken or unreasonable. Some well-known scientists, in fact, hold such a view (e.g. Julian Huxley, Pierre Teilhard de Chardin, Sewall Wright, Ralph Gerard), and the rest mostly leave the question to one side as not, at present, at least, a scientific question. It is not physicists or biologists, but philosophers without any special rapport with physics or biology, who have told me that panpsychism is not worth discussing. If the question is indeed a factual one, it appears that certain philosophers have discovered facts hidden from science, as well as from many of their fellow philosophers.

Is it perhaps analytic, or apparent from the mere rules of language, that not all of nature could consist of some form or manifestation of mind in the form of feeling? Then here, too, we seem to learn about more than mere words from analytic necessities. It must be understood that Whitehead knew as well as anyone that to say outright, 'Everything feels', would be to make the term 'feeling' useless. But this he by no means does say. Abstract entities (e.g. triangularity) obviously do not feel, and in his system such entities are taken as 'real', though of course, not as 'actual'. Also chairs and stones do not feel, though they are held to consist of processes whose unit-becomings are sentient. I should like to meet the person who can show that this theory is analytically false. And if the question is empirical, then it is worth remarking that science is not so treating it. What scientist as such stands up to be counted on the question, Where is the lower limit of feeling in the plant-animal series?, or even is willing to say that there is or can be a lower limit? And quite a good many are ready to be counted as denying such a limit. They, or some of them, do this not on a factual basis, but rather as a result of conceptual analysis. For they agree with Whitehead that the notion of a sheer absence of mind or feeling from any part of nature is probably a meaningless one. What criterion of such absence can be proposed?

There are indeed criteria for saying that certain particular entities 'do not feel', that is, are not singular subjects of feeling. For instance, it is reasonable to doubt (as even Leibniz did doubt) that trees feel, for, as Whitehead picturesquely puts it, "a tree is a democracy"—not so much a singular as a collective entity, like a swarm of bees. He is here speaking factually, and I know competent scientists who would agree with him. But it is a distinct question if a tree-cell is, in a similar sense, a mere 'democracy' of molecules; and if it is, still some level is implied on which dynamic unit *is* found. (For the disunity of the whole is relative to the unity of certain parts.)

Carefully reasoned criteria for the total absence of feeling from a portion of nature, both as a whole and in its constituent parts, have not been formulated. Until they have been worked out, the conception of 'mere matter' has not been given empirical meaning. I do not anticipate that they can be worked out in such a way as to justify the conception. But the problem is being dealt with far more by dogmatic proclamation or innuendo than by careful reflection. Whitehead, however, reflected upon it, over much of a long lifetime. So did Leibniz, Peirce, Clifford, and many another who reached much the same conclusion as he. My own conviction that reality is indeed an 'ocean of feelings' (Whitehead's phrase) was reached at an early age, without conscious reference to any philosophical writer or teacher, and was based, as I know from conversation Whitehead's was, upon an attempted analysis of immediate experience, where alone reality can be encountered. He found, as some of the rest of us have found, that no mere surd to feeling is ever given, but only certain sensory qualities whose affective character is, to be sure, less obvious than that of some other qualities, but (as I tried to show in my *Philosophy and Psychology of Sensation*) is nevertheless detectable. There is here an appeal to observation or intuition, and someone is a poor observer. The question is, Who?

(4) Determinism. Not much can be made out of Whitehead's philosophy by anyone who is unalterably convinced that the concept of absolute causal regularity (classical determinism) even makes sense. For in Whitehead's language, whose first principle is that of creative process, determinism can enter only as a limiting conception which could not be literally realized in any world. Hume (and many of his followers) believed that causal regularity is at least logically capable of taking an absolute form, and that we actually have good observational grounds for regarding this possibility as realized. Today, not many would say so, in the face of the evidence that laws, so far as knowable, are probably all of a statistical character. Thus Hume was mistaken in regarding his determinism as an empirical proposition. Is it then analytic? Some have thought so, but they, too, are few today. I cannot but think that on this matter time is strongly on Whitehead's side. Determinism is a waning idea. People say that the physicist Bohm has proposed a way to reinstate determinism in quantum mechanics. However, if they looked into his book, they would find Bohm declaring that chance is as real as law.[12] His proposal (which has not so far been accepted, I gather) is not motivated by a belief in absolute regularities, which indeed he denies, but (to put it very roughly) in the tactical wisdom of looking for such regularities, in order to make sure that we do not overestimate in a particular case the (admittedly genuine) role of chance.

(5) Naïve Realism. Contemporary writings on the theory of knowledge seem dominated by one rarely challenged assumption, that the alternative to the 'sense-datum' theory (generally viewed as discredited) regarding the *given* in perception can only be something like plain old-fashioned 'naïve realism' (so-called, for I agree with Lovejoy that the plain man does not hold this view). Since Whitehead holds neither of these doctrines, nor yet quite Russell's identity theory (that the sensation is the neural process itself), his distinctive and carefully elaborated theory of perception is not readily understood. Whitehead is a direct presentational realist—

---

[12] David Bohm, *Causality and Chance in Modern Physics*, London, 1957, pp. 132, 136, 153, 169.

but not of the naïve variety. He holds that the primary datum in sense perception is some phase of the neural process itself; but this does not mean that our sensory experience simply is the process. Human experiences consist of actual entities coming temporally just after the subhuman actualities constituting the cellular activities which are given in these experiences. There is a 'prehensive' relation of experience to its datum, and this relation is not that of identity. A temporal distinction is involved, and the datum, being prior, is quite independent of the particular human experience in question (though not of all earlier human experiences).

Against the contention that the neural process is given, we have the violent negation (again, I speak from experience): "Whatever may be given in normal vision, it is certainly not the optical process itself!" Is this denial an empirical or a linguistic statement? It seems sometimes to be intended as a species of the former; for we are reminded that until physiologists discovered neural processes no one knew there were such things, hence they could not all along have been given. Again we have an appeal to facts which, as interpreted, are known to certain philosophers only, but not to scientists, or to certain other philosophers. Granted, many truths about nerve cells were not known until physiologists discovered them; but just so, many truths about rocks (e.g. their crystalline structure) were not known until physicists and chemists discovered them, although, according to naïve realism, rocks had been directly experienced for ages.

But, it will be urged, at least men did know that there were rocks, and they did not know that there was nervous tissue, except by autopsies; hence in ordinary vision nervous tissue cannot be given. Answer: it cannot be given *as* tissue (or as anything so definitely categorized), for (as many forget) the directly given, merely as such, is not categorized at all, though there is feeling of its quality and spatio-temporal spread. It begs the question at issue to say that men do not directly experience some of the very qualities and shapes really characterizing nervous tissue. For the view which Whitehead holds (something like that of Spinoza, if I understand the latter correctly) is that the sensory quality and shape given in a sensation does qualify, first of all, a physical process going on inside our bodies, and only less directly and precisely the extra-bodily physical thing. To object that it is not *as* something inside our bodies that we experience that process is to forget that locating a process in public space involves correlating data from more than one sense, or it involves correlating processes actually given but not 'seen' (i.e. not reflecting light to our normally functioning eyes) with objects that are seen. The theory of the inner-bodily datum of visual experience does not mean that this datum, rather than the light-reflecting object, is what is seen. For to 'see'—Ryle is correct in this, of course—means to gain information about something, or adjust to it, by means of the light which it transmits to our eyes. But the theory in question holds that this information is an evaluation, which has become largely instinctive or automatic, of something still more directly had or possessed. It is a reading of reliable signs, not themselves noted as such (Whitehead's 'transmutation'); somewhat as when we read a book we take conscious note, not so much of the words as of the things meant, or as when we watch a cinema we often seem to observe people, not lights and shadows on a screen.

Now one current belief is that all this is obviously not so. We not only see the extra-bodily object, but that, and nothing within the body, is what is directly experienced. A possible source of this confident pronouncement seems to be a certain semantic confusion. Thus the yellowish-red patch which I experience when I see an orange in a tree is certainly given as outside the flesh-coloured expanse experienced in seeing my hand just before me, or any other part of my visual field similarly representing my physical organism. But on the neural theory, this is but the physiological truism that the part of the bodily process directly had in seeing the orange is spatio-temporally separate from the part had in seeing one's own body. There is no contradiction here of any kind, nor any conflict with known fact. Nor is it known fact that the 'orange' quality directly sensed (which does not mean, 'a certain wave length') is not any quality of a neural process. Science does not locate qualities, it uses qualities in our experience as signs of quantities, these being what it locates. As for the shape, a neural process does have spatio-temporal pattern, and so far as I can find out from physiology, the given patterns *may* all be represented in the inner bodily patterns. There are some apparent exceptions or qualifications, but I believe they are due to ambiguity or vagueness in the meaning of 'given', or to careless observation of perception.[13]

[13] See my "Professor Hall on Perception", *Journal of Philosophy and Phenomenological Research*, XXI (1960–1961).

It will perhaps be asked: if the inner bodily patterns are given, must it not be *certain* that they have the properties we directly experience? Hence how can the 'may' in the above sentence be in order? The answer is this: since the patterns are directly given, they must exist, and *that* at least is not to be put in doubt. But whether they exist inside or outside our bodies is a distinct question, to be answered only after we have considered carefully what we know about both the inner and the outer physical worlds, those inside and outside our skins. The physical and physiological evidence supports the view that there is no universal correlation between given patterns and any patterns existing outside the body; whereas the evidence is at least compatible with there being a universal correlation with the inner-bodily process. Since what is given cannot be in contradiction with what it is given as (by the meaning of 'given'), we are led to prefer the hypothesis that the spatial location of the given is in, not outside, the body.

Those who reject this reasoning land in the following predicament. They say that the seen oranges, and other external objects, are directly experienced, or at least, nothing else is, in certain cases, and so far as vision is concerned. But when we close our eyes and have an after image, or when we submit our eyes to intense stimulation and then suddenly put ourselves in total darkness, and yet for sixty or a hundred seconds perhaps experience brilliant light and colour qualities, what is it that we directly experience? Clearly nothing outside the body! There are then three possible interpretations: (1) we experience merely a succession of 'images', in other words, of sense data; (2) we experience merely our own experiences—of what? (3) we experience the highly stimulated neural process. The first two versions are, by all tests I can think of, indistinguishable from each other and equally absurd; the third is Whitehead's version. But, accepting this version, it would be strange to suppose that when we turn the light on again, the neural process suddenly ceases to be given at all. I cannot imagine any scientist finding this an attractive theory. For there is a straightforward account of the change from the one situation to the other which makes readily intelligible (*a*) how and why it is that in the second case we are, and in the first we are not, gaining reliable information about the extra-bodily world, although (*b*) in both cases the primary, directly experienced object is (in part at least) the same general sort of neural process. Under (*a*) we merely need the processes of learning plus the Darwinian scheme of natural selection and non-survival of organic structures and built-in impulses which fail to give the organism what it needs in order to cope with its environment.

I call attention to the fact that, in spite of all the brave talk about dispensing with mere sense data (and Whitehead could agree they should be dispensed with), not many of our contemporaries have really shown us *how* to dispense with them. Ryle's attempt to talk dreams and images out of existence is hardly a solution. *He* may have few of these things; some of us, at least, have had many, and quite indubitable, instances of them. And what else can one say of vivid visual images in darkness than that they are either mere sense data, or else neural processes directly experienced? And if this latter sort of thing happens at all, why not experiment with it in a general theory of sense experience? Is this not normal empirical procedure? And we have here little room for alternatives. For the mere sense-datum theory is semantically, not just factually, suspect. It seems to make experience constitute its own datum, and this looks like nonsense. The given is precisely—given; it is not created by, or a moulding of some wax-like substance of, the experience for which it is given. To experience is to experience something not just that very experience. At best, the sensum theory is likely to fall before Occam's razor. Thus Whitehead's view is, in one aspect, based upon logical analysis, and in the other aspect (that of locating the datum in space-time) it is a reasonable empirical hypothesis. But few are discussing it as such. Rather, dogmatism is regnant in current epistemology, the dogmatism of a slightly new linguistically furbished sophisticated naïveté: the axiom that the 'seen' and the sheerly given must be one.

(6) Inadequacies in Whitehead's method of justifying his view. It often seems as though Whitehead were merely 'telling us' things which, in some secret way, he has found out about reality. A well-known logician said to me: "I don't expect anybody to prove things in philosophy; this is impossible. But I do like them to half-prove things. Whitehead doesn't even do that." I can't entirely agree; there are a fair number of half-proofs in Whitehead. But still the complaint has some justification. Whitehead the metaphysician was elderly; he needed his energy to define his rather extensive stock of ideas; and he tended to skimp on the elaboration of reasons. For instance, why introduce God into the system? Whitehead

has reasons for this, and not one but a number. However, they are sketched, suggested, hinted at, not set out in neat, scholastic order. This can be done, however. And it needs to be done.

There is need also to meet the analytic-synthetic challenge. Whitehead says his method is 'descriptive'; but then he also speaks of 'necessity', not indeed for all of his cosmological views, because some of them merely claim to report matters of fact belonging to our 'cosmic epoch', but for those claiming 'ultimate metaphysical necessity'. This is a serious problem and cannot be left just where Whitehead left it. Yet I believe that here too a reasonable view can be worked out in general harmony with his thought.[14]

(7) Whitehead's Platonism, and (in so far) Eclecticism—Pepper's charge.[15] Our age is somewhat nominalistic and, as I personally think, in part for good reasons. With a number of others, I have always found 'eternal objects' either ambiguous or dubious. But anyone who sets out to refute the entire system, as some have tried to do, by showing the difficulties of 'Platonism' in this sense is overestimating the commitment of the system to this doctrine. Only minor changes are needed, I believe, to make the view decidedly more nominalistic. And so far from introducing inconsistencies, this, as I am not alone in believing, renders the system more consistent. The key to his philosophy, Whitehead says very plainly, is creativity, taken as 'creative synthesis'. This is scarcely Platonism. And it is not merely *a* Whiteheadian principle, but *the* principle—'the category of the ultimate'. Everett Hall showed long ago that a philosophy of process of this kind has no obvious need to entertain a set of eternal objects as a multitude of distinct entities.[16] Some eternal ideal or principle of process there is doubtless need for; but this is not necessarily, if even most plausibly, conceived as a set or multitude.

(8) Slips in exposition. Whitehead much of the time expresses himself with care and precision. But now and then he makes real 'blunders' (his own word, in this connection) in the language he uses. Thus he has sometimes spoken as though each thing in the

[14] See my "Some Empty though Important Truths", *Review of Metaphysics*, 8 (1955), pp. 553–68; "Metaphysical Statements as Nonrestrictive and Existential", *ibid.*, 12 (1958), pp. 35–47.

[15] See S. C. Pepper, *World Hypotheses*, University of California Press, 1942, p. 106.

[16] See his "Of what Use are Whitehead's Eternal Objects?", *Journal of Philosophy*, xxvii (1930), pp. 29–44.

universe, according to him, depended logically upon every other thing, no matter where or when in all space-time. All close students of Whitehead know that this is by no means what he wishes to say. Yet he did appear to say it occasionally, thereby obscuring the fact that what he himself refers to as 'external relations' are as essential to his doctrine as internal relations. Again, there are sentences about the Primordial Nature of God that seem really to refer more correctly to the Consequent Nature. There is the use, in two meanings, of 'transmutation' (one with reference to God), without discussion of the great difference between them. And so on.

(9) Whitehead's apparent ignorance of those who most nearly anticipated him. Whitehead knew the main philosophical and theological traditions well enough to know why he could not agree with them, and to avoid egregious 'straw-man' fallacies in his criticisms. He also found a good many of the anticipations of his doctrines, e.g. in Plato, Bacon, Descartes, Locke, Spinoza, Leibniz. But on some points he seems not to have known at all that certain Western thinkers before him (Socinus, Fechner, Lequier, to name only three) had held views with striking similarities to his own. He seems also not to have noted the particularly striking analogies between his theory of process, as more concrete than substance or being, and the entire Buddhist tradition. In some ways, indeed, he overstates his divergence from tradition, and in others understates it. As an example of the latter, he imputes a kind of flux to the divine, but in not a few expressions seems to lean back dangerously far toward the timeless deity of the Middle Ages. As an example of the former: a 'dipolar' notion, such as his, of deity makes it possible, as I hope to show elsewhere, to employ a revised form of certain traditional proofs for God. All in all, the relations of his doctrines to tradition need more adequate statement than he could give them.

III

However, I wish to correct an egregious misstatement in Collingwood's posthumous essay on *The Idea of Nature*, to the effect that Whitehead was unaware, until it was pointed out to him, that his view of God was essentially that of Aristotle.[17] As is carefully explained in *Process and Reality*[18] it is not God as conceived by Whitehead who is (nearly) coincident with God as thought by of

[17] R. G. Collingwood, *The Idea of Nature*, Oxford, 1945, pp. 169 ff.
[18] PR 9, 121–2, 484–97 [11, 134, 520–33].

Aristotle, but—a radically different thing—the Primordial Nature of God. No two entities could be more diverse, the one the purely 'abstract' form, radically empty or 'deficient in actuality', of Deity in its bare eternal identity, and the other the incomparable richness of the concrete divine actuality.

It is not among the best-known names in the history of western theology and philosophy that Whitehead's nearest analogues are to be found. Yet there are analogues, and we shall never attain proper perspective regarding the importance of Whitehead until we realize that what he did was neither merely to reiterate the 'great tradition', with minor deviations or corrections, nor yet to affirm a simply new conception, but rather to give more articulate development, in a great speculative system, to old religious and philosophical insights hitherto neglected by the great system-makers of the West, but long present in philosophy and theology, struggling for a more adequate hearing.

Whitehead once remarked to me that he was not unaware of his defects as a philosopher. "I have certain advantages", he said, "but I can readily imagine that one of you may say the things I ought to have said." My judgment now, after nearly thirty-five years, is this: while Whitehead's approach certainly does not exhaust the speculative possibilities open to us—and I hope personally to show before long that significant advances are immediately available—yet he does, with Peirce, and on the whole probably more than Peirce, represent our greatest speculative model since Leibniz. Like that philosopher he knew much of the exact science of his day, and yet was sensitive (indeed even more than Leibniz) to the totality of human interests. Like him he had, as few others in history have had, the 'architectonic' capacity to conceive philosophical inquiry as a definite, articulated whole. Like him, and unlike the post-Kantian idealists, he was able to think in terms of unambiguous logical patterns, so that the skeleton of the Whiteheadian view, like the Leibnizian, can be grasped most readily by seeing certain simple assumptions of a sharply logical kind.

Let us consider, as Leibniz's basic technical tenets: (1) sufficient reason, (2) *de inesse*, or the doctrine that no predicates of a concrete unit-reality or monad can be inessential or accidental, (3) logical independence of every monad from every other (lack of 'windows'), (4) monadic character of the human or animal soul, (5) universal validity of the psychical analogy between the human monad and any others (doctrine that monads, as such, have some form of perception and appetition), (6) timeless reality of God and hence of all truth. From these tenets there are deduced pre-established harmony and a logical impossibility that a given person or individual should ever, as that individual, have done otherwise than in fact it has done. Optimism too is implied: 'whatever is, is right'. It is these three consequences which give the system its air of artificiality. And they lead to a grand inconsistency: that the monads are closed to one another and yet open toward God, who also (this would not be admitted, but it follows from the meaning—any possible meaning—of cognitive perfection or omniscience) is open toward the monads. By pre-established harmony, the monads know of and in a sense influence each other; but God knows of and also influences them in some *absolutely* different way. Thus the system rests, as Whitehead saw very clearly, upon a principle which it never articulates and, without a fresh start, cannot articulate. And he also saw that the medieval systems differ from Leibniz in this respect only by being less clear and candid.

Whitehead carefully and brilliantly avoided these difficulties, while retaining, as no one else had been able to do, the basic insights whose one-sided expression had led to the impasse. The result is as follows: (1) Sufficient reason assumes a more moderate form, as we shall see. (2) *De inesse* is retained, because, properly understood, it is analytic, and only loose thinking ever led to its being denied. There cannot, on the most concrete level of 'subject', be two ways of having predicates: (*a*) that of requiring them for its, the subject's, identity, and (*b*) that of not requiring them. The distinction between 'essence' and 'accident' must lie on a secondary, somewhat abstract, level. It is the relatively abstract which can have inessential qualifications (the reason being that it does not really 'have' them at all, since this is but a way of talking about the characters of the more concrete). (3) Whitehead also retains a certain logical independence of the unit-realities, but yet, without contradiction, upholds their partial logical dependence.

He does this by making several changes in Leibniz. Thus (4) he drops, and in all his later writings (unless perhaps in a few passages about God), never forgets that he has dropped, the idea that the most concrete level of subject or entity is that of individual persons or other enduring individuals; instead he adopts, as apparently Leibniz never once dreamt of doing, but untold multitudes of Buddhists have done, the unit-becoming, or unit-event, as the concrete sample of reality.

Also he limits *mutual* independence to relations between contemporary events, of which neither is past or future to the other.

Again events are seen as related to their predecessors by 'prehensive' relations (corresponding in part, but only in part, to Leibniz's *petites perceptions*—see 5 above) which render the later event logically dependent upon the earlier, no matter to what enduring individuals or 'societies' the two belong. Here too, probably unknowingly, Whitehead repeats Buddhistic views. In contrast to Leibniz, Whitehead refuses to countenance the notion that the datum of experience can be simply a property of that experience itself; he refuses to treat a mind as a picture gallery to which something independent *might* correspond. The primary data for an actuality are other and independent actualities.

Finally, Whitehead denies prehensive relations forward in time, so far as concrete entities are concerned. No event prehends or depends upon a later event, as a concrete, particular actuality. I think he would not grant that psychic research could upset this prohibition; though there may well be some subtle and difficult questions to consider in that connection, as also perhaps with reference to the 'reversal' of time in quantum mechanics.

What is the result of these principles? That the world can be seen as a unified system of causal influences, every item, by its own nature, placing itself in a unique locus in the system ('identity of indiscernibles'), and yet every item being free and contingent. The necessity that a unit be where and when it is is not a necessity that it *be* or occur. The necessity is hypothetical: *if* that entity, then just there. But the entity was not prehended or logically required by its predecessors. The principle here is the familiar one, $\sim [(p \to q) \to (q \to p)]$, entailment is not necessarily (or normally) reversible.

What about pre-established harmony? It exists, but in the mild and reasonable form of statistical uniformities, relative regularities of behaviour inspired by the influence of Deity upon all prehending subjects. A certain amount of "disorder is as real as order". There is no implication that whatever is, is right. Yet the world has a basic coherence, and every item, by strict though hypothetical necessity, places itself just where and when it is.

Sufficient reason remains in this moderate form: looking back-ward, from effect to cause, we find a certain definite past to be implicated as furnishing the 'real possibility' of the sort of effect which has taken place; looking toward the future, the effect is implicated only as a kind, or class, of really possible effects, some instance or other of which must occur. If the effect is a decision, and concretely and in the singular it always is that, causation is 'creative', that is, not the mere unwinding of any necessity or pre-determination, or the mere consequence of any law. No matter what antecedently or externally given 'motive' may influence a decision, since any motive is more or less abstract and general (otherwise it would be the act itself), the act cannot be implied, but in its further particularity must be created arbitrarily.

If Whitehead had ever considered Leibniz's proposal that God would not have made a world at all were it not that one possible world is best, I imagine that he would have said, with typical good sense; "Since some world is better than no world, the suggested divine behaviour would be irrational, and downright peevish, just as the ass who starved because one bundle of hay was no better than the other, would indeed be asinine in its obliviousness to the superiority of eating over starving."

What then about the order of the world, which Whitehead holds expresses the influence of God upon things? This influence, like any influence in this philosophy, can only operate by the influencer getting himself prehended by the things influenced; and therefore, by the asymmetry of prehensive relatedness, there can be no strict entailment of the result. No matter what God decides for the world, the result, the world's prehensive response, involves an element of self-determination or creative freedom. Moreover, although the divine decisions manifest infinite 'wisdom', they yet cannot be deduced from any ultimate necessity because (a) they take into account previous cosmic epochs, and previous events in this epoch, all of which are contingent, and (b) there is no one best way for God to react creatively in a given situation (by the very meaning of creative), though there are, as I personally see it, ways of which it can be said that no other could have been better. Whitehead, no more than Leibniz, I think, would admit that God could ever have done better; yet since the world is in part self-created, the result could always have been better.

The timelessness of factual truth and of God (except in his most abstract aspect) goes by the board. The idea that both truth and divine knowledge receive additions is not nearly so new in theology as some think, nor I suspect is it so easily refuted.[19] Creative synthesis (or synthesizing) is here taken as reality itself, after two millennia of trying out the notion that pure being, non-synthesizing and non-creative in essence, is reality itself, or at least its primary and superior form.

That Whitehead has reinstated the rationalists' vision without its most obvious defects may be seen further by considering an item or two in the Kantian criticism of Leibniz. In Dreams of a Ghost-seer,[20] Kant rebukes those who had laughed at Leibniz's pan-psychist theory of matter; for, said Kant, if we are to look for a positive conception of physical reality as it is in itself, Leibniz showed us the only possible way to form such a conception. But, Kant went on to remark, if we took this path, we should then confront the impenetrable mystery of one monadic subject interacting with others to form a dynamic system, for instance in the human body. But this problem is directly and clearly solved (in principle) in Whitehead's modified Leibnizianism. A unit-reality *consists* of a complex act of prehending various other units; it is an experient occasion whose only possible concrete objects of experiencing are other such occasions. Clearly, to prehend X, to feel its feelings, is, in a certain definite way, to be influenced by X. There is no further problem or mystery of influence passing from one monad to another. Thus Kant was simply mistaken if he supposed (and clearly he did suppose) that what the Leibnizian form of monadism could not do, no other form could do either.

Again Kant (in the first *Critique*) criticized Leibniz for arguing that the concept of a divine nature consisting of all positive predicates or perfections could not involve any inconsistency, since contradiction requires negative as well as positive properties; on the contrary, said Kant, two positive properties may be 'really repugnant', even though both are equally positive—for example, velocities in contrary directions. Now Whitehead agrees with

---

[19] There is indeed a problem of relating this to the 'semantic concept' of truth accepted by formal logicians. But at least Waismann's attempt in ordinary language to refute the notion of new truths seems to me a failure. His supposedly unanswerable questions can be answered. See his essay, "How I see Philosophy", in *Contemporary British Philosophy*, Third Series, ed. H. D. Lewis, London: Allen & Unwin; New York: Macmillan, 1956, pp. 449–58.

[20] See the final paragraph of the first division of Part I.

Kant, but draws a more radical conclusion. God cannot, for nothing can, actualize every positive quality, or all possible value, since positive properties and values are typically alternatives to each other: red instead of blue or green, a sonnet instead of a ballad, or *vice versa*. But there is another way of defining perfection. We must distinguish between perfect and imperfect *capacities* for positive predicates. No being can have all positive properties, for they involve mutual incompatibilities; but a being can be capable disjunctively of *any* positive property and any compossible set of such properties. Properties accrue to an actuality through its experiences or prehensions: the divine capacity for prehensions is to be conceived as subject to no limitation whatever, as between various compossible sets of objects or events. God could not have all, but he could have any, among internally compossible sets of positive properties; in other words, no world state or positive actuality could be such that he could not experience it. This is his infinite *potentiality* for properties. His *actuality*, which must, like all actuality, be in some respects finite, is composed of his actual prehensions of the *de facto* cosmos. I call this the Consequent State (for 'Consequent Nature' is ambiguous, alas!). This state sums up without any loss or deficiency the total reality and value of the cosmos prehended, which is a partly new one with each new state of the prehending Deity. The cosmos is not only totally embraced, but the act of embracing it has its own supreme value, which is absolute in its adequacy, in the 'wisdom' with which the given totality is received into the divine reality.

This is a concept of divine perfection which never clearly dawned upon Kant, or even Hume—who came closer to it—but which has a long line of descent, at least from some religious thinkers of the Reformation, if not from some Patristic and Islamic theologians of centuries earlier. It can be shown, though not in this essay, that the theistic proofs must one and all be transformed if they are to be made relevant to this conception; and when they are thus transformed, it turns out that Hume's and Kant's critiques of the proofs are no longer, as they stand, decisive, or perhaps even pertinent. The whole issue is reopened, if we are intellectually candid and avoid reasoning according to 'guilt by association'.

Admirers of Kant will perhaps have asked themselves, What about the Antinomies? Has Whitehead properly considered the difficulties which appear when we try to conceive the space-time reality as a whole? I believe that he must have given this matter some thought, and I know that he had long meditated upon Kant's views. But I feel it as a defect that he did not more explicitly discuss the question of the infinity of the past, which he seems to take for granted, and of space, about which he has little to say, and of the regress toward the infinitely small, which he appears to reject. But one thing is clear to me: at least two of Kant's Antinomies depend upon the classical (deterministic) concept of causality which Whitehead rejects. He believes in real possibility in a sense which requires a reformulation of the very meaning of 'cause', or of occurrence 'according to rules'. But the relationships to Kant ought to be worked out by someone.

My conclusion is this: granted that Leibnizianism was fairly refuted, the revision of his doctrines in Whitehead has not been refuted, but only (by most of our contemporaries) ignored. Not even in principle or indirectly has Whitehead been disposed of. Those who reject metaphysics on the ground that necessary propositions 'assert nothing' (Wittgenstein) do not show us that and how they themselves avoid taking the Humian doctrine of universal external relations—or some other view on the basis of which Whitehead is rejected—either as an extra-linguistic yet *a priori* pronouncement, or alternatively as a factual statement, which is nevertheless vouched for by none of the sciences of fact and is widely disputed among philosophers. I submit: the status of Whitehead's metaphysics of process is a postponed, not an adjudicated, matter.

WILLIAM A. CHRISTIAN

SOME USES OF REASON

I

WILLIAM A. CHRISTIAN

SOME USES OF REASON

My main object is to explore some kinds of thinking that are involved in speculative philosophy. Since Kant and especially in recent years philosophers have often asked how speculative philosophy is like and unlike scientific inquiry. I propose to ask, instead, how speculative philosophy is like and unlike religious inquiry. Part I gives the skeleton of a theory of religious inquiry and deals with some uses of reason (analysis, construction, and judgment) in religion. Part II treats speculative philosophy in a similar way but at greater length. Part III applies some results of Part II to Whitehead's practice of speculative philosophy, and Part IV draws some conclusion about speculative philosophy and religion.

I

I shall discuss religious inquiry in a non-theological way. The Christian theologian has a problem about faith and reason, but his problem is more concrete than the problem I have in mind, for it is posed in the terms of a particular religious tradition. He has a specific conception of what faith responds to, and a specific conception of faith itself. Perhaps also his conception of reason is formed in harmony with a Christian conception of human nature. The problem I have in mind is a more abstract one, which is not to say it is more important. I only mean that it is not defined in the frame of a particular religious tradition. It can be interpreted in Christian terms; it might be interpreted in Jewish or Mohammedan or Buddhist or Hindu or Stoic or Neoplatonic terms as well.

Religious inquiries can be distinguished from other inquiries by the sorts of questions that are asked in it. Its questions are different from those asked in moral inquiry and from those asked in scientific inquiry, for example, though they might well be connected with moral or scientific questions in important ways.

Let us distinguish two types of questions which arise in the course of religious inquiry. As examples of one of these types we might take the following:

A. Is God a trinity?
B. In Nirvana does the self continue to exist?
C. Is the Koran eternal?
D. Are all the buddhas one?

Let us call these *doctrinal questions*, since they arise primarily within some more or less organized religious community and are concerned with what shall be taught in that community.

From these doctrinal questions we can distinguish questions of another type, such as the following:

E. What should human beings worship?
F. What is the supreme goal of life?
G. What is that on which we unconditionally depend?
H. What is it that is ultimately holy?

Let us call questions of this type *basic religious questions*. We can distinguish them from doctrinal questions in the following way. If an answer to a doctrinal question is a religious assertion,[1] then it presupposes an answer to a basic religious question. The point of a religious doctrine, then, is to expand and explain some answer to a basic religious question. For example, the point of a religious doctrine about the Koran is to expand and explain the Mohammedan answer (or, a Mohammedan answer) to a basic religious question, e.g. (for *E*) that we should worship Allah, whose prophet is Mohammed.

Let us look more closely at one feature of these basic religious questions, namely at what they presuppose. A question of this type presupposes that there is something to which its predicate truly applies, and it asks to *what* logical subject this predicate truly applies. So anyone who asks *G* presupposes that there is something on which we unconditionally depend, and anyone who asks *H* presupposes that there is something that is ultimately holy.

[1] A doctrinal question might be asked by a historian of religion without a religious interest. Then there would be some tacit or explicit qualification like (for A) "according to the Bible", or (for C) "according to standard Mohammedan theology". In these cases an answer to this non-religious question need not be a religious assertion. But an answer to a *religious* question about doctrine presupposes an answer to a basic religious question, and is thus a religious assertion.

A question of this type is not seriously asked unless the asker (i) supposes there is something to which the predicate truly applies, and (ii) does not know what this is.

It would be possible to ask a question of a different type, like "*Is there* anything human beings should worship?", and "*Is there* any supreme goal of life?". I suggest that these are not religious questions, though they are closely related to religious questions in the following way. Let us use the symbol P for predicates of the appropriate type. Then anyone who asks a question of the form, "Is anything P?", is asking the question either out of idle curiosity, or out of a religious interest. If he asks it out of idle curiosity, it is not yet a religious question. If he asks it out of a religious interest, then it is not the *real* question for the asker to ask, though he may utter it rhetorically, perhaps in vexation. For if he already has a religious interest, something in his experience has already suggested to him that there *is* something of the sort and he has already responded to this suggestion. So the real question for him to ask is of the form "What is it that is P?".

The next (logically speaking) phase of religious inquiry consists in the occurrence and the adoption of promising suggestions about what is P. Suggestions of this sort may occur in various ways, being mediated through various sorts of experiences, and being expressed by symbols of various sorts. A suggestion might be mediated by a natural object (like a vine, the sun, a stone), a human relationship (like sexual love, physical combat, parenthood, political authority), or a historical event (like a flood, the Exodus from Egypt, Gotama's enlightenment, the death and resurrection of Christ, or some other event in public history or in private history). Such objects, relations, and events introduce, in a concrete way, answers to basic religious questions. Incidentally, one fruitful way of differentiating various religions is according to the different suggestions they adopt.

Clearly a particular religious suggestion is adopted only if it has a meaning. But this meaning needs to be stated and elaborated in a set of propositions which answer doctrinal questions. The suggestion needs to be explicated into a (more or less elaborate) theory. This is what is done, in various religions, by prophets, teachers, and theologians, and the results are sometimes embodied in creeds. A doctrinal scheme may be more or less systematic, and may be tested, more or less rigorously, for consistency and coherence.

Finally the answer reached in this way, namely the suggestion as formulated and elaborated, may be compared with the facts of life. The question for inquiry then is whether the answer is adequate to all the relevant facts. For example, does it do justice to the fact that all human beings die? I cite conversions from one religious faith to another as evidence that this sort of question is sometimes asked, more or less explicitly. Some conversions involve serious reflection. And this is evidence that facts of some sort or other are being taken as counting in a crucial way for and against particular answers to basic religious questions.

With this sketch of religious inquiry in mind we are in a position to distinguish some uses of reason in religion. I shall call them analysis, construction, and judgment.

1. *Analysis in religious inquiry*

The sort of analysis *of* religious inquiry I have been giving is also important *in* religious inquiry. The difference is that in the latter case analysis is, we might say, self-analysis. Here we ask not "What sort of questions are people asking when they are engaged in religious inquiry?", but "What questions am I asking?"; and not "What is the role of suggestions in religious inquiry?", but "What suggestions have I, in effect, adopted?"; and not "How are suggestions explicated?", but "Is my theory self-consistent?", or, more generally, "What is the logical structure of my theory?". In as far as one is a member of a religious community, the 'I' of these questions becomes a 'we'.

Asking these analytical questions does not always make religious inquiry easier or more immediately successful. Instead they might —or might not—complicate inquiry and postpone the finding of good answers. For here, as elsewhere, self-analysis may become introverted and thus distract us from our pursuit. We might become concerned with phenomenological truth instead of religious truth. But this need not be so. Ordinarily these analytical questions are asked with a view to getting on with the inquiry. And often, in order to get on with the inquiry, it is necessary to ask them.

It is especially important to get a certain amount of reflective clarity about basic questions. "What question am I asking?" Only if we know what we *want* to know can we tell what our suppositions are, what sorts of facts might count for or against answers to our question, and how arguments might be constructed.

2. Construction in religious inquiry

I have said that, in religious inquiry, a theory is constructed by explicating a suggestion. This means beginning with a meaning which is concretely suggested by some object or relationship or event in experience. By saying these meanings are concretely suggested, I mean that they are most naturally and directly conveyed by non-propositional symbols. The problem is then to put these meanings into propositional form. For example, Buddhist philosophers explain, more or less systematically, the meaning of Gotama's enlightenment, Jewish theologians explain the (theological) meaning of the history of Israel, and Christian theologians explain the meaning of the life, and death and resurrection of Christ.

In this sort of explanation two kinds of abilities are brought into play. There is an intuitive grasp of the meaning of the suggestion. This we might aptly call, after Rudolf Otto, 'divination'. Or we might call it an act of constructive imagination. And this intuited meaning is put into logical form; it is expressed in statements, which are subject to the tests of consistency and coherence. Sometimes, in religion, we find resistance to systematic explication of suggestions, for example, in certain romantic or mystical or existential forms of religion. But in many of the major religious traditions the systematic explication of doctrines has been undertaken with great energy and skill.

It seems clear enough that this use of reason in religion has analogies in other inquiries. In any serious inquiry there is need for the construction of theories, and this calls for imagination as well as logic. The genius, in mathematics or physics or morals, sees a possibility that others may not see, at least not so clearly, and puts his vision into a communicable form. Sometimes he does not work out in detail the implications of the pattern he constructs. So there is room for Shankara as well as for the Upanisads, for Aquinas as well as for Augustine.

3. Judgment in religious inquiry

Finally we come to a third use of reason in religion. Suppose some particular suggestion has been adopted, and that it has been explicated reasonably well (i.e. amply and consistently). And suppose that a reasonable degree of reflective (analytical) clarity has been gained. Then there is room for a final question about this answer (i.e. the theoretically elaborated suggestion): Is it true?

I suppose that the truth-claim of a basic religious proposal is a claim to more than logical truth. So a judgment about such a proposal involves comparing it with facts. A judgment of this sort is a decision about the proposal in view of something other than purely logical possibilities.

We ask this question ("Is it true?") because what we have thought out (analytically, or constructively, or both) is not good enough. We want something more. We want our thought to be in harmony with the facts. This aim at a harmony of thought and reality might well be looked at as a function of reason. It means a seriousness about other-than-logical truth. We would rightly say, of someone who refuses to admit this question and take it seriously, that at this point he is unable or unwilling to reason in religion.

Of course he might justify himself by arguing that it is impossible to reason in religion at this point. He might argue that there are no rules of judgment for deciding such questions. This might be argued by a sceptic, but it might also be argued by an existentialist of a certain sort or by a mystic of a certain sort.

I do not wish to argue here against this view of religion, though I do not hold it. I suggest only that *if* truth-claims in religion could be taken seriously, in the way I have indicated, then asking whether some religious answer is true and trying to decide this question in view of relevant facts would be a function of reason.[2]

It might be argued that while religious judgments are indeed in some sense a function of reason, they are also a function of faith. It might be said that we cannot really *know* whether, in some particular case, we have achieved a harmony of thought and reality, of a theory and the relevant facts. Furthermore, it might be said, we cannot *know* whether such a harmony is possible. So, it might be argued, to make such a judgment is an act of faith as well as an act of reason.

This would not mean that these judgments are unreasonable. This would be different from saying they are *only* acts of faith. It is

[2] Of course terms like 'reason', 'reasoning', 'reasonable', 'rational', 'rationalist', and 'rationalistic', take on various colourings and have to be used with caution. It would be easy to construct various paradoxes, like "It is not reasonable to be rationalistic" (i.e. we have to take account of facts as well as of logic), and "Acts of judgment are not acts of reasoning" (i.e. a judgment is a result of inferences but is not itself merely the making of an inference).

not absurd to speak of a reasonable faith. There is indeed a kind of passion (in Kierkegaard's sense) in these judgments, a passion usually referred to as a love of truth. The point I would stress is that this passion involves a certain openness. It involves being open to revision of our theories, on one hand, and on the other hand being open to a better apprehension of the relevant facts.

Such judgments are only the final expression of an interest which controls a serious inquiry from the beginning. A serious question is not asked without it. Also, a suggestion is a promise of truth, and an adoption of a suggestion is a response to this promise. We judge whether a suggestion, explicated in thought and explored in action, gives what it promises. For we aim at a harmony of thought and being.

To keep these uses of reason in religion in perspective we might ask whether, in addition to this love of truth which judgments aim to satisfy, there are other features of religious inquiry which might aptly be called functions of faith.

(i) One feature of religious inquiry with an obvious claim to be called a function of faith is the adoption of a particular suggestion for an answer to a basic religious question. Here faith is a response to a particular possibility of religious truth. We do not need to construe this response as a merely intellectual act. Though it does involve a certain assent, it involves something more also. For we are considering a religious response. And one way religious responses differ from responses of other types is that, in principle, they involve more of the self.

This feature of religious inquiry suggests a general way of interpreting what, in theology, is called revelation. This would not be a theological interpretation of revelation. It would not take the place of a Christian doctrine of revelation, for example. But it would give a point of contact between what theologians mean by revelation and a general theory of religious inquiry. It would help those who do not hold a theological theory of revelation to understand its point.

The point is that something *like* revelation is essential in religious inquiry. Without the adoption of *some* suggestion or other, inquiry cannot proceed. And this is true also of moral inquiry, of scientific inquiry, and indeed of any type of problem-solving which is not merely a matter of calculation. So this feature of religious inquiry is not utterly peculiar to religion.

(ii) A second feature of religious inquiry which has a claim to be called a function of faith is the basic supposition of a religious inquiry. This claim may be less obvious than the former one, but it seems to be equally important. A basic supposition is a supposition that there is something holy, or that there is some supreme goal of life, or something to which some other basic religious predicate truly applies. And I suggest that such a supposition might be aptly said to be a matter of faith.

I do not wish to suggest that these suppositions are in any way unnatural. (In our ordinary usage of 'faith' we do not always suggest that it is an unnatural act.) Indeed, as is true of the adoption of suggestions, this is an essential feature of *any* serious inquiry which is not simply a matter of calculation. Thus I suppose that in as far as physics differs from mathematics on the one hand and from engineering on the other, some basic supposition or other is involved in physical inquiry, perhaps for example a supposition that there are some uniformities in nature (whether 'nature' is defined realistically or phenomenalistically) that can be precisely described. Similarly I suppose that serious moral inquiry involves a supposition that finding the right thing to do is a real possibility.

Calling such suppositions matters of faith does some justice to one of their features, the fact that they cannot be justified in the way a particular conclusion (a particular religious or scientific or moral theory) can be justified. These suppositions are not gratuitous; they are responses to something in our experience. But we cannot call them conclusions from evidence. Logically speaking they are much more primitive than that. If they should be challenged, the proper sort of response to the challenge would be more like an attempt to awaken an interest than like giving an argument.

One further feature of basic religious suppositions may be mentioned. They make it possible, both logically and psychologically, to admit questions about the validity of some particular answer to a basic religious question. Suppose, for example, it should be suggested to a Christian that Christianity is not true. The suggestion might be simply resisted, by what Peirce calls 'the method of tenacity'. Then the belief may become compulsive. It is then no longer an act of the whole self, and therefore no longer a free act. If on the contrary the question can be admitted, and given some answer, this danger may be avoided. The question can (psychologically and logically) be admitted only if the believer is in a position to say something to the following effect: "Fundamentally I am interested in what is true (about what is ultimate, or holy, or the supreme goal of life), *whatever* that is. As far as I can see, x is true. But it is not absurd to think it is not true. And if it is not true, I want to know it." I suggest that analogous basic assumptions have analogous functions in other types of inquiry, including moral inquiry and scientific inquiry.

Finally it should be noticed that neither of these functions of faith, if we should call them that, amounts to a mere leap in the dark. In each case, faith proceeds on some warrant.

Now I shall summarize these uses of reason and functions of faith, and comment briefly on their interconnectedness.

Uses of reason in religious inquiry:

R1. Analysis of the interest underlying the inquiry and the concepts arising within it. Analytical reason.

R2. Explication of suggestions. Reason as imaginative construction and theoretical elaboration.

R3. Reason as aim at harmony of life, at harmony of theory and fact, leading to judgments of truth-claims.

Functions of faith in religious inquiry:

F1. Faith as a fundamental supposition, responding to some intimation in experience that there is something to be inquired about, to which our formulations should conform. Faith as response to 'general revelation', we might say.

F2. Faith as response to 'special revelation'. Adoption of a particular suggestion, including commitment to exploration of the suggestion in thought and action.

These features of religious inquiry are interconnected. For example, the point of a suggestion (what it is *about*), which must govern both its explication (R2) and the analysis of this explication (R1), is given in the initial interest and reflected in the basic supposition (F1) of the inquiry. In similar ways it becomes clear that no one of these features can be understood without reference to each of the others. It would follow that reason and faith are not merely consistent with one another, but require one another. But I should emphasize once more that this is an *abstract* interpretation of faith and reason in religion. An interpretation of faith and reason from the standpoint of some particular religious faith would be another *sort* of interpretation, though it need not conflict with this one.

II

There are many questions we might well call speculative questions, for example:

Are all events pre-determined?
Are minds functions of material bodies?
Is history made up of cycles of events with identical patterns?
Are there any imperishable substances?
Are indiscernibles identical?
Does non-being exist?

Questions like these border on, but do not seem to belong to, the domains of history, psychology, physics, and logic. Also, although they appear to have connections with common-sense questions, they do not seem to be common-sense questions. From the point of view of ordinary experience, as well as from the points of view of the sciences I mentioned, these are odd questions.

Now it is conceivable that the domain of speculative philosophy consists of a multiplicity of such odd questions as these. And some philosophers say that speculative philosophy is indeed just a collection of such questions. It is important to ask whether or not this is the case.

The reason why this is an important question is as follows. Suppose we could reasonably construe these questions as something more than a collection. Suppose we could construe them as belonging to some *enterprise*, and hence as related to one another by virtue of some underlying interest they all reflect. Then, if we understood the point of this enterprise, we might understand better the points of these and other questions that might arise within that enterprise.

So it is important to ask what the point of such an enterprise might be. One possibility is to construe speculative philosophy as a productive enterprise, as an art. It might be conceived as the art of constructing conceptual systems with certain formal properties. But let us suppose that, though speculative philosophy may well be an art, in the sense that imagination, skill, and aesthetic judgment are required in it, it is also an *inquiry*, with a logical structure of some sort, in which we aim at making responsible decisions about whether something is true. Let us suppose that the speculative philosopher may hope to discover, or learn, or know something.

Now one way to tell whether speculative philosophy is an enterprise of this latter sort, namely an inquiry, is to see whether we can say what it attempts to discover. Here we would be asking, not what might be learned about incidentally in the course of the enterprise, but what the whole enterprise is aimed at learning about.

More specifically, if speculative philosophy is an inquiry and not a collection of odd questions, then it should be possible to formulate some question or other which the enterprise means to answer. This question would tell us the point of the inquiry. So let us ask whether we can formulate questions which might have, in speculative inquiry, functions analogous to those of basic religious questions in religious inquiry. This gives us a natural starting point for exploring one important use of reason in speculative philosophy, namely analysis.

1. *Analysis in speculative philosophy*

In recent years there has been a great deal of analysis *of* speculative philosophy. Analysis is also important *in* speculative inquiry, in somewhat the way in which it is important in religious inquiry. I shall bring this out mainly by showing the importance for speculative inquiry of being clear about its basic questions and suppositions. But in concentrating on these topics I do not mean to suggest that analysis of concepts arising in (logically) later stages is not also important. Also, though analysis is always in order, it is not the only use of reason that is in order. Construction of theories, and the formation of judgments, are also in order. At least, they are in order if speculative philosophy is an inquiry.

(*a*) *Basic speculative questions.* In search of clues to formulations of basic speculative questions, let us turn to what some speculative philosophers have said about what they were doing. Let us notice some remarks by Aristotle, Spinoza, Bradley, and James.

"It is generally assumed", Aristotle says, "that what is called Wisdom is concerned with *the primary causes and Principles.*" Later, after explaining how the prime mover causes motion by final causation, he says: "Such, then, is *the first principle* upon which depend the sensible universe and the world of nature."[3]

3 *Metaphysics* I 981 b; XII 1072 b. Loeb. ed. (Italics mine.)

Spinoza defines the supreme human perfection as "the knowledge of the union existing between the mind and the whole of nature". And among the necessary conditions of attaining this end is, first:

"To have an exact knowledge of *our nature* which we desire to perfect, and to know as much as is needful of *nature in general.*"[4]

And with this we may notice two passages in the *Ethics*:

"From the necessity of *the divine nature* must follow an infinite number of things in infinite ways—that is, all things which can fall within the sphere of infinite intellect."

"Nothing comes to pass in *nature*, which can be set down to a flaw therein; for nature is always the same, and everywhere one and the same in her efficacy and power of action; that is, nature's laws and ordinances, whereby all things come to pass and change from one form to another, are everywhere and always the same; so that there should be one and the same method of understanding the nature of all things whatsoever, namely, through nature's universal laws and rules."[5]

Now let us come to F. H. Bradley. In the introduction to *Appearance and Reality*, he says:

"We may agree, perhaps, to understand by metaphysics an attempt to know reality as against mere appearance, or the study of first principles or ultimate truths, or again the effort to comprehend the universe, not simply piecemeal or by fragments, but somehow as a whole."[6]

Then, in replying to objections against metaphysics, he says:

"How much we can ascertain about *reality* will be discussed in this book; but I may say at once that I expect a very partial satisfaction. I am so bold as to believe that we have a knowledge of *the Absolute*, certain and real, though I am sure that our comprehension is miserably incomplete."[7]

Finally, in the closing pages:

[4] *On the Improvement of the Understanding*, pp. 4, 8. (Italics mine.) In *Philosophy of Benedict de Spinoza*, tr. R. H. M. Elwes, New York: Tudor Publishing Co.   [5] *Ibid.*, pp. 53–4, 128. (Italics mine.)
[6] F. H. Bradley, *Appearance and Reality*, London, 1893, p. 1.
[7] *Ibid.*, p. 3. (Italics mine.)

"The Reality itself is nothing at all apart from appearances."[8]
"And Reality is one Experience, self-pervading and superior to
mere relationships."[9]

We may notice that 'the Absolute' and 'the Real' are used as
equivalents of 'Reality' and 'the Reality'.

Finally, notice a passage in William James's *Some Problems of
Philosophy*, in which he is explaining what metaphysics is:

"It means the discussion of various obscure, abstract, and
universal questions which the sciences and life in general suggest
but do not solve; questions left over, as it were; questions, all of
them very broad and deep, and relating to the whole of things, or
to the ultimate elements thereof."

He gives some examples, and then continues:

"One may say that metaphysics inquires into the cause, the
substance, the meaning, and the outcome of all things. Or one may
call it the science of the most universal principles of reality
(whether experienced by us or not), in their connection with one
another and with our powers of knowledge. 'Principles' here may
mean either entities, like 'atoms', 'souls', or logical laws like:
'A thing must either exist or not exist'; or generalized facts, like
'things can act only after they exist'."[10]

He thinks such definitions as these have only a 'decorative'
value, since the principles are so numerous, and the 'science' so
incomplete. In the book he proposes only to handle a few separate
problems. The 'serious work of metaphysics' is done over the
separate single questions.

Now, with these passages in mind as samples, let us ask what
questions are being posed (or discussed) by these philosophers. On
the surface, we can distinguish questions of two sorts. The first
passage from Aristotle, which is echoed in the passage from James,
might yield a question like:

   (i) What first principles are there?
Other questions of this type would be: What primary causes are
there? What sorts of things are there? What sorts of things are real?

   In contrast, the later passage from Aristotle, the passage from

[8] F. H. Bradley, *Appearance and Reality*, London, 1893, p. 551.
[9] *Ibid.*, p. 552.
[10] William James, *Some Problems of Philosophy*, New York: Longmans, 1931,
pp. 29, 30–31.

Spinoza's *Ethics*, and the last three passages from Bradley all suggest questions of a different logical type. These would be questions like:

(ii) What is the first principle?

Other questions of this type would be: What is the primary reality? What is nature? What is Reality? What is the Absolute?

So we have at least two possible ways of conceiving basic speculative questions. We might take the basic or fundamental questions of speculative inquiry to be like (i), or we might conceive them on the model of (ii).

An expression like "What is reality?" might be construed in either way. Though it might more readily express a question like (ii) (and thus be congenial to capitalization: "What is Reality?"), yet it might well be used to express a question like (i). In the latter case it would ask, in effect, "What things (or sorts of things) are real?". In this case it would be replaceable by "What is real?". This latter sense of the expression, in so far as it differs from "What is there?", might be explicated as follows: There are many things we can think about and talk about. Some of these things affect other things; others do not. Thus the sun affects other things; the number seven does not. What things and sorts of things affect other things? That is to say, "What things and sorts of things have power?" For to be real is to have power.

The main difference between these two types of questions is that questions like (ii) make unique references; questions like (i) do not. Questions like (i) present a predicate (like 'first principles') and ask to what logical subjects it properly and truly applies. Questions like (ii) present a unique logical subject and ask what can be said truly about it.

Before noticing the different suppositions made by questions of these types, let us look at some points of comparison with religious questions. "What is Reality?" is more like "What is God?" or "What is Nirvana?" than it is like "What is it that is Holy?"[11] or "What is the supreme goal of life?". This similarity might encourage us to treat questions like (ii) as doctrinal questions in speculative philosophy. Answers to these questions would then be speculative doctrines.

[11] Taking 'holy' in an eminent sense, which allows other things to be holy in a derivative sense. Hence the capitalization. God is Holy. The temple is holy because it is God's house.

Just as it is possible to discuss religious doctrines without formulating basic religious questions—and this is the case in many treatises in systematic theology—it is possible to discuss speculative doctrines without formulating basic speculative questions. For example, Leibniz begins his *Monadology* as follows:

"1. The Monad, of which we will speak here, is nothing else than a simple substance, which goes to make up composites; by simple, we mean without parts.
2. There must be simple substances because there are composites; for a composite is nothing else than a collection or *aggregatum* of simple substances."[12]

And he begins his *Discourse on Metaphysics* by saying:

"The conception of God which is the most common and the most full of meaning is expressed well enough in the words: God is an absolutely perfect being."[12]

In neither case does Leibniz begin by formulating questions to which the doctrines he will discuss, doctrines about simple substances, composites, and God, are supposed to be relevant. Sometimes it is possible to derive such a formulation from the philosopher's discussion. For example, we might derive from the second proposition of the *Monadology* ("There must be . . . there are . . .") a question like "What sorts of things are there?". But it is not necessary for a speculative philosopher to formulate a basic speculative question in order to propose a speculative doctrine, though often this would be helpful and enlightening.

The predicates used in formulating questions like (i) (e.g. 'first principle', or 'real') are not uniquely applying predicates, as basic religious predicates are. They can be applied to more than one logical subject without inconsistency. It is proper to say "*m* is a first principle *and n* is a first principle", or to say "*m* is real *and n* is real". (Of course it could be *argued* that only *m* is real.) But this is not true of the predicates used in formulating basic religious questions. It would not be proper to say "Nirvana is the supreme goal of life *and* (the vision of) God is the supreme goal of life", or to say "Yahweh is Holy *and* Brahman is Holy", or to say "Nature is

---

[12] In Leibniz: *Discourse on Metaphysics*, etc., tr. G. R. Montgomery. Chicago; Open Court, 1931.

that on which we depend unconditionally *and* God is that on which we depend unconditionally".

(*b*) *Basic speculative suppositions.* Construing basic speculative questions as questions like (i), we may construct a list of some of these questions, with a supposition corresponding to each, as follows:

What first principles are there?
Supposition: There are some first principles.
What primary causes are there?
Supposition: There are some primary causes.
What sorts of things are there?
Supposition: There are some *sorts* of things.
What sorts of things are real?
Supposition: Things of some sorts are real.

The relation between one of these questions and its corresponding supposition is that the supposition is needed to make sense of the question. Without the supposition the question has no point.

Of course one of these interrogative expressions might be used rhetorically by someone who did *not* make the corresponding supposition. "What first principles *are* there?" might be uttered sceptically. But in this case a better, because more explicit, formulation of the question that is being put would be: "*Are* there any first principles?" And this is a different sort of question from those listed above.

Questions of this latter type would be limiting questions. They would be analogous to questions like "Is there anything Holy?", which might arise in connection with religious inquiry. They are limiting questions because neither in religious inquiry nor in speculative inquiry is it possible to settle them by straightforward argument. In either case, an appropriate response to the limiting question would have to include an attempt to awaken (or to bring to consciousness) a certain sort of interest, a speculative interest or a religious interest as the case may be. Basic speculative questions, like basic religious questions, presuppose the sorts of interests expressed by their respective suppositions.

We might ask whether the principle of non-contradiction is not a first principle which does not depend on the context of any special interest for its meaning. And this might well be granted. But it is possible and indeed not unusual in philosophy to take it as a logical first principle and not as a speculative first principle. Certainly it is not clear that there could be inquiry of any sort without it. But a concern with this principle alone would not be sufficient to constitute a speculative inquiry.

What would a negation of a basic speculative supposition amount to? This would depend on the particular supposition that is being negated. "There are no first principles" might express a decision to the effect that 'the world' (or 'experience') is so protean that it cannot be categorized in any way. In this case, we might argue, some other speculative supposition is being accepted, perhaps "The world is utterly mysterious". Or, it might express a decision not to raise any speculative questions. ("Metaphysics is nonsense.") This might mean a resolution to restrict oneself, when making references, to phenomenalistic expressions. In this case the intention is to rule out all speculative suppositions. So, in one way or in another, the negation of a basic speculative supposition might be given some sense. And this is incidentally one condition, though not a sufficient condition, of giving the supposition some sense.

The suppositions of questions like (i) are very different logically from the suppositions of questions like (ii). "What is Reality?" supposes a unique referent of which something can be said. Questions like (i) on the contrary do not suppose a unique referent, but only that the predicate in question has *some* application. The former suppose the existence of a unique logical subject, and ask what may be truly said of it. The latter suppose the existence of *some* logical subjects to which the predicate may be truly applied.

To bring out this difference further let us take a borderline case, an expression which might be interpreted either as a question like (i) or as a question like (ii): "What is the nature of things?" If we should construe this as a question like (ii) we might put it as: "What is the Nature of things?" This would suppose the existence of some unique logical subject which is being asked about, perhaps in a Spinozistic way, or in a Bradleyan way. Suppose on the contrary we construe this as a question like (i). Then we might explicate it as "What sorts of things are there?", or perhaps by one of the other formulations listed above. In this case the supposition would be of a very different sort.

Some speculative questions may have more point than others do, and in this way may be less trivial than others. One way to tell whether this is so, for a given pair of questions, is to see how trivial their corresponding suppositions are. And one way to tell *this* is to see how significant it would be to deny one or the other of these suppositions. For example it seems more significant to deny that Reality exists than to deny that something exists.

Some questions might be shown to be prior to others. It seems, for example, that if someone asks, "What first principles are there?", then he has already answered implicitly the question "What sorts of things are there?". He is now supposing there are at least two sorts of things. There are first principles, and there are other things. So we might say that "What sorts of things are there?" is prior to "What first principles are there?". But I do not want to argue that there is some one basic speculative question which, in some such way, is prior to all others. Just as there may be more than one useful general theory of religion, from which basic religious predicates might be derived, so there may be more than one useful way of formulating basic speculative questions.

So one use of analysis in speculative inquiry is to reveal what questions are being asked, what sort of questions these are, and what their suppositions are. And analysis has other uses at other stages of inquiry. I see no good reason why speculative philosophers should not be hospitable to analysis of this sort. And it may well be that they have not been so unthinking in these matters as some of their critics have supposed. But it is only fair to expect more of speculative philosophers at this point than of, say, engineers or moralists.

As with religious inquiry, analysis *in* speculative inquiry is, in a way, self-analysis. One would ask, "Just what is it that I want to decide?", and "Just what am I supposing?". And this involves understanding the sort of interest that underlies the inquiry. There is no substitute for this sort of self-analysis. In the course of reading what other philosophers have said, and in the course of philosophical discussion, someone *M* may become acquainted with possibilities he had not thought of and consequences he had not seen. But only *M* can decide what he will do.

Of course analysis *of* speculative inquiries is also essential for the health of philosophy, which cannot be a *purely* private enterprise. And *M*'s own decisions, if he is serious and responsible, involve a readiness to *explain* what he is doing.

One possible result of this sort of analysis is that one may cease to ask a certain question. This might happen in either of two ways. The question might be simply abandoned. Or, one might find that the question being entertained is not the real question one wants to ask. Indeed it is possible that one might discover that the real question one wants to ask is not a speculative question, but instead a moral question or a scientific question or a religious question.

This is equally true of other inquiries. For example in scientific inquiry analysis may lead to the abandonment of certain questions, or to the discovery that the real question one wants to ask has been hidden by the question one has entertained, and that this real question is not a scientific question but instead a moral question or a religious question or a speculative question.

2. *Construction in speculative philosophy*

It is not plausible to suppose that a speculative scheme can be arrived at by a process of simple inductive generalization. It may be that we do arrive at certain theories in some such way in ordinary experience, as when we say there has been more rain this autumn than usual, and in the classificatory stages of some of the sciences, as when we give a provisional account of a species of insects by noting the common characters of a certain number of individuals. But the whole point of speculative philosophy is that it is an interpretative enterprise, and that its categories do not have their applications in so direct and simple a way. We cannot *give* examples of substances in the way we can give examples of rainy days or of boll weevils.

Nor is it plausible to suppose that speculative schemes are arrived at by a simple process of deduction from self-evident and necessary truths. Not many philosophers would claim that their premises are as clear and necessary, or that their conclusions are so inevitably true, as this view of speculative philosophy would suggest they should be.

Therefore it seems clear enough that a process of construction enters into the creation of speculative schemes. This is a use of reason that is common in ordinary experience, in religion, in the physical sciences, and in mathematics.

One way in which imaginative construction enters into speculative philosophy is by way of paradigmatic suggestions. In general,

c

we begin to answer questions (when something more than calculation is required) by starting with suggestions arising from
experiences of various sorts. Sometimes a suggestion will provide
a speculative philosopher with a paradigm for his scheme, a theme
or motif which gives shape to the scheme. Then the propositions
of the system articulate and elaborate this theme in a more or less
coherent way. In this case the suggestion determines the starting
point for the construction of the system.

The logical significance of the paradigm (in contrast with its
historical or psychological significance) is not that it is evidence for
the truth of the system. Rather it is a clue to the meaning of the
system. So interpretation of a speculative system by reference to a
paradigm need not be reductionist in intent or in effect. Suppose,
for example, we should look for the paradigm of Plotinus' system.
We might find reason to think that some self-unification, a unification of the multiple experiences of the self, was paradigmatic for
Plotinus. Or suppose we could identify Schopenhauer's paradigm
in some experience of, as he says, 'my will'. We might thus be
enabled to understand the content and structure of the system
better, without *having* to conclude that the system has only a
'psychological' significance. Nor need we suppose that speculative
philosophers are always clearly aware of their paradigms.

Now if a speculative question is like (i), then paradigmatic
suggestions are not in order. Questions of this sort are open-ended
questions. "What first principles are there?" logically excludes a
paradigmatic answer since it admits the possibility of a multiplicity
of first principles. Similarly, "What sorts of things are there?"
admits the possibility of a multiplicity of sorts of things.

If a speculative question is like (ii), however, then paradigmatic
suggestions are in order, whether or not they occur. "What is
Reality?" admits of being answered from a starting point in a
paradigmatic suggestion.

It follows that if a system is developed from some paradigm, then
the question which is being answered is a question like (ii) whether
or not some such question has been explicitly stated. Paradigmatic
thinking in speculative philosophy is a sign that a question like (ii)
is being (implicitly) asked. For this is the sort of question to which
a paradigmatic answer is logically relevant.

In *this* respect questions like (ii) are more like basic religious
questions than questions like (i) are. For basic religious questions,

like "What is Holy?", admit of paradigmatic answers, and answers of this type are common in religion.

We are considering here a use of *reason*, namely speculative construction. This involves imagination, but if it is a process of reason then it involves a disciplined imagination. What controls might there be in speculative philosophy, so that the construction of a speculative scheme is a serious and responsible act of thought? How is speculative construction disciplined?

I suggest two sorts of controls which might operate to prevent speculation from being irresponsible. One sort of control is a deep respect for facts of all sorts. This brings us to the border of the topic of truth-claims and judgments in speculative philosophy, a border we cross in the next section. But it needs to be mentioned here. For construction has to be undertaken with a view to satisfying the relevant factual conditions of inquiry. And this shows, incidentally, how the uses of reason we have been selecting for separate treatment cannot be isolated from one another as though each belonged in only one distinct phase of speculative inquiry.

There is some justice, however, in postponing a discussion of the factual controls of inquiry to the following section on judgment. For there is a danger that speculative construction may be, we might say, *illogically* restricted by a concern for the facts, or, we might better say, by a premature assessment of the facts. For the point of speculative philosophy is not to give a list of facts but to put the facts in some perspective and throw some light on their interrelations.

The other sort of control on speculative construction lies in the sort of analysis suggested in the previous section. And this is another reason why analysis is important *in* speculative philosophy. Responsible inquiry begins by trying to be clear about the questions one is asking. Just what are they? Are they *real* questions? Are they the questions one really wants to ask, and not just questions one has been taught to ask? Are they *good* questions? Does it make sense to ask them seriously? And particularly, What is their *point*?

Suppose, for example, one finds oneself asking a question like (i), "What first principles are there?". Then we should be clear what we are asking. First principles of *what*? Are we asking about the causes of events? of things? about premises of reasoning?

All this is important in speculative inquiry because only if we understand our questions can we avoid unreal questions and (logically) bad questions. Also, only if we know what we are asking can we have some (more or less explicit) rules of relevance. Only then can we know what sorts of facts are relevant to our questions. For if, when we think we are asking speculative questions, it should be the case that we are asking scientific or religious questions, then we are in for confusion and frustration.

Though constructive imagination in speculative philosophy must be disciplined in these ways, still a certain freedom of imagination is essential, as in any inquiry. For the enterprise of speculative philosophy has point only if scientific theories and religious theories do not completely determine answers to speculative questions, and only if the speculative schemes constructed by philosophers in the past leave at least something more to be done. So, if speculative questions are real questions and good questions, there must be new possibilities to be discerned and developed, not for the sake of novelty itself but for the sake of coming closer to the truth.

3. *Judgments in speculative philosophy*

If speculative philosophy is an inquiry, and not just a productive art (analogous to abstract painting, for example), then it includes a serious and responsible intention to make speculative judgments. Logical judgments, of course, are another matter. Judgments of logical compatibility and incompatibility, for example, are involved in the uses of reason we have already discussed, analysis and construction. But we have been supposing that speculative philosophers mean to learn something, not just to analyse and to construct logically possible systems. We are supposing that their analyses and constructions are features of a process of discovery. And if this is the case, then it must be asked whether theories constructed as answers to speculative questions are in fact true. That is to say, it is necessary to aim at speculative judgments.

Contrariwise, if speculative judgments are not in order, if it does not make sense to ask whether a speculative theory is true, then it would seem that speculative philosophy is not an inquiry but a productive art.

This means that if speculative philosophy is an inquiry then it involves a third use of reason. Along with analysis and construction there is, from the logical beginning of the inquiry, an aim at a harmony of thought and being. This aim shapes the course of the inquiry and requires speculative judgments for its satisfaction.

It is not inconsistent with this aim to suspend judgment on a theory until such time as a judgment may be warranted. Indeed, in suspending judgment, for want of sufficient evidence, we are supposing that a judgment is in order. But when this suspension becomes prolonged in spite of extensions of the range of experience, we may well begin to wonder whether we are in a blind alley. Is a judgment on *that* theory really in order? Then a new analysis of the theory, and of the question it is meant to answer, is needed. And *if* it should turn out that *all* speculative theories are blind alleys, then we would have to conclude that speculative philosophy is not an inquiry but a productive art.

What sorts of truth-claims are made by speculative theories, and how might these claims be judged? At this point I have only one or two suggestions that bear on this vexing problem. I can put them best by considering a question like (ii), "What is Reality?". One (partial) answer to this question might be: "Reality is an experience." Now let us consider one requirement it seems reasonable to make, which would need to be met before it would be clear that, in this answer, a significant truth-claim is being made. It seems that it must be possible to make some reference to Reality, the logical subject of the speculative doctrine we are considering.

Suppose we should ask of the philosopher who asserts this doctrine: "What is it that you are talking about when you say that Reality is an experience? Will you put me in mind of what you mean by Reality? What is it that you are referring to?" And suppose that the philosopher had nothing to say (which is not the same thing as saying nothing) in response to this request. Then would it not be fair to conclude that he is not making any significant claim to truth?

One defence might be that while he does indeed mean to talk about Reality, what he is talking about cannot be referred to. Reality cannot be singled out, in any of the ways we single out one logical subject from among others. The whole point is, he might say, that Reality is not a thing of any sort. So, in saying Reality is an experience, he had no intention of making any reference at all. The point is, he might explain, that whenever we *do* refer to anything, *if* we say of it that it is real, then we ought to say of it also that it is an experience.

Now if this is the case, then we need to ask whether the speculative *question* he is answering is not being put in a misleading way. Perhaps, instead of "What is Reality?", a better formulation of the question he is prepared to answer would be: "What sorts of things are real?" And his answer would then be: "Experiences." For, on his showing, in talking about Reality he really means to talk about a predicate and not about a logical subject.

This latter question would be like (i), not like (ii). It would be like "What sorts of things are there?". But it would fall at a later stage of inquiry, at a point where the scope of the inquiry has been narrowed down by leaving out whatever things there are, if any, that are *not* real.

Suppose on the contrary that the philosopher accepts our request for a reference. Let us notice three features of what he must then do. (1) He must take some factual starting point, and (2) he must employ some interpretative category (since an ostensive reference would not be appropriate) to move from this fact to the goal of the reference. For example, he might say: "Reality is what is behind the world we know through our senses." The starting point is the sensory world. The interpretative category is 'being behind'. There is also a third condition he must satisfy in order to make a successful reference. (3) Some context for the reference needs to be understood or given. Without supposing that the first two conditions are easy to satisfy, let us consider this third condition further.

Suppose that, in response to a request for a reference to God, it is said that God is the cause of the world. Now if the context is indeterminate, the point of the remark will be unclear, and therefore it will be unclear how 'the world' and 'cause' are to be taken. Would it be *in order*, for example, to object that the world was caused by an explosion five (or ten) billion years ago? Suppose however that it is reasonably clear, from what has been said already, or from the way the remark is made, or from other circumstances, that the remark has a *religious* point. Then we might be clearer about how its terms are to be taken and *how* other remarks (about a cosmic explosion, for example) are relevant.

Now we are supposing that speculative inquiry differs in some important way from religious inquiry. And if this is so then it is important to be able to *show* the point of a speculative reference. We need to be able to give the context of a speculative reference in order to show how its point differs from the point of a religious reference and from references of other sorts.

One way to give the context of a reference to Reality is to explain that this reference arises in the course of answering a prior question like "What sorts of things are there?". 'Reality' been has brought into the discussion in this way, the initial answer to this question being, perhaps, "(1) appearances and (2) Reality". This explanation would give us a context within which to understand both the point of the question "What is Reality (or Being, or Nature, or the Absolute)?" and the point of the reference to Reality.

From this it would follow again that questions like (i) ("What sorts of things are there?") are logically prior to questions like (ii) ("What is Reality?"). In order to explicate answers to questions of the latter type, we must put them into the context of questions of the former type. That is, it is questions like (i) which determine the context and the point of questions like (ii). This reinforces the suggestion that basic speculative questions are questions like (i). The fundamental problem is how answers to *these* questions might be judged.

Certain features of these basic speculative questions help us see more clearly the sort of truth-claims which answers to them might make:

(*a*) I have already suggested that questions like this ("What sorts of things are there?") do not make unique references, as questions like (ii) do. They do not present a particular logical subject.

(*b*) In the second place, I take it, common-sense answers (like "Tables, people, colours, etc.") and scientific answers (like "Electrons, elements, fields, cells, etc.") would not do. For if speculative philosophy is an inquiry, then it must be asking questions which differ from common-sense questions and from scientific questions, as well as from religious questions. They would have no point if they were just questions of these latter sorts in disguise.

(*c*) In the third place these questions call for schematic answers. That is, a mere list of sorts of things would not be a complete answer. These sorts of things (like substances, attributes and modes) need to be related to one another in some systematic way. Indeed, it is not really a matter of first thinking up some categories and *then*, after we have them, connecting them up with one another in some more or less ingenious way. They need, in a way, to be thought of *together*, as for example 'appearances' and 'Reality' are thought of together. A scheme is called for. Then some questions like (ii) may find their context within this scheme (though others may not) and thus their point may become clearer. Also it may be possible then to interpret, in terms of the scheme, some of the borderline questions mentioned at the beginning of this Part.

One way to see how speculative schemes might be judged is to study some one such scheme. In the next Part I shall ask how Whitehead's scheme might be judged. Here I only urge the importance of the question whether such judgments are in order. May we, or may we not, properly ask of a speculative scheme whether it is true of (is adequate to, truly illuminates, rightly orders) the world we apprehend in and around ourselves? What we make of this question and how we answer it will determine largely what we think of speculative philosophy. Certainly it seems that in the past serious speculative philosophers have thought speculative judgments were possible. They have meant to do something more than to analyse and to construct, for they have aimed at a harmony of thought and being. They have meant to say something that would be materially true; they have aimed at something more than logical truth. But it is equally clear that it is not easy to say just what sort of truth-claims are made in their schemes and just how speculative judgments are possible. It may be that the current analytical movement in philosophy will help us to understand speculative philosophy better. Also it may be that Whitehead's writings have exhibited a somewhat different mode of philosophizing than those to which we had been accustomed.

Finally a few general remarks on religious inquiry and speculative inquiry are in order, anticipating Part IV. I suggest, first, that these two inquiries are logically independent of one another in the sense that it is possible to ask a basic religious question (e.g. "What is it that is Holy?") without thereby (logically) committing oneself to ask a basic speculative question also, and that it is logically possible to ask a basic speculative question (e.g. "What sorts of things are there?") without (logically) committing oneself to ask a basic religious question. Very often it happens that, in a concrete case, both types of questions are being asked at once.

Hence the importance of analysis. Also very often concepts used in the construction of religious theories have been derived from speculative discourse, and concepts used in the construction of speculative theories have been derived from religious discourse. Hence again the importance of analysis.

It is particularly worth noting some similarities between basic religious questions (like "What is Holy?") and speculative questions like (ii) (e.g. "What is Reality?" and "What is Being?"). In both cases paradigmatic answers are in order, and such answers are often given—answers, that is to say, which are developed from some particular concrete suggestion in experience. And, as a matter of historical fact, the concerns which prompt questions of these different types sometimes have a strong family resemblance. Hence once more the importance of analysis.

Both in serious religious inquiry and in serious speculative inquiry, I have said, there is (along with analysis and construction) an aim at harmony of thought and being. Both religious doctrines and speculative schemes aim at being true. But this is also the case with all serious inquiries. And this does not imply that in having speculative truth we necessarily have religious truth also. For some speculative schemes do not readily yield answers to basic religious questions. Nor does it imply that in having religious truth we necessarily have speculative truth also. For some religious doctrines do not readily yield answers to basic speculative questions. But it might be that some religious doctrines are interpretable in terms of some speculative scheme or other. And a religious doctrine might help to shape the construction of some speculative scheme. So religious truth and speculative truth *need* not be either in conflict with one another or isolated from one another.

III

Whitehead has said a great deal about this own way of doing speculative philosophy, especially the first chapter of *Process and Reality*, and his remarks are highly illuminating if we take them together with what he has done. But here I propose to be guided primarily not by what he has said but what he has done. I would like to draw attention to the structure of what he proposes in speculative philosophy. His remarks *about* speculative philosophy

c*

may be helpful at certain points, but they are not my *primary* concern.

To see what sorts of truth-claims are made in Whitehead's speculative philosophy, we should begin by distinguishing his categoreal scheme (as concisely stated in Chapter Two of Part I of PR) and its systematic development from the pre-systematic and post-systematic statements in which the scheme is, so to speak, embedded.

By pre-systematic statements I mean statements of facts Whitehead means to take account of and do justice to in his speculative construction, for example:

> All things flow.
> Consciousness presupposes experience.
> There are many things.
> Things are interconnected.
> Aims are effective.
> Quanta of energy are associated with periodic laws.
> The primitive experience is emotional feeling, felt in relevance to a world beyond.

We might characterize these statements by saying that neither their logical subjects nor their predicates are expressed by terms taken from Whitehead's own categoreal scheme. Instead, their terms are taken from ordinary usage, from science, from religious discourse, or from traditional philosophical usage, and have the meanings they are given in those contexts. Such terms may be called non-systematic terms, meaning that they are not taken from Whitehead's categoreal scheme.

By systematic statements I mean statements of relationships within the scheme, for example:

> A prehension has a subject, a datum, and a subjective form.
> Eternal objects are ingredient in actual entities.
> Every actual entity is present in every other actual entity.
> A proposition is the datum of a complex feeling derived from the integration of a physical feeling with a conceptual feeling.

In statements of this sort all the terms are derived from the categoreal scheme. Both the logical subjects and the predicates of these statements are expressed by systematic terms.

By post-systematic statements I mean statements in which facts

and principles of various sorts are interpreted in terms of the
categoreal scheme, for example:

> The finite things that endure through time are not actual
> entitites but nexūs of actual entities.
>
> Feelings are the entities which are primarily 'compatible' or
> 'incompatible'. All other usages of these terms are
> derivative.
>
> The societies in an environment will constitute its orderly
> element, and the non-social actual entities will constitute its
> element of chaos.

In these statements some of the terms are non-systematic terms
and some are systematic terms. And the point of the statements is
to put the facts and principles expressed by the non-systematic
terms into a certain perspective. The systematic terms are used to
interpret non-systematic terms. Perceptual facts, scientific facts,
moral facts, and others are framed in terms of the categoreal
scheme.

So these three sorts of statements in Whitehead's writings
correspond to the phases of the flight of an aeroplane, which he
gives as a parable about speculative philosophy:

> "It starts from the ground of particular observation; it makes a
> flight in the thin air of imaginative generalization; and it again
> lands for renewed observation rendered acute by rational inter-
> pretation."[13]

Now it seems reasonably clear that different sorts of truth-
claims are made by these different sorts of statements. Pre-
systematic statements are themselves of very different sorts. Some
are scientific statements, some are statements of logical principles,
some are moral statements, some are common-sense perceptual
statements, and so on. So the sorts of truth-claims they make vary
widely.

Systematic statements are, we might say, analytical statements.
They state relationships within a scheme which has been *constructed*. So they do not follow in a straightforward way from the
pre-systematic statements. They are not strictly deduced from
the pre-systematic statements. Nor are they inductive generalizations from the pre-systematic statements. This can be put by

[13] PR 5 [7].

saying that the truth of a particular systematic statement, like "An actual entity has a subjective aim", does not strictly depend on the truth of any particular pre-systematic statement, nor on the truth of any conjunction of pre-systematic statements.

There is presumably a genetic relation between acknowledgment of the pre-systematic facts and the construction of the scheme. That is to say, the intention in constructing the scheme is to throw light on the facts. Also the applicability of the scheme will depend in part on some of the pre-systematic statements being true since, presumably, the truthfulness of a post-systematic statement presupposes the truth of some pre-systematic statement. This is a point we must return to later.

My main point at the moment is that systematic statements are not *directly* about the world. Systematic *terms*, like 'actual entity', are used in post-systematic statements to say something about the world. But systematic statements are directly about relationships within the categoreal scheme. This means that the entities mentioned in the categories of existence, for example actual entities, are what Whitehead says they are.[14]

So it is a mistake to take Whitehead's categories of existence (actual entities, prehensions, nexūs, subjective forms, eternal objects, propositions, multiplicities, and contrasts) in some simple way as names for perceptually isolable components in experience. When we see a table we do not see actual entities. We might say that when we see a table we are looking at a nexus of actual entities. But this would be a post-systematic interpretation of experience. Nor do we, in the act of seeing a table, experience our *seeing* it as itself an actual occasion. We do not have sufficient powers of discrimination to isolate, perceptually, any one of the multiplicity of actual occasions of which, on Whitehead's theory, our experience of seeing the table is composed. The *use* of the concepts in Whitehead's categoreal scheme is not to name perceptually isolable elements in experience, but to analyse and interpret our experience. The entities listed in his categories of existence are not intuited—though they may well have been suggested by elements in experience—or deduced; they are constructed.

[14] It would not make good sense to say: "I know that according to the scheme every actual entity has a satisfaction. But might there not be one or two actual entities somewhere, sometime, which do not have satisfactions?" Of course there are problems about what Whitehead does say they are. These are problems about the consistency and coherence of the categoreal scheme.

It follows that post-systematic statements are not straight-forward descriptions of what is experienced. We do not experience the 'fact' that a stone is a nexus of actual occasions. We interpret the stone as a nexus of actual occasions. So the kind of truth-claim made in the post-systematic statement is not the kind of truth-claim made by a straightforward description. We do not *see that* a table is a nexus of actual entities any more than we *see* an actual entity.

What then is the point of these post-systematic statements? And, since the purpose of the systematic construction is to make post-systematic statements possible, this is also to ask, what is the point of the construction of the scheme? What would be the value of being able to express our observations and beliefs in systematic language?

Presumably this would be something like the value of being about to express (some) of our observations and beliefs in scientific language, in which constructions are also important. But it would be different in the following ways:

(i) A speculative system would have a wider scope than science (the exact sciences taken together) does. A speculative system would enable us to express in a coherent way (*a*) the concrete perceptual experiences from which the sciences abstract; *and* (*b*) our moral and aesthetic and religious intuitions, which are embodied in practical activity, in works of art, and in religious experiences; *and* (*c*) well-founded scientific theories themselves. Its objective is "to put the various elements of our experience into a consistent relation to each other".[15]

(ii) For this very reason a speculative system is not subject to confirmation in just the same way as a scientific theory. Though the concepts of actual entities and electrons are both constructed, they are constructs of different sorts. It is not *in order* to offer statistical studies or the results of experiments in *direct* support of a speculative system.

These scientific facts do have an indirect bearing on speculative judgments, however, at least on judgments of Whitehead's system. For his scheme is meant to be applicable to well-founded scientific theories. It is meant to be both relevant to them and consistent with them. For example, he offers an interpretation of electrons in terms of routes of actual occasions. So, to the

[15] PR v [v].

extent that well-founded scientific theories are logically dependent on scientific data—to the extent that scientific concepts are shaped by scientific facts—to that extent these data are indirectly relevant to speculative judgments. If the speculative system is incapable of interpreting a well-founded scientific theory, then it is in that respect inadequate. So in this indirect way Whitehead's scheme is subject to disconfirmation by scientific discoveries.

(iii) Since Whitehead's system is proposed as an interpretation not only of scientific facts but of other-than-scientific facts as well, it is in one way more vulnerable to disconfirmation than scientific theories are. It must be defended on more than one front. It must be shown to be consistent with and relevant to all the other sorts of experiences referred to above. So the final test of a speculative system like Whitehead's, beyond the internal tests of self-consistency and coherence, is adequacy to all of our experience.

How might this sort of test be made? Aesthetic judgments of the system are of course in order, and no doubt one reason for the appeal of Whitehead's system is the impression of elegance, subtlety and scope it gives. But we are supposing for the sake of argument that speculative philosophy is not a productive art, and that therefore speculative judgments are not aesthetic judgments.

The first step in making a speculative judgment on Whitehead's system is to formulate, independently of the system, a statement in which we express some fact as clearly as we can. Since the system purports to be adequate to all of experience, no sort of fact is excluded. So the fact we express in the proposition may be a logical fact, a mathematical fact, a fact of perceptual experience, a fact apprehended in moral experience, or a fact of some other sort.

It is not enough to take some proposition which might come to mind without reflection, for example "Stones do not act". We must try to make clear to ourselves just what fact we mean to express by the use of this sentence.

Next we need to ask whether this fact can be expressed in Whitehead's systematic terms, by some set of post-systematic statements which might include for example "Stones do not have subjective aims, for stones are enduring objects and only actual entities have subjective aims". Does the complex post-systematic statement, which we construct by use of the categoreal scheme, adequately express the fact we mean to state? Is there any part or aspect of the fact which would *not* be expressed by the post-

systematic statement? Assuming that in the post-systematic statement we have exhausted the resources of the scheme for expressing
the fact, is there something in the fact to which the scheme is
inadequate? For example, can the scheme be used to express the
impression of inertia we get as we lift the stone? Again, does
the scheme yield an adequate interpretation of the theory of
gravitation?

The question is not whether Whitehead *has*, in his writings,
adequately expressed the fact in his systematic terms. This would
be a different question. It might turn out that his own post-
systematic interpretation of some fact, for example personal
identity, is incomplete. He may have failed to make full use of his
own resources. Also we must leave room for the possibility that he
has misused his scheme in some post-systematic interpretation.[16]

So the question here is not exactly whether Whitehead has given
an adequate interpretation of the fact we have in mind. The
question is whether the scheme *can* properly be used to give an
adequate interpretation.

So the formation of this sort of speculative judgment involves
exploration in two directions. It involves on one hand a pre-
systematic exploration of some particular fact, and it involves on
the other hand an exploration of the resources of the categoreal
scheme for interpreting the fact. Further, a certain dialectical
process is involved. To look at the fact in the light of the scheme
is to re-examine the fact.

We might call these judgments particular speculative judgments.
They decide whether or not some post-systematic statement is
true, that is to say, whether or not the post-systematic statement is
an adequate interpretation of the pre-systematic fact.

Now if a particular speculative judgment is negative—if we
decide that there is some part or aspect of the fact which is not
expressed by the post-systematic statement—then, assuming that
we have used the full resources of the scheme in constructing the
statement, we are deciding that the scheme is not adequate to the
fact.[17] And since the scheme purports to be adequate to *all* facts,
this means that the scheme is untrue. It has failed in its aim. This

[16] It is true that his post-systematic interpretations help us to understand the
structure of the systematic scheme. But they do not determine the structure of
the scheme and are thus on a different logical footing.

[17] A negative judgment may be annulled either by better understanding of the
fact or by better understanding of the resources of the scheme.

failure may be more or less important. The scheme may still be enormously suggestive. Indeed, it may come nearer to fitting all the facts than any other scheme at hand. Further, it may permit some reconstruction which would enlarge its resources. Still, as it stands it is untrue.[18]

Suppose that on the contrary we decide that the post-systematic statement is adequate to the fact. Then we are deciding that the scheme is *in so far* true. It has met this particular test of its truth. But many other particular speculative judgments have to be made, starting with other pre-systematic facts. For it purports to be a matrix sufficient for adequate interpretations of all facts.

Now suppose that a number of such affirmative speculative judgments have seemed to be warranted, so that the truth-claim of the scheme seems increasingly supported. Might we ever be in a position to make a *final* judgment of the truth of the scheme? This does not seem possible, for the reason that we never can be in a position to say that we have considered all the facts. Still we might be in a position to say that the scheme is true as far as we can see, meaning that it is adequate to all the facts we have considered. And this would be a great deal to say of any speculative scheme.

Now I would like to turn from this discussion of how speculative judgments of Whitehead's scheme are possible, to consider first, the sort of questions to which his speculative proposal is relevant and, secondly, its suppositions.

Primarily, I suggest, Whitehead's speculative proposal is an answer to a question like (i) "What sorts of things are there?". Part of the evidence for this is that his formal statement of the categoreal scheme really begins with a list of 'categories of existence'.[19] That

[18] Cf. PR 11 [12–3]: "If we consider any scheme of philosophic categories as one complex assertion, and apply to it the logician's alternative, true or false, the answer must be that the scheme is false. The same answer must be given to a like question respecting the existing formulated principles of any science."

[19] I say 'really' begins because 'the category of the ultimate' is not a systematic category in the same sense as the categories of existence, explanation and obligation. This can be shown in this way: Any statement referring to creativity can be expressed by a statement about entities. For example, for "Creativity is unending" we can substitute, "There is an infinite and unending multiplicity of actual entities". Strictly speaking, if something is not included in the categories of existence, then it is not an *entity* in Whitehead's scheme (see PR 27 [31]). And this means that there cannot be systematic discourse about it. For the function of entities in the system is to be the logical subjects of systematic statements. Since the use of multiplicities (category of existence vii) as logical

is to say, the first step he takes, in stating the formal categories of his scheme, is to give a list of different sorts of things. He presents a set of multiplicities.[20] This is not all he does, of course, but let us pause to note some of the implications of this fact.

It would follow from our analysis earlier in this essay that Whitehead's basic problem is not a religious problem but a speculative problem. This is more clearly true than it would be if his basic problem were like (ii), "What is Reality?" (I am not suggesting that he raises no question like (ii); I suggest only that his *basic* question is not of this type.)

It would follow likewise that a paradigmatic solution of his basic problem is not in order, though paradigmatic solutions may be in order for other questions he raises.

These conclusions are important, for they offer us a way of understanding how a speculative inquiry *might* be clearly different from religious inquiry. For it might turn out that a speculative inquiry does not *have* to ask a question like (ii). And since it is these latter questions that resemble religious questions, this would make it easier to conceive how speculative philosophy and religion *might* be distinct, though not necessarily unrelated, human interests.

In the course of his speculative inquiry Whitehead does ask other questions as well as questions like (i). And we need to see how these other questions arise and what they amount to. Among the entities mentioned in the categories of existence, actual entities have a certain primacy. Let us look at this primacy of actual entities and ask what sort of question it is relevant to and what sort of supposition is being made.

One way in which actual entities have a primacy over entities of other sorts in the categoreal scheme appears in Whitehead's systematic discussion of propositions. A proposition has one or more actual entities as its logical subject(s).[21] This means that any judgment of truth and falsity, when rendered into systematic terms, would deal with what is the case with some actual entity or with the actual entities composing some nexus.

The primacy of actuality appears also in the ontological principle, which means "that actual entities are the only *reasons*; so that to

---

subjects has to be qualified (category of explanation xvi), a multiplicity is not a 'proper' entity (PR 40 [45]). But creativity is not an entity at all, in this systematic sense. The term is a relatively non-systematic term.

[20] PR 29 [32–3].   [21] PR 364 [393].

search for a *reason* is to search for one or more actual entities".[22]
This means that an explanation of any fact, when rendered into
systematic terms, would point to some actual entity or entities as
the reason(s) for the fact.

The primacy of actuality appears in many other ways. For
example, the whole point of the categories of obligation is to state
the conditions which the concrescence of an actual entity must
satisfy. It appears also in Whitehead's interpretations of qualities
and relations,[23] and in his doctrine of eternal objects.[24]

It seems fairly clear that the primacy Whitehead gives to actualities (i.e. things that have power) reflects a judgment about
importance. It answers some question like, "Among the sorts of
things there are, what sorts are more important?". We may well
agree that this is a highly defensible judgment, but it is a judgment
nevertheless, a judgment which is built into the very structure of
the categoreal scheme.

Suppose it is granted that actualities are more important than any
other sort of entities (for example, forms, concepts, ideals). Then
it may be asked, "Of what sort are actual things?". Now this is
different from the basic speculative question "What sorts of things
are there?". But it is still in the framework of the basic question. It is
still not a question *just* like (ii), "What is Reality?".

Now Whitehead's own answer to this question ("Of what sort
are actual things?") is like answers to questions like (ii) in at least
one respect, namely he gives a paradigmatic answer to it. Certainly
this is his own interpretation of what he has done:

"Philosophic thought has to start from some limited section of
our experience—from epistemology, or from natural science, or
from theology, or from mathematics. Also the investigation always
retains the taint of its starting point. Every starting point has its
merits, and its selection must depend upon the individual philosopher.

"My own belief is that at present the most fruitful, because the
most neglected, starting point is that section of value-theory which

[22] PR 33 [37], category of explanation xviii.
[23] See William A. Christian, *An Interpretation of Whitehead's Metaphysics*,
Yale University Press, 1959, pp. 240–1.
[24] Cf. PR 363 [392]: "The very diversity of eternal objects has for its reason
their diversity of functioning in *this* actual world." This illustrates the far-
reaching importance of the ontological principle.

we term aesthetics. Our enjoyment of the values of human art, or of natural beauty, our horror at the obvious vulgarities and defacements which force themselves upon us—all these modes of experience are sufficiently abstracted to be relatively obvious. And yet evidently they disclose the very meaning of things."[25]

So he constructs actual entities on the model of acts of experience, more specifically acts of aesthetic experience, with subjective aims, prehensions, and satisfactions.[26]

Two comments are due on Whitehead's use of an act of aesthetic experience as a paradigm for his theory of actual entities. One has to do with its bearing on the construction of the categoreal scheme; the other has to do with its bearing on judgments of Whitehead's scheme.

(i) 'Experience' is not, strictly speaking, a systematic term. It is true that it is used very often, and that in *Adventures of Ideas* 'occasions of experience' becomes the standard term for actual occasions. This makes it all the more significant that the term 'experience' does not appear in the categories of existence, explanation, and obligation. It is as though Whitehead deliberately avoided using it to introduce his basic categories. Instead he speaks of 'feelings' (with quotation marks to indicate a systematic use) and immediacy. Now notice how these terms are introduced. A 'feeling' is defined as a prehension; a prehension is not defined as a feeling. The movement of thought, that is to say, is toward abstraction. Similarly the immediacy of an actual entity is explained as the significance of the entity for itself. "By this it is meant that an actual entity functions in respect to its own determination."[27] Again the aim is at concepts which might apply beyond the range of our ordinary use of terms like 'experience'. For the categoreal scheme is meant to apply to electrons and stones as well as to instances of human experience. Whitehead makes it perfectly clear that on his view prehensions are only rarely conscious.

So it would be misleading to say that Whitehead is attributing aesthetic experience (pre-systematically understood) to electrons and stones. We should take quite seriously Whitehead's aim at logical rigor in the construction of his scheme, and we should not

[25] "Analysis of Meaning", *Essays in Science and Philosophy*, Philosophical Library, New York, 1947, p. 129.
[26] Cf. RM [89, 104–5, 115]; PR 5 [7], 158 [172], 249 [268]; SMW [ix, 103]; MT 86.   [27] PR 34 [38], category of explanation xxi.

read into his systematic terms stronger meanings than they are given in the categoreal scheme. If Whitehead himself should be misleading on this point sometimes, we should judge this in the light of his own principles.

(ii) Using aesthetic experience as a starting point for construction of the scheme is different from using such experiences to support the truth-claim of the scheme. Here the question is not how Whitehead happened to get his vision of things, but whether the categoreal scheme he has constructed is in fact applicable and adequate to interpret all the facts. It is entirely in order to ask whether the scheme *is* adequate to aesthetic experiences of various sorts. The fact that Whitehead takes some such experience as a paradigm does not guarantee that the scheme *as constructed* will meet this test. It is equally important to ask whether the scheme can yield adequate interpretations of facts of other sorts, physical motions and moral resolutions, for example.

Now let us consider the suppositions made in Whitehead's speculative inquiry. A question like (i), "What sorts of things are there?", supposes there are some sorts of things, and Whitehead's basic question certainly makes a supposition like this. Again, Whitehead's assignment of primacy to actuality supposes, as we have seen, that things of some sorts are more important than things of other sorts.

There is another supposition which underlies Whitehead's speculative philosophy. In the categoreal scheme this supposition is reflected in the principle of relativity: "it belongs to the nature of a 'being' that it is a potential for every 'becoming' ".[28] The supposition underlying this principle is that there is nothing which is absolutely unconnected with everything else, or, to put it in another way, that there is nothing that is entirely beyond our experience, or, to put it in still another way, that there is nothing which is *absolutely* transcendent.

Again, as with the supposition that things of some sorts are more important than things of other sorts, this is a supposition with which we might well agree. But it is not an inevitable supposition. Kant, if I understand him, did not make this supposition— nor did he deny it. But certainly Whitehead does.

Now we may not want to call this, in Whitehead's case, a supposition, because he makes it quite explicit.[29] We might prefer

[28] PR 30 [33], category of explanation iv.   [29] Cf. PR 234 [254], 268 [288].

to call it an assumption. What is important about it is its function. It is the justification for constructing not merely a list of sorts of things but a categoreal *scheme*. More specifically, it is the justification for constructing a conception of actual entities from the paradigm of aesthetic experience. For this supposition makes it possible to say there is a 'logical harmony' of being.[30] With this supposition there can be an intellectual unification in experience which is something like the unity of an aesthetic experience.

The point I would stress is that, at most, this supposition would justify only the conception of a *logical* harmony of being. The kind of unity of experience it might, at most, support is a unity in thought. The supposition that all things are interconnected in some systematic way does not, of itself, justify us in going further and saying there is a harmony of being in some other and stronger sense.

Yet it is clear that Whitehead does go further. In the last Part of *Process and Reality*, in the final chapters of *Adventures of Ideas*, and elsewhere he speaks of a "Harmony of Harmonies"[31] which is both the basis of morality and the object of religious experience.

I have argued elsewhere that Whitehead's conception of God, though it is a "derivative notion"[32] is integral to his speculative scheme. His categories of explanation are logically ineffective without it. So I do not mean to suggest here that this conception is merely added to the basic notions of the categoreal scheme. On the contrary I suggest that something more than a speculative interest has operated in the construction of the categoreal scheme, I suggest that a religious interest has helped to shape the scheme.

For consider: If we find some religious proposal as the conclusion of an argument, is it not reasonable to suppose that there is some (implicit or explicit) religious premise which gives the conclusion its religious colour? Is it possible, strictly speaking, to derive religious conclusions from altogether non-religious premises, any more than it is possible to derive moral conclusions from altogether non-moral premises?

Now if some religious interest has helped to shape the construction of Whitehead's categoreal scheme, then along with the speculative questions noticed above, he has been asking a basic

[30] "This means that thought can penetrate into every occasion of fact, so that by comprehending its key conditions, the whole complex of its pattern of conditions lies open before us." SMW [39].

[31] AI 367.
[32] PR 42 [46], title.

religious question as well. And it is not difficult to formulate such a question by making use of Whitehead's religious conclusions. For example, in the eloquent passage at the end of Chapter Twelve of *Science and the Modern World*, he says, "The vision claims nothing but worship . . .".[33] This yields, as a formulation of a basic religious question, "What is it that rightly claims worship?". Again, when he introduces the conception of a primordial actual entity in *Process and Reality*, he says:

"It is here termed 'God'; because the contemplation of our natures, as enjoying real feelings derived from the timeless source of all order, acquires that 'subjective form' of refreshment and companionship at which religions aim."[34]

And this yields, as a formulation of a basic religious question: "What is the (ultimate) source of refreshment and companionship?"

So I suggest that Whitehead's speculative philosophy is not *pure* speculative philosophy, if this means a speculative philosophy proceeding *only* from a speculative interest.

Notice that, just as in Whitehead's speculative questions certain suppositions are made, so also in his religious questions certain suppositions are made, for example that there is something or other which claims worship and that there is a source of refreshment and companionship. The question, in either case, asks *what* this is.

IV

In conclusion let us reflect briefly on some resemblances between uses of reason in religious inquiry, on one hand, and in speculative inquiry, on the other hand. (*a*) In both cases analysis is important, to make clear (i) what questions are being asked and what their suppositions are, (ii) what suggestions are being adopted for the construction of theories and how these theories are structured, and (iii) how these theories might be judged. (*b*) In both cases construction is important, for the sake of obtaining categories of explanation. Without such categories no reasonable judgments can be made. (*c*) In both cases, when inquiry is serious, there is from the beginning an aim at harmony of thought and being, theory and

[33] SMW [268].   [34] PR 43 [47].

fact, to which analysis in the inquiry and the construction of theories are instrumental.

Notice also some resemblances between what we termed functions of faith in religious inquiry, on one hand, and, on the other hand, certain features of speculative philosophy. (*a*) Whenever, in speculative philosophy, some question is answered by use of a paradigm, we have something analogous to the adoption of a particular religious suggestion. The adoption of some particular starting point for construction of a speculative theory, whether this starting point is a mechanistic physical system, a biological organism, an act of will, or an aesthetic experience, involves a more-or-less-calculated risk. Before a theory of the appropriate type is constructed by use of the paradigm, it is not possible to know how fruitful the use of *this* paradigm will be. Yet there may be some questions in speculative philosophy which cannot be answered without the use of some paradigm or other, though I have tried to show that not all speculative questions are of this type.

(*b*) Speculative questions, like religious questions, make suppositions. And only if these suppositions are adhered to does it make sense to go on with the inquiry. Some suppositions have more point, are more significant, than others. And some suppositions are logically prior to others. The fundamental or basic suppositions are those which define the interest from which the inquiry proceeds and thus underlie the inquiry as a whole.

Because of these resemblances certain confusions, and even conflicts perhaps, between religious inquiry and speculative inquiry may occur. When a religious question is being asked along with a speculative question, then the adoption of a paradigm may bring about a problematical situation. For example, shall we say that the paradigmatic use of a mystical experience by a neoplatonic philosopher is a logical *alternative* to the paradigmatic use of the Exodus by a Hebrew prophet?

Again, when a religious question is being asked along with a speculative question, there may be a problem about the suppositions that are being made. For example, take the following passage from *Science and the Modern World*:

"Faith in reason is the trust that the ultimate natures of things lie together in a harmony which excludes mere arbitrariness. It is the faith that at the base of things we shall not find mere arbitrary mystery. . . . This faith cannot be justified by any inductive generalization. It springs from direct inspection of the nature of things as disclosed in our own immediate present experience. There is no parting from your own shadow. To experience this faith is to know that in being ourselves we are more than ourselves: to know that our experience, dim and fragmentary as it is, yet sounds the utmost depths of reality: to know that detached details merely in order to be themselves demand that they should find themselves in a system of things: to know that this system includes the harmony of logical rationality, and the harmony of aesthetic achievement: to know that, while the harmony of logic lies upon the universe as an iron necessity, the aesthetic harmony stands before it as a living ideal moulding the general flux in its broken progress towards finer, subtler issues."[35]

With some care we might be able to distinguish the supposition of a logical harmony from the supposition about an aesthetic harmony, and from the suppositions about the self and about the depths of reality that are being made in this passage. This may help us see what uses of reason are being proposed.

If we ask what are the natures of things and how they are related to one another (which is like asking for a schematic answer to "What sorts of things are there?"), we are supposing there are some determinate things and that they are related to one another in *some* way or other. Then we may *find* that things are 'together' in some particular way, for example that their togetherness is a kind of aesthetic harmony, or we may not. The interest expressed in the question might be satisfied equally well either way. For the question means that if things are not together in an aesthetic harmony we want to know it. Being rational in our thinking about the world does not itself require that the world be an aesthetic harmony. A concern for harmony of thought and being, in answering *this* sort of question, requires only that what we believe about the world should conform to what is true about the world, and that we do our best to understand the truth about the world, whatever that may be.

Suppose we do find the world an aesthetic harmony. Then another sort of response is involved. Another sort of interest than that expressed in the initial question has been awakened. Then we

[35] SMW [26–7].

enjoy the harmony we find in the world. Then and only then, is it in order to ask a question like "What are the conditions of the aesthetic harmony of the world?" or "What are the metaphysical implications of aesthetic experience?". For the interest which prompts these questions goes beyond the interest expressed in the question like (i). That question does not itself suppose the world is an aesthetic harmony. If we ask something more, we must have found something more which prompts us to seek what we seek.

But is 'finding' quite the right thing to say? We have an intimation that the world is an aesthetic harmony? And, responding to this suggestion, we *take* it to be so? But the taking cannot be an arbitrary taking. Faith, if this is a kind of faith, must proceed upon a warrant. And must it not be possible, if we are concerned for truth, to ask whether we are *right* in taking the world to be so?

There is yet another strand of thought in the passage. We 'ourselves' are being considered, and the 'depths of reality'. Here something more than aesthetic harmony seems to be involved. Here a question like "What is the ground of our being?" or like "What is the source of refreshment and companionship?" is being answered. Something more than aesthetic contemplation is at work.

My purpose in suggesting these distinctions has not been to suggest that speculative interests and religious interests are incompatible with one another, or that there is any incongruity in having them at the same time, or indeed that they cannot be satisfied together. There is no reason why, in the course of some particular inquiry which we begin by asking some question, a question of another sort should not also occur to us and interest us. My purpose is, instead, to show how we can understand better what we are doing. Neither theologians nor speculative philosophers can afford to overlook the religious questions which sometimes arise in the course of speculative inquiry and the speculative questions which sometimes arise in the course of religious inquiry, or to mistake one for the other.

FREDERIC B. FITCH

SKETCH OF A PHILOSOPHY

FREDERIC B. FITCH

SKETCH OF A PHILOSOPHY

If it is true, as Aristotle said, that philosophy begins with wonder, it is also true that it ends with wonder, because the complexity of the world and of man is so great that unfathomable mysteries are always bound to remain after philosophical investigation and speculation have done their best. Each man who tries to understand, as well as he can, the universe in which he finds himself, is being to that extent a philosopher. If he is also a teacher of philosophy, that is somewhat of an accident, and it makes him no more (or less) a philosopher than he would be anyhow.

As I see it, the world is made of a number of things. It contains not only 'cabbages and kings' (more of the former and fewer of the latter than in bygone days), but it contains in some sense such peculiar things as the square root of minus one, atoms that can split and fuse, theories about such atoms, and theories about all theories whatever. It also contains values, purposes, religions, wars, hatreds, loves; and theories about all these things too. It contains animals that are very much like men, and men that are very much like animals. In fact, there seems to be no sharp line between man and animal, between animal and plant, between plant and virus, between virus and so-called non-living matter.

It is the job of the philosopher, and of the ordinary man in his capacity as philosopher, to try to understand how this conglomeration of diverse things can somehow constitute a single world with a place for everything and everything in its place. We wish to understand the world not only because of the pure joy of understanding, but also for practical reasons. If there is an ultimate and real purpose in life and if we can know what this purpose is, we might decide to reorient all our practical activities in the light of such a purpose. In this connection, for example, we may well ask whether there is a human self or soul that in some way survives the death of the body, and whether such a self or soul will be rewarded or punished in an afterlife because of its performance in this life.

I believe that in some sense this is true, at least metaphorically, and that the great religions that have taught this have not been teaching unreasonable superstition but have hold of a profound philosophical insight. Even the religious beliefs of primitive men often contain valuable philosophical insights. It is true that primitive men have not had the advantages of modern science, or the use of that tool *par excellence* of modern science, mathematics; still, they have survived in a hostile environment for hundreds of thousands of years, and over those long periods of time many good philosophical minds must have appeared among them and left some trace in their religious traditions.

Not only did primitive man lack mathematics but he also lacked something that most philosophers of our present age have lacked, namely training in modern symbolic logic. I believe that symbolic logic will eventually make possible new advances in value theory, epistemology, psychology and philosophy which will be comparable with the advances that traditional mathematics, especially after the advent of calculus, has made possible in the natural sciences. One thing that will intensify the study of logical systems and the use of logical systems in fields of endeavour where they have been little used before is the important part that computing machines are coming to play in certain areas of our society and the fact that computing machines have such close theoretical connection with systems of logic. (Right now, indeed, I am engaged in writing a programme to cause one of the large IBM computing machines to solve problems in combinatory logic.) This stimulation that symbolic logic is receiving from its relevance to computing machines will hasten the day when at least some philosophical questions can be answered by putting these questions to a computing machine and asking it to reason out the answer with the help of symbolic logic. Imagine how pleased Leibniz would have been by this prospect. He hoped that some day philosophers could solve philosophical problems algebraically with pen and ink, but how much less tedious to have a machine do this work, and how many *hundreds* of philosophical problems could be solved by a machine in the time that it would take one philosopher to solve one philosophical problem algebraically by pen and ink.

In any case the study of logical systems is leading more and more philosophers to view the world in terms of relations, attributes, classes and propositions, and to study the structure of the world in terms of these categories, for these are the categories that modern logic is most concerned with.

I would now like to sketch out my present philosophical position, a position that surely reflects my interest in symbolic logic and in logical systems. Relations, attributes and classes are important entities in this philosophy, but so are events and substances. I follow Whitehead in regarding space-time as filled with small indivisible events which Whitehead would call actual occasions and which I shall call primary occasions. But this last statement must be qualified in several respects. First of all, although Whitehead's actual occasions are in a sense indivisible and atomic, he would say that potentially they are capable of divisibility into spatio-temporal parts, but are not actually so divided. Also he would distinguish genetic divisibility from co-ordinate divisibility. Whitehead seems to assume an antecedent plenum of space-time regions, each of which might have been exactly filled by an actual occasion of the right size and shape, whether or not it is actually so filled. But he never seems to give an adequate account of the metaphysical status of these regions. Now I said that my primary occasions, like Whitehead's actual occasions, also fill space-time. But this is not really an accurate way of speaking in the case of these primary occasions, because these primary occasions, by their relations to one another, constitute the space-time plenum, instead of filling it as if it were something antecedently there waiting to be filled.

Each primary occasion has other primary occasions as its immediate causal predecessors, and these are its immediate causal past. There is thus a relation of immediate causation holding among primary occasions and ordering them into a space-time somewhat like that envisaged in Einstein's General Theory of Relativity, so that we may speak of the total causal past of each primary occasion, and also of its total causal future. The way in which the primary occasions are related to each other by this relation of immediate causation, and by certain other relations, makes space-time what it is, makes it more curved in the vicinity of some primary occasions than in the vicinity of others, and even makes it lose its ordinary character altogether in special cases where the primary occasions have become related to one another in certain unusually complicated ways, as perhaps in the nuclei of atoms or in the central nervous systems of higher organisms.

Each primary occasion is a spatio-temporal unit in the sense that there is no meaning to speaking of spatio-temporal parts of it. If space-time is simply the relatedness of primary occasions, there can be no meaning to the notion of spatio-temporal part of a primary occasion. An aggregate of primary occasions *does* have as parts the primary occasions that belong to the aggregate, and it also has as parts smaller subaggregates of primary occasions, but the primary occasions themselves have no spatio-temporal parts.

The relation of immediate causation holds from each primary occasion to each primary occasion that is in the immediate causal future of the former. A whole chain of primary occasions related serially by the relation of immediate causation constitutes a causal chain of primary occasions. Another important relation among primary occasions is the relation of immediate substantival predecessor. This relation holds from any primary occasion to the next primary occasion that is an occasion of the same substance. A whole chain of occasions joined together serially by this relation constitutes a substance enduring through time. Every such substantival chain, or substance, is also a causal chain, but not every causal chain is a substance. Now causal chains can converge into a single causal chain and can branch into separate causal chains, thus giving rise to complex causal networks. I am inclined to assume that substantival chains, or substances, can branch too, as when a fundamental particle splits into two fundamental particles, or two fundamental particles fuse together to form a new fundamental particle. Similarly, when a living cell divides into two cells, or when two cells fuse to form a single cell, there is a branching of a substantival chain in the former case and a joining together of two substantival chains in the latter case.

In the case of any so-called complex substance, such as a living cell, which is a complex of molecules, or such as a molecule itself, which is a complex of atoms, I assume that there is one principal substance which provides the unity in the complexity. It is this unifying substance which branches into two unifying substances when the cell divides into two cells, or when the molecule divides into two molecules. In the case of higher living organisms there is also a dominant unifying substance, the self or the soul. There may be several such unifying substances which alternately take control of the body, as in the case of split personality. The various alternative personalities might fuse into a single personality when the split is healed, or one might establish itself as dominant over the others. I assume that no substance ever terminates except in the sense of dividing into new substances or fusing with others into a new substance. At the death of the human body I assume that the dominant substance, or soul, continues to exist in nature in some other role. Possibly it splits into many substances.

A natural question to ask is, Where in the human body is the dominant substance located? This is a question which inquires for a specific space-time location for the dominant substance or soul, as if, for example, it could be said to reside in the pineal gland as Descartes claimed. But only provided that the relevant primary occasions are arranged in a certain fairly common and normal way can they give rise to a normal and familiar kind of space-time in which each of the substances involved has a space-time location of the usual sort. In the case of the dominant substance or soul of a human being or of an animal there is such complexity of relationship of this dominant substance to the other substances and primary occasions of the body of the living creature that the dominant substance cannot be said to have any precise location in the body. In other words, the relatedness among substances and primary occasions gives rise to, or constitutes, space-time, but it does not always give rise to a space-time in which every substance or every primary occasion has a precise location. If the relatedness is unusually complex, the resulting space-time may provide only a vague location for some substances that are especially intimately involved in this high complexity. Thus, in a sense, it is meaningless to ask precisely where in the human body the human soul or self is located.

Let us see, however, what meaning can ordinarily be given to space distances between substances and between primary occasions, and to time intervals between primary occasions. I do not assume that we have at hand ready-made co-ordinate systems from which to make measurements of time and space. We have to define co-ordinate systems in terms of the relatedness among substances and primary occasions, rather than explain this relatedness in terms of antecedently given co-ordinate systems.

Certain causal chains will be called light-ray paths, or more briefly, light paths. Any two *successive* primary occasions of a light path are such that there is no other chain joining them than the light path itself. We may think of electromagnetic waves as

D

moving along paths of this kind. Such waves can be viewed as qualifications of the internal structure of the primary occasions constituting such paths. Now for any causal chain, whether it is a light path or a substantival chain (that is, a substance) or some other sort of causal chain, there exists a unique number associated with any two primary occasions on that chain, namely the number n of primary occasions lying between them on that chain. Consider two such occasions on a substantival chain, that is, consider two occasions in the life-history of a substance and consider the number n of primary occasions lying between them serially in that life-history. This number n can be viewed as a measure of the absolute amount of time elapsed between those two occasions in the life-history of that substance, as from the standpoint of that substance itself. This is the basis for saying that time has magnitude and is measurable. It is also possible to find a basis for saying that spatial distance is measurable, in particular the spatial distance of a primary occasion from some substance which it lies outside of. Again take two primary occasions lying on the substance in question, but choose them so that a light path passes from the earlier occasion to the occasion outside the substance, and so that another light path passes from that outside occasion to the second or later occasion that lies on the substance. Thus the substance and the two light paths form a sort of triangle, and the time interval n between the two occasions lying on the substance will be proportional to (and a measure of) the distance of the outside occasion from the substance. Thus in this case the number n may be viewed as a measure of spatial distance. Furthermore, any primary occasion lying on the substance temporally half-way between the earlier and later occasions on the substance can be said to be simultaneous with the outside occasion that we have been considering. Thus we have a criterion for the simultaneity of spatially separated primary occasions, as well as a measure of the distance between a substance and a primary occasion. This criterion and this measure, however, are relative to the choice of a substance, just as measurements of space and time in relativity theory are relative to co-ordinate frames. Now that these concepts have been established, there is no difficulty in defining what would be meant by an aggregate of substances that retain the same mutual distances from one another. Such an aggregate of an appropriate kind can be used to play the role of a reference frame or co-ordinate system. From this standpoint it is possible to define a space-time structure that agrees in important respects with that presented in Einstein's General Theory of Relativity. This can be done by use of some ideas of Dr Richard Mould that were set forth in his doctoral dissertation.[1] However, Mould used a space-time made of space-time points rather than of primary occasions, so that he was dealing with a continuous space-time rather than a discontinuous one. The apparent discontinuity of the space-time of primary occasions is not as objectionable, however, as it may at first seem. For example, the internal relatedness among the primary occasions constituting a substance or substantival chain gives a very deep-seated continuity to the substance that overshadows the outward appearance of discontinuity. The same may be said of all causal chains, and not merely those that constitute substances. In what follows something will be said about this internal relatedness.

Let us turn to some epistemological and valuational aspects of the system of philosophy that I am sketching. The concept of ingredient or ingression is crucial in this connection. This concept has close affiliations with concepts of combinatory logic, as I have tried to show elsewhere,[2] and this is another point where the application of symbolic logic to philosophy seems to be both possible and desirable. Such a symbolic logic analysis of the concept of ingredient will not, however, be attempted in this paper. But here again, just as in the case of the theory of relations, logical systems become closely relevant to metaphysical analysis.

Following Whitehead, I view primary occasions, like his actual occasions, as possessing a complex structure of a non-spatio-temporal sort. Each primary occasion possesses many ingredients of various kinds. In the first place, all the primary occasions belonging to the causal past of a given primary occasion are ingredients in that primary occasion. They are in the primary occasion as ingredients of it, but they are not in it in a spatio-temporal sense, for then the past would be simultaneous with the present. Also ingredient in each primary occasion are various universals, some of them abstract and others of them concrete. Whitehead would treat all universals as abstract, and he calls

[1] Richard A. Mould, "An Axiomatization of General Relativity", *Proceedings of the American Philosophical Society*, vol. 103 (1959), pp. 485–529.

[2] F. B. Fitch, "Combinatory Logic and Whitehead's Theory of Prehensions", *Philosophy of Science*, vol. 24 (1957), pp. 331–5.

them 'eternal objects'. I would also include in the universe universals which are not abstract, for example the attribute of being contiguous to a given primary occasion, or the attribute of being in the causal past or the causal future of a given primary occasion. I also regard relations and propositions, as well as attributes, as being universals, and some of these too are concrete and some are abstract. Generally speaking any entity, whether it is a universal or not, may have other entities as ingredients. Propositions, in particular, have as ingredients those entities the propositions are about. Any entity that has at least one concrete ingredient is itself concrete. Hence, any proposition about a concrete entity is itself a concrete proposition.

When one entity, say A, is an ingredient in another entity, say B, we may express this fact by the notation, $B=F(A)$. Here the letter F may be taken to express the *mode* of ingression of A in B, that is, the *respect* or *way* in which A serves as an ingredient in B. If B is a proposition, then writing B in the form $F(A)$ indicates that we are viewing A as the subject of the proposition and F as its predicate. Any ingredient of a proposition may be viewed as the subject of that proposition, and the predicate is then the mode of ingression F of that ingredient into that proposition. Thus in the proposition $F(A)$ the F is both the mode of ingression of A into $F(A)$ and is also the predicate assigned to A by the proposition.

In case B is not a proposition but is a primary occasion, the equation $B=F(A)$ still indicates that A is an ingredient in B, but in this case the mode of ingression F is called a prehension rather than a predicate. Thus we say that the primary occasion B prehends A by way of the prehension F. If C and D are two different ingredients of a primary occasion B, then we may have two equations,

$$B=G(C)$$
$$B=H(D)$$

where G and H are the modes of ingression or the prehension corresponding to the ingredients C and D.

Perception can be treated as one kind of prehension, and belief as another but closely similar kind. A believed proposition may be said to be prehended by way of a belief prehension, and a proposition perceived or intuited to be true may be said to be prehended by way of a perceptual prehension. Such propositions are ingredients in the primary occasion that prehends them, and the belief prehension or the perceptual prehension is simply the mode of ingression, that is, the way in which they are ingredients. The primary occasion which is my self at a particular moment will have among its ingredients those propositions which I perceive as true and also those which I actively believe at that moment.

In the case of perception the prehended proposition must always be true. Furthermore it must be a proposition which does not mention any primary occasions which are not in the causal past of the perceiving primary occasion. Thus the principal object of perception is not a sense datum or a substance, or an attribute or a relation, but a true proposition, that is, an actual state of affairs. In the case of belief the object of the belief is also a proposition, but it may be a false proposition, and it *is* a false proposition when the belief is erroneous. Purely abstract propositions, such as general mathematical and logical laws and principles, and propositions about logical systems, may be objects of belief and even objects of perception in the sense that they are directly intuited as being true. Logical systems themselves, incidentally, may be viewed as being abstract universals, and in fact as being classes of or relations among other abstract universals.

Propositions come to be believed in virtue of a recognition of relations they bear to other propositions already believed and ultimately to propositions already perceived. The recognition of such relations among propositions is itself by way of prehensions of propositions about propositions. In some cases these propositions about propositions may be directly perceived and in other cases may themselves be merely believed.

Just as perception and belief are kinds of prehension, so is knowledge itself. A proposition may be said to be known by a primary occasion if it is prehended by a belief prehension and is a true proposition and if the belief prehension arose by way of recognition of relations of logical relevance of various perceived propositions to the believed proposition.

Propositions may also be prehended by evaluative prehensions, as when a possible state of affairs is in some sense 'sought for' by a primary occasion and thus in a way serves as a kind of 'final cause' for it. An evaluative prehension may thus express the tendency of the prehending occasion to realize, or make true, the proposition thus prehended, or in the case of negatively evaluative prehensions, it might seek to make the proposition false. Some evaluative prehensions, moreover, are intrinsic and others are extrinsic. In the case of intrinsic evaluative prehensions, the proposition sought for is sought for for its own sake, or if it is being avoided, it is being avoided for its own sake. Such evaluative prehensions are analogous to perceptions since they need not arise from recognition of relationships of the prehended proposition to other propositions. In the case of extrinsic evaluative prehensions, on the other hand, the prehended proposition is sought to be realized or sought to be avoided, not because of its own internal nature but because of recognition of logical or other relations it bears to other propositions and ultimately to intrinsically evaluated propositions. Thus intrinsic evaluation is to extrinsic evaluation somewhat as perception is to belief.

In the case of those substances that dominate and unify atoms, molecules and the simpler living organisms, the evaluative and epistemological kinds of prehensions probably occur only in trivial or in very simplified ways, and it is only in the case of higher organisms that prehensions of these kinds reach full complexity and importance. But even in the case of atoms there are probably some minor activities of the form of evaluation, perception, and belief. Otherwise these activities would have to be attributed only to certain living organisms and not to others, or only to living organisms and not to non-living things. But the differences between different kinds of living creatures admit of all degrees without sharp breaks, and the same now seems true of the differences between living organisms and non-living things. Hence it seems unreasonable completely to exclude evaluative and epistemological activities from non-living things. In other words, no substances are completely dead, but all possess some evaluative and epistemological activities at least of a minor sort.

This completes the brief sketch of my view of the nature of the universe, depicting the world in its spatio-temporal, epistemological and evaluative aspects. Logical systems have their place in this scheme, as well as cabbages and kings, and as well as theories about all these things. Even this particular theory or philosophy that I have been enunciating has its place in this scheme as a certain complex proposition. The emphasis on relations, classes and propositions reflects my interest in logical systems, and ultimately I would treat the concepts of ingression and prehension by way of those logical systems which constitute what is known as combinatory logic. In many ways this account agrees with Whitehead's views, but contrary to Whitehead, space-time is viewed as depending explicitly on the actual relatedness of occasions. The theory of universals also differs from Whitehead's theory of universals because cognizance is taken of concrete universals as well as abstract universals. Furthermore, purely abstract propositions are admitted as a special kind of abstract universal, whereas for Whitehead all propositions contain factors of concreteness. Finally, the notion of substance is granted a more central position than in Whitehead's philosophy, and indeed the whole theory of space-time structure is made to depend on the notion of substantival chain, or substance.

CHARLES HARTSHORNE

METAPHYSICS AND THE MODALITY OF EXISTENTIAL JUDGMENTS

III

CHARLES HARTSHORNE

METAPHYSICS AND THE MODALITY OF EXISTENTIAL JUDGMENTS

What is metaphysics? One may use the word variously. I use it to refer to the study which seeks to clarify our conceptions of the absolute, necessary, strictly universal, infinite, or perfect. These terms are not synonymous; but they all have this in common, that they transcend empirical evidence, in any normal meaning of 'empirical'. No experiment can show that there is, or is not, anything absolute, necessary, strictly universal, infinite, or perfect. That we find no exceptions to a law establishes not the slightest rational presumption that none ever will be found by any cognitive being. Some of the Greeks took the stars to be absolute in relation to all lesser things, that is, wholly unaltered by changing relations to these things; but this they could not possibly have had cogent empirical grounds for doing. Nor, I should suppose, could cosmology as an empirical science ever prove, or give any reason for holding, that the cosmos is infinite in space. Or again, we may have evidence that a certain thing is a 'perfect' specimen, in some loose sense. However, 'perfect' in the strict metaphysical sense means not merely, as measured by this or that concept or standard, but (in some way), by any legitimate concept or standard. It means good, not simply for this or that purpose, but—in whatever way, if any, this can be so—for every possible purpose. No such thing could be empirically detected. The mystic may perhaps experience the Perfect reality, but he cannot 'observe' it, in the sense of an empirical science.

The denial of metaphysics consists simply in the assertion that everything so far as knowable (or even conceivable?) is relative, contingent, finite, imperfect, and less than strictly universal.

Metaphysics is distinctive both in subject-matter and in method. The absolute, infinite, necessary, or perfect must be very extraordinary indeed; and the manner in which such a thing could be known to exist, or not to exist, or even to be unknowable or nonsensical, may be expected to reflect this uniqueness. To proclaim a flat monism of intellectual method applied to both this problem and ordinary ones is to try to settle the issue by fiat and definition.

There are two seldom-noticed ambiguities in the foregoing account of metaphysics. The confusions which have clustered about this subject are in no small part due to these ambiguities.

(*a*) It is one thing to speak of a concrete particular thing as necessary and another to say that there is an idea, property, or *kind* of thing which must necessarily be exemplified in some suitable concrete particular thing or other, no matter what so long as it exemplifies the idea or property.

In extensional languages, the concept of 'individual', or lowest-level object, must be exemplified; but this does not mean that any particular such object is taken to exist necessarily. We have rather a class which is not allowed to be empty, though the members of it which exist might have been replaced by others. The class of 'contingent things' is taken to be necessarily non-empty. There is, I maintain, no contradiction in this.

The same sort of distinction applies to the characterization 'absolute'. The validity of the concept of 'relative thing' (thing dependent upon certain relations, which might not have obtained) need not itself be relative, but may in a strict sense be absolute. Thus perhaps the truth, 'There are relative things', obtains, not relatively to this or that, but in any possible case and relative to nothing, or (the same) to anything you please. 'Nothing is absolute except relativity' might, taken in this sense, be close to the last word concerning both the absolute and the relative.

In some such way the long strife between 'absolutists', or believers in 'the absolute', and 'relativists', or believers in the proposition, 'There are no absolutes', might be resolved. Again, with respect to finite and infinite the same ambiguity appears. Are we to think of some actual infinite thing, or is infinity rather a function of the finite as such, and in this manner perhaps: the totality of *conceivable* finite realities is precisely and absolutely infinite? What else could it be? Finitude is the cutting off of possible finite things. To be just this length is not to be just that length; every limit is alternative to various other limits; and thus the totality of possible limits can only be rigorously unlimited.

(*b*) There is another distinction we need to make. It is one thing to say necessary, infinite, or absolute, and another to say Perfect. 'Perfect' is a value-term, and we have learned in recent discussions how unsafe it may be to confuse such with neutral terms. If by 'necessary' we mean, 'in all respects non-contingent', this is not synonymous with 'Perfect', unless every form of contingency is to be viewed as a disvalue. This is a further question, needing consideration on its merits. Again, 'infinite' may be taken as equivalent to 'Perfect' only if every form of limit is regarded as bad, a disvalue. But what about the conviction of the Greeks, and perhaps of every artist, that the good is something like the beautiful, and that the merely unlimited is the formless, hence the unbeautiful? Beauty is harmony in contrast; but in sheer infinity there are no definite contrasts and no definite harmonies; there is only the totality of all possible contrasts and harmonies, which is the same as sheer confusion, if taken as actualized. To create beauty is to select, to renounce some possibilities in favour of others. God creating a world must, it seems, do this very thing, and hence he must also select among possible roles for himself as creator and lover of his world: shall he create and love as actual this world or that instead? If then God is Perfect as Creator, he is not in every respect infinite; for if he were he would be the mere totality of his possible roles as creator, but not any actual creator at all. And if you say that he would then be no less good than he is, you are saying that the world adds no value whatever to reality, and that from the definitive or divine point of view it is exactly the same, in terms of value, whatever we do or fail to do. Perhaps (I hope not!) this is good Hinduism, but that it should ever have passed for Christianity is one of the curiosities of human history. A God who 'loves' the world cannot be merely indifferent to its existence, and this is true, no matter how 'analogical' the term 'love' may be here. There is no analogy whatever, on the assumption. To love x is at least to prefer x to nothing at all.

My conclusion is that 'Perfect', in the religiously relevant sense, cannot be identified with 'in all respects infinite, absolute, or necessary'. Rather we should say, somewhat as we did under (a), that the Perfection of God must be the *absoluteness of his relativity*. His essential or generic manner of being relative, in contrast to our way of being relative, is itself non-relative, independent of all things; and this, not his mere absoluteness, is his Perfection. (To see a contradiction here is to overlook the distinction of logical levels involved.) Again, God's infinity must be something like the infinity of his possible finite roles, not of his actual role. All other individuals are finite, not only in their actual, but also in their possible roles. God could relate himself to any conceivable world; whereas in some worlds you and I would be nothing. However, not even God can relate himself to all conceivable worlds as actualities. For not all are actualities.

Let us now apply these considerations to the main topic of this essay, the modality of existential judgments.

It is a commonplace in logic that ordinary existential statements are contingent. Thus that there is something with the character of being an elephant is true merely in fact, not by any logical necessity. This contingency of ordinary existential statements is by many writers generalized to cover all existential statements. Yet there are good reasons for questioning this generalization. In some logical systems, at least, it is permissible to infer $(Ex)fx$ from $(x)fx$. In other words, a predicate applying to all objects must apply to some object; or, again, the universe of discourse cannot be empty. The extensional interpretation of language seems to make this requirement inevitable. But it follows that the contingency of ordinary existential statements arises not from their existential reference but from some further characteristic. Moreover, the assertion that thought is contingent if it refers to existence prompts the retort, to what else could it refer? Language? But this is nothing except as a factor in what exists. 'Possibilities', 'essences'—ditto. It is existing things, or really occurring processes, which make certain other things or processes possible or conceivable. It is instances which alone give universals any foothold in reality—if nothing else, an instance of the universal, 'someone thinking of the universal'. It has been said that even mathematics is 'the physics of everything', a study of the forms which the cosmic process might conceivably take.

If contingency does not derive from existential reference alone, from what does it derive? Let us consider what 'contingent' means. It means that what is asserted selects among the conceivable possibilities, affirming some and excluding others. To say that some individuals are elephants excludes a world consisting entirely of individuals other than elephants. And such a world is easily conceivable (and doubtless once did exist). If, however, we say, 'Some individuals are self-identical', what do we exclude? We exclude only the case of there being no self-identical individuals, which is the same as no individuals at all. (I use 'individuals' here in a sense neutral to the distinction between particular things and particular events.) In what sense is this verbally possible case genuinely conceivable? It is by definition incapable of being known (not only by man, but by any being); for it could not be true that, although there were no individuals, there was an individual knowing this to be so (nor even, that it had 'once' been so). Thus whereas 'no elephants' might describe a positive and knowable world-state, 'no individuals' appears not to describe such a state. And whereas the existence of an elephant excludes from some portion of space-time various otherwise possible kinds of objects, the existence of an individual of wholly unspecified kind does not exclude anything from existing.

It does not exclude universals; for, as Aristotle argued, the universal can exist in individuals, and even those who deny this will contend that the universal exists in its own way or realm, in no fashion interfered with by the reality of individuals. Thus the total emptiness of the class of individuals is (i) unknowable and (ii) purely negative, without any positive bearings of any kind.

I suggest that these two traits, unknowability and lack of positive significance, come to the same thing and that what they indicate is lack of consistent meaning. To know is to know something positive, and the knowledge itself must be something positive. Hence any statement which excludes only a mere negation excludes no genuine possibility, and since contingency means selective exclusion of existential possibilities, affirming some and denying others, a statement which excludes only negations cannot be contingent. I propose then, as criterion of non-contingency, the absence of any positive meaning for the denial of a statement, or —the same thing—the failure of the statement to exclude any positive state of affairs. *There are individuals* excludes no such state; hence it cannot be contingent. Yet it is not meaningless, since in fact there are individuals. Thus the statement is significant, true, and non-contingent. But this is the definition of necessity, in the absolute sense.

There are, then, three modal forms of existential statement: those which contradict every positive existential assertion; those which contradict some positive existential assertions but agree with others; those which contradict no such assertions. In the first case, any conceivable situation would make the statement false, hence it is impossible (there is a contradiction or logical absurdity somewhere); in the second, some conceivable situations would make the statement false and others would not, hence it is empirical or contingent; in the third case, nothing could make the statement false, hence it is necessary or metaphysically valid.[1]

That the necessary excludes no positive existential assertion is entailed by the common logical dictum that the necessary gives no information about the state of the world. To exclude something from the world is certainly to give such information. But I am proposing that we may convert the rule, 'What is necessary is without positive exclusiveness', so that it runs, 'What is without positive exclusiveness is necessary'. If the rule is held not to be convertible, I ask, why not? To me this denial is 'counter intuitive'.

We have now to note that although a statement which denies no contingent possibility also affirms no contingent possibility, yet it does not follow that it affirms nothing at all, and 'says nothing about the world'. The necessary is indeed compatible with any affirmation you please, but not with any negation you please. Rather it is exclusively positive. It affirms that about the world which would be real no matter what possibilities were actualized, and which therefore cannot be denied except by impossible formulae. If 'information' means a description of what distinguishes one state of affairs from other conceivable states, then necessary statements are not informative; but if 'information' includes reference to the factor which all possible positive states of existence have in common, then necessary statements are informa-

---

[1] Karl Popper's lucid classification of existential statements as impossible, empirical, or metaphysical—in *The Logic of Scientific Discovery*, New York, 1959, p. 633—according as they contradict all, some, or no positive observation statements ('basic statements') is equivalent to ours, except that for his purpose there was no need, and for ours there is need, to subdivide the empirically nontestable statements into those whose 'unfalsifiability' is relative to human perception, and those which are unfalsifiable absolutely, or relative to any form of positive perception or knowledge, whether human, subhuman, or superhuman. The latter statements may be termed absolutely transempirical or metaphysical. They are sheer necessities. Since I read some parts of Popper's great book years ago in the earlier (German) edition, it seems just possible that in the recesses of memory I owe my idea of this matter to him. I wish also to salute Popper for his wisdom in having refused, from the outset, to identify the meaningless and the humanly untestable. Such identification is one form of the attempted deification of human nature, which is not the measure of all things. This mistake was original only in ancient Greece.

tive. And when we refer to such a common aspect of all possibilities, are we talking merely about language? Or has it really been proved that the contrast between what is and what could be is a mere linguistic artifact? If not, then for all that has been shown, the necessary—or that in which all possibilities agree—is also extra-linguistic.

We now take up the most important issue connected with the modal question, the issue of the Ontological Argument. Can a being which is conceived as the source of all contingent being also be conceived as a mere contingent being? If the idea of such a source makes sense at all, it describes the ground of all real possibilities; and the unreality of this ground cannot then be one of the possibilities. The idea of 'creator of all things, himself not possibly a creature', is contradicted if it is taken as a mere possibility which might, or might not, be actualized. For while to be a creature is to be an actualized possibility, to be the universal or ultimate creator is not. There can be no such thing as the possibility of the ultimate creator; there can only be his necessary reality, prior to all contingent alternatives. For it is the Alternativeness itself, the indeterminate-determinable potentiality for possible worlds. So far, at least, the Ontological argument seems to be in the right. Moreover, our test of non-exclusiveness supports the view that the existence of the creator cannot be contingent. A being absolutely unlimited in creative and cognitive capacity cannot, by existing, conflict with the existence of any possible thing; for *a state of affairs which the existence of deity would exclude must be a state which deity could not bring about or know. Both the creative power and the cognitive capacity of the divine would thus be conceived as less than perfect!* So we infer that whatever the idea of God may mean or fail to mean, it cannot mean a being whose mere existence would be exclusive in any respect. It follows from this, together with our theory of contingency as exclusiveness, that the question of the divine existence does not concern a contingent fact, positive or negative, but only a necessity, positive or negative.[2] Deity is logically im-

---

[2] According to M. Lazerowitz, a necessary proposition is one such that a proposition falsifying it has no descriptive use. Very well, I maintain that 'world without God', or 'state of affairs such that there is no God' has no such use. It does not distinguish one conceivable world from another. That it cannot do so is deducible from the definition of God. (See M. Lazerowitz, *The Structure of Metaphysics*, London, 1955, pp. 265–71. Also Alice Ambrose, in "Proof and the Theorem Proved", *Mind*, 68 (1959), p. 439.)

possible or necessarily real. Either the divine by existing must exclude everything, or it could exclude nothing; but in the latter case, nothing could make its existence false, while in the former, its existence is a logical impossibility.

It may be argued that the existence of God should at least limit the possibilities of evil in the world, and thus exclude something. Nor would this something be mere negative; since evil is, in some instances, a positive opportunity for heroism, courage, and other good things. And it may be asked if the existence of a deity ideally powerful and good must not exclude this opportunity, by guaranteeing perfect harmony and happiness in all the world. This, however, presupposes that the perfect Will, in creating, would or could choose the details of the world, leaving nothing for the created wills to determine. And this, in turn, means that the created will would differ from the supremely creative will, not as imperfect or limited power of choice from perfect or unlimited, but as total helplessness from complete competence, or as zero from infinity. But thereby the very meaning of 'choice' or 'will' as used in the two cases is destroyed. (Several recent writers on the problem of evil overlook this point.3) We can attribute the perfect form of causally-undetermined power of choosing contingent details to deity only because we too have a real, however imperfect, form of this power (for which a clearer name than 'freedom' is 'creativity'). That the divine is the ideal form of creativity cannot mean that ours is, or could be, a mere sham. We may have little, or poor, capacity to select among genuinely open alternatives, and God may have much, or in some sense infinite, or all possible, capacity to select among alternatives, but we cannot have none and he all, if our concepts, as used in making the comparison, are to have significance. Accordingly, the supreme Creativity cannot be conceived as an all-determining or monopolistic force, and in so far, its existence cannot guarantee complete harmony. Not that God is 'weak', but that *the ideal 'strength' is not a monopoly of strength*. 'All-powerful' properly means, 'having power extending to all things', and able to do for them everything compatible with the element of self-determination without which they would have

<hr>

3 E.g. A. Flew, in *New Essays in Philosophical Theology*, London, 1955, pp. 145–69, esp. 153. For a detailed discussion of the issue, see my "Freedom requires indeterminism and universal causality", *Journal of Philosophy*, 55 (1958), pp. 793–812, esp. 799–800. (The 8th line of this essay should be deleted, and the 9th should begin with "insight", not with "sight".)

no individual reality. It follows that the existence of perfection does not exclude the existence of evil, since a multiplicity of (partly) self-determining individuals implies innumerable hazards of conflict and discord. Nor is this argument refuted by pointing out that some evils do not result from human freedom. The argument, fully thought out, is entirely general: the creatures as such must be free.

Nevertheless there is a serious difficulty with the Ontological Argument. For we have seen that the concrete or particular is contingent, while only the universal or (in one sense at least) abstract, e.g. 'something exists', is necessary. And yet it seems that God is thought of as no mere general abstraction, but as a particular and concrete reality, an individual. Indeed, the entire concreteness of the world must be summed up in the divine knowledge. This knowledge must be precisely as particular and exclusive as the world. For if God knows that elephants exist, then this knowledge, being infallible, logically excludes the state of the world free from elephants which otherwise conceivably might have obtained in this geological age. Accordingly, God as including his concrete knowledge is exclusive, and hence, by our principle, contingent.

At this point theologians and philosophical theists, apparently ninety-nine per cent of them, insisted upon what I can only regard as a grave error. They held that not only the existence of deity but also his entire reality were necessary. They refused to make any effective distinction between divine 'essence' and divine actuality. But then the Ontological Argument would imply that something concrete, particular, and exclusive was yet necessary, and therefore non-exclusive, and this defies the logic of contingency and necessity altogether. So it was a sound intuition which kept most thinkers, theistic and otherwise, from accepting the Argument. But it is not the Argument which is to be rejected, it is the standard view of God. There is indeed no basis for the dogma that 'existence', in an undetermined sense, cannot be a predicate; but there is a basis for the denial that concrete, particular exclusive existence can be so. Moreover, as we have seen, divine knowledge that certain contingent things exist is exclusive of alternative possibilities, and hence can only be contingent, like the things. If proposition p is contingent, then so is the knowledge that p is true; for since p might have been false, there might not have been the knowledge (and could not have been, had p been false). What the possible contradicts cannot be necessary, and 'the non-existence of this world' contradicts 'God knows that this world exists'.

If we admit, what seems obvious, that any knowledge of the particular, exclusive, and contingent is itself particular, exclusive, and contingent, then it need not and cannot be the full actuality of an all-knowing God which is declared necessary by the Ontological Argument; it can be only his abstract essence, and his bare existence as defined by this essence. God must exist (if deity be logically possible, an assumption I have not tried to justify in this essay), and very likely he must know some world or other perfectly; but he need not have existed knowing *this* world, for this world need not have existed to be known. The particular actual concrete 'state' of the divine knowledge is no more required by the necessity of the divine existence than the particulars of the world are required by the necessity that there be some particulars or other. Not the concrete things, but concreteness as such, is necessary; and not the divine concrete states, but divine concreteness, as such, is what the Argument demonstrates to be non-contingent. God must (assuming his logical possibility) be concrete somehow, but not exactly as he in fact is.

It is an old saying that God is not a member of a class. There is only one God, and he is not a merely possible or contingent God, but rather the one necessary God. We can interpret this as follows: the divine essence is embodied in contingent states, but cannot fail to achieve embodiment in some such states or other; moreover, any such state will be connected with all others so as to form a single personal life, what Whitehead calls a 'personally-ordered society', or a sequence of states interconnected by ideally complete memory and continuity of purpose.

Some readers will say that I do not understand the elementary principle that the divine is not temporal, or subject to the distinction between individual and state, or past and future, or potential and actual. During the past forty years I have encountered this view perhaps a thousand times; however, I have also learned that another, less popular, conception has for centuries had its defenders. After reflecting for many years upon the question, I still see the more usual view as a philosophical and religious blunder.

The divine self-identity or individuality is necessary because it alone is, in its essence (not in its full actuality), free from all particularity or exclusiveness. There is no conceivable world whose existence God could not tolerate and know; and for this very reason there is no world which he must have rather than any other. The divine individual alone has strictly universal functions, and hence it alone, in abstraction from its concrete actual embodiments, is wholly unparticular, non-exclusive, or necessary. It cannot be contingent.

Is God then not a 'particular' individual? No, certainly not; he is the universal individual. What do I mean here by 'individual'? I mean the unity of a sequence of concrete states of consciousness each connected with the others in the most truly ideal way by omniscient memory and steadfastness of purpose. This is plainly analogous to 'individual' in the everyday sense, except that this individual, being universal in his role, is unique and without competitor. Being non-localized, he occupies no place from which he excludes other beings, as each of us does at every moment. There is no function exercised by God which any other being could take over in his stead. He is the sole non-competitive, non-exclusive, conscious agent—in his necessary essence quite as general as being itself, but in his contingent actuality containing all the exclusive particularity and concreteness of the real.

Thus the Ontological Argument can be freed of its basic paradox, that it appears to derive the concrete from an abstract definition. On the contrary, the individuality whose existence the argument shows to be necessary is no less abstract than the definition of perfection which furnishes the starting-point of the argument. God merely *qua* necessary is infinitely less than God in his fullness of actuality. This fullness we cannot know by any abstract argument; and we cannot know it at all, except vaguely, fragmentarily, and uncertainly, and even then, only be reacting to all our experience and knowledge in a fashion for which words can never be adequate.

In this respect, the Zen masters, other mystics, and Wittgenstein are right. There is that which, though it can perhaps in some faint and fragmentary way be 'shown', cannot be said. But this something is not any 'essence', even the necessarily somehow-existing essence of God—the most independent, abstract or general, hence the most sharply definable, of all individual characters—but is rather the unimaginable states by which the worlds, as they come into being, are omnisciently grasped and immortalized. These states constitute not merely that, but *how*, God exists. No such state can ever be known—save to another such state. It can be felt, 'prehended'; and indeed we cannot avoid prehending the concrete deity, but with an overwhelming preponderance of 'negative prehensions', such that they bury in hopeless obscurity all but an infinitesimal portion of the wealth prehended. The God demonstrated by a correct ontological proof, or any other proof, is unspeakably less than the actual God. However, this very truth that there necessarily is an actual God who is unimaginably more than our proofs can describe, this too is proved, if the proving process succeeds at all.

Thus Anselm is vindicated in his contention that we can conceive God as incomparably greater than anything we can (explicitly) conceive. We can understand that we cannot understand the content of omniscience, and that necessarily the existing divine necessity (the common denominator of possibilities) fails to compare in richness of contrast and beauty with the ever-growing integrated totality of contingently actualized possibilities which is the divine consciousness.

According to G. E. M. Anscombe, the ontological argument is a mere fallacy since it amounts to this: $(x) Gx \rightarrow EEx$ [my notation]. "For all x, if x is God, then x has eternal existence. We can . . . still ask, 'But is there such a being?'."[4]

This is not the argument, even as in Anselm, much less as we can put it now. Instead of the somewhat evasive 'eternal existence' Anselm has "such that thou canst not be conceived not to exist". Moreover, Anselm argued not from God, existent or not, but from the *idea* of God taken as admittedly an existing idea. The question then concerned the status of this idea, as exemplified or unexemplified. He held that the only exemplification which would not contradict the meaning of the idea must be necessary exemplification, without conceivable alternative of non-exemplification. Further, that which cannot be contingently exemplified cannot be contingently non-exemplified either. Hence, assuming that there is a genuine idea (that divinity is logically possible), it follows that divinity exists necessarily, since the other three relations to existence have been excluded: the three being contingent exemplification and non-exemplification, and necessary non-exemplification (impossibility).

4 See her *Introduction to Wittgenstein's Tractatus*, London, 1959, p. 15.

One should also remember that it is a respectable, even though not universal, doctrine in modal logic to hold that $\sim N \sim Np \rightarrow Np$: *if a proposition could be necessary it is necessary*. Hence if a predicate is such that the assertion of its exemplification could be necessary, then it is necessary, and since $Np \rightarrow p$, the necessarily true is true, the predicate is exemplified.

What Anselm discovered was that, whereas for some predicates or functions it makes sense to say:

$\sim (Ex)fx$ & $\sim N \sim (Ex)fx$ (The function is contingently un-exemplified) also to say,

$(Ex)fx$ & $\sim N(Ex)fx$ (The function is contingently exemplified) for other functions what makes sense is only:

$N(Ex)fx$ V $N \sim (Ex)fx$ (The function is either necessarily exemplified or necessarily not exemplified—i.e. impossible).

If all language is taken as extensional, as requiring some realm of objects to refer to, then some function must be such that it necessarily denotes objects, say the function of 'being an object'. But note: 'infallible knower of all objects, whatever they may be', is just as general, as noncommittal among objects, as the mere idea of 'object' itself. True, it adds the idea of 'knowledge', but this, too, is a universal correlate of objects, unless one wants to try to make sense out of 'absolutely unknowable objects'. As for 'infallible', this simply prevents 'knows' from being subject to qualification or diminution. We know save so far as we do not know but are ignorant; God, however, knows.

What Anselm intuitively grasped was the complete abstractness or neutrality of the idea of perfection; had he become clearly conscious of the nature of his discovery he must have seen that no such neutral entity could be the total actuality of the supreme existent; he must have altered his idea of deity as necessary through and through, or in all properties.

It is important not to forget that the values of x in existential formulae need not be individuals; they may be states of individuals, 'actual entities'. With reference to deity this distinction not only does not disappear, it becomes uniquely important. For *here alone the individuality has a different modality from the actual states;* elsewhere both are contingent, here, only the states. This is, I submit, the only way—if there is a way—to remove logical absurdities from the idea of God, and to clarify at last the so long misconceived logic of the Ontological Argument.

In the foregoing I have sought to show, not that the traditional Ontological Argument is conclusive, but that the nature of the issues which it raises has been incompletely understood, both by its defenders and by its critics. In a prospective publication, *The Logic of Perfection*, it will be argued that of twenty criticisms to which the Argument has been or can be subjected some are irrelevant and the remainder are at best inconclusive, when applied to the reformulation of the reasoning, and of its conclusion, which I propose.[5] The problem for the future is this: what is the relation between our criterion, *degree of positive exclusiveness*, as mark of modal status, and the criterion for analytic, non-analytic, and analytically false, relative to a specified language system, as given by certain authors, e.g. Richard M. Martin.[6] I have some vague guesses about this, but no more. Upon one point, however, I am tolerably clear: the answer is not furnished ready-made in the pages of Kant, Hume, or the many who do little more than repeat their dicta on this matter, with the *ad hoc* incorporation of a trick or two from modern logic. We face here large systematic syntactical and semantic issues such as cannot be disposed of by minor revisions of the old shortcuts and dogmas, whether speculative or sceptical, theistic or non-theistic. No more in metaphysics than in physics or biology can we identify our problems with those of the seventeenth or eighteenth century. And the concepts of modality

---

[5] In a remarkable number of cases these rebuttals of the standard objections are duplicated (I assume independently) by Norman Malcolm, in his admirably reasoned article, "Anselm's Ontological Arguments", *Philosophical Review*, 69 (1960), pp. 41–62. My discussion was completed before I knew anything of Malcolm's; and some of his main points are to be found in my writings of many years ago. I am delighted, however, to have his support. Perhaps now our profession will begin to realize that we cannot rely upon Kant to do our thinking for us in this matter. But Malcolm does not refute the objection that the argument, when used by traditional theists, implies the derivability not only of 'existence' but of concrete actuality from an abstract definition. All Malcolm does is to charge the objection with a confusion between 'concrete' and 'contingent'. This will not do; for the burden of proof is on the man who holds that there is any alternative to 'concrete and contingent' except 'more or less abstract', and in the extreme case of the completely abstract, 'necessary'. What can the necessary be if not what all possible concrete states of affairs have in common (a necessary proposition is entailed by any and every proposition), hence a residuum of omission, a deficient mode of reality, if taken merely by itself?

[6] See R. M. Martin, *The Notion of Analytic Truth*, University of Pennsylvania Press, 1959.

and logical validity will have to be clarified well beyond what has yet been achieved before we can say that the possibility of a cogent Ontological Argument has been proved or disproved.

However, I do venture to regard it as already manifest that the argument not only could not support, it could only tend to refute, the way of defining deity which Anselm, Descartes, and even Kant had in mind. Only a genuinely different type of theism offers any hope of finding a positive use (or perhaps even of evading a negative or anti-theistic use)[7] for the brilliant suggestion of Anselm. Such a new theism also, I believe, offers the only hope of achieving clarity concerning the various remaining theistic arguments—and counter-arguments. It is not the classical theologians, but certain heretical ones, Socinus, Fechner, Whitehead, and a number of others, who point the way to the avoidance of the confusion between abstract and concrete ('the fallacy of misplaced concreteness') which is the pervasive error of much traditional thought and is found among persons of very diverse religious and anti-religious persuasions. The Great (or 'perennial') Tradition in metaphysics or speculative philosophy is one thing, and metaphysics as such (and its possibility or impossibility) is quite another; very much as Classical Physics is one thing, and physics is another. Is there anything very odd or irrational about this distinction? Is not the refusal to make it the attitude which deserves to be branded as odd, nay, in principle obscurantist, a 'blocking of the path of inquiry'?

---

[7] See J. N. Findlay, "Can the existence of God be disproved?" *Mind* LVII (1948).

A. H. JOHNSON

WHITEHEAD ON THE USES OF LANGUAGE

IV

A. H. JOHNSON

WHITEHEAD ON THE USES OF LANGUAGE

Introduction

A recognition of the impressive competence of Alfred North Whitehead in many areas of human experience naturally gives rise to the question: Did Whitehead investigate the uses of language? This question is particularly relevant in view of the intense contemporary interest in this topic.

As a matter of fact Whitehead was greatly concerned with the problem of symbolism in general and the uses of language in particular. As one might expect, in a philosophy stressing organic interrelatedness, Whitehead's discussion of the uses of language is not to be found in any one chapter or any one book or article. His treatment of this topic is interwoven with his discussion of many other major questions.

It is the purpose of this study to: (*a*) survey and systematize Whitehead's remarks subsequent to 1924, concerning the uses of language, thus making them readily available for careful examination;[1] (*b*) compare Whitehead's position with some other (actual and possible) views concerning the uses of language. Implicit, and explicit, in this analysis is the judgment that Whitehead's treatment of the problem is sound, and superior in some respects to the other views under consideration.

The Uses of Language

A statement in *Modes of Thought* is typical: "Language is the triumph of human ingenuity, surpassing even the intricacies of modern technology."[2] Whitehead regards language, spoken or written, as an instrument devised by men to aid them in their adjustment to the environment in which they live.[3] Language is

[1] Hence there are numerous references to the widely scattered source materials which are involved. This discussion deals only with Whitehead's writings subsequent to 1924, because the books and articles written in this period constitute his mature philosophical position.

[2] MT 44.   [3] See MT 53; also Symb [87].

used for *many* specific purposes in the process of this adjustment.

The most primitive type of language is "merely a series of squeaks".4 When it first arises in human experience, language is used to (*a*) express emotions, and (*b*) signal (i.e. communicate). Even in its most sophisticated contemporary forms 'speech' retains these functions.5

Whitehead, in his discussion of the communicative function of words, notes a "double symbolic reference:—from things6 to words on the part of the speaker, and from words back to things on the part of the listener".7 This process of symbolic reference becomes increasingly complex as the reference of language changes from the particularity of concrete objects to generalities and abstractions. As this development takes place, *written* language becomes more prominent in human experience.8

Words (spoken or written) are employed not only to refer to data (and to express emotions). They may be used also to record (and hence retain) experiences, and thoughts about these experiences. This use of words makes possible, or at least facilitates, recall. Words also function as instruments in the organization of experiences as they are considered in retrospect. Thus words free us from the bondage of the immediate. We can deal with the past, the distant (in space) and make predictions concerning the future. Further, thanks to the instrumentality of words, we can not only converse with others but also hold that internal conversation of self-examination which is essential to self-development. Here then is a factor which has an important bearing on freedom of thought and the development of the spirit of reflective criticism, of the most healthy sort. In short: "Human civilization is an outgrowth of language, and language is the product of the advancing civilization."9

Among the many impressive chapters in Whitehead's *Aims of Education* is one entitled "The Place of Classics in Education". Here he provides excellent illustrations of the uses of language in recording facts and experiences, making them subject to easy recall, organizing them so as to provide the basis of civilized life,— in particular providing stimuli and directives to guide human

---

4 PR 374 [403].   5 See MT 52.
6 The term 'thing' refers to any type of datum, physical object or mental state.
7 Symb [12].   8 See MT 53.
9 MT 49. See also MT 46; Symb [68].

action. In the case of Rome it was an "habitual vision of great-ness".[10]

This reference to the inspiration exercised by Rome (through the medium of its language) brings into focus an important use of language. Whitehead would have us realize that words are used not only to (a) express emotions, and (b) refer (also record, organize and in general facilitate communication) to objects (physical and mental). Another important use (c) is to influence action. "The particular direction of individual action is directly cor-related to the particular sharply defined symbols presented to him at the moment."[11] Words not only exert an influence on the private life of individuals. They also, when charged with emotion, may arouse a common purpose in a large number of persons and hence serve as the foundation of national unity.[12] Orders, promises and questions are also illustrations of the use of words to influence behaviour. The relation between words and the instinctive phase of human behaviour is discussed in the context of the influence of words on action. Specifically words can be used to bring into focus of attention *urges* which would otherwise be neglected. It is obvious that these urges can not be controlled unless they are first identified and understood. Both these operations are greatly facilitated by the use of words.[13]

The use of language to express emotions is aptly illustrated by a quotation from Shakespeare. England is referred to as:

> ". . . this little world,
> this precious stone set in a silver sea."

Such words uttered by a patriotic Englishman, obviously involve an outpouring of intense emotions.

Whitehead's discussion of the three main uses of language may seem far removed from some contemporary treatises on the uses of language. There are some philosophers who, while they agree that language has many uses, seem to be primarily concerned to point out that when a person is using certain important words he is not really saying what he seems to be saying but rather something else. For example, if a person says 'I know', he is not referring to a mental process, the so-called act of cognition. The phrase 'I know' is really being used to state 'I am trustworthy'; 'You can

---

[10] AE 106.

[11] Symb [73].

[12] See Symb [68, 73].

[13] See Symb [69].

rely on me'.[14] Whitehead is not unaware of the significance of this particular aspect of human behaviour. He notes that when a person uses the East Asian concept of God (i.e. there is an impersonal order to which the world conforms) he is really saying something about the world. Also, concerning the pantheistic concept of God, "when we speak of the world we are [really] saying something about God".[15] (It is true, of course, that many philosophers would prefer not to talk about God, while Whitehead does.)

The service of language to thought has been noted (e.g. it records and serves as a basis for recall). In a moment of rash exuberance Whitehead remarks: "The souls of men are the gift from language to mankind." More soberly, he states that "the mentality of mankind and the language of mankind created each other".[16] Specifically, what he really means to say is that while *language is not the essence of thought* yet it is one very important method of expressing thought.[17] He bases this opinion on the argument that if a sentence is to be identified with a thought then it is impossible to translate from one language to another, or from one sentence to another in the same language. "If the sentence is the thought, then another sentence is another thought."[18] Further, we struggle to find words to express ideas. We have the ideas, we do not have suitable words. Hence it is impossible to identify words and thoughts. Nevertheless Whitehead contends that "the notion of pure thought in abstraction from all expression is a figment of the learned world".[19] There are activities older than thought, namely actions and emotions, of a fairly complex sort. When the activity of thought emerged in human experience it appeared as an agency in the process of the organism's adaption for the environment. Thought receives expression through the medium of these older activities.

Whitehead's statement that words are the most important way of expressing thought, thus brings into focus the point that Whitehead is well aware of the fact that words are not the only type of symbolic expression. There are other instruments which can be used to (a) express emotions, (b) refer to objects (physical or mental), (c) control human behaviour. Chief among these other symbols are actions and art. Gestures sometimes are more effective than words. The symbolism of a great painting may also, in some instances,

[14] See J. Austin, "Other Minds", *Proceedings of the Aristotelian Society*, Supplementary Volume, XX.

[15] RM 58 [69].   [16] MT 57.   [17] MT 48-9.   [18] MT 49.   [19] MT 50.

exceed the power of words. The smell of incense, giving rise to a rich aesthetic experience, may be a more influential religious symbol than a spoken or written creed. Religious ritual, combining action and aesthetic experience is highly effective in expressing emotion and in controlling behaviour.[20]

It is not surprising to find that Whitehead, a mathematician of eminence, reminds us of the value of that form of symbolism known as mathematics. Indeed, he terms it a type of language distinct from the ordinary language of words.[21]

Symbols of various sorts, words, actions, aesthetic phenomena, mathematics, are so much a part of our intellectual environment that we tend to forget that these instruments are the result of the creative initiative of a very few minds. Whitehead aptly remarks that there is little genuinely novel, creative symbolic expression in the world. The symbols used by the vast majority of men are merely repetitions of symbols invented, or first used, by a few creative geniuses. These initiators, in the realm of symbolism, usually flourish in a restricted but congenial environment: Goethe in Weimar, Shakespeare in Elizabethan England. Yet despite this apparent provinciality, "they deal with what all men know, and they make it new".[22]

Whitehead's delineation of three main uses of language should not be interpreted as suggesting that they are to be separated in any ultimate sense. As he remarks: "A thought is a tremendous mode of excitement. Like a stone thrown into a pond it disturbs [influences] the whole surface of our being."[23]

Meaning

Implicit in Whitehead's discussion of the uses of words (and other symbols) is a theory of meaning. His most comprehensive and explicit definition of meaning is as follows: "The human mind is functioning symbolically when some components of its experience elicit consciousness, beliefs, emotions, and usages, respecting other components of its experience. The former set of components are the 'symbols', and the latter set constitute the 'meaning' of the symbols. The organic functioning whereby there is transition from the symbol to the meaning will be called 'symbolic reference'."[24]

[20] See PR 258 [278]; RM 10–13 [20–3].   [21] See Symb [2].
[22] RM 121 [136]. See also RM 119–20 [133–4].
[23] MT 50.   [24] Symb [7–8].

E

For example the word 'tree' has as its meaning the object tree. It is very important to notice Whitehead's contention that a component which is a physical object (or a mental occurrence) may be either a meaning or a symbol. Which it is depends on the situation in which it is used. More specifically it depends on the person who uses the word. If the word 'forest' suggests trees, then the word is the symbol and the trees (as objective facts) are the meaning. If however the existing trees suggest the word 'forest' to an observer, then the trees are the symbol and the word 'forest' is the meaning.[25]

In order to understand the meaning to which a word refers, it is sometimes very important to appreciate the system of thought within which a person is operating. The phrase 'the Fatherhood of God' has a meaning, i.e. a datum to which it refers. But the full significance of the datum will vary from ancient Rome to modern America. Fathers are thought of differently in these two cultures.[26]

There is a difficulty involved in an apparently simple statement such as: '1 plus 1 equals 2'. Confusion will arise unless we know what kinds of data these symbols are specifying. This mathematical statement is a way of referring to a certain type of one thing which when joined with another thing of a specific type will give you two things of a specific type. One apple and one orange constitute two pieces of fruit. But one spark and one pile of gunpowder do not add up to two objects.[27]

Whitehead points out that one word may have several meanings, i.e. refer to several different data (objects). For example, the word 'Caesar' may refer to (a) the man Caesar at one moment of his existence, (b) the entire extent of this man's life, (c) the characteristic pattern of this man's behaviour.[28]

Whitehead suggests that the difficulty in apprehending the meaning of a word is sometimes greater in the case of spoken words than in the case of written words. The phrase 'a warm day' as *written* has a meaning which can be specified in fairly exact scientific terms involving a reference to the rotation of the earth and the location of the sun. But the *spoken* words are more likely to be at the mercy of local conditions. The phrase refers to one set of data at the Equator and another set at the North Pole.[29]

[25] See Symb [10–12]; PR 257 [277].   [26] See RM 115 [130].
[27] See Imm § XVIII.   [28] See Symb [27–8]; PR 374–5 [403–5].
[29] See MT 54.

In his discussion of meaning, Whitehead notes that the emotions which have become associated with a word may be transferred to the object to which the word refers (i.e. to its meaning). This process may occur as the result of reading great literature. The emotional charge which is carried by words may be used, with consummate skill, by a great literary artist to suffuse with a new dimension of meaning a situation which when described by ordinary men using 'limp' words seems drab and unimportant.[30] A comparison of the description of a convict written by an uninspired jailer and Victor Hugo's analysis of the inner life of Jean Valjean, would serve to illustrate Whitehead's point.

Paralleling his three-point analysis of the uses of language— (a) to refer to data, (b) to express emotions, (c) to influence behaviour—Whitehead identifies *three types of meaning*. The first type has been the topic of the preceeding discussion of meaning, i.e. meanings are data (mental and physical) to which words refer. The second type of meaning is the emotions expressed (not referred to as an object).[31] The third type of meaning is the pragmatic type, i.e. the fact that a word may be used to arouse or direct action. This influencing of action is a type of meaning.[32] The type of meaning called 'theoretical' seems to belong within type one. In the case of theoretical meaning the data referred to are vaguely experienced 'ultimate reasons'.[33]

It is obvious from Whitehead's discussion of meaning that *he does not place the primary emphasis on the function of rules in determining proper usage, hence meaning*—as is the case with some contemporary philosophers. Indeed Whitehead's discussion of meaning invites comparison with the theory of meaning advocated by the so-called 'Oxford Philosophers'.[34] Strawson, for example, *denies* that meaning requires referring. Meaningful words (or sentences) are those which have "rules, habits, conventions governing [their] correct use, on all occasions".[35] Ryle's influential paper on "Ordinary Language" focuses attention on the importance of rules in this theory of meaning. "Learning to use expressions, like learning to use coins, stamps, cheques and hockey-sticks,

[30] See Symb [83].   [31] See AI 290–1; also 312.
[32] See Symb [74].   [33] See Symb [74].
[34] This is a convenient label commonly used to refer to Ryle, Strawson, Austin and men of like disposition, despite the fact that they tend to disavow the existence of a well-defined group with common characteristics.
[35] P. F. Strawson, "On Referring", *Mind*, Vol. LIX, p. 327.

involves learning to do certain things with them and not others . . . Among the things which we learn in the process of learning to use linguistic expressions are what we may vaguely call the 'rules of logic'; for example, that though Mother and Father can both be tall, they cannot both be taller than one another; or that though uncles can be rich or poor, fat or thin, they can not be male or female, but only male."[36] It seems to Whitehead justifiable to inquire whether the final court of appeal should be the laws of logic or the facts concerning existing parents and uncles.

It can be argued that the word 'meaning' may be used (*a*) to refer to data as Whitehead does or (*b*) to involve approved ways of putting words together, as the 'Oxford Philosophers' do. Indeed (*c*) it can be argued that the meaning might be the *process of referring* a symbol to an object. All three uses of 'meaning' are found in ordinary usage. (This is to say men use the word 'meaning' in these three fashions.) Be that as it may, the very important issue remains: What is the ultimate justification for putting words together in sentences? Are rules the final authority; or are the rules merely convenient summaries of what is required in the complicated process by which the human organism adjusts to a complex environment?

Implicit in Whitehead's position is the contention that the attempt to equate the use of language with the use of coins, stamps and hockey-sticks involves serious danger *if excessive emphasis* is placed on the analogy of *playing games*. It is of course correct to say that playing a game, or using coins and stamps, involves following rules. Similarly, in using language one must follow rules. But, games and the usage of coins and stamps are characterized by a degree of arbitrariness which may be carried to dangerous lengths. Further, the process of using coins for commercial purposes may lead to disaster if the economic system of the country is not sound. The use of words, *if* the game mentality is too strong, may also involve grave dangers simply because, for most people, life is not a game and language is an instrument used in the serious 'business' of living. If it be objected that it is unfair to assign this 'game mentality' to serious philosophers (despite the apparent justification), then it might be suggested that they abandon this unfortunate analogy.

Whitehead states: "The meaning, in the form of actual effective

[36] G. Ryle, "Ordinary Language", *Philosophical Review*, Vol. LXII, 1953, p. 173.

beings reacting on us, exists for us in its own right."[37] In short, meanings are data. It is wrong to "trust to mere syntax to help you out".[38] It is of course necessary to assign a superior status to rules in dealing with algebraic symbols. But the case is entirely different in dealing with ordinary language and non-mathematical technical terms. It is correct to say that rules are useful in guiding employment of language. Further, "general terms require a permanent literature to define them by their mode of employment".[39] *However, these rules do not legislate meaning.* They are summaries of how words are used. The question of meaning goes out beyond the question as to *how* a word is used in a sentence to the question as to *why* a word is linked with a meaning, i.e. a datum.

In so far as a reliance on rules tends to stress the arrangement of words, a comment by Whitehead is relevant. "The sentence is a sequence of words. But this sequence is, in general, irrelevant to the meaning. For example 'Humpty-Dumpty sat on a wall' involves a sentence which is irrelevant to the meaning. The wall is in no sense subsequent to Humpty-Dumpty."[40] In so far as reliance on rules as the final authority tends to produce a rigid attitude, Whitehead's remark that rules of all sorts require revision is relevant. "Free men obey the rules which they themselves have made. Such rules will be found in general to impose on society behaviour in reference to a symbolism which is taken to refer to the ultimate purposes for which the society exists. . . . The art of free society consists first in the maintenance of the symbolic code; and secondly in fearlessness of revision, to secure that the code serves the purposes which satisfy an enlightened reason."[41]

There remains the final question concerning meaning: If meaning is not determined ultimately by rules, what is the basis of its determination? In short, how does it come about that a word elicits consciousness, beliefs, emotions, images and usages respecting other components of experience, i.e. its meanings? More specifically why is it that a specific component of experience is selected as the meaning of a symbol component? Whitehead contends that "considered by themselves the symbol and its meaning do not require . . . that there shall be a symbolic reference between the two. . . . The nature of their relationship does not in

[37] Symb [57].   [38] Symb [2].   [39] RM 23 [34].
[40] MG § IX.   [41] Symb [88].

itself determine which is symbol and which is meaning." In general, "symbolic reference is the active synthetic element contributed by the nature of the percipient".[42] However, this statement may be misleading. Whitehead's final answer to the question (Why does a specific meaning become linked with a word in symbolic reference?) seems to be this: In the process of adapting to the environment, human beings link words with other experienced data. There is a general agreement as to the linkage of specific words and specific meanings because this facilitates the process of adjustment by individuals to the complex social and physical environment. Rules of language are, to repeat, summaries of the uses of words during the course of adjustment to the environment, in the process of self-development.[43] How these symbols are used to form sentences is determined ultimately by the structure and nature of the data to which they refer since these symbols are ultimately instruments used by human beings in their adjustment to the environment. This environment can not be neglected in any thorough or consistent fashion. An element of arbitrariness in the use of symbols is possible. But in due course the stern necessities of survival place limitations on our conventions and arbitrary stipulations.

This apparent serious-mindedness on the part of Whitehead does not imply that he would refuse to admit as meaningful statements about fictitious or imaginary persons or events. He agrees with Plato that on occasion one must have recourse to myths rather than statements which are literally true or factual. In similar fashion he approves of imaginative dramatic performances and literature. It would seem then, that he would accept as meaningful references to 'round squares' and 'the present King of France'.[44]

Dangers in the Use of Words

Whitehead's discussion of language includes a number of cogent warnings concerning the deficiencies of language, and hence the

[42] Symb [9–10].

[43] Whitehead's highly technical discussion of some forms of symbolic reference (in terms of causal efficacy and presentational immediacy) will not be dealt with in this study, because the terms of this technical analysis are designed to deal with the problem of perception. An inclusion of these terms would unnecessarily complicate this discussion of the uses of language.

[44] See MT 14, 17–18. For a more technical discussion see PR on 'propositions'. See also: A. H. Johnson, *Whitehead's Theory of Reality*, Boston, The Beacon Press, 1952, pp. 83–5, 102–4.

need for great care in the use of words. "Experience does not occur in the clothing of verbal phrases."[45] Language developed gradually. For the most part we have created words designed to deal with practical problems. Attention focuses on the prominent features in a situation, in particular the changing aspects of things. With reference to such data our words are relatively adequate. However, this issues in an unfortunate superficiality. The enduring, the subtle, the complex and the general aspects of the universe do not have adequate verbal representation. In short, "language is incomplete and fragmentary, and merely registers a stage in the average advance beyond ape-mentality". "Our understanding out-runs the ordinary usage of words."[46] The difficulties we have in discussing human personality or expressing the nature of God are illustrations of the limitations of words, to which Whitehead refers.[47] Since some fundamental human problems can not even be stated adequately in available language, it should be obvious that these problems can not be solved by ingenuous manipulation of available language.

Words have an unfortunate tendency to distract our attention from facts. If we manage to escape the blinding effect of words we are inclined to pay little or no attention to facts for which we have no words. A related danger is that the apparent simplicity of a verbal formula (which is correct as far as it goes) may veil the vast complexity of the facts to which it refers, e.g. the economic interpretation of history. The supreme danger implicit in the use of words is that excessive devotion to verbal facility may engender a type of intoxication. Men become bemused by the rhetorical flow of their own unimpeded verbosity. Hence there arises "the triviality of quick-witted people".[48] In developing these interrelated themes, Whitehead refers to the fact that "the college senior has lost the things that correspond to the words. His mind is occupied by literary scenery".[49] Thus, in general, Whitehead deplores the second-handedness of book learning, because he believes that first-hand experience is essential for efficiency in life. With characteristic irony he remarks that "the second-handedness of the learned world is the secret of its mediocrity. It is tame because

---

[45] *Whitehead's American Essays in Social Philosophy*, ed. A. H. Johnson, New York: Harper, 1959, p. 167.

[46] AI 291 and MT 68. See also AI 209; RM 23 [34].

[47] See AI 209; RM 66 [78].   [48] MT 55.

[49] *Whitehead's American Essays in Social Philosophy*, p. 168.

it has never been scared by the facts."[50] Words may not only turn us away from facts or blind us to them. There is also the danger that words may arouse emotions, beliefs and actions which are quite irrelevant to the actual state of affairs.[51]

Despite all these deficiencies of language, ordinary and technical, Whitehead is prepared to admit that on occasion it is a source of sound information even about matters of some complexity and philosophical generality. The organic theory of nature, in particular the close linkage of mind and body, and of the human body with the rest of the world, is recorded in ordinary language.[52] As Whitehead once remarked: It sounds very strange for a person to say: Here I am and I have brought my body with me.

Whitehead's general approach to the problem of dangers involved in undue reliance on language is very effectively expressed in his comments on (a) the need for new symbols to deal with new experiences, and (b) the need for revision of presently available symbols. "The symbolic elements in life have a tendency to run wild, like the vegetation in a tropical forest. The life of humanity can be easily overwhelmed by its symbolic accessories. A continuous process of pruning, and of adaptation to the future ever requiring new forms of expression, is a necessary function in every society. . . . The society which cannot combine reverence to their symbols with freedom of revision, must ultimately decay either from anarchy, or from the slow atrophy of a life stifled by useless shadows."[53]

Whitehead's general examination of the uses of words receives focus and illustration in his discussion of the uses of words in philosophy.

Philosophy and the Uses of Words

Whitehead's position concerning the uses of language in philosophy is stated with pungent directness: One of the (two) main errors to which philosophy is liable "is the uncritical trust in the adequacy of language".[54] More specifically, "Conventional English is the twin sister to barren thought".[55] This deficiency is not the unique characteristic of English. As Whitehead fairly remarks, Greek bears witness to the same defect. Whitehead

[50] AE 79.   [51] See Symb [6].   [52] See MT 157.
[53] Symb [61; 88].   [54] AI 293. See also PR viii [viii].
[55] A. N. Whitehead, "Remarks", *Philosophical Review*, Vol. XLVI, p. 183.

quotes from John Stuart Mill: "They (the Greeks) had great difficulty in distinguishing between things which their language confounded, or in putting mentally together things which it distinguished. . . . Accordingly, scientific investigation among the Greek schools of speculation and their followers in the Middle Ages, was little more than a mere sifting and analysing of the notions attached to common language. They thought that by determining the meaning of words they could become acquainted with facts."[56] Whitehead maintains that "Language is thoroughly indeterminate, by reason of the fact that every occurrence pre-supposes some systematic type of environment".[57] Philosophic language should be designed to express profound insights and vast generalities. "It is for this reason that language, in its ordinary usage penetrates but a short distance into the principles of meta-physics."[58]

Since ordinary language does not do justice to the generalities, profundities and complexities of life, it is obvious that philosophy requires new words and phrases, or at least the revision of familiar words and phrases. Proceeding to develop this theme Whitehead remarks: "Words and phrases must be stretched towards a generality foreign to their ordinary usage."[59] In the same vein Whitehead refers to the need to realize that language which is the tool of philosophy needs to be redesigned just as in physical science available physical apparatus needs to be redesigned.[60] The procedure then is to start with words and phrases which in their ordinary usage are ill defined. Their vagueness must be then clarified in the only fashion which is effective, an appeal to the direct experience of the basic facts in the situation. This is an act of intuition, i.e. a type of immediate experience which penetrates to the depths and complexities of human experience in so far as that is possible.[61] As Whitehead expresses the matter: "No language can be anything but elliptical, requiring a leap of the imagina-tion to understand its meaning in its relevance to immediate experience."[62] The imaginative leap referred to is not a foolish flight of fancy. It is a way of obtaining adequate insight concern-

---

[56] PR 15-6 [17-8].　　　[57] PR 16 [18].　　　[58] PR 234 [254].
[59] PR 4 [6]. See also: "Remarks", *Philosophical Review*, Vol. XLVI, p. 178.
[60] See PR 14 [16].
[61] See A. H. Johnson, *Whitehead's Theory of Reality*, pp. 9-11.
[62] PR 17-8 [20].

E*

ing the facts to which the word refers. "Imagination is not to be divorced from the facts: it is a way of illuminating the facts."[63]

An illustration of Whitehead's procedure in stretching and redesigning ordinary language will clarify his point of view. The word 'subject' is used in ordinary language[64] to refer to a human person as a perceiving, feeling, willing, thinking agent (or to a topic for discussion). Whitehead stretches and redesigns the terms to apply to the basic elements which go to make up the universe. Thus the physical world is composed of subjects (Whitehead offers evidence to support this contention).[65] In ordinary language usage one subject (person) is regarded as quite distinct from another subject. Whitehead redesigns the word to stress interrelatedness rather than exclusiveness. In traditional philosophy the exclusiveness of distinct subjects is reflected in the theory of mental substances. In Whitehead's 'reformed subjectivism' the traditional exclusiveness of substances is completely abandoned. Complete and exclusive substances are replaced by events in developmental organic inter-action. This interpretation of the universe results from a careful examination of immediate experience. For example, the life of a human mind during a period of time required to pronounce the phrase 'United Fruit Company' is composed of three interrelated events: the process of experiencing and uttering (a) 'United', (b) 'Fruit', (c) 'Company'. The transition from one to the next is an experienced fact as is the experience of development within each moment of experience. In this fashion, Whitehead's 'reformed subjectivism' corrects the *genuine* errors (noted by Ryle in *The Concept of Mind*) in Descartes' doctrine of mental substances. However, Whitehead disagrees with Ryle in that he (Whitehead) accepts the legitimacy of an appeal to a reformed type of introspection, i.e. intuition. Whitehead finds ample evidence for the existence of a type of inner mental life which is denied by the logical behaviourism favoured by the 'Oxford Philosophers'.

Whitehead not only stretches and redesigns old terms. He also invents new words. For example, he employs the word 'prehension' which he considers more acceptable than the word 'relation', in view of such difficulties as those pointed out by Aristotle in his 'third man' discussion, and the claim of the Absolute Idealists that relations can not relate unless there is an all-inclusive being

[63] AE 139.   [64] As recorded in a standard dictionary.
[65] See AI 237; PR 163 [178], 248–9 [268]; MT 205.

to bring this about. The term 'prehension' refers to the process by which events are interrelated. Other new technical terms used by Whitehead are: 'eternal object', 'subjective aim', 'subjective form', 'presentational immediacy', 'God's primordial nature', 'God's consequent nature', 'God's superject nature'.[66]

There are those who suggest that the proper language for philosophy is the technical languages of natural science, mathematics and symbolic logic. Whitehead replies that these languages and symbols are useful in their proper places. However, they are completely inadequate to perform the broad tasks of philosophy. "Under the influence of mathematics, deduction has been foisted on to philosophy as its standard method, instead of taking its true place as an essential auxiliary mode of verification whereby to test the scope of generalities."[67]

As far as the problem of factual reporting is concerned, mathematics is defective because it is characterized by abstraction. We are thereby cut off from "any consideration of any particular entities".[68] Sometimes the crucial fact in a situation is a particular fact. Mathematics can not do justice to this particularity. This same objection applies to the use of the abstract symbols of logic. If it be objected that Whitehead actually is very optimistic about the applicability of symbolic logic to all phases of human experience— a careful examination of the relevant remarks is recommended. It is true that Whitehead once stated: "Symbolic Logic . . . will become the foundation of aesthetics. From that stage it will proceed to conquer ethics and theology."[69] However, this statement must be placed in its total context. Whitehead is referring to "the distant future" when symbolic logic has expanded to examine patterns other than those of quantity. It will consider "real variables". Even then it will be only the *foundation* of aesthetics, not the statement of all particular, factual phases of aesthetics, or ethics or theology. Whitehead's final published words about the inadequacies of symbolic logic are: "The conclusion is that Logic, conceived as an

[66] See relevant sections in PR and A. H. Johnson, *Whitehead's Theory of Reality*.

[67] PR 14 [16]. Since this study is not concerned primarily with Whitehead's metaphysics, it is not appropriate to discuss, in detail, Whitehead's reformed subjectivism. A treatment of this topic and a comparison of Whitehead's position with that of Descartes will be found in A. H. Johnson, *Whitehead's Theory of Reality*.

[68] SMW 25 [30].   [69] "Remarks", *Philosophical Review*, Vol. XLVI, p. 186.

adequate analysis of the advance of thought, is a fake. It is a superb instrument but it requires a background of common sense. . . . My point is that the final outlook of Philosophic thought cannot be based upon the exact statements which form the basis of special sciences. The exactness is a fake."[70]

The reference to special sciences involves not only logic but also natural and social sciences. Taken by itself any special science can not provide a language adequate for the purposes of philosophy. "The experiences on which accurate science bases itself are completely superficial."[71] Accurate science concentrates on the clear and distinct data of sense experience and the abstractions of mathematics. It is Whitehead's contention that the vague and obscure data of experience are sometimes the most crucial. After all scientists have had their say about a man like Schweitzer, there remain the vague and obscure depths of personality which defy clear awareness or exact statement.

The adequacy of the language of prose and poetic *literature* is referred to briefly by Whitehead. In so far as a piece of literature remains within the limits of ordinary language, it suffers from the inadequacies of ordinary language. However, Whitehead remarks that philosophy is akin to poetry in that both employ language which goes beyond the limits of ordinary language. In this vein he refers to meanings revealed by great literature.[72] The very perceptive chapter in *Science and the Modern World* entitled "The Romantic Reaction" provides a number of excellent illustrations of this contention. For example, he points to the remarkable efficacy of Wordsworth and Shelley in conveying a sense of the organic interrelatedness of the facts of nature. In the case of Shelley there is also the profound insight that while things change there is also the factor of endurance, and the eternal.

In formulating his philosophy Whitehead uses many classes of words: *nouns* (subject, eternal object, God); *verbs* (feels, rejects); *adjectives* (good, angry); *adverbs* (slowly, quickly); *prepositions* (at, in, of). All words which he employs he regards as symbols which refer to or involve data discoverable in experience.[73]

One last point must be made concerning Whitehead's use of words in his philosophical speculations. He does not claim com-

---

[70] Imm § XIX.   [71] MT 41.   [72] See AE 91; PR 14 [16]; MT 69.
[73] The scope of this study ("Whitehead on the Uses of Language") does not permit an exposition of the basic concepts of Whitehead's metaphysics.

plete adequacy for the new, or stretched or redesigned words. They are, in his opinion, a very great improvement over ordinary language or the language of science, mathematics or symbolic logic. But, to repeat, they are not completely adequate. "Philosophy can never hope finally to formulate these metaphysical first principles. Weakness of insight and deficiencies of language stand in the way inexorably."[74]

[74] PR 4 [6].

NATHANIEL LAWRENCE

TIME, VALUE, AND THE SELF

V

NATHANIEL LAWRENCE

TIME, VALUE, AND THE SELF

The splendid rhetoric in the closing pages of the *Apology* moves sentiment so strongly that a philosophical point of profound importance is likely to be ignored. Stated in its most provocative form, this point is that the past can alter.

Let us see what Socrates tells his judges. He condemns them of injustice in finding him guilty. Theirs is an act of injustice, although it can not harm him. However, let them trouble his sons as he has troubled his accusers, if his sons are vain or if they care for anything more than for virtue. Should his accusers do this, says Socrates, then he and his sons will have received justice at their hands.

Superficially this passage is open to a variety of interpretations. (1) Hard practical sense may claim that speculation should not be misled by sentiment. Much of our moral and legal activity aims at rectification or equity. Should anyone damage me or mine, I may go to the law and, on principle, obtain rectification. Even in the delicate world of manners, if you are rude or offensive, decency requires that you make amends. The righting of wrongs is not mysterious. Why see in it a paradox about the reversibility of time itself? One does *not* turn back the clock. One *does* try to compensate for the value consequences of the events which have taken their shape in the irrevocable past.

Such sturdy common sense will not meet the case at hand, since the consequences here include the destruction of the inspirited flesh which is the historical Socrates. Today a reversal of the judgment of the court would open the way for a lawsuit by Xantippe and her sons. Tangible aspects of *their* loss would thus be theoretically recoverable; something closer to justice might be done *them*. But neither in Athens nor in Metropole can justice be done to *Socrates* without some reconsideration of what the name 'Socrates' designates. Socrates himself, of course, in the *Phaedo* undertakes just such a revision of what the term 'Socrates' designates, and there is a close relation between Socrates' closing remarks in the *Apology* and the major theme of the *Phaedo*. But the problem comes to this: How can a man who is dead share in justice with the living, the same justice which is theirs? Not mere rectification, but the justice of just treatment? Even in common sense we shall have to take a new line.

(2) A second line of thought will be something rather more vague to materialist ears, yet fortunately known to common thinking. We may suppose that what is meant is that if Socrates' principles live, then Socrates lives. And his 'death' is either an illusion or a misunderstanding. Surely this is implied in what is said, and the theme is clearly developed in the *Crito*. However, the mere survival of principles is not enough. It is this time-structured creature, Socrates the man, not a sheer collection of pretty principles, who claims that he will have received justice, *post mortem*. We must look further for something that will continue to be Socrates, not merely in the realm of ideal forms, of high purpose and noble character, but something which can stand at last before the court of circumstance and receive justice. There must be an earthly repository, however partial.

(3) There is an ancient conception of a fleshly immortality. It is this conception to which Crito appeals when he makes his strongest case for seducing Socrates into escape. The same conception permeates the Levitic law of the ancient Jews and survives today in our laws of family inheritance. To that conception Socrates addresses himself. What is required is not merely a conception of value, in this case the moral value, justice, "laid up in heaven", surrounded by a choir of principles, but a theatre of actuality, an arena, in which value must actually occur. But Socrates' perspective on immortality was not confined to the idea of family continuity. For example, in the *Crito* the care of his sons, to which Crito appeals, is put to one side, lest by attending to it nearsightedly Socrates threaten the life of the laws themselves. However, by introducing his sons at the end of the *Apology* Socrates makes his point without arguing its presuppositions. That a man was in some measure immortalized through his sons needed no defence to an Athenian audience. This simple appeal is a powerful exemplification of how Socrates' thought values occur, *actual concrete values*. "I and my sons", he says, "will receive justice." Nevertheless, Socrates will be dead. How then is the clock turned

back? In what sense can the past alter? Socrates' principles are impersonal, and his historical identity is about to be ended.

In order to see in what sense the past may be said to be alterable, a great deal of groundwork must be laid. (i) To this end, I shall begin at an apparently remote point, the exposure of the value element in experience as primary. It is only on consideration of the factual elements of experience as being the primary ones that physical time becomes the standard against which all other modes of time are measured. Physical time best lends itself to the concept of irreversibility. Any effort to show that the past can alter must expose the factuality of experience as derivative rather than primary. (ii) I then turn to the idea of the self, conceived in terms of its survival and integration. (iii) In the third part of the essay I examine the subject of the ingression of value, showing why it is necessary to delineate least temporal units in terms of the temporal extent required for the value to appear. (iv) In the fourth section the self is then interpreted in terms of the values which define it. (v) In the final section I re-examine the significance of Socrates' extraordinary claim.

I

The primacy of value experience

Concrete values are never properties of things, that is, of substances in the classical sense. The reason for this is essentially a Whiteheadian one: substances are not concrete. In explication of this claim, however, I wish to emphasize certain aspects of the claim which Whitehead might regard as of secondary importance, might even wish to modify or reject.

The demand for concreteness in philosophy is commonly a demand for fixity. We want reliability, a starting point. We also want something rich enough to accept the total range of human curiosity. *Reliability* and *richness*: either without the other is inadequate. Pure phenomenalism is not possible; if only richness be pursued, then the predictability and the manipulability of the world, and with them knowledge, fade to nothing. Sheer reliability, however, is no more adequate than sheer richness. When sought monocularly, it results in deductive rationalism, in which a universal principle is expected to produce derivative principles that are disciplinary for the whole of reality. Such a principle is the contemporary delusion that all meaning must be reducible to sense-meaning, a stipulation not likely to contribute much, except hilarity, to the public view of academic philosophy.

It is the joint demand for richness and reliability that commends events as the fundamental stuff of the world. (1) The richness rests in this, that when we speak of an event we do not propose to eliminate from what is meant by 'concrete event' any factor that might be inconvenient to some established scheme of explanation. (2) An event's reliability is rooted in its temporal pastness, its being over and done with. Thus the reliability of an event demands for its warrant fairly specifiable temporal boundaries. It is especially important that the event demonstrate closure as definite; otherwise its incompleteness disqualifies it ontologically as an event and procedurally as reliable. It is perfectly safe to say, then, that in human experience events are all that there is, provided we keep before us these two standards: that of reliability, which wants closure for an event, and that of richness, which will not permit us to stipulate in advance the depths of its meaningfulness. As a consequence of the foregoing, the root of the conception of value lies in expressed value, the significance one event has for another. To say that all other notions of value must be brought back to this consideration is not to commit the reductionist fallacy which has been attributed to positivism. Positivism not only claims that meaning requires reference to experience, but also proposes to issue warrants of acceptability and inacceptability among the various aspects and types of experience.

What does it mean to say that human values are always embedded in human experience? It means perhaps nothing more than what Kant meant by saying that all knowledge begins in human experience and further requires explicit reference to human experience. It does *not* mean that value so discerned can not be dissociated from its encounter, treated distinctly and explicated against only a vague backdrop of reference to fact. Any discernment of aesthetic realization, of moral value, or of religious worth plucks value out of the flow of experience, looking for that which abides through the temporal flux. However, that it abides through time does not mean that it is independent of time. The pursuit of fixity thus leads us from what is 'fixed' in the sense of being 'completed' to the conception of what is 'fixed' as being 'intransient'. The fixity of a lost value, unable to survive the flow of time, discommends it as satisfactory for human motivation.[1] Mere facts are worthless except by reference to some understanding of value. To say that facts are intrinsically worthless is only to assert an analytic proposition. Before a fact can serve as a worthy object, before the discrimination of the worth of one fact over another can even be undertaken, some system of value, however primitive and implicit, must be present. The degree of arbitrariness or confusion in the system of value introduces a corresponding unconvincingness in the importance of the facts which are placed before us.

No one should suppose this problem of confusion in the standard of value to be a purely theoretical one. For instance, consider the current problem of education in the democracies. The best that could be expected of a widespread and intensive *factual* scientific education, Meeting the Challenge of the Russians, would be the stabilizing of a power imbalance. Such stabilization may be a condition of peace. It is not, and it could not be, peace. Any neglect of education in the realm of *value*, in so far as education successfully shapes the young citizen, is destructive of that understanding upon which alone peace may firmly rest. Human knowledge and therefore science, *in any sense of the term*, has as its broadest frame human valuation. It was this truth that led Socrates to ignore physical science and to claim that the unexamined life was not worth living, as it led Kant to assert the supremacy of practical reason. It led Whitehead, generalizing in his anthropomorphic way, to the extreme statement that " 'Value' is the word I use for the intrinsic reality of an event".

Summary. I have argued thus far that the philosophical enterprise has at its centre two needs. (1) Its data are not those of some special discipline. They must be broad enough to serve as *philosophical* data. The data must exhibit what I have called richness. This means full, fat, opaque events. (2) The data need some sort of reliability. The most primitive kind of reliability is exhibited by the event which is effectively *done with* in time, but such primitive

---

[1] The notion of value as intransient before time is a foundation stone of Greek ethics and underlies also the extreme formulation of Kant. The universality of the Categorical Imperative is time-transcendent. It is therefore a principle of reason and not of understanding. Plato's society was culturally homogeneous as to art and artifact but heterogeneous in its speculations about the nature of the physical world. For this reason, at least, the notion of a stable value norm did not seem so remote to him as it does to us. The form of all forms is thus designated by a value term, and one with moral connotations at that, ἀγαθον.

'fixity' is not enough. What we need at the second level of the demand for reliability is something in the event which *survives* temporal passage: Aristotle's substance and/or material substrate, Plato's intransient form, Kant's hierarchy of principles of the understanding and of reason, the physicist's physical law and material stuff.

I have further insisted that bare facts are worthless, and that the only way to exhibit the worth of a fact is by referring it to some pre-accepted system of value for which it is a relevant datum. The term 'relevance' itself implies the presence of a standard of value. (1) Value has its living roots in value experience. The experience is primary. (2) Moreover, the *value* aspect in experience is primary in the sense that sheer factuality provides no standards of relevance, order, discrimination. Withdraw these value-elements, and experience collapses into an infinite rubble heap of what is merely, at best, true.

In the vast web of value experience, strands of identity come and go. Such chains of identity give rise to the abstractions, 'thing' and 'self', the two 'substances' of Descartes. We cannot go far with 'value' without encountering the idea of the 'self'.

II

The idea of the self

In so far as an awareness of value is expected to induce motivation, it always makes sense to ask wherein lies the arousing character, from which an imperative may be derived, of the value claim. The imperative consequences of value assertions are even sometimes made to do the whole work of the assertion, as in R. M. Hare, *The Language of Morals*.[2] But to ask "What is that to me?" is not only to ask "What should I do?" but "Why should I?" and there is no way of responding to that latter question unless there be some conception of what the speaker means by 'I'.

Everything turns on what is designated by the 'I'. The possible range of meanings for this term defines the range of significant answers that can be given to the question, "Why should I?". It is

---

[2] I have argued elsewhere, in "Ethics as Mandate" (forthcoming in *Mind*), that to say that "Value statements when they are action-guiding, entail imperatives", is virtually a tautology, especially when 'imperative' is interpreted in its grammatical sense, as in Hare, and that the imperative needs something other than a prior imperative or a system of imperatives in order to recommend it.

characteristic of the present era that this fact has been well understood, although variously construed, by psychologists, literary men, and theologians. Of movements within contemporary philosophy, only existentialism has been consistently alive to its importance.

'I' is a variable, a dependent function, whose dimensions of dependency virtually defy analysis: the age of the person, the time of day, the needs of the moment, the accidents of the environment, the chemistry of the body, the habits of the past, the ideals for the future. Such variability is chaotic for all pretty logics and detailed ethics, yet it is commonplace. Clinical psychology and sensitive literature never bother to defend, for instance, the conviction that the 'same' self can both love and hate another. And casuistry must always step in, therefore, when the question, "Why should I?" is asked. The same ten-year-old on the same day may rightly get such answers as, "I will punish you if you don't", "You won't be liked if you don't", "You won't learn well if you don't", "You'll have more self-respect if you do", "In order to be fair", and so on. The task of summarizing all of these responses under a single ethical principle is not a promising one. Every effort in ethical theory to assert such a principle has either explicit or overt recourse to practical judgment as the means of its instrumentation.

At this point it should be noticed that we are still investigating a narrow range of value. We need to notice in passing that the subject of value has been thus far sharply limited and must remain so, by the opening remark of this section, to what is "expected to induce motivation". By this restriction I wish not only to confine attention to *ethical* valuation (although the phrase might include areas of aesthetics and religion as well), but further to put aside investigations concerned with such things as the rightness of killing Caesar or the worth of democracy in Pakistan. A developed ethical theory needs to show how these remoter judgments are related to the problems of personal choice, but we must limit our study to the smaller topic.

The problem of value conceived as the end of motivation, then, rests on a relational consideration. The relation is of an odd sort; it relates the actual self, however ill-defined, to a possible situation. I now want to stipulate two demands which the self normally recognizes. (1) The first of these is expressible in familiar terms, *the demand for survival*. This demand can be countermanded, as a ruling factor in choice, for instance by situations in which physical or spiritual pain is intolerable. It is nonetheless natural, as natural as the breathing upon which it depends. It can also be hopelessly inexpert and unconscious, as in the case of the newborn babe. (2) The second I shall call *the demand for integration*. Success in the latter task is usually partial and fragile. For instance, shrewd torture can scatter a man's mind and cause him to renounce his profoundest convictions. Roman Catholic sanctification rightly discerns something superhuman in the spirit which refuses to yield in the latter way. Together these two demands are simply the demand to be. Collapse of the first terminates existence; collapse of the second dissolves it.

The two demands are, however, genuinely interdependent. For example, the schizophrenic can be said to survive, but he *exists* only in the biological or animal sense, not in the fully human sense. Consequently we ignore certain of his immunities and privileges. Some future anthropologist, discovering the schizophrenic's skull, will say that a man 'existed' in 1960; but such 'existence' is only a condition of the existence which I am here discussing.[3]

A non-living entity may be defined as one whose survival is identical with its existence. But such survival is not adequate for a living being. The living being is in a constantly altering relationship with its environment, whether or not the environment is stable. The demand for integration, then, is commonly the challenge to meet a self-created crisis. Where creativity is low, the crisis is small and the standard of integration is relatively simply satisfied. At this level even the issue of life or death, with its fringe of anthropomorphic meaning, becomes difficult to decide. For instance, when the individual paramecium divides into two paramecia, did the first one live or die?

But human life does not develop by instinctive response. As William James says, "Man is born with a tendency to do more things than he has ready-made arrangements for in his nerve-centres. Most of the performances of other animals are automatic. But in him the number of them is so enormous, that most of them must be the fruit of painful study."[4] The fulfilment of these

---

3 After I had written this passage I came upon a discussion, by a psychologist, of an autistic child. He was existing, not living, she said. (Mira Rothenberg, "The Rebirth of Jonny", *Harper's Magazine*, Vol. 220, No. 1317, February 1960, p. 62.)

4 *The Principles of Psychology*, New York, 1950, I, 113.

functions brings the art of humanity to the otherwise automated process of becoming a mature animal; but such fulfilment requires the larger social environment, with its incredible resources for the protection and preservation of the great reservoir of past human value and the provision for survival and integration in the future. We notice that the social whole survives and integrates also. To the extent that the social whole exhibits this tendency to survive and to integrate, it merits some status as a self. Exaggeration of this fact leads to totalitarian politics. Ignoring of it leads to the enthusiastic conception of liberty to be found in Mill's *Essay on Liberty*. Rousseau was wrong. Men are born in chains. They are strictured by eruptive need coupled with personal incapacity.

To return to our demands. Integration prerequires survival. Conversely, survival for a living being means meeting the constant challenge to integrate. The challenge would be overwhelming in its complexity if it were not for habit, which leaves a place for creative self-enlargement. The mechanisms stabilized by habit are of many types, some of them very close to the purely physical. But very early in the developing child, other needs appear, and from that point on merely physical habits do not exhaust the nature of the self.[5] Roughly speaking, we may say that the more clearly physical the needs, the more unreflective and shallow the self-consciousness which is associated with them. Precisely because physical needs are of a compelling sort, little choice is involved, and where choice is not a prominent factor in action, self-conscious identity flickers low.

The theme which I am here developing is relatively simple, and must be stated abruptly, at the risk of flanking attacks from psychologists of habit, motivation, and even the unconscious. It is this: whether choice be habitual, critical, or somewhere in between, it exhibits the self. Moreover, any particular choice may be a composite outcome of many subordinate choices, or sets of such series. The dimensions of choice are various and want investigation, preferably not under the exclusive guidance of animal psychologists. *But whenever choice appears, it is directed toward some conceived value and proceeds from a conceived or accepted self.* Finally, *every act of choice, from the most habitual to the most reflectively considered, is self-building and self-defining.* For Hinduism and Buddhism the knowledge that this is so is the beginning of wisdom. This knowledge is embodied in the doctrine of *karma*.

---

5 Feral children are apparent exceptions.

Summary. The self is defined in terms of the value it discerns and conceives, especially as this discernment and conception determines choice, whether the choice be exemplified in acts of belief, mode of life, response to particular situations, espousal of moral standards, or what you will. This is true both statically and organically; that is, the self during any time slice is so defined, and so is the total self thought of as an organically developing—or degenerating—entity. The self begins with a set of explosive internal needs and possibilities, dominated by the internal basic motive to be, and is exposed to a complex intrusion of external influences. This basic motive is differentiable into a demand for survival and integration. The integration is confronted with diversity, both of the internal self and of its external environment, and it aims at achieving a harmonizing of the values inherent in these diversities. Thus, the effort to fragmentize general axiology into distinct and autonomous fields of value is treacherous if turned into practice. It is an invitation to the self to disperse itself into a kind of corporate committee whose best hope for unity, that is, integration, lies in wary compromise. Clarity so purchased is of slight importance.

I have indicated the 'stipulations' which the self recognizes: to survive and to integrate. Over against these stipulations stands the barrier of death with its apparently contrary mandates to perish and to dissolve. If the locus of the living self is both individual and material and nothing more, these mandates mock the stipulation. If the locus of the living self is not individual but is material, as in the tribal and racial unity of ancient Judaism, then a meaningful ethic is possible. Or if the locus is individual but not material, as in classical Christianity, then an ethic and a doctrine of immortality are possible.

Where does Socrates' view stand in relation to this problem? He is on the threshold of death. He is not as individualistic as the early Christian; he is not as materialistic as the ancient Jew. Before we can proceed further we must inspect the subject of the ingression of value.

III

The ingression of value

No modern philosopher with an understanding and love of science has seen so clearly as Whitehead that the internal realities of the world are best described as "'values'". "'Value'," he says, "is the word I use for the intrinsic reality of an event."[6]

It should be clear that the term 'value' has been chosen deliberately and must not be taken narrowly. Whitehead's use of the term, to be fully persuasive, requires a separate essay. I shall present a skeletonized introduction to such an essay, in order to consider the problem of the ingression of value.

The language of philosophy is anthropomorphic. Whitehead's philosophy is no exception. Metaphysics undertakes to frame or exploit its vocabulary in such a way as to minimize the dangers of anthropomorphism. Categories must be devised which transcend the arbitrary aspects of human experience. Physical science, for instance, which is a special branch of metaphysics, conceptually presents the ultimate nature of the material world as devoid of colour, since colour evidently arises only in the presence of a complex sensing mechanism possessed by a restricted group of entities. Without urging the point further, I propose that this kind of procedure is best understood as an effort to raise the concept of 'fact' up to the level of metaphysical generality where more anthropomorphic 'facts' like "'The sky is blue'" can be interpreted in terms of the less anthropomorphic facts. Whitehead's effort, lest reductionism play endlessly with the hopeless task of conjuring up values out of valueless facts, is to generalize the admittedly anthropomorphic term 'value' in such a way as to show *human* value as a restricted and complicated case of value. This enterprise is in keeping with the same metaphysical impulse which spurs the physical scientist to transcend the anthropomorphic conception of 'fact'. The introduction of this conception of value ultimately entails similar enlargements of related terms, like that of mind into the notion of every event as having a 'mental' pole, and that of apprehension into 'prehension', etc. In the latter case there is a deliberate addition to the vocabulary, designed etymologically to exhibit its human specification, 'apprehension', as a restricted case.

I have earlier spoken of Whitehead's 'anthropomorphic way'. It is this generalization of vocabulary to which I referred.

A question remains, however. Why give the priority to the term 'value', so enlarged, as opposed to 'fact', similarly enlarged? Undoubtedly it is partly a matter of deliberate contrariety to the prevailing tendency, a case of overcorrection of a common bent of

[6] SMW 116 [136].

mind. In addition, however, three more important factors are surely present. (1) The doctrine of 'significance' of the earlier works already contains within it the suggestion that an event has a kind of interiority which in its initial phase, to use the language of the later works, appropriates aspects of antecedent events and grades them as to their relevance to its becoming. The event, before it has anything to offer to the future, becomes something for itself. It has a unique self-identity, which is its self-constituting response to the available environment. (2) We are thus led to another anthropomorphic term, 'feeling', used as an alternative term for 'prehension'. 'Feeling' suggests both evaluation and interiority. (3) In our own self-conscious experience not every fact has equal status for the ongoing self. There is a classless democracy of truths about facts, but there is a hierarchically arrangeable relevance of values. *That a fact should play any role in our lives at all depends upon its value as a certain sort of fact.* What we need is a generalization from this feature of human experience to cosmological processes generally. I am here reading freely between the lines of *Science and the Modern World*, e.g.:

"The name '*event*' [is an abstract word which] cannot be sufficient to characterise what the fact of the reality of an event is in itself. . . . But conversely, nothing must be left out. Remembering the poetic rendering of our concrete experience, we see at once that the element of value, of being valuable, of having value, of being an end in itself, of being something which is for its own sake, must not be omitted in any account of an event as the most concrete actual something. 'Value' is the word I use for the intrinsic reality of an event. Value is an element which permeates through and through the poetic view of nature. We have only to transfer to the very texture of realisation in itself that value which we recognise so readily in terms of human life."[7]

Two points are clear. (1) Whitehead explicitly wishes to 'transfer' to 'realisation' itself the things "we recognise so readily in terms of human life". Whitehead's anthropomorphism is here explicit. (2) We can now see that what is being said is that value is the *intrinsic* reality of an event, as opposed to its *extrinsic* reality, which is factual. So there is no final priority of value, but only a priority

[7] SMW 116 [136].

in the order of becoming. This theme is worked out in great detail in *Process and Reality*.

We may now return to the subject of the ingression of value.

The fundamental building block of the universe, as Whitehead sees it, is the actual occasion, "the limiting type of an event with only one member".[8] The term is exchangeable with 'actual entity' except when the latter term is used to denote God.[9] A substantial portion of *Process and Reality* is devoted to showing that within the actual occasion, the temporal pattern and the qualitative content are given 'all at once'. It is, in Whitehead's terms, co-ordinately divisible but not genetically divisible. It will submit to mathematical, i.e. conceptual, dissection without limit; however, genetically, that is in point of its genesis, its parts do not exhibit any priority to one another. They are simultaneous (not instantaneous) with one another in the act of becoming. Whitehead's own use of the notions of 'earlier' and 'later' in the analysis of the phases of the actual occasion is such a conceptual device, one which may mislead the hasty critic. Thus if we ask how time becomes, the answer is that time becomes continuously and abstract time can be divided as fine as you like, but the concrete becoming from which it is abstracted is composed of least temporal units.

It is a curious thing that Whitehead never asks himself, "How big is an actual occasion?". If the actual occasion be an electronic one, its temporal extent will be measured in terms of microseconds. But what of the actual occasions of the human sort? Human consciousness seems to come in larger chunks than does an occasion of vibratory energy. For instance, if any given least temporal unit of consciousness be dominantly perceptual, the perception must be relatively sustained in order for the conscious aspect and the perceptual aspect to be temporally coextensive. Subliminal advertising is a negative case. Here the perception is so fleeting that it does not enter the level of conscious discrimination at all, although it may insinuate itself at a deeper level of motivation. But even subliminal perception seems to require thicker moments of existence than those of the electron in order to become an ingredient feature of the entity on which they intrude and to which they contribute. At the level of conscious intellection the actual occasion would seem to be huge by comparison with its 'physical' counterpart. Whitehead himself tacitly admits this:

[8] PR 101 [113].   [9] Cf. PR 122 [135].

"In human experience, the most compelling example of non-sensuous perception is our knowledge of our own immediate past. I am not referring to our memories of a day past, or of an hour past, or of a minute past. Such memories are blurred and confused by the intervening occasion of our personal existence. But our immediate past is constituted by that occasion, or by that group of fused occasions, which enters into experience devoid of any perceptible medium intervening between it and the present immediate fact. Roughly speaking, it is that portion of our past lying between a tenth of a second and half a second ago. It is gone, and yet it is here. It is our indubitable self, the foundation of our present existence."[10]

I do not see how one can avoid the implication that actual occasions come in different sizes according to their type. Moreover, if it is from groups of actual occasions considered *seriatim* that we distil our abstract conception of time, a complexity in the nature of time is introduced, upon which Whitehead has hardly touched.

Let us investigate this complexity a bit further. The intrinsic reality of an event is called by Whitehead 'value'. And this value is definable as the way in which the actual occasion expropriates past actual occasions for its own satisfaction and completion. What was, that is, is externally so, becomes *internally* significant for the new occasion. The past then appears—in perhaps too simple terms—as *actually so* and *potentially valuable* in terms of possible future significance for oncoming actual occasions. In *Process and Reality* the actual occasion's state of being internally complete and finished while remaining externally available for future occasions is called its 'objective immortality'. Subjectively it has perished.

Summary. Whitehead uses the anthropomorphic term 'value' to refer to whatever internal concrete organization a self-constructing actual occasion achieves. Suppose now we conceive of time (we never perceive it this way, of course) as an abstract medium capable of infinite division. On this scale, some values will require a comparatively great extent of time, in order to ingress. Other values will mature in a briefer span. Since the actual occasion is definable in terms of the values it apprehends, I infer that it is greater or smaller owing to its type. I propose to join the development of this inference with the themes which have been previously pursued in this essay.

[10] AI 232–3.

IV

The self in terms of its values

The ego is a fleeting entity. Whitehead says it is an actual occasion.[11] The 'he' which transcends the individual actual occasion is either an eternal object or a string of actual occasions. Whitehead allows both.[12] I reject the idea of 'he' as an eternal object, with its suggested determinism for personal identity. The 'he' is what purposively and serially integrates myriads of actual occasions—which as mere data are merely factual—into a more or less ordered system of relevant values. For one 'he' a primrose by the river's brim is merely a primrose; for another it is a microcosm.

The self is thus always defined in terms of its values. If the values be transient, so is the self. If the values be intransient, so is the self. If the values be dispersed and incoherent, so is the self. If they are organized and integrated, so is the self. In the former case the person is analysable, with little or no loss, into the small and disorganized values which comprise his life. He lends himself to a deterministic theory of human nature, and the psychoanalyst rightly presumes him to be the *product* of his past. *In the latter case, the exact converse holds.* The unified self by definition can not be understood in terms of his constituent parts as dissected away from one another. Instead of his being understood exclusively as the outcome of his environment, the environment can only be understood in terms of him. His very capacity to organize what might otherwise be discordant values puts him in a position of causal primacy.

Since values define the self, it simply will not do to try to divide an intransient self, shaped in terms of its intransient values, into its transient subordinate elements, for these subordinate elements are determined by it, not *vice versa*. If the only way in which I can explain the individual units of a man's consciousness and behaviour is in terms of the abiding purpose which dominates them, then that purpose does not arise exclusively from them. *They have their being, their value status, in it.* To ignore this fact is to commit a fallacy, either the fallacy of composition or the fallacy of division. If a series of actual occasions composing the conscious life of a person exhibits a purposive value collectively, it simply does not follow

[11] PR 104 [116]; cf. PR 165 [180], where the subject is repeated in a somewhat whimsical context.   [12] PR 104 [116].

that this purpose can invariably be understood in terms of the values which the individual members of the series exhibit. The result is a failure. It is the failure of a certain method of analytic procedure to do the job that it set out to do, namely, to expose the nature of the thing that it investigated.

Many units of value ingression are 'molecular', that is, divisible into subordinate parts but not without a destruction of their identity. Corresponding to this molecular value ingression there is a molecular self definable in terms of the temporal extent of the value to which it is committed. A man's stature is measurable in terms of the temporal extent of his values. If his ruling motivation is of the sort that attends to temporal impulse, for instance those of appetite and momentary gratification, his personal stature in so far exhibits its parameters. More abiding commitments are those of friendship, family, country, society, mankind. It should be noticed that I have here spoken of a man's *stature*. We must include men whose genius is evil according to some given moral code. Effective fanatics, ruthless conquerors, 'amoral' aesthetic giants, are men of stature. It may be that their immortality finally wanes by reason of its disruptive strength. Such a question is of the gravest importance, but we are here concerned primarily with the metaphysics of immortality, not its axiology. It is a weakness of western conceptions of immortality that they slide often from the one consideration to the other with too little care. The result is that we often can give no account of the immortality of Alexander and the mortality of some simple Christian of Pompeii.

The dominance of purpose as the ruling element in the definition of self directed toward value has been brilliantly appreciated and exploited in so-called 'depth psychology'. Here the probe exposes the buried attachment or revulsion, the cherished hurt, the unrewarded fascination, and the frustrated would-be conquest. One may only praise such an undertaking—but the sucesss of the venture needs to be exposed against a backdrop of its intentions, which are primarily toward the alleviation of pathology. Psychoanalysis explains why things go wrong, not why things go right. As a result, it can never be made to do the task of giving a broad understanding of the self without an enlargement of its objectives.[13]

[13] Consider the tragic spectacle of Freud, at the end of one of his most famous works, crying aloud for relief from his own pessimism by invoking the image of an Eros which has been present all along in spite of civilization and its discontents.

There is something blinding about the chronic occupation with human ills; the image of humanity is fragmented and distorted.

To return to the conception of molecular value ingression and the molecular self which is defined by it, in one sense the molecular value ingression can be analysed into its parts, and so can the self which corresponds to it. But there is an analytic difficulty. The difficulty is not merely that we "murder to dissect". It is that in dissecting we introduce an arbitrary mode of differentiation which is not suited to the subject-matter. The fallacy in murdering to dissect lies not exclusively in the fact that we kill the cat to discover what makes him purr and thus stop his purring; it is that when we are done with the dissection an inventory of contents does not disclose anything like 'the sight of food', 'the stroke of a hand', or 'the appearance of a familiar face'. Instead we have a dismantled laryngeal mechanism, which is less instructive than a broken bit of stone from an ancient ruin. Nor is it the case that our analysis has been too gross. Were we to disengage the whole mechanism, part by part, down to the last jiggling electromagnetic field, we should be even further from our answer.[14]

Thus a simple formula emerges. In a sense a man is identical with his purposes. However, these purposes, during what is normally called a lifetime, require a dominantly physical vehicle, the immediate locus of which is his own body, with its incorrigible mortality.

When the body is lifeless, its unity is gone, its mechanisms no longer function, no longer interrelate. The living body is liable to a variety of types of analysis. (1) There are the least physical particles, electrons, protons, neutrons, and the like. In the endurance of each of these particles each actual occasion is a pulse measured in microseconds. The pulses are of greater extent as we move up to atoms, molecules, cells, etc. (2) A major size jump occurs when we think of the living body as a perceptual being. Whitehead speculates on the minimal unit's being somewhere between half and a tenth of a second. This means that the actual occasion of perception, as the focus of selfhood, exploits the resources of much more 'physical' entities than itself. These more physical units, e.g. a

---

[14] Notice the analogy with the atomic and molecular treatment of sentences. Currently the passion for exactness emphasizes isolable meanings of words and expects them to hold these meanings stable in spite of context. The term 'logical constants' exhibits this simple-mindedness in one form.

F

complete vibratory period of an electron, appear and disappear much more swiftly than do the units of perception. As I read a single word hundreds of them are born and die in the ongoing life of the submicroscopic entities which 'compose' my body. The immediate past, present, and future of the microscale is all one specious present, here-now, on the macroscale of perception. (3) When we make another jump from perception to the more active aspects of consciousness which involve memory, attitude, disposition, foresight, planning, prediction, etc., the scale of the occasions becomes vastly enlarged again.

All consciousness rests on memory, and memory bridges physical time, drawing together in one present consciousness the significance of past events. The significance of past events is indeed grounded in their completeness, their having subsided; but their significance also depends just as firmly on what use present consciousness puts them to.[15] The way in which memory expropriates the past is one species of what Whitehead calls the 'objective immortality' of completed events. The fact that memory integrates aspects of diverse occasions warns us of the molecular character of conscious actual occasions. The diverse occasions exhibit no inescapable coercive force which determines consciousness. They converge in one consciousness, but not exclusively through their own agency. Their significance for one another is always contextual and the context always includes consciousness. And if we ask what events prior to *this* moment of consciousness are responsible for the selective disposition that has operated *now*, we are driven back to previous occasions in which prior consciousness is the integrating factor. In pathological cases the train of conscious occasions tends toward the extreme of deterministic analysability, but not all consciousness is pathological. Even in pathological cases, however, psychoanalysis itself presumes that conscious recognition of past influences will loosen their hold on present volition. Psychoanalysis is deterministic only in its diagnosis. Its practice is directed toward freeing the consciousness from its entrapment in a submerged past.[16]

The actual occasions of present consciousness are molecular. We

[15] I simplify here, dealing only with conscious, cognizable memory. Depth analysis requires a more elaborate account.

[16] This point is pursued elsewhere in a different context; see "Causality: Causes as Classes", *The Review of Metaphysics*, Vol. 12, 1958, pp. 161–185.

can not explain this unity in terms of their contents. As dissociated parts they carry within themselves no adequate explanation for their convergent unity.

The living person is thus differentiable into many kinds and orders of component parts. (1) We can deal with him as a swarm of fundamental particles. In so far as we do, we find that his life continuity rests in the overlapping sequences of minute actual occasions, themselves comprising the continued existence of these particles. These microprocesses, however, are seemingly endless in their occurrence, pre-dating and post-dating their engagement with this or that supervenient organism. The continuity of these processes is substantially duplicated in the more complex organisms which they comprise. As we rise through levels of complexity we come to the great organism, the body itself, complete with the continuously functioning autonomic nervous system. This system is perhaps faintly accessible to volitional consciousness,[17] but for the most part it leads an automatic existence. (2) We can deal with the person as a string of more or less passive perceptions. These processes, as we have seen, require larger chunks of time to appear (on the physical scale of time) and tend to be discontinuous. The gross cases of such discontinuity are sleep, coma, etc. (3) We can deal with the person as a purposive consciousness, characterized by evaluation, volition, attitude, disposition, etc. Here even larger extents of time are embraced, and the discontinuities are even more marked.

The general pattern is thus quite clear. The more predominant the element of consciousness, the more discontinuous it is as compared to the continuous functioning of the physical elements to which it belongs. The element of consciousness is also less predictable; its activities are less inclined to be law-like, even in pathological cases. It is more free. Men can not add one cubit to their physical statures by taking thought. But they *can* add to their spiritual statures by so doing. This is the cornerstone of what Socrates meant by saying the unexamined life was not worth living. Shy of self-examination, life comes perilously close to its routine physical counterpart, which survives continuously and then at last dissolves when its comprising parts lose their power of organic interrelation.

---

[17] Some fakirs are said to be able to stop heart beat through an act of " 'will' "; ulcers are said to arise from worry, etc.

The drive for survival must turn elsewhere, if it is to avoid temporal eclipse. *The self is determined in terms of the values according to which it subordinates and integrates the rest of its values.* Such values must be transpersonal, for individual personality as we know it must at least sublimate when its physical components lose their organic unity. Yet these values can hardly be trans-human, for we expect them to be proper lures for human moti-vation.

Suppose such a value to be stated as a principle. The principle could not set a precise limit on human growth, nor explicate a positive prescriptive value for all humanity. But it *could* prescribe what must be avoided by any man who did not wish to perish. And in doing so it would offer a course of action, a mode of existence.

V

Time and the types of process

We may now return to Socrates and consider his statement of an enduring principle of enduring humanity: that the unexamined life is not worth living. Socrates is seen as a man who puts aside the rather fleeting values of the temporal body, including its perseverance as an entity—which is foredoomed anyhow. He also puts aside the love of universal acceptance among men, a somewhat less fleeting value. He even puts aside his devotion to his friends, for as a corpse he will hardly be a satisfactory companion. He puts aside that fleshly immortality, with its tempting promise of spiritual continuation as well, which is the devotion to one's children. He puts aside that form of patriotism which places its country's current anaesthetic happiness above all other considerations. He identifies himself with the one principle that the unexamined life is not worth living. If we realize that this identification is conceived by Socrates as a real act having profound metaphysical significance and not merely a superb gesture of a determined man, who will throw his life across the counter rather than be shaken from the position that he has taken, then the rest of the *Apology* and the *Crito* fall into place. For this reason, the emotions of his judges must not be treated to the unguents and intoxicants of a sweet rhetoric or the spectacle of a prostrate wife and children. For this reason Socrates cannot leave Athens, nor still his questioning, nor propose any penalty which suggests an admission of wrong-doing.

For this reason he cannot violate those laws which in their imperfect way represent the imperfect struggle of a half-blind society toward enduring principle. Poor though the laws may be, and badly administered, they are of the kind of effort which Socrates would most encourage men to make. Finally, by devoting himself to the principle that the examined life is that which is the most completely worth while, by genuinely identifying himself with that conviction, he leaves the way open for justice for himself and his living sons. Should that principle be pursued, there is a thin truth in the interpretation of Socrates as having substituted principle for physical life as an object of motivation. The deeper truth is that the living historical Socrates is, in his own eyes, caught up, as are his sons, as living beings in the enduring value expressed in the principle. They are not abrogated by it, but fulfilled through it.

Temporal passage, as Newton deals with it, is abstracted from processes whose component units are so minute that the irreversibility of time is virtually assured. What we do is to peg our conception of temporal passage to the succession of dominantly physical events, each of which is a complete phase in the endurance of the physical object. But philosophically there should be no special primacy about this type of process. Other processes are composed of units whose temporal requirements for becoming actual are gigantic, as compared with the physical microprocesses. Consciousness, even as possibly perceptual, is such a process. If we try to divide the basic unit of consciousness into subordinate parts of smaller size, we are left with a collection of much more nearly physical processes, mere end-products of dissective analysis, having no explicative power within themselves to show the integral character of the conscious unit. Explanation degenerates into physical description of the physical aspects of human consciousness. Actively purposive consciousness, concerned with the realization of value, proceeds by even larger temporal blocks. It may take days or weeks to bring justice into a courtroom. All the while, lesser processes deliver their much less reversible results into the overarching occasion which is the huge single event, the ingression of justice. Taken by themselves as complete and having no significance for the network of processes in which they are embedded, they are irretrievable. But in their context of the larger process, that is, considering not their internal completeness, but their external significance, their external significance is never done until all the contributing elements have come into being. The reversibility of time lies in this, that *what is over and done with, in its relation to some particular temporal process, may quite easily be as yet incomplete with respect to some supervenient process* whose unit blocks are temporally longer, and for which it may have significance still. The past is irrevocable only if the perspective on it be arbitrarily confined.

Socrates is in court; so he speaks the recognizable language of fleshly immortality to the popular mind. "I and my sons." The issue of justice in this court is not finished by the myopia of his judges, unless Socrates affirms his values only in terms of his personal existence. That the ingression of justice is not to be measured in terms of his sons' existence alone is shown by the fact that Socrates will not allow himself to be distracted from his purpose by Crito's mention of his sons. But they do make the point for the popular audience, showing the way to the vaster conception, abiding value, in terms of a phrase which every father could comprehend. In his last public minute Socrates teaches. Socrates did not die for his value and the principle which embodies it. He identified his selfhood *with it* rather than with his "old bones", as he calls them in the *Phaedo*. In this identification he *lived* for his value in the only way that immortal man can live.

Socrates functions as Plato's Achilles. But his courage is exhibited not in terms of mere headlong determination, even where such determination is backed up by great physical endowment and great spiritual perseverance. To get a better view of Socrates, let us look at Gilgamish. Gilgamish, like Achilles, was a great warrior, a man of superb courage and great physical endowment. Like Achilles he weeps when his beloved companion is killed. But Gilgamish has another layer to his soul. From his youth he has been troubled by death and the transiency of things. And when his friend dies, he goes in search of immortality or its secret beyond Mount Mashu. Beyond Mount Mashu the wife of the Babylonian Noah tells him where to find the plant which will give him immortality, and how and when to eat it. With his great physical endowments Gilgamish gets the plant and then, in a moment of human inadvertence, loses it while taking a bath in a cool spring. His fate is that of Achilles, but his vision is that of Socrates. Socrates successfully resists at the moment of his crisis, and in culmination of his life, the full array of the temporal allurements that lead to mortality.

IVOR LECLERC

FORM AND ACTUALITY

VI

IVOR LECLERC

FORM AND ACTUALITY

When Plato, as the culmination of a long development in Greek thought, enunciated his theory of form, he exposed and brought to the fore one of the most profound of philosophical issues which, in one guise or another, has played a fundamental role in all subsequent philosophical thought. This issue is that of the nature and status of form, and of its relation to actuality. I use the term 'form' here in its most general connotation, and not with any restricted meaning such as might be attached to it by some particular theory of form; so that the term covers also a nominalistic conception of form.

One of the highly interesting features of the history of thought in so far as it involves this issue, is that it reveals a persistently cyclical character. There has been a recurrent movement from a strong emphasis on form, culminating in ascribing to it an 'eminent' status, round to the opposite extreme, in nominalism, of attributing to it the very contrary status; and then back again to the other attitude of increasing emphasis on form as somehow fundamental.

Sometimes the cycles have been smaller ones, cycles within cycles, as is, for example, exhibited in the development from Plato through Aristotle. This has features of very great importance for the inquiry into the philosophical issue which is the topic of this essay. I shall start by briefly bringing out the cyclical character of the Platonic-Aristotelian development. Later, in the context of modern thought, some of the main philosophical problems here involved will be raised and examined.

The initial discovery of form is probably to be ascribed to the Pythagoreans and Socrates. The latter grasped, even if not with perfect clarity, the crucial relevance of form to the philosophical problems of ethics and epistemology. But it was Plato who realized the full philosophical import of the discovery. He recognized that it raised the metaphysical problem of the nature and status of

F*

form. The combined ethical, epistemological, and metaphysical considerations of form led Plato to the famous theory of forms of his 'middle' dialogues. That is to say, the consideration of form in its relevance to the fundamental philosophical problems—ethical, political, epistemological, and metaphysical—drove Plato to the conception of form as the ὄντως ὄν, the truly real. This meant relegating all else to a metaphysically different and subordinate status. In his later dialogues, from the *Parmenides* onward, Plato wrestled with the implications and difficulties of this conception.[1]

Aristotle came to reject this doctrine according to which forms are οὐσίαι. He argued powerfully that forms could not be independent existents in their own right. Aristotle was completely opposed to any kind of 'two-world' theory; there is one world, the world in which we live, with which we interact, of which we are part. But Aristotle was far from wishing to deny the supreme importance of forms; in one aspect of the emphasis on form, Aristotle was in full accord with his predecessor Plato. The forms however, he maintained, must be within the world; they must be the *forms of* the things constituting this world. It is these things which are the οὐσίαι. More strictly, in Aristotle's view, the οὐσίαι are those things, such as individual men, individual horses, etc., which have 'nature' (φύσις) in the full sense.

But in the course of the working out of his position, a highly interesting development takes place. The analysis of οὐσία, of that which is, reveals more and more that form is fundamental. In the analysis of οὐσία into 'matter' and 'form', it is form which is basic: (*a*) matter is undetermined in itself, and receives its determination from form; (*b*) matter as such is unknowable, and the οὐσία is known through its form; (*c*) it is not matter but form which constitutes the 'essence' (τὸ τί ἦν εἶναι) of οὐσίαι; (*d*) matter is not a 'this' (τόδε τι), and it *is* only 'potentially'[2]; (*e*) it is form which is a 'this'[3], and it is form which finally turns out to be 'actuality' (ἐνέργεια) and end.[4] Thus it has come about that, as Sir David Ross has put it, "the general tendency of ZHΘ is to carry Aristotle away from his earlier doctrine that the sensible individual is 'primary substance', to one which identifies primary substance with pure

[1] Cf. Gottfried Martin, *Einleitung in die allgemeine Metaphysik* (English translation *An Introduction to General Metaphysics*, London: Allen & Unwin, 1961) for an illuminating discussion of the development of Greek thought from Socrates to Aristotle.

[2] *Metaphysics*, 1042 a 26–8.   [3] 1017 b 23–6, 1042 a 29.   [4] 1050 a 4–25.

form and with that alone".⁵ Aristotle found himself increasingly driven to ascribe 'act' (ἐνέργεια) to form,⁶ and when he came to develop his doctrine of the prime mover, who is eternal and the supreme actuality, he had to conclude that such an actuality must be pure form, devoid of all matter—for matter is potentiality, and the supreme instance of actuality could not be the prime mover, the cause of all motion, the ultimate final cause, if its being included potentiality.⁷

Admittedly this makes the Aristotelian forms different from the Platonic forms, as Aristotle was constantly at pains to stress; for the Platonic forms, Aristotle argues, do not act,⁸ but are universals⁹ and potentialities.¹⁰ But what is of significance from our point of view is that Aristotle, who had started by maintaining, in opposition to Plato, that form must be the 'form of' οὐσίαι, ended with a conception of pure form as itself the οὐσία.

This cyclical development is the more interesting in view of the subsequent history of philosophy in which, in various ways, it is a recurrent feature. Thus in this respect the history of thought suggests strongly that the notion of 'form' is not to be got rid of, and that it must be one of the most important tasks of metaphysical inquiry to work at the problem of the nature and status of form.

In our own time the dominant trend has on the whole been in the direction of a depreciation of the status of form. In this the philosophy of existentialism has been in accord with the prominent positivistic and near-positivistic movements. But there have also been contrary trends, exemplified by such thinkers as Nicolai Hartmann and George Santayana in the generation just passed, and by Paul Weiss among others in the present. This trend is also to be found, very significantly, in some of the most advanced thought on the philosophy of nature, which has once again been bringing thinkers —scientists¹¹ as well as philosophers—round to an emphasis on structure, pattern, i.e. on form, as in some respect basic. In this trend Whitehead has a prominent place; his thought has indeed by many even been regarded as a resuscitation of Platonism. This trend, arising from a consideration of the problems of the philosophy of nature, is especially interesting in contrast with the

---

⁵ W. D. Ross, *Aristotle's Metaphysics*, A Revised Text with Introduction and Commentary, 2 Vols., Oxford: Clarendon Press, 1958, p. ci.

⁶ Cf. 1050 a 3–25.   ⁷ Cf. 1071 b 11–26.   ⁸ Cf. 1071 b 16.

⁹ Cf. 1040 b 27–34.   ¹⁰ Cf. 1050 b 34–1051 a 2.

¹¹ Such as Erwin Schrödinger and others.

dominant view of the last two to three centuries, today still largely adhered to, and underlying the whole positivistic climate of thought of our time, that modern science has finally laid the ghost of 'Platonism', and that the ultimate 'real' is indubitably constituted by those entities which are the subject of investigation in the laboratories of the scientists.

In this context Whitehead is of special importance. Of those who have been prominently affected by scientific considerations, Whitehead has been far in advance, not only of his own generation, but also of subsequent ones, in having developed the implications of this trend, and in having worked them out to their full philosophical conclusion. It was considerations deriving from scientific problems which initially determined Whitehead's approach to the issue with which this paper is concerned, and which shaped the view at which he arrived. In his later thought, however, as in that of Plato, it was the essentially philosophical problems involved which occupied his attention, and which produced not only the unfolding and development of his system, but also some highly important modifications of his conceptions as they had earlier been maintained under the influence of science. It must therefore be of considerable moment for the general inquiry into the nature and status of form to attempt to get clear as to where exactly Whitehead stands in regard to this historic issue, whether he has introduced any significant novel ingredients into the age-old struggle with this issue, and if so, whether these assist to any appreciable extent in resolving the enormous difficulties which have haunted thought on this problem.

It seems to me a serious misunderstanding of Whitehead's doctrine to regard it as 'Platonic', in the sense that he maintained a theory of forms (in Whitehead's earlier terminology, 'objects', and in the later, 'eternal objects') as constituting a realm of independently existing entities transcending the realm of 'temporal existents'. In this respect Whitehead's position has from the beginning been much closer to that of Aristotle. While, like Aristotle, he certainly did emphasize the importance of form, he equally strongly, again like Aristotle, insisted that form does not constitute an independent realm of existents, but that form exists only as ingredient in actuality. This is clear from the following passages, from the earlier to the latest works.

In the *Principles of Natural Knowledge* Whitehead argued for a "diversification of nature" into 'events' and 'objects';[12] by this he meant that these two types of 'element'[13] are to be discovered *in nature*.

"The relation of extension exhibits events as actual—as matters of fact—by means of its properties which issue in spatial relations; and it exhibits events as involving the becomingness of nature—its passage or creative advance—by means of its properties which issue in temporal relations. Thus events are essentially elements of actuality and elements of becomingness. An actual event is thus divested of all possibility. It is what does become in nature."[14]

"Objects convey the permanences recognised in events, and are recognized as self-identical amid different circumstances; that is to say, the same object is recognized as related to diverse events."[15] "The object is permanent, because (strictly speaking) it is without time and space; its change is merely the variety of its relations to the various events which are passing in time and space .... Events (in a sense) are space and time, namely, space and time are abstractions from events. But objects are only derivatively in space and time by reason of their relations to events."[16]

"Whatever is purely matter of fact is an event. Whenever the concept of possibility can apply to a natural element, that element is an object."[17]

"The continuity of nature is to be found in events, the atomic properties of nature reside in objects."[18]

The full implications of this position were by no means clear to Whitehead at that stage of his thought. But what was clear to him was that, although objects as a type of entity are to be distinguished, and to be distinguished as of an essentially different type from events, objects are nevertheless definitely *in* nature. He states this explicitly in *The Concept of Nature*:

"Objects are elements in nature which do not pass."[19]

"An object is an ingredient in the character of some event. In fact the character of an event is nothing but the objects which are ingredient in it and the ways in which those objects make their ingression into the event. Thus the theory of objects is the theory of the comparison of events. Events are only comparable because they body forth permanences. We are comparing objects in events whenever we can say, 'There it is again'. Objects are the elements in nature which can 'be again'."[20]

"I am using the term 'ingression' to denote the general relation of objects to events. The ingression of an object into an event is the way the character of the event shapes itself in virtue of the being of the object. Namely the event is what it is, because the object is what it is; and when I am thinking of this modification of the event by the object, I call the relation between the two 'the ingression of the object into the event'. It is equally true to say that objects are what they are because events are what they are. Nature is such that there can be no events and no objects without the ingression of objects into events."[21]

By the time Whitehead came to write *Science and the Modern World*, considerations of the properly philosophical problems had resulted in an appreciable clarification. As before he maintained that:

"We must start with the event as the ultimate unit of natural occurrence. An event has to do with all that there is, and in particular with other events. This interfusion of events is effected by the aspects of those eternal objects, such as colours, sounds, scents, geometrical characters, which are required for nature and are not emergent from it. Such an eternal object will be an ingredient of one event under the guise, or aspect, of qualifying another event."[22]

Careful scrutiny of this passage reveals, however, that there has occurred some modification of the earlier position. A greater emphasis has come to be placed on events as 'actuality'. Nature is still seen as essentially 'in passage'; nature is still a 'process' of 'creative advance':

"Thus nature is a structure of evolving processes. The reality is the process. It is nonsense to ask if the colour red is real. The colour red is ingredient in the process of realization. The realities of nature are the prehensions in nature, that is to say, the events in nature."[23]

But this 'process' is now seen more precisely as 'organic', and the event as a 'unit of realization'. That is, "these unities, which I call

[20] CN 143-4.   [21] CN 144.   [22] SMW 129.   [23] SMW 90.

events, are the emergence into actuality of something".[24] Thus, he argues:

"The organic starting-point is from the analysis of process as the realization of events disposed in an interlocked community. The event is the unit of things real."[25]

"An event is the grasping into unity of a pattern of aspects."[26]

It becomes clear that an event must not only be conceived as a 'unit', but also as an 'activity', an organic agent:

"Cognition discloses an event as being an activity, organizing a real togetherness of alien things."[27]

The development of Whitehead's thought in *Science and the Modern World* has, therefore, resulted in an important modification of his earlier view according to which "the continuity of nature is to be found in events, [whereas] the atomic properties of nature reside in objects".[28] The 'atomic' character of nature is now found in the events as 'units', which he begins calling 'actual occasions' in the later chapters of *Science and the Modern World*.

This development necessitated a corresponding modification to Whitehead's theory of form. He abandoned the theory of various kinds of 'atomic' objects ('perceptual objects', 'sense objects', 'material objects', 'scientific objects', etc.). Form continues to be identified with 'possibility', and it is still the 'character' of the actual: an actual occasion is what it is by virtue of the 'ingression' of what Whitehead now terms 'eternal objects'. But in this new position, in which "eternal things are the elements required for the very being of the process",[29] the notion of form has been fully generalized as the 'form of' actuality. Therewith Whitehead attained his mature philosophical position which, in this respect, remained unmodified to the end:

"It is the foundation of the metaphysical position which I am maintaining that the understanding of actuality requires a reference to ideality. The two realms are intrinsically inherent in the total metaphysical situation."[30]

This is the position which is presented also in his last book, *Modes of Thought*, and in the final lecture he delivered, the Ingersoll

---

[24] SMW 116. [25] SMW 189. [26] SMW 149.
[27] SMW 187. [28] PNK § 15.4. [29] SMW 135. [30] SMW 196–7.

Lecture on "Immortality". In the former he maintained that analysis discloses two types of existence which "can be named respectively, The Type of Actuality, and The Type of Pure Potentiality. These types require each other, namely Actuality is the exemplification of Potentiality, and Potentiality is the characterization of Actuality, either in fact or in concept."[31] And in his final lecture he propounded the same doctrine of "the ultimate character of the Universe. This ultimate character has two sides—one side is the mortal world of transitory fact acquiring the immortality of realized value; the other side is the timeless world of mere possibility acquiring temporal realization."[32]

Thus while Whitehead throughout maintained a strong emphasis on form, at no time, in either the earlier doctrine or the later, did he regard form as constituting an independent realm of existents. Like Aristotle, Whitehead distinguished form as a metaphysically ultimate ingredient in that which exists actually. True, he speaks of eternal objects as 'transcendent entities',[33] but by this he does not mean that forms are themselves οὐσίαι, actual existents in their own right. Forms are 'transcendent' in not being reducible to, and exhaustively explicable in terms of actuality. He expressed this in calling them 'abstract':

"Eternal objects are thus, in their nature, abstract. By 'abstract' I mean that what an eternal object is in itself—that is to say, its essence—is comprehensible without reference to some one particular occasion of experience. To be abstract is to transcend particular concrete occasions of actual happening. But to transcend an actual occasion does not mean being disconnected from it. On the contrary, I hold that each eternal object has its own proper connection with each such occasion, which I term its mode of ingression into that occasion."[34]

Indeed, this designation of form as 'abstract' is a deliberate consequence of Whitehead's definite realization of his position, and it makes that position explicit. For to be 'abstract' is to be abstract by contrast with what is 'concrete', and it is to be 'abstracted from' that concrete. The 'concrete' is constituted by the actual occasions.

In *Process and Reality* Whitehead made his metaphysical position fully clear by his enunciation of what he termed the 'ontological principle', which he referred to as "the general Aris-

[31] MT 96.   [32] Imm § VI.   [33] Cf. SMW 197.   [34] SMW 197.

totelian principle . . . that, apart from the things that are actual, there is nothing—nothing either in fact or in efficacy".35 His doctrine is that

"Thus the actual world is built up of actual occasions; and by the ontological principle whatever things there are in any sense of 'existence', are derived by abstraction from actual occasions."36

In this respect Whitehead's position is in close accord with that of Aristotle. But Whitehead diverges from Aristotle by going further in a direction in which Aristotle only displayed hesitant tendencies—Aristotle was too close in time to Plato, and it was thus difficult for him to move too far in this direction without seeming to capitulate to what he had rejected in Plato. Whitehead saw clearly that if forms are to be the 'forms of' actualities, and yet not be reducible to actualities, then we must regard forms as a kind of entity which is 'transcendent', as a kind of entity whose nature in an essential respect 'transcends' actuality. That is to say, forms are not to be regarded simply as features disclosed in the analysis of actuality; forms must constitute entities of a distinct categoreal type. Whitehead maintained this position throughout his later work, from *Science and the Modern World* onward. In that book he spoke of them as a "realm of entities which transcend" actual occasions—a designation apt to give rise to misapprehension, as William Christian has brought out.37 In *Process and Reality* Whitehead held that among the "eight categories of existence, actual entities and eternal objects stand out with a certain extreme finality",38 a position which he maintained to the end, as the two quotations above from *Modes of Thought* and the lecture on "Immortality" sufficiently evidence.

The problem is how forms can be metaphysically distinct and yet not themselves be οὐσίαι; how forms can be 'transcendent' and yet be the 'forms of' actualities. Is it possible consistently and coherently to hold this position? Will it not in the end be necessary either, maintaining the ontological principle, to abandon the metaphysical distinctness of forms, thereby moving closer to a nominalistic position, as has been done by even some followers of Whitehead; or to abandon the ontological principle, as Paul Weiss

35 PR 54 [64].   36 PR 101 [113].
37 Cf. William A. Christian, *An Interpretation of Whitehead's Metaphysics*, 1959, Ch. 14.   38 PR 29 [33].

has done with his doctrine of four equally ultimate modes of being?[39]

Whitehead's own position in respect to this problem must be investigated in further detail. We can perhaps most usefully commence this by bringing out a very important, perhaps the fundamental, difference between the conceptions of Whitehead and Aristotle. In the final Aristotelian doctrine, form is not only ἐντελέχεια, the full reality, but form is also identified with ἐνέργεια, 'act', and stands in contrast to matter, which is δύναμις, 'potentiality'. Whitehead virtually reverses this position.[40] He decisively rejects any identification of form and act. For Whitehead, *form does not in any respect 'act'; for him all activity belongs to actuality*.[41] This is quite basic to Whitehead's position, and must not for a moment be lost sight of, especially in view of what I shall subsequently point out, namely the closeness of the relation of form and actuality in Whitehead's doctrine.

What Whitehead has done is to put 'act' in the place of the Aristotelian 'prime matter'. It must be explicitly understood that Whitehead has not *ascribed* activity to matter; matter cannot act— on this Whitehead and Aristotle are in complete agreement. But whereas Aristotle saw no alternative in that case but to ascribe act to form, Whitehead abolishes 'matter' entirely, and in its place puts 'act' or 'activity', pure creative activity. That is to say, Whitehead replaces the Aristotelian category of 'prime matter' by the category of 'creativity'.[42] It should be noted that Whitehead thereby completely disposes of anything of the kind of 'matter' or 'stuff'; and with it goes every characteristic attaching to matter, excepting for one. This is that activity, creativity, like the Aristotelian matter, is that which takes on form, that which is characterized by form. But there is, in this respect, nevertheless an essential difference from the Aristotelian matter: creativity, in contrast with matter, "is divested of the notion of passive receptivity".[43] The point is not simply that the notions of 'activity' and 'passivity' are contraries. It is that if one ascribes 'passive receptivity' to that which is formed, then either the factor of 'act' must be ascribed to form (as it is done by Aristotle) or to some transcendent agent (as is done by Plato in the *Timaeus*, and afterwards by many philo-

---

[39] Paul Weiss, *Modes of Being*, 1958.   [40] Cf. my paper on "The Analysis of 'Act'", *Proceedings of the 12th International Congress of Philosophy*, 1958.   [41] Cf. PR 42 [46]; AI 253-4.   [42] PR 29 [32], 42 [46].   [43] PR 42 [46].

sophers who were strongly affected by the main tradition of Christian theology). Whitehead rejects both these alternatives as unable to produce a coherent metaphysics. Whitehead's own solution is to make 'activity' as such the "Category of the Ultimate". Therewith Whitehead has introduced a novel feature of the highest importance into the philosophical scene.

This means that in place of the conception of some sort of primal 'stuff' which takes on form, Whitehead has the conception of 'pure activity' which is of some or other definiteness. In other words, οὐσία, that which is, an actual entity, is to be analysed into 'activity' with some definite character or form. What is *concrete* is 'activity', not 'stuff': "The sole concrete facts, in terms of which actualities can be analysed, are prehensions."[44] And 'prehensions' are primarily 'acts'. "In Cartesian language, the essence of an actual entity consists solely in the fact that it is a prehending thing (i.e. a substance whose whole essence or nature is to prehend)."[45]

It must be clearly appreciated that when Whitehead maintains the concrete, the οὐσία, to be an '*acting* entity', he does not mean that there is an entity which is, as such a completed existent, *and* which acts; that is, an entity whose existence is antecedent to its acts, with its acts ancillary to *it*. To grasp Whitehead's conception we have explicitly to abandon the customary way of thinking in terms of a substance which has qualities, a subject with its predicates. The entity *is* its acting: "*how* an actual entity *becomes* is *what* that actual entity *is*. . . . Its 'being' is constituted by its 'becoming' ";[46] "the process [of acting] itself is the constitution of the actual entity".[47] It would be more correct to say that the concrete is *the acting*, than to say that the concrete is 'something' *which acts*. Whitehead is here decisively rejecting the widely held—though usually implicit—conception that 'acting' is a 'property' of the existent, i.e. the conception that an actual entity has a complete 'real internal constitution' describable apart from its acts, and that its 'being' is to be found in that constitution, that it exists by virtue of that constitution.

In Whitehead's doctrine, the actuality not only exists 'in the acting', but it exists *by virtue of* acting. *Its acting is its existing.* 'Acting' is 'being', and 'being' is 'acting'. In this identification of 'being' and 'acting' Whitehead is close to Aristotle. We recall

---

[44] PR 411 [444]. Cf. also PR 31 [35].   [45] PR 56 [65].
[46] PR 31 [34-5].   [47] PR 309-10 [335].

Aristotle's words: "For the action (ἔργον) is the end, and the actuality (ἐνέργεια) is the action (ἔργον). And so even the *word* 'actuality' (ἐνέργεια) is derived from 'action' (ἔργον), and points to the complete reality (ἐντελέχεια)."[48] But there is this vital difference with Aristotle. While for Whitehead the ἐντελέχεια, the actual entity, is the 'acting' entity, he does not, like Aristotle, identify ἐνέργεια, act with form. For Whitehead the being, the existing, of an actual entity is due to its acting, and not to its form.

But although the Whiteheadian doctrine in this way identifies 'being' and 'acting', and would thus appear to minimize sharply the status of form, in fact this very identification of being and acting necessitates bringing form into great prominence. The Whiteheadian analysis, like the Aristotelian, elicits the fundamental status and role of form. And many of the reasons produced by Whitehead are essentially the same as those urged by Aristotle.

In the first place, the ultimate activity is undetermined of itself. That is to say, if *pure* activity, activity as such, be taken as a metaphysical ultimate, it must, as such, be undetermined. In this respect 'activity' or 'creativity' is strictly analogous to the Aristotelian 'prime matter', which too is undetermined of itself. "Creativity is without a character of its own in exactly the same sense in which the Aristotelian 'matter' is without a character of its own."[49] This means that activity as such cannot be the metaphysical source of determination. While the *being*, the *existence*, of an actuality is due to activity, the *character* of actuality, *what* it is, can in no respect be due to or derive from activity as such. The character of actuality must have a different metaphysical ground. This calls for the recognition of *another* metaphysical ultimate as well, and for Whitehead, as for Aristotle, this is 'form'.

Thus because to exist, to be actual, requires determinateness, and determinateness means to be definitely this or that, i.e. to be of some definite character, and because the Whiteheadian creativity, analogously to the Aristotelian matter, is undetermined of itself, form is necessitated as the metaphysical basis of determinateness. On this point Whitehead and Aristotle are in full accord. And in this way Whitehead, like Aristotle, brings form into a metaphysical prominence of the first order.

A highly important implication of this should be noted. This is that Whitehead is in agreement with Aristotle that there can *be* no

---

[48] 1050 a 22–3. Ross translation.   [49] PR 42 [47].

actuality without form. That is, *form is necessary to being*. Thus for Whitehead the relation of form and being is much closer than might at first have seemed as a result of his reversal of the Aristotelian position in regard to form and act, and of his identification of being and acting.

It is just here that the similarity of and the difference between the Whiteheadian and the Aristotelian positions is specially illuminating. Aristotle, clearly realizing that being involves acting, as well as that form is necessary to being, concluded that, since matter cannot act, act (ἐνέργεια) must be ascribed to form. Thus Aristotle brings the three (being, act, form) together: form is identified with being, and thus with act. For him this constitutes one metaphysical ultimate, which he sees as one pole in the total metaphysical situation, of which the other pole is matter. Aristotle, however, as we have noted, was unable, in the end, to maintain both poles. Matter had finally to be dropped from the metaphysical 'first rank', and form, as being and act, remained supreme.

Whitehead, on the other hand, replacing the Aristotelian matter by act, identifies being and acting, and seeks to maintain acting and form as two ultimates constituting two poles in the total metaphysical situation. We have to inquire whether Whitehead is any more successful than was Aristotle in being able to maintain two poles. This investigation will necessitate our entering into further detail of Whitehead's theory. At this point, however, it is well to note that, considered in reference to *being*, acting and form are, for Whitehead, much closer than might perhaps appear to be the case. We shall have to examine just what that relation is.

Although Whitehead did not, like Aristotle, give great prominence to purely epistemological considerations in the argument for the fundamental status of form, he did certainly take them into account, and an examination of his writings, early and late, shows that they played an important part. But on the whole the epistemological considerations were, in Whitehead, subordinated to the metaphysical. He saw that the problem of knowledge is but an aspect of, an item within, the general metaphysical problem of the relationship of actualities to one another. The latter is the problem which received his primary attention, and it was to the solution of this that he found form to be essential.

The problem, in its most general terms, is *how* actualities are related. This involves asking what must be the nature of actualities such that they can be in relation, and what must be the nature of that relation. Explicit attention to these questions, Whitehead argues, compels us to reject any conception of an actuality "as complete in itself, without reference to any other substantial thing",[50] an actuality as thus having purely external relations.

"Such an account of the ultimate atoms, or of the ultimate monads, or of the ultimate subjects enjoying experience, renders an interconnected world of real individuals unintelligible. The universe is shivered into a multitude of disconnected substantial things, each thing in its own way exemplifying its private bundle of abstract characters which have found a common home in its own substantial individuality."[51]

Relations between actualities must be 'internal': "there can only be evidence of a world of actual entities, if the immediate actual entity discloses them as essential to its own composition. Descartes' notion of an unessential experience of the external world is entirely alien to the organic philosophy."[52]

The crucial problem which therefore arises is *how* actualities can be internal to each other. This problem is fundamental to knowledge, as was quite clear to Aristotle. For in knowing, in experiencing, the object known is somehow immanent in the knower. Descartes' statement[53] epitomizes what, despite theory, we perforce presuppose and act upon:

"Hence the idea of the sun will be the sun itself existing in the mind, not indeed formally, as it exists in the sky, but objectively, i.e. in the way in which objects are wont to exist in the mind."

Two points are relevant here: (*a*) the known exists immanently in the knower, and (*b*) this existence as immanent is a mode of existence different from the 'formal', i.e. 'actual', existence of the known; by contrast with the latter, the existence of the known as immanent is 'objective'. It will be noted that this involves epistemological realism: the knowing makes no difference to the *actual* existence of the known; in other words, the knower is externally related to the known, whilst only the known is internally related to the knower. But the 'actual' existence of the known cannot be its sole mode of existence; as known, it must exist 'objectively' in the knower. And further, although the 'objective' existence of the

[50] AI 169.   [51] AI 169–70.   [52] PR 201 [219–20].   [53] *Reply to Objections* I.

known is a different mode of existence from its 'actual' existence, nevertheless it must in a fundamental respect be *the same* entity existing 'actually' and 'objectively', for otherwise *knowledge* of *other* actualities would not be possible.

Thus the issue is primarily a metaphysical one. What is required is a metaphysical explanation of the distinction between 'actual' and 'objective' existence. To provide this, Aristotle maintained that form is essential: the immanence of the actuality known in the knower is effected by the *form of* the known existing in the knower. Again we find Whitehead in agreement with Aristotle. For Whitehead too immanence is effected by form, in basically the same way as it is in the doctrine of Aristotle. That is, the same form which is inherent in the entity as it is *in actuality*, as the 'form of' that actuality, becomes inherent in the knower, and thereby the actuality known is 'objectively' in the knower.

This theory of the objective existence of the known is decisively opposed to the Kantian and any other phenomenalistic doctrine of 'objective' existence. For, as Whitehead has repeatedly emphasized, the phenomenalistic doctrine entails a radical gap between the 'actual' existence of the known and its 'objective' existence. On the one side there is the 'phenomenal object', and on the other there is an 'actual' entity which, as *Ding an sich*, is completely separate from the 'phenomenal object'. Strictly, it is gratuitous to speak of *it* as 'actual' and as 'phenomenal', since an entity as 'actually' existing is entirely beyond the range of knowledge. There is no one entity both as *Ding an sich* and as 'object'; all we are able to *know* is a 'phenomenon'—and we cannot know that it is an 'appearance of' anything. Whitehead rejects this position as creating insuperable philosophical difficulties, not only epistemological, but more importantly, metaphysical, for in the end it can provide no explanation of interrelationship, and of knowledge as an outcome of interrelationship.

Whitehead's doctrine is therefore that "an interconnected world of real individuals" necessitates internal relatedness, and that this involves that actualities must be immanent as 'objects' in other actualities. Whitehead secures the latter with this theory of prehension. The 'act' which is the being of an actuality is an *act of prehending*. Every actual (acting) entity prehends other (past) actualities, thereby 'objectively' including them in itself, synthesizing them into a novel unity which is the acting entity itself.

It is important to the proper understanding of this theory to appreciate that the doctrine of 'being' as 'acting' necessitates the conception of an actuality as an 'epochal becoming'.[54] That is, the 'being' or *actual* existing of an οὐσία is constituted by an epochal prehensive act of becoming, at the termination of which the 'actual' existence of the entity ceases—the entity, as Whitehead puts it, 'perishes'. Its 'actual' existence is its existence as a subject acting. Since it exists 'as actual' only in the acting, when its act of becoming has achieved its end, its 'subjectivity' as an 'actual' (i.e. acting) existent terminates, and it is then capable only of 'objective' existence. It exists then as an 'object' for superseding prehending subjects; that is, it exists 'objectively', as immanent in the constitution of the superseding actualities, through their prehensive activity. Whitehead points out that this doctrine

"directly contradicts Kant's 'First Analogy of Experience' in either of its ways of phrasing (1st or 2nd edition). In the philosophy of organism it is not 'substance' which is permanent, but 'form'. Forms suffer changing relations; actual entities 'perpetually perish' subjectively, but are immortal objectively. Actuality in perishing acquires objectivity, while it loses subjective immediacy. It loses the final causation which is its internal principle of unrest, and it acquires efficient causation whereby it is a ground of obligation characterizing the creativity."[55]

"Thus 'perishing' is the assumption of a role in the transcendent future. The non-being of occasions is their 'objective immortality'. A pure physical prehension is how an occasion in its immediacy of being absorbs another occasion which has passed into the objective immortality of its non-being. It is how the past lives in the present. It is causation. It is memory. It is perception of derivation. It is emotional conformation to a given situation, an emotional continuity of past with present. It is a basic element from which springs the self-creation of each temporal occasion. Thus perishing is the initiation of becoming. How the past perishes is how the future becomes."[56]

The 'objectification' of actualities, as is evident from the former passage, is effected by form. The role here played by form

---

[54] Cf. my paper on "Being and becoming in the philosophy of Whitehead", *Kant-Studien*, Band 51, Heft 4, 1959/60.

[55] PR 40 [44].

[56] AI 305.

is crucial, and the implications of this are of the greatest significance. Whitehead makes clear that

"The organic philosophy does not hold that the 'particular existents' are prehended apart from universals; on the contrary, it holds that they are prehended by the mediation of universals. In other words, each actuality is prehended by means of some element of its own definiteness. This is the doctrine of the 'objectification' of actual entities. Thus the primary stage in the concrescence of an actual entity is the way in which the antecedent universe enters into the constitution of the entity in question, so as to constitute the basis of its nascent individuality."[57]

In this doctrine each actual entity is an acting of a particular definiteness or form. That form is the form of that acting; thus that form is the form of that entity 'as actual'. Upon perishing, that "actuality is prehended by means of some element of its own definiteness" or form; that is, by this means the actuality, objectively, "enters into the constitution of" the prehending subject. Thus the form, which determines the definiteness of the entity 'as actual', in objectification becomes an element in the definiteness of the prehender.

It is important to be clear on the following points. The first is that form, the same form, is ingredient in the entity 'as actual' and in the superseding prehenders. As Whitehead says in the quotation above, forms are "permanent" and "suffer changing relations". But, secondly, it is not simply the case that a form, as such, has multiple ingression; that is, the form is not simply a universal. The form in question is the 'form of' a particular actuality. So, thirdly, it is not the form as such which "enters into the constitution of" the prehender; it is *the form of the prehending actuality* which so enters. Thus, fourthly, in this way it is *the prehended actuality* ("the antecedent universe") which enters into the constitution of the prehending actuality.

For our purposes we do not need to enter into the discussion of Whitehead's theory of how this entry is effected—his theory of re-enaction.[58] That theory does not alter nor add anything essential to the basic point which has now clearly emerged, namely, that form, in objectification, is identified with the actuality prehended. The form is the objectified actuality, and the objectified actuality is the form. Once again, in Whitehead's doctrine, the relation between form and actuality is seen to be extremely close—here indeed to the point of identification: in one respect at least, the form is the actuality.

This identification, we must be clear, will be impossible if form be simply a universal. Whitehead does not himself so regard form, as we shall see in more detail—despite the statement in the passage last quoted that particular existents "are prehended by the mediation of *universals*"; the word is used here as synonymous with 'form'. In Whitehead's theory of objectification, form cannot be a pure universal (though it will have aspects of universality), for if it were a pure universal it could in no sense *be* actuality. Basically, the form in question, as the *form of* a particular individual, must be what Aristotle calls τόδε τι, 'a this'—by contrast with 'a such'. Whitehead did not himself explicitly pursue in this way the implications for the notions of form and actuality which his theory of objectification involves. But his position, as he elaborates it, is on this point fully in accord with Aristotle, who had very carefully examined the implications of the identification of form and actuality (οὐσία). Aristotle saw clearly that, in that case, form could not be a universal:

"it is plain that no universal attribute is a substance (οὐσία), and it is plain also from the fact that no common predicate indicates a 'this', but rather a 'such'. If not, many difficulties follow and especially the 'third man'."[59]

But on the other hand, Aristotle also saw that form as a 'this' cannot simply be a 'singular', for it is by the form that we have knowledge of the οὐσία, and knowledge entails universals.[60] Form, therefore, as a 'this', must have an aspect of universality. All this is true also of Whitehead's theory of objectification.

But this holds not only with regard to form in objectification. It applies also to form as the 'form of' individuals *as actual*. That is to say, it is equally true that the form which is the *form of the acting* cannot be a pure universal. Whitehead persistently and completely rejected the conception of a universal qualifying a particular. As the form of the acting, that form must be a 'this' and not a 'such'.

When we investigate this conception of 'the form of the acting', the explicit repudiation of the mode of thinking of 'universal

<hr />

[59] 1038 b 34—1039 a 1. Ross translation.   [60] Cf. 999 a 24–31.

qualifying particular' brings to light further implications. The acting is not some kind of 'substance', some kind of 'stuff', which 'has' form. Instead we have to think of the acting as an 'enacting of a certain character'. The character is not a 'property' of something; the *character* is 'enacted'. And the *concrete* is precisely *that enacting of that character*. That is, that *character or form in enaction* is the concrete real, the οὐσία, the entity which is in the full sense 'actual'. In other words, the individual 'as actual' is the enacting of a form; the enacting of the form is the 'real internal constitution' of the actuality. Which is to say that the *actuality* is the enacting of a particular character or form; and that character or form being enacted *is* the actuality. Thus we see that for Whitehead form is identified with actuality, not only as 'objective', but also as acting.

It is evident that this point, namely that in Whitehead's doctrine form is identified with actuality in the basic sense of actuality, i.e. in the sense of the fully existing, acting οὐσία, is of the utmost significance, and that we have to try to see what exactly it involves.

It will be helpful in assessing Whitehead's position if we again consider it in comparison with Aristotle's. It is clear that in view of Whitehead's identification of form with actuality in the basic sense, there is a close analogy between his position and that of Aristotle in respect of the fundamental metaphysical importance and status accorded to form. But does this mean that Whitehead is in the end forced, like Aristotle, to abandon the conception of the total metaphysical situation as involving two ultimate poles, and that for Whitehead too form in fact turns out to be supreme?

To reject this conclusion at the cost of denying the foregoing analogy between the Whiteheadian and Aristotelian positions in regard to the status of form would, it seems to me, be erroneous. Not only does Whitehead's position definitely involve that identification of form and actuality, as I have endeavoured to demonstrate, but the fact of the analogy and agreement between Whitehead and Aristotle on this point seems to me of considerable interest and significance.

On the other hand, to draw the above conclusion from this analogy and agreement seems to me also definitely erroneous. For this conclusion can only be upheld by ignoring the fundamental difference, which I have sought to bring out, between the positions of Aristotle and Whitehead respectively. Form cannot, for Whitehead, be supreme, the one metaphysical ultimate, for precisely the reason that it can be that for Aristotle. This reason is that Aristotle identifies act and form, whereas Whitehead rejects that particular identification. In other words, whereas Aristotle ascribes act to form, Whitehead holds that form as such cannot act. Whitehead thus maintains that both poles are requisite if we are to have an adequate metaphysics.

Further, Whitehead holds, both poles are integrally necessary to each other. Our examination of what this entails, however, has shown that form is identified with actuality. It is evident that we have to be careful as to how exactly this 'identification' is to be understood.

In the first place, it does not involve a reduction of either to the other. Nor does it involve an *equating* of the one with the other. On the contrary, we must here clearly bear in mind that it is the essential and distinctive Whiteheadian doctrine that creativity (act, activity as such) is the 'category of the ultimate'. This means that being, existence, is ultimately grounded in creativity, in 'act'. The relevance of this to form is crucial. It means that form, as such, cannot *be*; the being of form is the enacting of form. And this enacting is not due to form; form 'is enacted' —form does not enact itself.

Form in enaction is actuality. The enacting of form is the coming into being of actuality. And as having been enacted, that form is that actuality 'objectively'. The point to be noted here is that form is not simply as such to be identified with actuality. The 'enaction' is the crucial factor. When we take this into account it is clear that the 'identification' of form and actuality is not an 'equating' of them. To say that form is identified with actuality does not mean that form is *equivalent to* actuality. The denial of equivalence to form and actuality is part of what is entailed in denying that form, as a 'this', is a 'singular'.

Another vitally important reason why 'identification' is not 'equivalence', that is, why form as a 'this' is not a 'singular', is that form, in its own nature, 'transcends' actuality. Aristotle went some way toward recognizing this in maintaining that form has an aspect of universality. Whitehead, however, goes much further. It is essential to appreciate that in Whitehead's doctrine form is not wholly confined within the realm of the actual—it is not merely an aspect of the actual, appearing as a factor in the analysis of the actual, a mode in which the actual can be analysed. Whitehead explicitly conceives form as a metaphysical ultimate which, considered in abstraction from actuality, has a nature of its own. In this respect form is 'transcendent'.

Form conceived thus 'in abstraction' is the totality of every possible aspect of structure, pattern, character, definiteness, "ways of composition".[61] The adequate elucidation of this theory of the nature of form, though very important to a full treatment of the topic of this essay, will clearly take us far beyond the scope of a single paper.[62] Here I can only state that in this theory form is conceived as constituting a total structure of continuous abstract relatedness. This involves that every individual form or eternal object is in essential structural relatedness with every other form. Whitehead has spoken of this as the 'relational essence of eternal objects'.[63]

The relevance of this conception of the 'abstract' nature of form becomes clear when we consider form 'as actualized'. Form as actualized is in this theory the enactment not of a single form, in isolation, but the enactment of a particular 'perspective' of the total structure of form. This was Whitehead's doctrine already in *Science and the Modern World*, but it comes out most clearly in *Modes of Thought* with his explicit use there of the "notion of perspectives of the universe".[64] This perspective theory means that every actualization involves the whole realm of form. This doctrine, it is evident, brings the two metaphysical ultimates into the most intimate and essential relationship in the total metaphysical situation. The further assessment of this doctrine, however, must await a full investigation of the theory of form in its abstract structure.

[61] MT 112.
[62] I have discussed some aspects of the theory in a forthcoming article on "The Structure of Form".
[63] Cf. SMW 198, MT 92.   [64] MT 92.

VICTOR LOWE

THE APPROACH TO METAPHYSICS

VII

VICTOR LOWE

THE APPROACH TO METAPHYSICS

In the last book that Whitehead wrote there is a passage which every April brings to my mind. He is insisting that all human understanding is partial, but without permanent limits.

"For example, we know about the colour 'green' in some of its perspectives. But what green is capable of in other epochs of the universe, when other laws of nature are reigning, is beyond our present imaginations. And yet there is nothing intrinsically impossible in the notion that, as years pass, mankind may gain imaginative insight into some alternative possibility of nature, and may therefore gain understanding of the possibilities of green in other imagined epochs."[1]

In what other philosopher's writings could we expect to find what the professionals call a 'sense-datum term' being used at once to call attention to the immediate value of sensory experience, to remind us of our ignorance, and to set forth the ideal of ever enlarging our conceptual horizons? My purpose in quoting the passage, however, is not to contrast various uses of sense-datum terms. It is to indicate one of the kinds of caution which a good metaphysician should have. What he hopes is a quite general theory of existence may, for all he knows, be quite as special as three-dimensional Euclidean geometry. This caution is consequent upon a bold imagination concerning possibilities. The boldness makes trouble; there are obvious difficulties in the idea of a presumably infinite variety of cosmic epochs, and (for me) in the idea of an eternal object, like green. I shall look at the second later. My present point is only that a metaphysics which does not boldly make a generous allowance for forms of existence "beyond our present imaginations", is in danger of a dogmatic provincialism.

Besides imagination, passion appears to be indispensable in metaphysical work. This should not surprise us; it is generally, if

[1] MT 59.

G

not quite universally, true in other fields of constructive endeavour that only those who entertain some ideas with emotional intensity have anything to say. All Whitehead's philosophical writings manifest this intensity. The Harvard students who came to the Whiteheads on Sunday evenings remember it too. What he talked about, he cared about; the care was so evident in his voice, that those who wanted a dialectical game coolly played, or who were too young to own (or too timid to show) philosophical convictions of their own, as well as those who were enjoying a flirtation with logical positivism, would say that he pontificated—which he did not.

Proper caution in metaphysics mainly has to do with temptations to stray from an objective in which one ought to be passionately interested. It depends on an active conscience, more than on detachment. Of course everyone who in reading metaphysics is doing more than going through the motions of reading, brings his metaphysical conscience to bear. When an idealist author uses the proposition that ideal knowledge defies reality, the realist reader cries 'foul'. The moralistic tone of the nominalist's "We do not believe in abstract entities" is unmistakable. Whitehead's repudiations were fervent.

I too have my notions of what should be permitted in metaphysics and what should not. Of course none of us has charge of the permissions in this field. But one may clear the air by setting down what one would, and what one would not, with good conscience permit one's self; what does, and what does not, arouse one's scepticism when it is read in others; and why. The 'whys' I have in mind are not comparisons with the one true metaphysics (a standard not within human reach); they are comparisons with a definition of the metaphysical enterprise that has been made explicit and can be explicitly defended. This is what I propose to do now. I shall be both using Whitehead's work, and reacting against it.

I

To avoid getting bogged down at once in hopeless verbal dispute, we must agree on an initial identification of metaphysics. The major tradition in Western 'metaphysics' seeks a general theory of existence.[2] The minor tradition aims at a clear, coherent conscious-

---

[2] It is wise to avoid the ambiguities inherent in 'being'.

ness of our ways of thinking and talking about the world. Such consciousness is obviously desirable; and it appears to be sufficiently attainable to make the pursuit worth while. Let us give it (though not necessarily all forms of it) our blessing, and turn to metaphysics in Whitehead's sense, already suggested by the language of my first page—as aiming at a general theory of existence.

The most useful brief description of this business which I know is given by Whitehead's phrase, "the effort after the general characterization of the world·around us". I am taking this phrase, which appears in the second sentence of *Nature and Life*,[3] out of its immediate context, which is a discussion of our general concept of Nature—but not out of the wider context which Whitehead before many pages explicitly provided, that is, the fusion of Nature with Life in a new conception of the evolving universe. For present purposes I take 'the world' to mean the totality of all existence, including whatever gods exist. But as Whitehead's most frequent name for this totality is 'the universe', and as it has the advantage of not automatically suggesting a contrast with God, I shall substitute it for 'the world' in our defining phrase.

I am accustomed to using the several words in this definition as so many reminders of what I seek and what I would avoid in the pursuit of metaphysics. (They do not suggest all that needs to be said.)

I would first of all avoid the suggestion that metaphysics is an established body of principles about the universe—principles doubtless subject to refinement, and the set of them perhaps to some enlargement; but still, established, so that a student can take Metaphysics down from a bookshelf and learn it. If we begin our definition, "Metaphysics is . . .", we must immediately bring in a term like *effort* to forestall the natural expectation that we are defining something which is *there*, awaiting inspection. Naturally I do not mean that metaphysics is pure effort, without results and progress. But all this has been set forth admirably by Whitehead in the opening chapter of *Process and Reality*.

The word *characterization* reminds us that the metaphysician's task is to describe something; as I like to say, existence in its most general features is the *formulandum* to which his formulations must be faithful. In talking about metaphysics, where the gap between

³ MT 173.

the two is most formidable, 'characterize' and 'formulate' are better words than 'describe', because they carry a positive suggestion of this gap. 'Characterize' also implies that the primary aim is not to express or evoke experiences, whether private and special or widespread and socio-cultural. Of course a metaphysics may have interest and value when it is read as an intellectual expression of cultural aspirations or forces; and some of the words used should be capable of arousing in the reader the feelings (about certain aspects of existence) which stirred the writer. But for all that, metaphysics is meant to be a kind of telling. Only when a metaphysics ignominiously fails to help us understand the experienceable world may we assign it, as Dewey once assigned philosophy in general, to the realm of cultural meaning (along with drama and Athenian civilization) rather than to the realm of difficult, partial truth. Such reassessment must be separately made for each distinct metaphysical system, as a system. I have not seen any argument to show that all metaphysics is really something else, that did not either beg the question, or ask for too much.

General is a word of degree. The metaphysician is to get as high up the ladder of generality as he can. We have no trouble in recognizing relative heights, but much, if we try to define the ladder in a way which will not spoil the rest of our definition, e.g. by directing us from the universe around us to universes of discourse. The only direct clarification of that supreme generality which metaphysics seeks, I find in Whitehead's explanation (in terms of experience and its interpretation) of the *adequacy* of a metaphysical scheme. I shall come back to this shortly.

The universe, one should not need to say, is the biggest possible subject-matter. One merit of insisting upon this term when defining metaphysics is that its use gives notice that no mere philosophy of man is to be advanced as a metaphysics. The history of modern philosophy shows, I think, that it is on this point much more than on the distinction of science from metaphysics that lapses must be guarded against. Also, we think of the universe as, relative to man, not only an ongoing, but an antecedent reality. Metaphysics, so far as it is successful, is a form of knowledge which resists Dewey's claim that the object known in knowledge is not an antecedent reality but is constituted by the consequences of directed operations, of changes instituted. It would be ridiculous to suppose that the operations of any metaphysician institute changes in the general characteristics of the universe.

The universe to be characterized is *the* universe, the one and only actual universe—not a 'possible world', and decidedly not 'all possible worlds'. The usual meaning of 'possible' in connection with worlds (or universes)[4] is 'consistently thinkable'. Different applied meanings then arise, depending upon what one intends to be consistent with. Consistency with what is known marks out what ought to be called 'epistemic possibility'. For example, I know that there is now some money in my pocket, but I do not know how much. Suppose it is $11.30. Then a world which is just like the one I suppose actual, except that I have $11.35 in my pocket, is a possible world. Plainly, I can think of an indefinite number of worlds which are possible in this sense. But this plurality is already noticed and left behind in our statement of the metaphysical purpose as a *general* characterization of the universe. And that is the better way to describe the situation, because 'possible' is too tricky a word in philosophical discussion to be used when it isn't needed. It *is* needed in the theory of human thought,[5] and in some types of metaphysics; but to say that metaphysical propositions, if true, are true of all possible worlds (where 'possible' means 'thinkable in terms which are self-consistent and consistent with our present empirical knowledge'), and 'world' is meant in the inclusive sense stipulated above (not as denoting a sub-world such as the 'created world' of Leibniz), is an unnecessary, misleading and gradiose way of saying that these propositions present the most general facts about the actual world.

Like Whitehead, I cannot understand actuality without making reference to possibilities. But even if one could understand them otherwise than as within the universe of actual entities, it would still be the case that the subject-matter, for the sake of understanding which they were introduced, was that actual universe and not being in any other mode.

One reason why I have devoted a bit of space to a notion as indefensible as the notion that metaphysics has for subject-matter

[4] In discussing this point I revert from 'universe' to 'world', to be in accord with the customary phraseology.

[5] E.g. C. I. Lewis has shown this need in the theory of the meaning of terms and propositions: see Chap. III of *An Analysis of Knowledge and Valuation*, La Salle, Ill., 1946 (my illustration is a true-life form of his on p. 56); also my paper, "The Concept of the Individual", *Methodos* V, 1953, especially pp. 158 ff.

not what is but what might be, is that it represents the bold romantic way, in contrast to divers cautious ways, in which philosophers try to find a distinctive work to do during this age of science. It was ardently presented as the path of glory by the late William Pepperell Montague, who pleaded with philosophers to give the earth to the scientists and devote themselves to exploring the ocean of possibilities. By imagination and vision philosophy should propose possibilities, and let science dispose of them. An emphatic subsistentialist metaphysics underlay this simple notion of the division of labour between science and philosophy. The necessity of imagination in metaphysics is undeniable. But is it addressed to anything but the actual world? It is truer to say that a first-rate metaphysician loves the world (and so is motivated to construct a vision of it), than that he becomes a metaphysician by casting off from it.

". . . the universe *around us*." The last two words remind us of a fact on which the very possibility of the metaphysical effort depends, namely, that the universe is the metaphysician's environment, indefinitely extended. His subject is not out beyond the bounds of space and time; it is all around him—under his nose, in his dreams, in his memories.[6] What is commonly called 'experience' is his foothold in his environment, his point of departure for imaginative thought. It is his datum, what he must interpret; and the testing ground to which he must return. It is careless to say that metaphysical systems are so many 'interpretations of the world'. 'Interpret', carefully used, takes as object something which is a datum and so may be inspected and consulted. The world to be characterized is no such datum; only conscious experience can play that role. In short, we interpret our conscious experience by characterizing the universe or some part of it; and conversely. Whitehead's repeated statements that the actual world is the datum for philosophy, and is what we experience though we are conscious of much less, will mislead unless we remember that only what can emerge in consciousness (e.g. the conscious sense of a vague totality, and the corresponding, consciously noticeable characteristics of everyday language), can be suggestive for thought or be empirical evidence for or against what we think.

---

[6] "The universe around us" is meant in the sense in which it would normally be understood, namely, as including ourselves—not in the exclusive sense in which it might be literally taken.

Whitehead argued that all experience-events partake of and pass on a general 'texture', causal and purposive, which we can discover if we permit our attention to be drawn away from details. I find this entirely convincing. In additional respects given experience is for Whitehead alive with suggestions which quietly start an empirical philosopher's interpretations of it in just one direction. I do not find all these suggestions binding. Still, given experience7 is for metaphysical purposes much more than the epistemological absolute which a pure theorist of perceptual knowledge (e.g. C. I. Lewis) demands.

Our interpretations of experience naturally vary with our purposes. In that way many equally true characterizations of existing things can arise. When the purposes are identical, this latitude disappears. Even if all metaphysicians pursue the same purpose, their imaginative powers are so limited by the varying special characteristics of their first-hand experience, their intellectual period, etc., that we must expect great differences between metaphysical systems. In attending to the purpose of metaphysics we are concentrating upon the source of those other large differences, which are theoretically, though not practically or perhaps always desirably, eliminable.

II

The metaphysical objective, then, is a general characterization of the universe, capable of making every type of experience intelligible; a scheme of ideas such that (in Whitehead's words) "everything of which we are conscious, as enjoyed, perceived, willed, or thought, shall have the character of a particular instance of the general scheme"8—when that scheme is applied under the circumstances (planetary, human, etc.) of the experiences we have, or believe others to have had. The test of metaphysical truth is the 'general success' of the system in such applications.

The desired *scheme* of ideas is not revealed to us by any rational, or mystical, power of intuition. There is nothing for it but to try to frame one, and see if it will interpret diverse areas of experience

7 The adjective which Whitehead usually attaches to 'experience' is not 'given', but 'concrete'. Experience, for him, is not a flat display; it has depths and meanings which may be caught intuitively by poets and others. There is a good deal of truth in such a conception of experience; but the dangers which it presents to the ordinary thinker are obvious. 8 PR 3 [4].

better than earlier systems did.[9] The first positive act of the cautious metaphysician is to grant permission to speculate—not at random, but under conditions of which Whitehead has given the classic statement.[10]

The permission to speculate is also a permission to go in thought 'behind the scenes' (as a hostile critic would say)—to explain what is perceived by something conceived. This sounds very bad to many modern ears, but is not. Our everyday thought interprets conscious experience by characterizing some part of the universe; for example, we interpret a sound when we conceive what produced it, and how. The phenomenalist language, which some philosophers try to insist upon, generally gives way to causal language when they try by illustrations to convince us that their doctrine can be applied. An intelligible conception of the sources of experience must of course maintain analogies with what is experienced; for example, no event can be explained by reference to an ultimate being which in its own nature does not involve temporality.[11]

It is not so much in relation to sense perception as in relation to the emotional and practical demands of human beings that the approach to metaphysics calls for an attitude of restraint. William James wrote in his first notable pragmatistic essay, "The Sentiment of Rationality": "Man needs a rule for his will, and will invent one if one be not given him."[12] It is the business of a complete philosophy to give him a rule—but not the business of metaphysics. James of course argued the contrary. Each and all of the "great periods of revival, of expansion of the human mind", he wrote, ". . . have said to the human being, 'The inmost nature of the reality is congenial to *powers* which you possess' ".[13] James's statement is very likely true; but the question of what general characterization of the universe makes it most congenial to man, is pertinent only to our understanding of man.

There are other ways in which illegitimate requirements of this

[9] This is of course a very simplified statement of proper metaphysical procedure. A more adequate one will be found in Ivor Leclerc's summary of Whitehead's position: see *Whitehead's Metaphysics: An Introductory Exposition*, London and New York, 1958, pp. 42–50.   [10] PR Part I, Ch. I.

[11] The difficulties and requirements of empiricism in metaphysics are briefly discussed in my paper, "Empirical Method in Metaphysics", *Journal of Philosophy*, XLIV (1947), pp. 225–33.

[12] *The Will to Believe and Other Essays in Popular Philosophy*, London: Longmans, Green & Co., 1937 (first published in 1896), p. 86.

[13] *Ibid.*, p. 86; italics in text.

sort have been imposed upon the metaphysical effort. John Dewey wrote a classic description of one, and himself eagerly embraced another. Men, as he often said, seek stability in a precarious environment; and philosophers have depicted 'reality' as

"what existence would be if our reasonably justified preferences were so completely established in nature as to exhaust and define its entire being and thereby render search and struggle unnecessary. . . . Then the problem of metaphysics alters: instead of being a detection and description of the generic traits of existence, it becomes an endeavour to adjust or reconcile to each other two separate realms of being."[14]

Namely, the realms of actual experience, and of the 'reality' depicted. Dewey never hid his own non-metaphysical motive for being interested in what, quite misleadingly, he called "the generic traits of existence". His discussions of them are entirely concerned with those features of man's situation in nature which are both irreducible matter of fact, and always important for the experimental art of controlling human affairs. In the end, fortunately, Dewey stopped calling the detection and description of such traits 'metaphysics'.[15]

In Whitehead's metaphysics there are two worlds—a world of finite existents and a divine being—but both are equally real, and everything he says about them is shaped by the requirement that they be in communion with each other. Also, Whitehead never tried to conceive 'reality' in such a way as to render human search, struggle, and experiment unnecessary. But there is a disturbing element in the exposition of the theistic side of his metaphysical system. In some passages he seems to be suggesting that the satisfaction of our deepest emotional cravings is an added merit in a metaphysics. Whitehead's thought is much more complex than this, and some examination of the way he handles the mutual relations of metaphysics, religion, and types of human experience is highly desirable. His way of handling any topic is unusually instructive in one way or another. The few pages which follow are a poor substitute for the book-length study which in this case is wanted.

[14] *Experience and Nature*, 2nd ed., Chicago: Open Court Pub. Co., 1926, p. 54.
[15] "Experience and Existence: A Comment", *Philosophy and Phenomenological Research*, IX (1949), p. 712.

G*

With fine insight Whitehead describes two cravings which seek to be somehow jointly satisfied. One is, that the future which is bound to follow upon the present shall bring novelty, freshness. The other is the craving for permanence: ". . . the culminating fact of conscious, rational life refuses to conceive itself as a transient enjoyment, transiently useful."[16] The final chapter of *Process and Reality*, "God and the World", gives Whitehead's solution. One aspect of God—his unchanging primordial nature—is the instrument of novelty for the temporal world (which is itself the instrument of novelty for God); and "the process of the temporal world passes into the formation of other actualities, bound together in an order [God's consequent nature] in which novelty does not mean loss".[17] The last sentence of the book reads:

"In this way, the insistent craving is justified—the insistent craving that zest for existence be refreshed by the ever-present, unfading importance of our immediate actions, which perish and yet live for evermore."

What Whitehead offers here is no bland assurance in the face of our mortality; his tone is suggested by the phrases, "tragic Beauty", and "the sense of Peace", which he uses in the last paragraph of *Adventures of Ideas*. And he is not injecting any of the traditional theologies into his world-view. He is offering something which, if true, is of the utmost value. Its truth, as he so wisely (and more than once) says, is nothing that can be demonstrated by logical argument.[18] Neither, to be sure, is the truth of a formulated metaphysical system so demonstrable. But in all four of his books which deal with this subject he indicated a distinction between "a metaphysics which founds itself upon general experience"[19] and further metaphysical notions whose source is religious experience. General experience includes—indeed, first of all *is*—an enjoyment of value here-now, and acknowledgment of value-existence elsewhere in the temporal world. The broad contribution of religious

---

[16] PR 481 [516].   [17] PR 481 f. [517].

[18] I regret to note one apparent exception, the passage in which Whitehead offers this argument for the consequent nature of God: "there can be no determinate truth, correlating impartially the partial experiences of many actual entities, apart from one actual entity to which it can be referred." PR 17 [19]. Not even Whitehead could produce a valid version of the argument from the 'existence' of truth to the existence of God!

[19] RM [149.] See, in SMW, Ch. XI, first paragraph; in PR 482 [517]; in AI 379.

experience to metaphysics, according to Whitehead, is a widespread direct apprehension of a character of rightness and a unity of value in the universe. There is also the possibility of supplementing this with more definite content drawn from exceptional intuitions, provided they are trustworthy.

Whitehead wisely insists that the verbal formulation of any religious intuition is always imperfect and fallible. If it expresses something more than strong emotion, it must be capable of integration with the (also imperfect) formulations of the nature of existence which are suggested by the general texture of general experience. Assuming that this is possible, the philosophic use of an exceptional intuition rests upon this argument (stated by Whitehead in setting forth the culmination of his philosophical theology):[20]

"It must be remembered that the present level of average waking human experience was at one time exceptional among the ancestors of mankind. We are justified therefore in appealing to those modes of experience which in our direct judgment stand above the average level."

No special intuitive experience, I take it, is justified for all time; any one may be superseded by finer intuitions. The many intuitions of an omnipotent perfection, reported in religious literature, have been superseded in Whitehead's eyes; and they fail to pass the test of being formulatable in a metaphysical system which is self-consistent and consistent with general facts of experience.

Whether widespread or special, religious intuitions vividly arise only because "religion is the longing of the spirit that the facts of existence should find their justification in the nature of existence. 'My soul thirsteth for God', writes the Psalmist".[21] One reason for prizing Whitehead's philosophical theology is that his language often reflects perfectly the peculiar character of those religious cognitions which have metaphysical meaning. For example: "the higher intellectual feelings are *haunted by the vague insistence* of another order, where there is no unrest, no travel, no shipwreck: 'There shall be no more sea' ".[22] It would be vain to object that the

---

[20] AI 379 f. The argument applies also to the corresponding exposition in PR; the passages with which the discussion of Whitehead in this Section began are drawn from it.

[21] RM [85].

[22] PR 481 [516]. (My italics). Note also "the notion of redemption through suffering, which haunts the world". PR 495 [531].

phrasing is ambiguous, to ask whether it refers to an intuition or a craving. The language is accurate as it stands.

This mutual involvement of craving and insight inevitably makes the value of religious evidence for metaphysics problematic for those who have had no personal experience of insight. The occurrence of just such experience demands explanation, but does not indicate the mode of explanation. We know too little about ourselves to eliminate the possibility that no religious experience, frequent or infrequent, reveals anything about the universe.

Whitehead himself was an agnostic for many years,[23] including the years of his collaboration with Russell. The latter has written, in connection with the death of Whitehead's son Eric in 1918: "The pain of this loss had a great deal to do with turning his thoughts to philosophy and with causing him to seek ways of escape from belief in a merely mechanical universe."[24] When I wrote in 1941 of Whitehead's turning toward metaphysics,[25] I made the safe guess: "Probably the national tragedy and the personal tragedy of the war of 1914 to 1918 played a part in extending the horizon of his thoughts." But I wish to withdraw the next sentence: "There is, however, no evidence that his metaphysics might, under other cicumstances, have taken on a different character." That was rash. Some day, I hope, biographers will find out what can be known, and will particularly spell out or qualify Russell's implication that Whitehead at one time favoured a mechanistic world-view.

The metaphysics which Whitehead drew from general experience and speculatively formulated as the philosophy of organism[26] was not only not mechanistic; it was definitely theistic. A "properly general metaphysics"[27] must be more than merely consistent with additions drawn from religion, unless it is willing to hand over religious experience to the philosophy and sciences of man. Whitehead gave the undeniable reason for this: "For nothing,

[23] Sir Edmund Whittaker used the phrase, "an outspoken and even polemical agnostic"—*Obituary Notices of Fellows of the Royal Society*, VI (1948), p. 293.

My discussion of Whitehead in this Section assumes that when he wrote about God and religion he was really writing about God and religion. I mention this because it has been seriously asserted that when he wrote about God he was really writing about the logical structure of space-time!

[24] *Portraits From Memory*, London: Allen and Unwin, 1956, p. 93.

[25] "The Development of Whitehead's Philosophy", in *The Philosophy of Alfred North Whitehead*, ed. P. A. Schilpp (The Library of Living Philosophers), p. 89.

[26] In SMW and Parts I–IV of PR.   [27] SMW 215.

within any limited type of experience, can give intelligence to shape our ideas of any entity at the base of all actual things, unless the general character of things requires that there be such an entity."[28] His exposition of the general nature of things also has this character: it is dominated by a profound and wholly ingenuous temporalism.

"All relatedness has its foundation in the relatedness of actualities; and such relatedness is wholly concerned with the appropriation of the dead by the living—that is to say, with 'objective immortality' whereby what is divested of its own living immediacy becomes a real component in other living immediacies of becoming."[29]

"Philosophers have taken too easily the notion of perishing. . . . Almost all of *Process and Reality* can be read as an attempt to analyse perishing on the same level as Aristotle's analysis of becoming."[30]

Throughout the elaboration of his general metaphysics, Whitehead makes us feel the sole value and the creativity of immediate life, and the poignancy of the fact that time is a "perpetual perishing". And that *is* the way things are. But it is hard for most of us to read this account without experiencing a strong emotional need for a concluding conception of 'another order'.

If a thinker produces a theistic metaphysics which, among other things, justifies an insistent religious craving, this result does not discredit the metaphysics. There is after all a type of experience to be explained—in this case, "the zest of self-forgetful transcendence belonging to Civilization at its height".[31] Whitehead offered an explanation in his concept of God, particularly of God's consequent nature and its immanence in the World. More: the general success of the system as a whole in explaining other things is a strong argument for the theistic concept, if the theistic concept is so integral a part of the system that without it we could not apply the system to anything. And that is the case with the philosophy of organism. If you start to use its fundamental categories—creativity, actual entities, and eternal objects—in the manner prescribed by Whitehead's categoreal scheme, you cannot avoid introducing an

---

[28] SMW 215-16   [29] PR viii–ix [ix].
[30] *Essays in Science and Philosophy*, New York: Philosophical Library, 1947, p. 117.   [31] AI 381.

actual entity which from eternity to eternity holds the entire multiplicity of eternal objects in its conceptual experience. And once you have this primordial nature of God, the completeness of the system in its own terms necessitates some doctrine of God's consequent nature. I think that the marvellous coherence of Whitehead's completed metaphysics constitutes the strongest argument for the theistic element in it—provided this general characterization of the universe has any considerable success as an interpretation of mundane experience, which to my mind it does.

It would be unrealistic to suppose that any human being can produce a substantial work of metaphysics which is motivated simply and solely by desire to frame a general characterization of the universe around us, capable of making every type of experience intelligible. Being an emotional animal and a civilized animal, he is bound to desire one kind of characterization more than another. This additional motive shows, whether you consider Spinoza, or Bergson, or Russell—or any philosopher. But the coherence and the empirical verification of the system are the only grounds for accepting it. The satisfaction of a mere craving—any craving— cannot be an added *metaphysical* merit of a general theory of existence. We are justified, then, in giving special scrutiny to those elements in a philosophy which make the universe support what the metaphysician, or mankind at large, cherishes; and we are always saddled with this task. There is also a danger that, leaning over backwards, a metaphysician might fall over backwards, as Nietzsche might be said to have done.

Whitehead nowhere, so far as I can remember, says that the universe is 'just', or demands that it be just; he was too wise and too loving to take that line. But Lecture Six of *Modes of Thought* is entitled "Civilized Universe", and begins, "In this lecture we seek the evidence for that conception of the universe which is the justification for the ideals characterizing the civilized phases of human society".[32] I shudder to think of what metaphysics could become if this sentence and title-phrase were to be widely adopted as guides in man's approach to metaphysics. Whitehead kept his discussion, for the most part, genuinely metaphysical, by founding it upon discernible features of the general texture of our experience —beginning with the vague, omnipresent sense of maintenance or discard, and the differentiation of this value-experience into the

[32] MT 143.

feeling of the ego, the others, and the totality. This level of experience, Whitehead rightly insisted, is much more fundamental than the clear discrimination of sense data. A refusal to use it would be a case of misplaced caution.

The cautious metaphysician may be strongly tempted to secure himself in advance against all kinds of wishful thinking, by laying down the broad rule that *no* value-concept is to be introduced in philosophy beyond the boundaries of the philosophy of man, or of sentient beings generally. He will appeal to common sense: is it not silly to try to think up a value-concept with general ontological application? Now this is quite a different question from that of the cosmic significance of religious experience and human ideals. It concerns intrinsic value; but not in the forms which are most familiar in moral philosophy, like pleasurable experience—nor does it concern value as any object of any interest. The question is whether we are so surely right when we habitually characterize most of the population of the universe as sheer matter of fact devoid of intrinsic value.[33] Probably we are simply being unimaginative, and substituting a parochially human point of view for a metaphysical one. The world-view which sits easiest with our desires is just the one which *restricts* the occurrence of intrinsic value to ourselves, the higher animals, creatures like us and them who may exist on planets of other suns, and God if he exists. Of course, it *would* be absurd to ascribe any kind of intrinsic value to an object like a typewriter. The great challenge for 'pan-valuism'— if I may introduce an awkward label—is to devise a conception of what the individuals of the universe are if all possess some definable for-itself character. Whitehead devised such a conception, which to my mind definitely supersedes the panpsychisms of the history of metaphysics. In general: the question whether value in some form is an ontological attribute, is one which in the approach to metaphysics should be looked upon as an open question. As there is no empirical evidence against the possibility of pan-valuism, we are not debarred from favouring a hypothesis of this type when indirect reasons for favouring it appear—the superior coherence of a metaphysical system of which it is a part, for instance.

By way of contrast, consider a type of metaphysics which, because of the unwarranted transfer to metaphysics of a necessity in the theory of perceptual knowledge, has sometimes been said to

[33] This is what Whitehead called "vacuous actuality".

be the only possible one. I mean the respectable view that the things, not ourselves, which make up the world (or including ourselves, in James's world of strands of "pure experience") are just those sensa which are given in sense perception, plus unsensed sensa; or are aggregates of these. This view is rendered improbable by a mass of physiological and psychological evidence to the effect that sense perception is a transforming, partly creative, agency. That thinkers should strain at intrinsic value as an ultimate feature of actualities while swallowing a phenomenalistic *ontology*, is one of the curiosities in the history of tough-mindedness among philosophers.

What is the general significance of essential features of human *practice* for metaphysics? Whitehead said, "Metaphysics is nothing but the description of the generalities which apply to all the details of practice".[34] The word to underline here is *generalities*. Then we may give this Whiteheadian illustration of the principle: a metaphysics that does not in a generalized form embody our practice of expecting a future which will continue some characteristics of the present and deviate from others, does not describe the world we live in. It is obvious, however, that the burden of explaining our practices (more generally, of interpreting our experience) never falls on metaphysics alone. It falls on a complex conjunct, consisting of the general theory of existence, plus the philosophy of man, plus the biological and cultural sciences of man. If some invariable feature of human practice contradicts, or stands in no relation to, this conjunct, some member of the conjunct is defective. It is not always easy to say which one this is.

III

Let us turn to alleged necessities of language and of thought, in their relation to the metaphysical effort.

Do necessities of speech have metaphysical significance? Plainly, the universe is under no obligation to be such that *homo sapiens* can talk about it. He *can* talk about it—for the same reason that he can talk about Poltergeists: he possesses a conceiving brain, vocal chords, and culture. Any universe in which these can arise is one that can be babbled about. The real problem is how it is possible for some of these babblings to approximate truth.

[34] PR 17 [19].

We should look with the utmost suspicion on every dilemma of the form, "Either you accept this metaphysical position, or you deny the possibility of meaningful speech"—or as people used to say, "of significant discourse". The necessities posed may reflect nothing more than the limitations of the author's vocabulary or the properties of the language in which he writes. Hence the potential value of new ways of talking metaphysics. Not that we can ever hope to possess a perfect metaphysical language; but we may hope to continue the progress which has occurred. It is an achievement to show that some things cannot be said in English without paradox, but it is mere intellectual conservatism to anathematize all efforts to talk in new ways. As Whitehead somewhere says, our language was formed for the market-place, not for metaphysical purposes. His reminders of the inadequacies of language have been misunderstood as complaints and condemnations, and said to be "completely nongenuine"[35] because he saw the redesigning of language as an endless task. What other view of the relation of language *to metaphysics* would be sensible?

In Whitehead's view, this endless task serves another process of endless approximation, that of constructing an adequate network of metaphysical concepts. The nature of things outruns human thought, and thought may outrun speech. When some metaphysical thesis is presented to us as a logical necessity and we find no logical mistake, we should remember that the author is not the universe but a human thinker. The necessity flows from his initial concepts, his meanings. So we search our stock of concepts for better beginnings. And we may never assume that this stock is perfect.

In contrast to particular alleged necessities of thought, which are always in reality hypothetical, stands the broad requirement of consistency. But it is a genuine necessity for metaphysics only because of our daily evidence that the world is not literally "a fiction . . . made up of contradiction". I have never heard anyone report that for a moment he saw something as both red and blue all over. If the universe were in large part made up of contradiction, consistency would be a demerit in a metaphysical system, though it might still be a convenience to an occasional reader.

[35] Alice Ambrose, "The Problem of Linguistic Inadequacy", in *Philosophical Analysis*, ed. Max Black, Ithaca, N.Y.: Cornell University Press, 1950, pp. 15–37 esp. pp. 15–20.

A second broad necessity for metaphysics is coherence, in Whitehead's sense: the general features of existence are to be so formulated that the full understanding of any one, as formulated, will take you to the others. Otherwise your system falls into unrelated parts (as Descartes' did). So far this is only coherence as an ideal of the understanding. To be more than that, the coherences which the system exhibits must be findable in experience, and pervasive enough to warrant generalization to a metaphysical status. This is generally the case with Whitehead's metaphysics. The immediate experience which is myself now, includes a feeling of its own derivation from other actualities, which collectively compose its environment; and also includes appetition for unrealized potentialities. This single sentence must suffice here as a sample of Whitehead's empirical warrant for developing his theory of the coherence of the universe, as that of a process in which 'actual entities' come into being by prehending other actual entities and 'eternal objects'.

That the universe, or being, is intelligible, is often said to be an indispensable and undeniable premise of metaphysics. But Whitehead has shown how the matter can and should be conceived:[36]

"That we fail to find in experience any elements intrinsically incapable of exhibition as examples of general theory, is the hope of rationalism. This hope is not a metaphysical premise. It is the faith which forms the motive for the pursuit of all sciences alike, including metaphysics.

In so far as metaphysics enables us to apprehend the rationality of things, the claim is justified. It is always open to us, having regard to the imperfections of all metaphysical systems, to lose hope at the exact point where we find ourselves. The preservation of such faith must depend on an ultimate moral intuition into the nature of intellectual action—that it should embody the adventure of hope."

I wish next, and finally, to note and briefly consider necessities for definiteness and distinctness. The human animal cannot think clearly without defining the object of his thought. This introduces a danger for metaphysics. Actualities are bigger than human concepts; the moment a metaphysician forgets this he ascribes to existence some limitation of his thought, and makes the universe foot the bill for his own clarity. It is not too much to suggest that

[36] PR 57 [67].

whatever he clearly and distinctly conceives to be the case cannot be the case in the universe—unless his thought has been as obedient to the coherences intimated in experience, as to Bishop Butler's "Everything is what it is, and not another thing". That dictum is a dangerous rule for metaphysical discussion because it is too easily used to sanction the erection of fences which may not exist in reality or in given experience but only between our concepts. The obvious example of such dictatorial thinking is the out of hand rejection of Bergson's metaphysics on the ground that it is sheer confusion of concepts to imagine that any kind of 'interpenetration' can occur in the temporal world. I do not suggest and do not believe that his metaphysics should be accepted; I am saying only that conceptual thought has no business forbidding one existent from embodying something of or from another. Furthermore, it is not a genuine necessity of thought to do this. James showed the preposterousness of it in his protest against the attempt of some monistic idealists to rule out pluralism with the argument that when you say there are many individuals in the universe you are logically bound to say that no connections exist between them. But in *A Pluralistic Universe* James professed to find no positive alternative other than one drawn largely along Bergsonian lines.[37] The man who, by doing it full-scale, showed that perfectly definite ontological concepts of intrinsic connection between individuals can be framed, was Whitehead.

He has often been charged with abandoning the intellectual ideals of clarity and definiteness in his metaphysics of process. If our civilization is allowed to continue, the historians of philosophy two hundred years from now are likely to find this reckless charge amusingly misplaced. It is a bit like saying that the designers of the first submarines did not believe in travel by water. A thoroughgoing conceptualization of process—done with an insistence on the absolute self-identity of concepts rather than by making each turn into its opposite—is odd evidence of disloyalty to the intellect.

It would be more sensible to inquire whether his approach to metaphysical construction was not in one sense too intellectualistic. I am thinking of his category of eternal objects, which roughly

37 See William James, *A Pluralistic Universe*, Lectures II, VI, VII. My paper, "William James's Pluralistic Metaphysics of Experience", in *In Commemoration of William James: 1842–1942*, Columbia University Press, 1942, reviews the varying positions James took in his published and unpublished writings.

corresponds to the historic category of universals. The use of universals is of course no vice of the intellect but a necessity of thought. I pass by the old question of whether they must also be considered a category for metaphysics, in order to discuss briefly the larger form which that sort of question takes concerning Whitehead's eternal objects. (Professor Christian in his recent book has included a needed reminder of the ways in which Whitehead dissented from the traditional view at the base of the old disputes— the view that the main use of universals is to classify individuals into genera and species.[38])

Things have characters. Some philosophers will not budge from the thesis that the characters of particular things are particulars rather than universals. That seems an untenable extreme view. Whitehead went all the way in the opposite direction. In his metaphysics the actual world is a process composed of individual processes; but he insists that none of these, nor any group of them, nor any element in any one of them, nor *anything* in the world, could be a definite entity *unless* it exemplified a form of definiteness which bears in itself no temporal limitation. To Whitehead this is obvious, and probably always appeared obvious.[39] It is not quite obvious to me. Granted that an existent has a character, and that at least component characters of this character can be exemplified elsewhere, I am not convinced that in conceiving them as eternal objects we are being faithful to their mode of existence in the universe. We may be converting a normal step— possibly a necessity—of conceptual thought into a necessity for metaphysics. We must remember that Whitehead's eternal objects are "ideal entities", and "in themselves not actual", but "such that they are exemplified in everything that is actual, according to some proportion of relevance".[40] We must not think of them as things which do something in the world; Whitehead's position is the sound one that eternal objects are abstract entities, and only actual entities act. Nevertheless his language, in all the books in which he writes about eternal objects, is half the time suggesting either too much or too little: that they *are* 'agents', or that they 'express' the definiteness of actualities. Plainly, Whitehead's

[38] William A. Christian, *An Interpretation of Whitehead's Metaphysics*, Yale University Press, 1959, Chap. 13.

[39] See Part II of his pre-metaphysical book, *Principles of Natural Knowledge*, and Note II to the Second Edition.   [40] RM [90].

doctrine that eternal forms of definiteness are exemplified in actualities is his way of expressing the definiteness of actualities. He often claims that without such forms no rational *description* of actual things is possible. If this were true, it would of course not prove that forms of definiteness are eternal in the universe, but only that if they are not, we must either write metaphysics as if they were or not write metaphysics. But I doubt that Whitehead's assertion is altogether true.

If every form of definiteness is eternal, it must be because each always has some relevance to whatever is happening, no matter how far that happening, or the whole universe in that stage of its history, may be from realizing this form. That which is relevant to a process but not certain to be realized in it must be called a potential for it. Now the metaphysician has not only to note that there are actual things and that they have characters; his formulations must describe the general way in which, in arising, they get their characters. This means using some notion of potentiality. Those who refuse to do this are abstracting from ongoing time— looking at the universe (either in their approach to metaphysics or at some point in their construction) as if it were a completed whole, spread out before them. They can then announce that it consists of the totality of actual things and nothing else; that is 'what there is'. But the universe we face is not like that. It has a tomorrow. Thus we need the notion that today contains potentialities (one or many) for tomorrow. The notion will take different forms, depending upon whether we think that new existence arises by efficient causation or by final causation or by both. In no case may we eliminate the notion of potentiality when we undertake to write the metaphysics of an ongoing universe.

However, I do not think we *need* carry to this task the full sweep of the notion, as Whitehead did. He introduced his forms of definiteness as 'pure potentials', each to all eternity a potential for every process. It is the maintenance of this eternal potentiality which first required a concept of God in Whitehead's system. Whatever we may conclude about this conception of the universe, we are bound to admit its magnificence. Of course his boundless realm of possibility staggers the imagination. I can't quite believe in it; but I don't find it an unintelligible notion. One alternative, which I do not think has been mentioned by any of Whitehead's unconvinced admirers, is that we may just possibly be able to construct a metaphysical theory of potentiality which does not assume eternal objects, by exploiting (with alterations) another of his categories of existence: 'propositions'. These are *limited*, 'impure' potentials, "matters of fact in potential determination". They are not timeless logical entities, but natural entities which come into being in the history of the universe.[41] Perhaps we can think of such propositions as embodying all the effective potentiality that there is. Some of them may be for practical purposes almost eternal, but none completely so.[42] The notion of an unrealized form of definiteness would appear in such a metaphysics as that of a component abstracted from a proposition; and the eternalization of such a form (a quality, relation, or pattern) would be a further abstraction which is performed by human thought and discussed in the philosophy of man, not in metaphysics. There are surely problems here, e.g. the problem of the status to be given to mathematical propositions, and to what we are pleased to call the 'metaphysical propositions' which we entertain in our stabs at characterizing the universe. We shan't know how difficult these problems are until someone works with this approach.

Whitehead was always warning against turning inabilities of our imagination into limitations of the universe. Metaphysics has also to remember that in some ways our thought tends to go beyond what is effective in the process of the universe.

IV

It is mainly because of its tendency to slight the difference between metaphysics and the philosophy of man that I do not like to use an approach to metaphysics which can quote Whitehead's authority but differs from the approach sketched in this essay. It conceives of philosophy as Henry Sidgwick did, in a remark which Whitehead quoted with approval: "It is the primary aim of philosophy to unify completely, bring into clear coherence, all depart-

[41] See, in PR, the sixth Category of Existence, the third and fifteenth Categories of Explanation, Section I of Chap. IX of Part I, and Sections I and II of Chap. IV of Part III.

[42] It should go without saying that any revision of *Whitehead's* metaphysics in which the category of eternal objects was eliminated would affect everything in his system; if a consistent scheme could be thus constructed, it would be no more than half Whiteheadian.

ments of rational thought . . ."[43] A statement of this sort does not tell us what to look for in the various fields, or how to put what we find to metaphysical use. It is really only a beginning for a definition. Whitehead's way of completing it is suggested by his statement that it is one of the functions of philosophy "to harmonise, refashion, and justify divergent intuitions as to the nature of things".[44] This brings the ordinary thinker up against the question, What intuitions are genuine? Suppose we substitute a weaker notion, e.g. that of the *point of view* which is characteristic of a field, e.g. of jurisprudence, or ethics, or physics. Unfortunately it is not true that all recognized 'departments of rational thought' are co-ordinate in their possible metaphysical significance. Those which deal with human peculiarities must be somewhat discounted, and the notion of the universe brought in. Whitehead remarked that "The various human interests which suggest cosmologies, and also are influenced by them, are science, aesthetics, ethics, religion".[45] If ethics be replaced by sociology, this is a fair list of the areas which Whitehead himself drew upon. Other thinkers with wide sympathies will prefer a different list. Under the modern departmentalization of knowledge, the whole 'integration of diverse fields' approach to metaphysics is in constant danger of encouraging a mere reconciliation of the different human standpoints embodied in the current division of labour. Its value for philosophy lies chiefly in the reminder that philosophy is to be a constant and constructive critic of abstractions; its value for metaphysics, in the insistence that the physicists' perspective of the universe around us must be confronted with other perspectives.

If you ask a scholar to define the metaphysical effort, he will take you first to Aristotle: "There is a science which investigates being as being and the attributes which belong to this in virtue of its own nature." He may elucidate this as meaning inquiry into the nature of that which has 'being' or 'existence' in the primary and full sense of the term, to which all other being, such as (for Aristotle) the being of Platonic Forms, refers. A conception of this sort is to be found also in Whitehead's *Adventures of Ideas:* "It [philosophy] seeks those generalities which characterize the complete reality of fact, and apart from which any fact must sink into

---

[43] From *Henry Sidgwick: A Memoir*, Appendix I. Quoted in SMW, 176; see also 23, 108.

[44] SMW, ix.   [45] SMW, ix.

an abstraction."[46] This Aristotelian definition of metaphysics is not easy to understand. And probably the statement from Whitehead, which looks somewhat clearer to me, means little to readers who know nothing else in Whitehead. Most descriptions of the metaphysical enterprise, naturally enough, refer to something historical, like Aristotle's difference from Plato, or to something other than existence (as Aristotle's description[47] referred to the different ways in which we *say* that things have being), or to our sense of contrast between 'concrete existence' and 'abstract existence', or to the contrasting words, 'appearance' and 'reality' (whereby we are nudged into an epistemological approach to metaphysics). All these definitions, carefully used, are helpful. In this essay I have tried to define metaphysics in a way which requires no such auxiliaries, and is understandable by anyone who has a living general wonder about existence. (You may call it the naïve approach to the subject; I have tried to show that fidelity to it requires more than naïveté.) It embodies, I hope, the spirit in which Whitehead wrote of philosophy in the opening sentences of *Nature and Life:*

"Philosophy is the product of wonder. The effort after the general characterization of the world around us is the romance of human thought."

And on his last page:

"Philosophy begins in wonder. And, at the end, when philosophic thought has done its best, the wonder remains. There have been added, however, some grasp of the immensity of things, some purification of emotion by understanding."[48]

---

[46] AI 187. Ivor Leclerc has shown how Whitehead's metaphysics may be read as a systematic modern investigation of the metaphysical problem as conceived by Aristotle. See especially pp. 17–34 of his book, *Whitehead's Metaphysics, An Introductory Exposition*, London and New York, 1958.

[47] *Metaphysics*, Bk. IV, 1–2.   [48] MT 173, 232.

GOTTFRIED MARTIN

METAPHYSICS AS *SCIENTIA UNIVERSALIS* AND AS *ONTOLOGIA GENERALIS*

VIII

GOTTFRIED MARTIN

METAPHYSICS AS *SCIENTIA UNIVERSALIS* AND AS *ONTOLOGIA GENERALIS*[1]

Aristotle, in a well-known and much discussed manner, divides metaphysics into the theory of *ens qua ens* and the theory of *ens primum*. In this distinction the connection of metaphysics with theology is operative, for the theory of *ens primum* is to be regarded, in a certain sense, as *theologia naturalis*. That is why Aristotle could explicitly speak of metaphysics as 'theology'. But Aristotle recognizes yet a second division in metaphysics, distinguishing between the doctrine of principles on the one side, and the doctrine of *ens qua ens* on the other. These two possibilities of metaphysics can be called 'theory of principles' and 'theory of being'. For this distinction the Latin terms *scientia universalis* and *ontologia generalis* are available. It must, however, be noted that these two terms were never used jointly by one and the same thinker. *Scientia universalis* was a general concept for Leibniz, whilst *ontologia generalis* was used by his pupil Christian Wolff in his attempt to systematize the Leibnizian philosophy. It is my intention to elucidate both the relation and the difference between these two possibilities of metaphysics, and I shall do so by tracing how this distinction was handled by the great thinkers in the history of metaphysics.

Aristotle explictly formulates both possibilities as the task of metaphysics. For him philosophy is the doctrine of *ens qua ens*, and philosophy is also the doctrine of principles. One might say that the Aristotelian *Metaphysics* as we have it today sometimes stresses one, sometimes the other function. For instance, Chapter 2 of Book X is exclusively directed to the question of being. Book IV concentrates on theory of principles, in particular on the law of contradiction as the fundamental principle. Book XIII, again, is essentially theory of being, in the investigation of Ideas as well as

[1] Translated from the German by Eva Schaper.

in the investigation of numbers: the concern is explicitly with the being of Ideas and the being of numbers.

Aristotle's theory of principles embraces the doctrine of first principles, in particular the doctrine concerning the law of contradiction, and it embraces the theory of principles in a narrower sense. The theory of principles in the narrower sense presents itself as the familiar doctrine of the four causes ($\dot{\alpha}\rho\chi\alpha\dot{\iota}$).

The first Book of Aristotle's *Metaphysics* especially throws light on our problem. After the first two introductory chapters—which have always been rightly regarded as a masterpiece of Aristotelian philosophy—Aristotle presents a history of Greek philosophy under the perspective of the four causes. The ancient philosophers, according to Aristotle, discovered the principle of $\ddot{\upsilon}\lambda\eta$, material cause. The Pythagoreans initiated, and Plato elaborated the discovery of the second principle, $\epsilon\hat{\iota}\delta\sigma$, formal cause. Various tentative analyses were also made of efficient cause and of $\tau\acute{\epsilon}\lambda\sigma$, final cause, but systematic investigation of these two had to wait for Aristotle, who completed the doctrine of the four principles or causes. Seen thus, the history of Greek philosophy constitutes one great movement of thought in the theory of principles, culminating in Aristotle.

Despite the dominance of theory of principles in its general structure, Aristotle's *Metaphysics* nevertheless contains considerations, in Book I, Chapters 6 and 9, which properly belong to theory of being. In these chapters Aristotle investigates the theory of Ideas and Plato's ontological interpretation of it, in particular the interpretations of the Ideas as $o\dot{\upsilon}\sigma\dot{\iota}\alpha\iota$. What Aristotle said about numbers might be adapted to summarize this investigation of the theory of Ideas: not *whether* there are Ideas, but *how* the Ideas are —that is the question. These investigations of the doctrine of Ideas are theory of being in the specific sense. The fact that Aristotle included such a treatise on the being of Ideas in his presentation of Greek philosophy (which proceeded mainly from the viewpoint of a theory of principles) shows how closely connected these two functions of metaphysics were for Aristotle.

Materially, we find this duplication of function already in Plato, but there it is not yet thematically nor terminologically developed. We see it in the different treatment the doctrine of Ideas receives in the *Phaedo* and the *Republic* on the one hand, and in the *Parmenides* and the *Sophist* on the other. The theory of Ideas as such s a species of the theory of principles, as Aristotle quite correctly saw. It belongs to the nature of Ideas to be of high generality, that s to say, it is the nature of Ideas to be principles. In some of Plato's own investigations, theory of principles becomes explicit. Among these we should count the question as to whether or not there be a supreme Idea, and thus a supreme principle—a question which has not, as far as we can see, received adequate treatment in the Platonic dialogues. Further, there is the question as to the connection between the Ideas: can they be systematically exhibited by the method of division, and in particular by the method of dichotomy, and are they to be represented as a pyramid of concepts? Questions such as these we find towards the beginning of the *Sophist*, and there are interpreters who regard the doctrine of this interrelation of Ideas as the essential outcome of Plato's philosophy. Another possibility is that the Ideas are connected in the manner of a net, as it is proposed in the *Sophist* towards the end of the discussion of the five highest kinds. It is with regard to such questions, i.e. questions belonging to theory of principles, that Plato speaks of his doctrine of Ideas as 'dialectics'. Nevertheless, the doctrine of Ideas in this form is still in a certain sense unreflective; this holds in particular for the form it takes in the *Phaedo*.

But one day Plato must have realized that he could no longer evade the question as to what exactly it *was* he had discovered when he discovered the Ideas. It is with this in mind that the arguments in the first part of the *Parmenides* and in the middle section of the *Sophist* have to be understood. For instance, when Plato considers whether the Ideas could be mere conceptions in the mind, and when he rejects this view as untenable, he is asking a question about being, and he is asking it in the first place as a question about the being of Ideas. One can well imagine that these investigations first developed from discussions which Plato had with his friends and pupils about the Ideas. Thus the question about being in the specific sense of *ontologia generalis* first emerges as the question about the being of Ideas, of the Platonic Ideas. This origin will always remain important for *ontologia generalis*.

Furthermore, the chronological relation between the *Phaedo* and the *Republic* on the one hand, and the *Parmenides* and the *Sophist* on the other, exhibits something which is decisive for the structure of *ontologia generalis*. Ontological thinking is a kind of reflection; only when there is first a statement with a certain content can the essentially ontological reflection begin. This is completely transparent in Plato. First comes the thesis: there are Ideas. Only then can ontological reflection enter with the question, What are Ideas? First natural laws have to be found and tested. Then only can the question be asked, What are natural laws? This relation between the Platonic dialogues is repeated in the relation between the *Principia Philosophiae Naturalis* and the *Critique of Pure Reason*. Seen thus it becomes clear that Aristotle's critical assessment of Plato, which occupies such a prominent position in Aristotle's philosophy, is not only a coming to terms of a philosopher with his teacher in the course of historical supersession; it is also one of the mainsprings of the Aristotelian metaphysics.

If we now consider the problem of the relation between *scientia universalis* and *ontologia generalis* in the modern period, Newton first of all is of importance. It is certainly correct to say that Newton was not a philosopher in the narrow sense of the word, and that he had no intention of being one. Nevertheless, Newton's axioms constitute an excellent exemplification of the theory of principles, not only in natural science, but also an exemplification of the theory of principles in its most original and most effective form. It is certainly correct to say that Newton devoted himself mainly to the elaboration of principles and their consequences; his great work therefore bears the title *Principia Philosophiae Naturalis* with full justification. And yet, theses in the specifically ontological sense are by no means lacking. The thesis of the absolute reality of space and time is such a specifically ontological thesis, and it is formulated as such. One cannot overlook, though, that Newton himself does not press the ontological statements any further than is necessary under the scientific aspects of theory of principles. The thesis of the absolute reality of space and time suffices for him, and he goes little further. In any case, he evades every explicit examination of what is involved in such a thesis. His famous dictum, *hypotheses non fingo*, is presumably not least meant with regard to the ontological problems. It is all the more remarkable that a thinker who was in such an explicit way concerned with principles only, could not entirely avoid ontological considerations.

Investigations by Leibniz in the theory of principles are as numerous as they are far-reaching. It is thus not surprising that his explicit discussion of the tasks of metaphysics in the *Nouveaux*

Essais arises almost exclusively from theory of principles. Meta-physics is the doctrine of the whole and the parts, the doctrine of the most general relations, the doctrine of the structure of matter, and the like. It is understandable that Leibniz should explicitly fix this range of functions of metaphysics terminologically: *scientia generalis*, *scientia universalis*, *characteristica universalis*. Numerous studies belonging to theory of principles have been found in Leibniz's opus posthumous, and even in the works published by Leibniz himself, he returns again and again to theory of principles. In his theory of principles, what is fundamentally given are con-cepts; judgments and propositions represent the unfolding of the connections existing between the concepts. Thus for Leibniz the system of principles is a system of fundamental concepts, and in this respect Leibniz is very close to Plato. Leibniz was convinced that such a system of basic concepts existed, even though he did not claim to have himself discovered this system of basic concepts, or even a single one of such concepts. The system as such exists, according to Leibniz, and the philosophical research directed towards it is therefore for him a proper and fundamental task.

To *ontologia generalis*, on the other hand, belong all Leibniz's assertions about the phenomenal character of the objects of mathematics and the natural sciences, and the corresponding assertions about the real character of individual living beings, the monads. As regards the problem of phenomenality, Leibniz first maintained the phenomenal character of secondary qualities, then, in a second step, the phenomenal character of primary qualities too, and finally, in radical adherence to this standpoint, also the phenomenal character of space, time, and matter. Here we have decisive problems for Leibniz: how to construe the concepts of reality and phenomenality, how to formulate the theses resulting from this, how to justify them and how to investigate them in their significance and range. In this Leibniz differs essentially from Newton. In the exchange of letters with Clarke, Leibniz attacks Newton again and again for maintaining the absolute reality of space and time and then failing to provide a reasoned basis for such a thesis, failing even to investigate the possible meanings of the thesis.

Let us try to see clearly in what proportion metaphysics for Leibniz is divided between *scientia universalis* and *ontologia generalis*. It may well be that the impressive studies of Couturat,

Russell, and Cassirer have very much pushed to the fore the
theory of principles. It is also correct that the conception of
metaphysics as the theory of *ens qua ens* is mainly to be found in the
Dissertatio de Principio Individui which is still deeply rooted in the
tradition. *Scientia universalis* is particularly strongly represented in
the *Inedita*—for which we are still without reliable dates. It looks
as though work belonging to *scientia universalis* dominated before
1700, whilst after the turn of the century the ontological considerations gained in prominence. That is why the considerations of
reality and phenomenality in the exchange of letters with Clarke
and in the two late presentations of the monadology are of such
importance. All considered, I am inclined to believe that Leibniz's
early writings are dominated by ontology, albeit in a very traditional sense, that it was *scientia generalis* which mainly absorbed
Leibniz's interest and energy during the productive middle
period, whilst during the last twenty years the specific problems of
ontology once more came to the fore. Of course, Leibniz was able
to base his late thought in ontology on an enormous life-work in
logic, in mathematics, in the natural sciences, in *scientia generalis*.

For Kant too these two tasks of metaphysics are closely connected. The *Critique of Pure Reason* is theory of principles as well
as theory of being. It is theory of principles in the doctrine of the
system of categories and principles; it is theory of being in the
doctrine of the phenomenal character of space, time, and nature,
and in the doctrine of the noumenal character of the freely acting
and productively thinking ego.

Seen as theory of principles, the *Critique of Pure Reason* is even
of a rather extreme kind. Although a complete system of basic
concepts and of the derivative principles was believed by Leibniz
to exist, Leibniz did not claim to have exhibited this system, or
even to be able to do so. Kant, however, explicitly claims to have
discovered and presented a complete and necessary system of the
basic concepts and principles. The proof of the completeness and
necessity of this system is the aim of the middle part of the *Critique
of Pure Reason*, the Transcendental Analytic. This prominence
of theory of principles explains why German Idealists and neo-
Kantians have tried again and again to interpret Kant's philosophy
exclusively as theory of principles.

In the *Critique of Pure Reason*, however, the completeness and
the necessity of this system of principles are gained and even made

possible at the cost of an ontological limitation. The principles are not valid for the totality of all being; rather, there are principles for noumenal being, and there are principles for phenomenal being. The difference becomes clear by comparison with Leibniz. For Leibniz the principles transcend the ontological distinction between real and phenomenal being. The doctrine of the whole and the parts, for instance, as intended by Leibniz, is valid for the real being of monads as well as for the phenomenal being of (say) matter. The system of principles in the *Critique of Pure Reason* on the other hand is valid only for the phenomenal being of nature. For instance, the causal law as here developed and argued is only valid for phenomena. When Kant deals in a specific manner with the problems of principles, he shows a distinct preference for the title 'metaphysics'. The two relevant works, *Metaphysical Principles of the Science of Nature* and *Fundamental Principles of the Metaphysic of Morals*, clearly exhibit the differentiation of the theory of principles. However great the claims of the *Critique of Pure Reason* to completeness and necessity, the limitations of this system, produced by its restriction to phenomena, are as great.

In the doctrine of the categories and principles, the *Critique of Pure Reason* is essentially theory of principles. But in the distinction of phenomena and noumena, in the distinction of appearances and things-in-themselves, in the doctrine of the phenomenal character of space, time, and nature, the *Critique of Pure Reason* is essentially theory of being. It may well be that the distinction between appearance and thing-in-itself, between phenomenon and noumenon, must be counted among the greatest difficulties of Kantian philosophy. But it would be a mistake to aim at an interpretation of the Kantian philosophy which eliminates this distinction. Interpretations attempting this, such as those of German Idealism and neo-Kantianism, are surely one-sided. Rather, one gains the impression that theory of principles and theory of being are finely balanced in Kant. We have already seen that Kant's theory of principles, by virtue of the restriction of some principles to certain realms of being, necessarily presupposes theory of being.

In our own time, we find a close connection of theory of principles and theory of being in Nicolai Hartmann's work. In the lofty structure of his ontology, theory of principles and theory of being occupy various positions in the progressive development of his

H

system. Theory of principles, as I understand it, appears later in the total work. Here too the theory of principles culminates in systems of categories and principles; its proper method, for Hartmann, is categoreal analysis. The outcome is the differentiation of being into spheres and levels. Hartmann claims to have found in categoreal analysis for the first time a genuinely valid method which enables us to differentiate being, and to provide the necessary reasons for it. As belonging to theory of principles in Hartmann, we must also count his doctrine of modalities with its development of the specific concepts of possibility, reality, and necessity, and the setting out of the corresponding modal laws.

On the other hand, as belonging to theory of being in Hartmann, we must especially count the first volume of his Ontology. This theory of being culminates in the thesis: "Being is independent of being thought". In many passages this realism of Hartmann's is very extreme, not infrequently appearing as absolute realism. Nevertheless Hartmann did not want to see himself as an absolute realist, and for this he has rightly been criticized from the standpoint of absolute realism. It is the aporematic problems which, for Hartmann, stand in the way of an absolute realism. If aporematics does not merely have a pedagogical significance, but beyond this a philosophical significance—as I believe it to be the case for Hartmann—then it necessarily leads to a critical version of realism.

A metaphysics which is exclusively theory of principles can be found in the work of Heinrich Scholz. He has presented it under the title of "Metaphysics as a Strict Science".[2] Scholz, with Leibniz, takes his starting-point from the conception of possible worlds. If one distinguishes the real world from the totality of all possible worlds, then there are statements which hold only for the real world. But according to the philosophical standpoint adopted, statements are also conceivable which hold for every possible world. For Leibniz, these are the statements of logic (in its wider sense), of arithmetic, and of geometry. For Scholz, this range of statements valid for all possible worlds has shrunk. First, geometry drops out. Once it is recongized that there are non-Euclidean geometries which are logically equivalent to Euclidean geometry (in the sense that they are equally free of contradiction) then, on the basis of Leibniz's and Scholz's assumptions, there must also be worlds in which non-Euclidean geometry is valid. For Leibniz, any

[2] Heinrich Scholz, *Metaphysik als Strenge Wissenschaft*, 1941.

geometry other than the three-dimensional Euclidean was self-contradictory, and therefore three-dimensional Euclidean geometry could hold for each of the possible worlds. For Scholz, non-Euclidean geometries are also free of contradiction, and therefore there must be—and on such logical assumptions, there would also have been for Leibniz—possible worlds in which such geometries hold. Similar assumptions, if somewhat more complicated ones, restrict arithmetic for Scholz. There are possible worlds in which only finite things exist, and in such worlds, according to Scholz, an arithmetic with infinitely many natural numbers could no longer hold. As valid for every possible world, however, there remains logic. Here logic is not restricted to syllogistic logic, but is understood in the wider, modern sense. As an example of a proposition valid in every possible world, Scholz mentions: "If a is different from b, then b is different from a". This proposition holds for every possible world, as long as such a world has at least two elements. Now the totality of propositions which are valid for all possible worlds is the theme of metaphysics. If and only if metaphysics sticks to this task, can it be a 'strict science', such as the title of Scholz's work demands.

This thesis is presented with all the power of conviction which always was at Scholz's disposal. Nonetheless I find it surprising that we are here asked to restrict the function of metaphysics to theory of principles. This is all the more surprising since Scholz himself was a dedicated Platonist. Would not a thinker so deeply committed to Platonism be obliged to give a reasoned account of his standpoint? I fail to see how Scholz would classify such an undertaking. Certainly not as belonging to 'metaphysics as a strict science', and there is, of course, no trace of such an inquiry in the book which bears this title. Such a reasoned account of the Platonic standpoint would certainly be relevant to metaphysics as a strict science, as understood by Scholz. For the principles too—and the principles above all—have to be conceived in Plato's sense, if one wants to be a Platonist at all. It is inconceivable that Scholz could have been of the opinion that the Platonic standpoint was incapable of being founded on a reasoned account. But where should such a reasoned account find its place, if metaphysics as a whole is handed over to theory of principles?

Whatever solution to this problem may be found for Scholz, the conception of metaphysics presented by him clearly shows the two possibilities with which we are here concerned. Scholz restricts metaphysics to theory of principles. Metaphysics as a strict science must present the totality of principles valid for all possible worlds, and it must give reasons for this presentation. Metaphysics as theory of being would have the wider task—indispensable in my opinion—of presenting the Platonic conception of these principles, and of giving reasons for it.

In Whitehead we find an especially pregnant connection between theory of principles and theory of being. In the first place, White-head's metaphysics is largely theory of principles. This comes out clearly, for example, in Chapter X of *Science and the Modern World*. At the beginning of this chapter Whitehead explicitly draws attention to the fact that he is now entering metaphysics. Readers "who find metaphysics, even in two slight chapters, irk-some"[3] are advised to skip these chapters. Looking into them, we find that Chapter X deals almost exclusively, excepting for a few sentences, with theory of principles, whilst Chapter XI presents itself already in its heading, "God", as *theologia naturalis*.

That metaphysics for Whitehead is so largely theory of principles is based upon his great logical optimism. Whitehead assumes the existence of a supreme system of principles, even though he con-cedes that this system can never be adequately grasped, but only approximately.[4] (Here as throughout this essay, the word 'system' must be understood in a very general sense. It means no more than, say, 'totality', but without specifying any requirements as to the structure of this totality.) In addition to this logical optimism we have Whitehead's conviction of the homogeneity of all that is real, on the basis of which he calls his philosophy a 'philosophy of organism'. By this he expresses his view that not only beings in the traditional sense, but also electrons, atoms, molecules, and other physical entities are organisms. This means that the same basic concepts and the same principles hold for the totality of all that is real, since every real thing is an organism. It is immediately evident that on such far-reaching assumptions the theory of principles must again assume special prominence. To remove false principles which have infiltrated into the sciences in their development, and to find correct ones to take their place—this then becomes the important task of metaphysics.

But Whitehead by no means neglects the theory of being—as

---

[3] SMW 195–6.   [4] Cf. PR 4–5 [6].

Leclerc's presentation of *Whitehead's Metaphysics*[5] impressively shows. To theory of being, for Whitehead, belongs on the one hand the doctrine of individual beings as organisms, and on the other hand the doctrine of eternal objects, conceived in a Platonic sense. Whitehead's theory of being culminates in the thesis: the individual being is the only reality. Apart from the reality of individual beings, and of the eternal objects rooted in them, there is no reality. The eternal objects, i.e. the Platonic modifications of individual entities, derive their specific reality from their realization in individual beings. This is a standpoint which connects the late Platonic dialogues with the Aristotelian metaphysics. One might say that here we have an ontological standpoint taking up those theses which are common to the late Platonic dialogues and the Aristotelian metaphysics.

Thus metaphysics as *scientia universalis* and metaphysics as *ontologia generalis* make their appearance in varied forms, both in their connection with and in their difference from each other. If one were to make a decision, I should be inclined to conceive metaphysics essentially as theory of being, that is to say, essentially as *ontologia generalis*.

Such a preference for *ontologia generalis* is determined by objections which can, in my opinion, be raised against *scientia universalis*. A general theory of principles, such as it is intended by Leibniz, by Scholz, and by Whitehead, contains assumptions which are very far-reaching and which cannot easily be verified. It must be assumed that the totality of everything real be so homogeneous as to allow for the same system of principles to cover everything real. One sees this clearly in Whitehead who, consequently, holds that even electrons, atoms, and molecules are organisms. But does this not extend the concept of 'organism' so much that it loses its original significance? This seems to me a valid objection, and I cannot see how Whitehead could meet it. It seems probable that even the far more guarded assumption of Kant's is untenable. Kant distinguishes the principles valid for nature, and those valid for acting human beings. But he still upholds the assumption that at least nature as a whole is determined by one system of principles, and that this system of principles has a specific systematic structure. However, he restricts even this assumption once more by considering new principles for living things in the

5 Ivor Leclerc, *Whitehead's Metaphysics*, London and New York, 1958.

Critique of Judgement. But perhaps the Kantian assumption doe
not even hold for inorganic nature. Perhaps the development o
physics, as it has already happened, and as it is very likely still t
come, will force us to introduce into the subject-matter of physic
such strong differentiations that different systems of principles wil
have to be adopted even in this field.

Further, there are the methodological difficulties of a *scientia
universalis*. It seems to me that these are most clearly seen in
Scholz—and here I believe Scholz formulates explicitly wha
Leibniz implied. The thesis that the principles are to be valid fo
every possible world contains well-nigh insuperable difficulties
This is obvious in the example used by Scholz. It may well be tha
the proposition, "if *a* is different from *b*, then *b* is different from
a", holds in every possible world in which it can at all hold. But I
cannot see how such a range of validity could be proved—and or
what other basis could one assume it? Scholz in any case has no
given a proof of the validity for the totality of all possible world
of even this one proposition, and one cannot see how he could have
proved it. On account of difficulties such as these I am inclined
to believe that only regional systems of principles are possible, tha
is to say, that there are only systems of principles which are relevant
to particular realms of being. If this assumption be correct, it
would be advisable to regard the systems of principles as belonging
to the fundamental questions of the respective sciences. If we are
dealing with very general systems of principles, and with general
questions about systems of principles, then these had best find
their place in theory of science or in logic—logic here understood
again in the modern extended sense. Considering Scholz's investigations with this in mind, one comes to the conclusion that they
would best be described as belonging to logic. In that case, however, instead of "Metaphysics as a Strict Science", another title
might have been more appropriate.

And yet, it is precisely Scholz's inquiry which seems to me to
make it plain that *ontologia generalis* constitutes a task which is
independent of all assumptions and all standpoints, since it is
precisely the meaning and significance of assumptions and standpoints which are its theme. With a sufficiently wide conception of
metaphysics as *ontologia generalis*, such a task is always necessary.
One must only take care to frame the conception of metaphysics
sufficiently wide so that also, for instance, a nominalistic stand-

point falls under it. Whatever standpoint one takes up oneself, be it that of nominalism or that of Platonism, it will always be necessary to scrutinize the meaning and range of such a standpoint and to give a reasoned grounding of the standpoint itself. I should therefore consider it appropriate to loosen the old bonds between *scientia universalis* and *ontologia generalis*, between theory of principles and theory of being. It would be in accord with these considerations to assign theory of principles to logic in its wide sense, and to concentrate metaphysics essentially upon the task of theory of being.

W. MAYS

THE RELEVANCE OF "ON MATHEMATICAL CONCEPTS OF THE MATERIAL WORLD" TO WHITEHEAD'S PHILOSOPHY

IX

W. MAYS

THE RELEVANCE OF "ON MATHEMATICAL CONCEPTS OF THE MATERIAL WORLD" TO WHITEHEAD'S PHILOSOPHY

I

The Importance of the Memoir

In 1906 there appeared in the Philosophical Transactions of the Royal Society Whitehead's memoir "On Mathematical Concepts of the Material World".[1] It had been read before the Society some months earlier. Its object was to show how one could construct alternative concepts of the physical world. It should be pointed out that although Whitehead had worked in pure mathematics and logic, his Fellowship dissertation at Trinity[2] had been on Clerk Maxwell's theory of electromagnetism, in which he seems to have retained an interest throughout his life. In this memoir he brings together axiomatic theory and the physical view of nature in terms of continuity assumed in electromagnetic theory. These two strands of thought are to be found running through his later writings, namely, an interest in abstract structure and its relation to the physical world.

This memoir is of considerable importance. It is the meeting place of (1) Whitehead's studies in geometry, (2) his PM work and (3) his interests in physical science. In it are also to be found the germs of both his nature philosophy and his metaphysics. The

[1] Read before the Royal Society, December 7, 1905. Published in the Philosophical Transactions of the Royal Society, 1906. All references will be to the reprint in *Alfred North Whitehead: An Anthology*, ed. F. S. C. Northrop and M. W. Gross, Cambridge, 1953, pp. 11–82. Hereafter the Memoir will be referred to as MC.

[2] Russell in *My Philosophical Development* (London: Allen & Unwin, 1959) after discussing the view that matter was a plenum pervading all space, states (p. 43) "This book [Clerk Maxwell's] had been the subject of Whitehead's Fellowship dissertation", and Whitehead urged Russell to prefer its views to those of Boscovitch. When Russell adopted this view he gave it a Hegelian dress "and represented it as a dialectical transition from Leibniz to Spinoza, thus permitting myself to allow what I considered the logical order to prevail over that of chronology".

axiomatic method is used here in all its rigour. The closely packed lists of definitions, axioms and derived propositions, make, for example, Carnap's work seem simple by comparison. Lowe reports that Whitehead thought that this was one of the best pieces of work that he had done.[3]

Despite the importance of the memoir it made little impact on the world of learning at the time of its publication. This is not surprising; expressed, as it is, in PM symbolism it must have seemed highly esoteric when it appeared six years before PM was launched upon the world. What must be remembered is that this was not the product of the idle fancy of a young man. Whitehead was then forty-five and had twenty years' mathematical teaching and research behind him.

To indicate the nature of the symbolism used, as there was as yet no PM to be referred to, he pointed out that Peano's chief symbols are used in the memoir. "The changes and developments from Peano, which will be found here, are due to Russell and myself working in collaboration for another purpose. It would be impossible to disentangle our various contributions."[4]

Not very many philosophers have indicated the connection of MC with Whitehead's later work. It also seems to have had little effect on physical thought. The axiomatization of physics, apart from attempts by von Neumann and Reichenbach in the field of quantum theory, has not been readily acceptable by physicists, possibly because of the rapid advances made in the subject. However, Whitehead is not trying to formalize a fragment of some specific physical theory such as quantum mechanics, but the foundations of the subject needed for any physical theory. He is not blind to the fact that the working physicist relying largely on insight and intuition, may not be willing to accept such a formal basis for his science. In physical research, he points out, so much depends on a trained imaginative intuition that it seems unlikely that existing physicists would gain by deserting familiar habits of thought.[5]

At the time of writing MC, Whitehead was, as we have seen, in

[3] The Philosophy of Alfred North Whitehead, ed. P. A. Schilpp, p. 34. [4] MC 18.
[5] MC, cf. p. 12. On another score Whitehead's memoir must have seemed very academic at the time of writing—namely, in the application of logical systems to concrete subject-matters. Logical systems have now been applied to a large range of topics, genetics, nerve-networks, computers, etc. Whitehead was a pioneer in this field.

the midst of writing PM. He was also about to publish his texts on Descriptive and Projective Geometry. *Universal Algebra* had already appeared some eight years previously, in which he tried to show the connection between logic and geometry.[6] But it was to be another ten years before his paper "La Theorie Relationniste de l'Espace", in which the 'Method of Extensive Abstraction' is stated for the first time, was to be seen in print.

As we have noted, this memoir has had little effect on the interpreters of Whitehead's later philosophy. Yet in some ways it is much more of a speculative endeavour than is his philosophy of nature. He was constructing what in effect were different cosmologies—a topic he comes back to in his later writings. *Process and Reality* when it appears does not come, if we understand this, as a bolt from the blue. It had already been heralded by MC.

II

The Axiomatic Method

Whitehead in MC might be said to be engaging upon a mathematical (or logical) investigation of various possible ways of conceiving the nature of the material world. Different axiom systems, or models of the material world, are constructed, from each of which geometry is derivative. There seems a certain resemblance to Leibniz's doctrine of many possible worlds, each of which is self-consistent, except that in MC we are limited to five main types and a number of variants.

Whitehead makes it clear that he is engaged in constructing logical models, rather than describing some actual physical situation. He points out that he is not concerned with (*a*) the relation of a concept of the material world to a perceiving mind, or (*b*) the philosophical problem of the relation, if any, of these concepts to existence.[7] His account is a purely hypothetical one.

In writing this memoir, Whitehead seems to have been influenced by the concept of alternative systems of geometry, in which, starting from different postulates, we can build up various non-Euclidean geometries. It was once assumed that Euclid's geometry was based on self-evident axioms from which all the theorems

---

[6] *A Treatise on Universal Algebra*, p. 32: "The result of it is that a treatise on Universal Algebra is also to some extent a treatise on certain generalised ideas of space." [7] MC, cf. p. 13.

followed deductively. The elaboration of non-Euclidean geometries in which the parallel postulate does not hold, has shown that different geometrical systems can be constructed upon axioms other than Euclid's. In a somewhat similar manner Whitehead constructs a number of alternative cosmologies which are hypothetical in character, and from which in each case Euclidean geometry may be constructed.[8]

The axiomatic method is succinctly described by Wilder as follows: It consists in setting forth certain basic statements or axioms about the concept to be studied, using certain undefined technical terms as well as the terms of classical logic. In proving theorems from axioms, the rules of classical logic are employed. To set forth an axiom system, say for plane geometry, we first select the basic undefined terms, perhaps point and line, and by means of which the more complex geometrical elements are defined. Next we select the basic propositions or axioms of the geometry with regard both to their simplicity and adequacy for proving the ones not selected.[9] Among the desiderata of a set of axioms, is that they should be simple, few in number, consistent and independent of each other.

The statements in an axiom system may also be about familiar concepts (or subject-matters) occurring in arithmetic, physics and zoology. Axioms can be set down for some such concept, and we can see what theorems are logically deducible from them. In practice, Wilder tells us, the concept comes first—the axioms later. We first select the concept, then the undefined terms and the statements that we wish to use to form our axioms, and finally we prove the theorems.[10]

The axioms from which in each concept of the material world geometry is derived, are themselves defined in purely logical terms. Some discussion of these logical notions and the symbolism in which they are expressed is therefore necessary before Whitehead can proceed to construct his various concepts of the material world. This he does in the section of his memoir on "Explanation of Symbolism",[11] in which he gives a concise introduction to some of the basic logical notions of PM. Whitehead starts with an account of the logical operators, such as negation, implication and disjunc-

---

[8] Non-Euclidean geometries can also be constructed if somewhat different axioms are used.

[9] *Introduction to the Foundations of Mathematics*, by Raymond L. Wilder, 1952, cf. pp. 9–10.   [10] *Ibid.*, cf. p. 20.   [11] MC, cf. pp. 18–23.

tion, and then proceeds to discuss propositional functions, class-membership, cardinal numbers, the theory of relations, etc.

The symbolism is used, Whitehead tells us, for the sake of its conciseness and (above all) its precision. The exact statement of any concept of the material world is therefore always to be sought in the symbolic alternative form. In the verbal account the proofs have been translated out of the symbolic form in which they were elaborated. In stating the proofs verbally, he admits that he has to some extent sacrificed precision to lucidity. Hence they may not always convey the precision of the ideas expressed symbolically.[12]

III

The Definition of a Concept of the Material World

Whitehead explains what he means by a Concept of the Material World.[13] It is in a sense a two-fold notion. Each such concept can be expressed in terms of (a) a set of fundamental relations and the axioms they satisfy, and (b) the class of entities which form the fields of these relations, i.e. the class of ultimate existents—points, lines, instants, etc.

The fundamental relations belonging to each concept are: (1) *The Essential Relation*, (2) *The Time Relation* and (3) *The Extraneous Relations*. (1) is a single polyadic relation of linear order by means of which the various geometrical entities are defined. (2) is a dyadic serial relation similar to that generating the series of positive and negative numbers, and having for its field the instants of time. (3) deals with the way material particles are related to points and instants of time, and in terms of which the laws of dynamics are determined.[14]

Whitehead, as we have noted, constructs five main concepts of the material world. He starts with the classical Newtonian concept and ends with specially constructed concepts where the basic elements are linear entities rather than points of space. In each concept he is primarily concerned with the essential relation and the axioms defining it, which take on different properties according to the particular concept involved. Whitehead states this problem

---

[12] MC, cf. p. 18–19.   [13] *Ibid.*, cf. p. 13.

[14] The essential and extraneous relations would seem to be the forerunners of the essential and contingent relations of his later philosophy. In his later work the essential relations relate events to other events in nature, whilst the extraneous relations concern the objects implicated in these events.

abstractly as follows: "Given a set of entities which form the field of a certain polyadic (i.e. many-termed) relation R, what 'axioms' satisfied by R have the consequence, that the theorems of Euclidean geometry are the expression of certain properties of the field of R?"[15] He is trying to show how from a certain set of entities and the axioms concerning the relations between them, geometry follows as expressing certain properties of these entities.

It will be noted that the essential relation appears in one form or another in every concept of the material world. There is some resemblance here to the extensive concepts of *Process and Reality*, which he thinks are persistent characteristics to be found in every epoch. These are exemplified in the notion of an Extensive Continuum, which we are told is one relational complex in which all potential objectifications find their niche.[16]

Whitehead now outlines the logical procedure to be followed in the study of any concept of the material world, and for that matter, he adds, any investigation respecting the axioms of geometry or physics viewed as deductive sciences. Four stages are distinguished.

(1) The definition of the entities capable of being defined in terms of the fundamental relations; e.g. a straight line is defined in terms of a class of points between which the essential relation R holds.

(2) The deduction of the various properties implicit in those definitions; e.g. statements about lines and planes derived from the above.

(3) The selection of the group of axioms which determines that concept of the material world; e.g. axioms concerning the properties of R.

---

[15] Though he adds (MC 11): "In view of the existence of change in the material world, the investigation has to be so conducted as to introduce, in its abstract form, the idea of time, and to provide for the definition of velocity and acceleration."

[16] He enlightens us as to what is meant by an Extensive Continuum when he says (PR 91 [103]) that it is "a complex of entities united by the various allied relationships of whole to part, and of overlapping so as to possess common parts, and of contact, and of other relationships derived from these primary relationships".

The extensive relation of *Process and Reality* has undergone a considerable evolution from the simple notion of intersection which is a property of the essential relation in Concept V. In this concept the notion of a system of abstract relationships is only at the most hinted at.

(4) The deduction of propositions from the initial axioms; e.g. the ordinary propositions of geometry which in Euclid are the derived theorems.

Psychologically, he points out, the order of these studies tends to be inverted. We first choose propositions of stages (2) and (4) and then stages (1) and (3). What Whitehead is essentially concerned with in each such concept is to exhibit states (1) and (3), i.e. the selection of the definitions and axioms of the system. Or putting it another way, in our ordinary experience we are intuitively familiar with the properties of geometrical figures. When, however, we put geometry (or any other concept) on to a purely formal basis, the geometrical propositions are now shown to be derivable from more basic propositions. They can, as for example in Veblen's axiomatization of geometry, be constructed from a set of points and a triadic serial relation.

IV

Dualistic and Monistic Concepts

The chief task of this paper will be to outline the various concepts of the material world elaborated by Whitehead in MC. This may be done without going into the more technical aspects of the memoir. Apart from the derivation of points and dimensions, which involves the use of a fairly technical logical apparatus, the essential features of Whitehead's account can be stated in non-symbolic terms.

Whitehead begins with a critical examination of the classical Newtonian concept. This, he says, arose in an age when Geometry as derived from the Greeks was the only developed science. The application of geometry to the physical world led to the acceptance of the absolute theory of space, upon which was superposed a theory of the motion of matter in time.

Three mutually exclusive classes of 'objective reals' are then posited in this concept: points of space, instants of time and particles of matter.[17] To these correspond three sciences. (*a*) Geometry,

---

[17] Whitehead takes over Russell's logical analysis of the nature of matter. Cf. *The Principles of Mathematics*, p. 468.

On this analysis (1) a simple material unit occupies a spatial point at a moment and persists through time, (2) two units cannot occupy the same point at the same moment, (3) their positions at intermediate times must form an intermediate series. Matter itself is a collective name for all pieces of matter, as space is for all points and time for all instants.

which concerns itself with a study of the relations between points. (*b*) Chronology—the theory of time as a one-dimensional series ordinally similar to the series of real numbers. (*c*) Dynamics, which deals with the movement of matter in space and time.

Whitehead objects to the classical concept on the ground that it bifurcates the world into separate elements, namely, space and the matter occupying it. It thus involves an unnecessary duplication of physical entities. Starting from Occam's principle that "Entities are not to be multiplied without necessity",[18] Whitehead believes that there is an intuitive preference for a monistic concept of the material world. In a monistic concept space and matter are unified so that only one class of entity can occur. Such a concept is termed by him Leibnizian, since for Leibniz points of space are not conceived as existing in themselves, but rather as denoting an order of co-existing things.

We would seem to have here the beginning of his later criticism of 'simple location' and 'the Fallacy of Misplaced Concreteness'. It is interesting to note that Whitehead's arguments for a monistic concept in MC are based on logical simplicity rather than on his later view that nature is perceived as a relational whole. Although, as we shall see, there is some ground for believing that this approach may have been brought in for physical rather than logical reasons.

A somewhat similar criticism of the classical concept is found in *Principles of Natural Knowledge*, where by way of an introduction to his own 'philosophy of nature' Whitehead compares the classical concept with what he calls the 'principle of relativity'. He links this up with the question, "What is a physical explanation?". The orthodox reply, he answers, was in terms of "Time (flowing equably in measurable lapses) and of Space (timeless, void of activity, euclidean), and of Material in space (such as matter, ether or electricity)".[19] Since the same material exists at different times, the notion of a state of change must be included.

On the other hand, according to the 'principle of relativity'

---

[18] This is amplified in AE 218: "Occam's razor. *Entia non multiplicanda praeter necessitatem*, is not an arbitrary rule based on mere logical elegancy. Nor is its application purely confined to metaphysical speculation. I am ignorant of the precise reason for its metaphysical validity, but its scientific validity is obvious, namely, every use of hypothetical entities diminishes the claim of scientific reasoning to be the necessary outcome of a harmony between thought and sense-presentation. As hypothesis increases, necessity diminishes."   [19] PNK 1.

which forms the basis of his own view, the properties of space are merely a way of expressing relations between things ordinarily said to be in space. All spatial entities, such as points, straight lines and planes are mere complexes of relations between things. Starting from this position, spatial concepts are defined in terms of the relations between material things.

Whitehead in MC also contrasts the classical concept with what he there calls Leibniz's theory of the relativity of space. From a wider standpoint, however, Whitehead sees this theory as a protest against dividing the 'objective reals' into two parts, (a) points of space, unrelated to instants of time, and (b) material particles which have a time-reference. In this sense, he states, it may be said to be a protest against exempting any part of the universe from change.[20] Not only is he then criticizing the view that space can exist apart from things, but also that it can exist unchanging and out of time.

In effect, what this comes to on a monistic concept of the material world, is that instants of time are included as terms within the essential relations from which geometry is derived. In such a system geometrical statements have therefore a time reference. There is already a certain similarity here to Whitehead's later doctrines, that geometrical forms are derivative from process, and that the fundamental entities are events which change and pass. But there is this difference; space and time are still regarded as independent of each other. They are not, as in his nature philosophy, fused together in the form of events.

In MC there is no attempt to derive time from something more primitive epistemically. Whitehead does, however, include instants of time among the 'ultimate existents of every concept'. It is only in his nature philosophy, where a doctrine of events is put forward, that he clearly states his belief that the absolute theory of time, i.e. an ordered succession of durationless instants, is implausible. When he examines his own experience he is unable to find anything corresponding to the bare time of the absolute theory. Time for him then is but an abstraction from the passage of events and the relation of extension which events have to each other. Thus the fusion of time with space, and the dropping of its unique seriality involves, he argues, the necessity of looking on ultimate fact as essentially a process.

[20] MC, cf. p. 14.

V

Punctual Concepts

Whitehead's discussion of Concept I is largely a straight investigation of Euclidean geometry. Veblen's axiomatic system, which bases Euclidean geometry on one class of undefined entities—points—and one undefined serial relation between points, is taken over and adapted to Whitehead's concept of an essential relation. The essential relation R of Concept I is triadic, namely, R (*a*, *b*, *c*), i.e. *the points a, b, c in a linear order*.[21] The relation may be varied so as to make the resultant geometry Euclidean or non-Euclidean.

But geometry thus derived has to apply to a changing world. A class of particles is therefore postulated, making up the fundamental stuff moving in space, and a class of triadic extraneous relations holding between a particle, a point of space and an instant of time. These relations provide for the definition of velocity and acceleration in terms of which the laws of dynamics are defined. Whitehead terms these relations 'extraneous' since they are superposed upon the geometrical entities and are not intrinsic to them.

Concepts II and III are monistic variants of I. In both geometry is brought into closer contact with physics. In II, the triadic relations by which particles are related to points of space at instants of time are transformed into dyadic ones between points of space and instants of time. A material particle becomes a mode of relating a point of space to an instant of time. This concept is suggested by Russell when he gives an abstract logical statement of what rational Dynamics requires its matter to be: "the only relevant function of a material point is to establish a correlation between all moments of time and some points of space, and that this correlation is many-one".[22] As Whitehead believes that 'matter' was only introduced to give the senses something to perceive, this concept, since it reduces 'matter' to the form of a relation, has for him an advantage over the classical one, if relations can be perceived.

In III the essential relation from which geometry is derived is tetradic. This is symbolized as R; (*a b c t*), i.e. *points a, b, c in the R order at the instant t*.[23] The geometrical definitions are the same as in I except that any geometrical proposition now involves a reference to an instant of time. The points of this concept are

---

[21] MC, cf. p. 25. Twelve axioms concerning this relation are stated, and from which he is enabled to derive Euclidean geometry.

[22] *Principles of Mathematics*, p. 468.   [23] MC 30.

assumed to be in motion, i.e. they have different relations to each other at different instants. The whole of space is then made up of moving points (or particles), the positions of which change at different instants. The persistence of matter is explained by motion alone.[24]

To show how different points can have the same position at different instants, he introduces a single extraneous relation S. When S ($u\ t\ v\ w$) holds t is an instant of time, and u, v, w are intersecting straight lines mutually at right angles (which are the kinetic axes). This enables him to define velocity and acceleration.

Two variants of III are stated. IIIA, in which the same points persist by continuing in the same special type of motion.[25] IIIB, where persistence refers to the *type of motion* of the points in some volume, but not necessarily of the same points, since they may disintegrate. The identity of a corpuscle, or volume made up of moving points whose motion persists at different instants, is then defined in terms of the continuity of motion of the corpuscle as a whole.[26]

VI

Linear Concepts

In Concepts IV and V, the terms related by R are linear in character, and points are classes of these simple linear entities. A linear objective real is conceived after the fashion of a single unity underlying a straight line, which has a particular direction (i.e. a vector character). Whitehead empirically identifies these linear entities with 'lines of force' in physics, which he takes to be the "ultimate unanalysable entities which compose the material universe".[27] Geometry is to be regarded as a study of a certain limited set of their properties.[28]

Linear objective reals, we are told, however, have "no properties

[24] It was, Whitehead says (MC 31), a dictum with some eminent physicists of the nineteenth century that 'motion is of the essence of matter'. This concept takes them sharply at their word.

[25] He states (MC 31) that Kelvin's vortex ring theory of matter can be adapted to such a concept.

[26] The persistence of an electron would be defined by a persistence of type and continuity of motion. This suggests his later view of a relatively permanent body as a succession of events having a similar pattern.

[27] MC 32.

[28] Compare the above, for example, with his statement (AI 258): "The peculiar relationships (if any) diffused systematically between the extensive groups of an epoch constitute the system of geometry prevalent in that epoch."

analogous to the properties of the ends of lines of force",[29] i.e. they are presumably infinite in character. The statement that they have no ends is a little cryptic. In some ways it resembles Whitehead's later account of durations (or complete wholes of nature), which have no maximum nor minimum extent. On this account the continuity of nature arises from the fact that every duration is part of other durations. If the analogy between linear entities and durations holds, it would mean that these lines are in some way co-extensive with each other and thereby form a continuum. In MC Whitehead only discusses the way classes of linear reals are related by the essential relation in a serial order. He does not indicate how such complexes are systematically connected with each other. Nevertheless, it is reasonable to suppose that the totality of linear reals taken as a system, will, like the lines of force making up the material world, form a field or a continuum.

In IV and V the essential relation is a pentadic one. It is symbolized by R $(a\,b\,c\,d\,t)$, i.e. *linear real a intersects linear reals b, c, d in that order at time t.*[30] As we shall see below, the notion of intersection has some slight resemblance to his later notion of extension. Not only has geometry in these concepts to do with points of space, but also with their relation to linear reals from which they are derived. If time or passage were injected into these linear entities, we would come pretty close to Whitehead's later doctrine of events. It is interesting to note that in *Process and Reality* the fundamental experiential elements or 'prehensions' also have a vector character.

Concept IV has two alternative forms, IVA and IVB. Both concepts are initially considered under the heading of Concept IV. Points are derivative from classes of linear reals and are not posited as basic entities as in I. Motion is defined in terms of one extraneous relation (as in III), determining the kinetic axes, and by reference to which all motion is measured. Points on this concept do not persist from instant to instant, i.e. they disintegrate. Any material corpuscle (i.e. volume made up of points) has passing through it moving linear reals which make up the ether[31] lying between the material corpuscles.

---

[29] MC 32. [30] MC, cf. p. 39.
[31] He is in PNK frankly sceptical of the existence of an ether (p. 25): "The material called ether is merely the outcome of a metaphysical craving. The continuity of nature is the continuity of events."

The 'action at a distance' controversy becomes, he thinks, irrelevant on Concepts IV and V. "In one sense there is something, not mere space, between two distant corpuscles, namely, the objective reals possessed in common; in another sense there is a direct action between two distant corpuscles, not depending on intervening corpuscles."[32] He explains what he means by this in more detail in "The Anatomy of Some Scientific Ideas".[33] Scientific objects, such as electrons, he points out, are now thought of as complex, i.e. as fields of force. The electron and its emanations form an essential whole—namely, a certain distribution of scalar and vector quantities throughout space. Both views of causation, 'action at a distance' and 'transmission through an intervening medium' are hence included in this account. If we concentrate on the focal regions of the electrons, i.e. on their character as corpuscles, there appears to be a direct action between them, but if we regard them as fields of force there would seem to be a transmission of influence through a medium.

IVA is a hybrid concept. It postulates not only linear reals, but also a class of particles (positively and negatively charged entities) associated at each instant with points of space by triadic extraneous relations, as is the case in I. These particles make up the matter occupying space. Laws of motion are stated both for the particles and the linear reals, which mutually influence each other.

In IVB each triadic extraneous relation between an instant of time, a particle and a point is replaced, as in II, by a dyadic relation between a point and an instant of time. This concept is therefore monistic, since the particle is now reduced to a form of relationship.

It will be noted that in his account of the linear concepts, Whitehead postulates a class of entities which he believes corresponds more closely to the basic physical elements than do points. At the time of writing, he thought that Maxwell's electromagnetic theory had made a linear concept more likely than a punctual one. But he realizes that in more recent physics atomicity in the form of electrons and protons has again emerged into importance. Nevertheless, he believes that these two contrasted aspects of nature, continuity and atomicity, are both essential for our descriptions of nature.[34]

[32] MC 34. [33] Chap. IX in AE.
[34] AI, cf. pp. 238–9.

VII

Concept V

Concept V seems to have been uppermost in his mind when writing this memoir. Although put forward as the final concept, it looks as if Whitehead first arrived at it by reference to electromagnetic theory rather than as a result of purely logical deliberations. What he does in this concept, which is a monistic one, is to derive geometry from postulated linear entities, which can be given an empirical interpretation in terms of physical notions (i.e. lines of force). As in IV, the essential relation is pentadic. One extraneous relation is also required for the purpose of enabling velocity and acceleration to be measured.

Seventeen axioms are postulated, in contrast with the twelve of Concept I. This arises from the larger field to be covered which includes physics. Thus in a monistic concept, although the number of undefined entities are reduced, there may be an increase in the number of axioms and derived theorems. Points in V are defined in terms both of the theory of interpoints and the theory of dimensions. To explain how a parallelism may be established between linear reals, Whitehead brings in the concept of cogredience.[35] This has some resemblance to the relation of cogredience in *Principles of Natural Knowledge*, namely, the relation between an event 'here present' and its associated duration.[36] However, in one case we deal with a parallelism between linear reals which have the same geometrical order, in the other with a parallelism between an event and a duration which are both happening together.

At the end of this memoir Whitehead sketches a possible development of Concept V. "The complete concept", he tells us, "involves the assumption of only one class of entities as forming the universe. Properties of 'space' and of the physical phenomena 'in space' become simply the properties of this single class of entities." In order to simplify the axioms of V, "the ideal to be aimed at would be to deduce some or all of them from more general axioms which would also embrace the laws of physics. Thus these laws should not presuppose geometry, but create it".[37]

We seem to be given here a preview of his later position that geometrical relations arise from the physical details of the cosmic

[35] MC 64.   [36] PNK 70–1, 128.   [37] MC 82.

epoch in which we live. In *Process and Reality* this shows itself in his belief that the order of nature presupposes the mutual interdependence of the real things to be found in nature. Since the laws of nature depend on the characters of these things, as the things change so will these laws also change.

What should be noted is that although in Concept V Whitehead says he is putting forward a monistic concept, it is only monistic in the sense that it does not postulate two types of entities, points and material particles. However, this concept is dualistic in another sort of way, since it postulates both essential and extraneous relations, as does the classical concept. There is thus still a dualism between the relations determining geometrical order and the relations determining changes of motion in the world, and from which the laws of dynamics are derived. It is interesting to see that a similar dualism is to be found in his later writings when he compares the world of permanences and the world of change.

In view of the statistical basis of modern physics and the substitution of cause by chance in physical explanations, it is doubtful whether physicists would accept such a frankly causal account as that of Concept V nowadays. Concept V and the whole tenor of MC is determined by the fact that Whitehead conceives nature as continuous and made up of logical linear entities resembling lines of force. Whitehead's model is constructed with Clerk Maxwell's theory of electromagnetism in mind, which seems to fit more naturally on to a causal macroscopic level than a statistical microscopic level.

The lesson to be learnt from this is that physics advances and one's models require continually to be adjusted to changes in physical theory and subject-matter. Whitehead recognizes this in *Adventures of Ideas* when he admits that the more punctual discontinuous side of nature has shown itself again in quantum physics. He believes, however, that his theory can take account of such discontinuities in nature. And in *Process and Reality* he states that his cosmology is consistent with the view that the physical laws are statistical in character.

Whitehead could also argue that the basic elements assumed in physics—space, time and matter—have remained the same, though the kinds of matter postulated and the laws they follow may have changed. It is these notions that he is trying to express in logical terms—to reduce their number and to derive them from more basic logical concepts. The whole rationale of Whitehead's argument is then in a sense a logical one—to reduce the number of basic concepts physics starts from. He might argue that the advances in physics have led to the need of a change in the different kinds of extraneous relations in terms of which the physical laws are stated, rather than in the essential ones from which geometry is derived. If this is the case, the MC account suitably modified should be applicable to different physical theories of nature.

VIII

The Derivation of Points

In the past, the Method of Extensive Abstraction, by means of which Whitehead arrived at the notion of points in his nature philosophy, has been misunderstood. This partly arises from the widely-held belief that it was based exclusively on empirical foundations. It has been assumed that its task was to show how abstract geometrical entities could be directly constructed from sense-perceptions. Critics of the method have therefore had no difficulty in showing that the attempt to deduce points, conceived as infinite classes of classes, from sense-perceptions which have a minimum extent, involves one in inconsistencies. This criticism, however, seems to lose its force if, as appears to be the case, Whitehead uses this method largely as an illustrative device or mathematical model.

To understand the origins of this method it is well to go back to Whitehead's paper "La Theorie Relationniste de l'Espace",[38] which may be said to mark the transition between MC and his nature philosophy. The relational theory of space, and the manner in which points may be derived by the Method of Extensive Abstraction are already to be found there.

In this paper Whitehead first distinguishes four senses of the word 'space': (1) immediate apparent space, which is fragmentary and differs with the perspective of each individual; (2) complete apparent space, which seems to be a construction, since it is the space common to all percipients; (3) physical space, which is, as he puts it, the space of a hypothetical world—the same for all of us; (4) abstract space, the space with which geometry is concerned.

His treatment of the relativistic theory of space which follows is strongly reminiscent of MC. We are told that this theory starts

[38] *Revue de Métaphysique et de Morale*, Vol. 23, May 1916, pp. 423-454.

from the fundamental idea of a 'class of relations σ'. A world founded on such a class is called a 'world σ', whilst the class of entities forming its field is called the 'class of objects σ'. Unlike MC, however, these relations and relata can be given either a perceptual or physical interpretation. In the 'complete apparent world', σ is the class of relations between a possible perceiving subject (the class of actual and possible subjects) and the perceived and extended objects. In the 'physical world' σ is the class of direct relations between physical objects.

Whitehead now defines a derived relation Eσ (inclusion σ) analogous to the relation of whole and part, which enables him to define points, and other geometrical elements, by means of a convergent series of enclosure volumes.

Whitehead notes that in apparent space a point is practically an area or a sufficiently small volume. Such perceptual points (or *minima sensibilia*) lack neither surface nor volume, only the stability for further sub-division. Similarly, in a volume of physical space a point is practically an area or a sufficiently small volume. But both these notions, Whitehead argues, are only approximations to the geometrical concept of a point.

Geometrical points and lines are then on Whitehead's theory derived by means of a convergent series, in which the areas and volumes containing each other exist only (beyond a certain perceptual limit) as possibilities of sub-division. In general, then, a point or a line, or other geometrical element, is simply the possibility of a series of such sub-divisions, in which only the earlier members of the series have a perceptual interpretation.

Nicod[39] has brought out the similarity of the Method of Extensive Abstraction in Whitehead's nature philosophy, where he deals with events having the character of volumes, to that of geometry of volumes translatable into one of points. Nicod argues that even if geometry requires points as ultimate terms, a point need not be taken as simple. In analytical geometry, for example, a point is a class of three co-ordinates. There are systems which posit the point as complex and which are composed of terms easier to interpret in nature.

According to Nicod, Whitehead starts from an analysis of the terms and relations that nature presents, and looks for a combination of those entities which yields the properties of the geometrical

[39] J. Nicod, *Foundations of Geometry and Induction*, cf. pp. 40–3.

points. This turns into a geometry, for the natural entities already possess the geometrical properties of volumes. Where we otherwise call a volume a certain class of points, we now have to call a point a certain class of volumes. Whitehead's construction can then be taken not as an analysis of the real world, but as a pure geometry, i.e. as a mathematical model.[40]

That the precursors of the Method of Extensive Abstraction have largely the character of mathematical models may be particularly seen in Concepts IV and V of MC, where the basic elements are hypothetical linear reals rather than event-volumes. One of the methods used by Whitehead to derive points from such linear entities, is based on the concept of the projective ideal point (or point at infinity) defined in terms of an infinite class of lines.[41] There is a close analogy between a converging series, or sequence of nested rational intervals, defining an irrational or complex number in algebra, and the class of parallel lines defining a projective (ideal) point.

Only a shift of emphasis is then required for Whitehead to pass from the MC definition of a point on the lines of a projective point, to its definition in *Principles of Natural Knowledge* in terms of whole and part enclosure relations. The Method of Extensive Abstraction, by means of which this definition is affected, uses the principle of convergence to simplicity with diminution of extent, and involves the assumption of a convergent series.

This change in the manner of derivation of points no doubt arises from Whitehead's introduction of the areas and volumes of the apparent world in "La Theorie Relationniste de l'Espace" in place of the linear reals of MC. As events have more the character of volumes than straight lines, one can see why Whitehead used the notion of a convergent series as a basis for the Method of Extensive Abstraction rather than that of a family of parallel lines determining a point at infinity. Nevertheless, he still used the MC method as an auxiliary device in "The Anatomy of Some Scientific

[40] It is interesting to note that the relation of extensive connection in *Process and Reality* holds between regions which have the character of abstract volumes, i.e. they are not events. In MC the linear elements have also a logical character.

[41] According to Russell, *Principles of Mathematics*, p. 403, "the highly complex notion of a sheaf of lines—an infinite class of infinite classes—is philosophically very widely dissimilar to the simple notion of a point. But since classes of sheaves can be formed, having the same relations to their constituent sheaves that projective lines and planes have to projective points, a sheaf of lines in descriptive space *is*, for mathematical purposes, a projective point."

Ideas". After defining points in terms of enclosure objects there, Whitehead finds himself faced with the difficulty of defining points in empty space, i.e. where there are no objects to stand in relation to each other.[42] He proceeds to do this by means of the concept of the ideal projective point.[43]

IX

Interpoints and Dimensions

In MC where Whitehead is concerned with the question, "How can a point be defined in terms of lines?",[44] he tells us that the Theory of Interpoints and the Theory of Dimensions give two different answers to this question.[45] He goes on: "The well-known definition of the projective point, as a bundle of lines, assumes the descriptive point. The problem is to define it without any such assumption."[46] Or, as he puts it in a somewhat different way, the following difficulty occurs with linear concepts. "A point is to be defined as the class of objective reals 'concurrent' at a point. But this definition is circular. How can this circularity be removed?"[47]

Whitehead's method of removing this circularity seems to be to assume that all points, descriptive or otherwise, are now complex in character. He thereby, as he says, abolishes the descriptive point in terms of which the projective point is defined. What this comes to on his account, is that he regards the descriptive (or ordinary) point itself as being complex, and as derivable from linear reals which he considers to be more fundamental than the points and lines of geometry. In the Theory of Interpoints this shows itself in the definition of a point in terms of a class of linear entities having among their properties that of a 'similarity of position'. In the Theory of Dimensions, where he is concerned to construct a three-dimensional geometry, he takes up a somewhat different position.

[42] His later doctrine of an ether of events which enables him to get over this difficulty does not seem to have as yet been elaborated.

[43] Whitehead proceeds as follows (AE 219): "Define 'material lines' to be complete collinear classes of collinear points. Consider now the set of material lines which contain a certain material point. Call such a set of lines an ideal point. This set of lines indicates a possibility of position, which is in fact occupied by that material point common to all the material lines." If it is unoccupied then the ideal point merely indicates a possibility of spatial relations which has not been realized. This, it will be seen, has a direct resemblance to his MC account, where a set of lines also indicates a possibility of position.   [44] MC 12.

[45] Whitehead notes that the main object of this memoir is the development of the Theory of Interpoints, the Theory of Dimensions and Concept V.

[46] MC. 12.   [47] MC. 33.

Starting from our ordinary geometrical ideas, he proceeds to define a point in the manner of an ideal point in projective geometry. The whole construction of points in MC is then to be regarded as a piece of pure logic.

In the Theory of Interpoints the definition of points (or interpoints) starts from the essential pentadic relation R; $(a\ b\ c\ d\ t)$, i.e. *linear real a intersects linear reals b, c, d in that order at time t.* The notion of intersection satisfies four axioms.[48]

(1) a is not a member of R; $(a\ ?\ ?\ ?\ t)$, i.e. a is not a member of the class b, c, d, since it intersects them all.

(2) R; $(a\ b\ c\ d\ t)$ implies R; $(a\ d\ c\ b\ t)$, i.e. b and d may be substituted for each other.

(3) R; $(a\ b\ c\ d\ t)$ and R; $(a\ c\ b\ d\ t)$ are inconsistent, i.e. the linear order cannot be changed.

(4) In R; $(a\ b\ c\ d\ t)$, b and d are distinct, i.e. they do not overlap.

The notion of 'intersection' has some slight kinship to that of 'extension' in *Principles of Natural Knowledge* in terms of which points are defined there. However, in MC it is only the linear real a which intersects linear reals b, c, d. As b and d are distinct, they do not overlap each other, nor do either of them overlap c. In contrast to this, in the relation of extension each event overlaps other events and is in its turn overlapped by others.[49]

The definition of a point in the Theory of Interpoints depends rather on the allied notion of 'similarity of position' in a relation.[50] This is expressed symbolically as R; $\left(\dfrac{a???t}{x}\right)$, which denotes the class of lines x, y, z, with positions similar to that of x at t in R. In other words, x, y, z are substitutable for each other, provided the linear order is retained. A spatial position is thus defined in terms of a class of entities which have a similar property, namely, the possibility of occupying the same position. This resembles the logical definition of a number as the class of all classes similar to it, e.g. the class of all couples will be the number 2.

In the actual definition of an interpoint,[51] the above notion of 'similarity of position' is related to that of intersection. An interpoint is thus defined in terms of the total class formed by the linear

[48] MC 37–8.

[49] The relation of extension is transitive, asymmetrical and with its domain including its converse domain.

[50] MC, cf. p. 35.   [51] Point or intersection point.

real a and the class of linear reals x, y, z having a 'similarity of position' which a intersects.[52]

Having in this way arrived at points which are complex, White-head next defines a class of interpoints having an interpoint order at a time t, namely R_{in}; $(B\ C\ D\ t)$. This resembles the essential relation of Concept I, except that the geometrical points are now complex, and refer to instants of time. Starting from this relation of interpoint order, Euclidean geometry can be constructed much in the same way as in Concept I. The punctual lines and planes of geometry are now series of interpoints having a temporal reference.

It is interesting to compare Whitehead's definition of a point with Leibniz's idea of a place from which, according to him, the notion of space arises. Leibniz says: "To give a kind of definition: *Place* is that which is said to be the same for A and for B, when the relation of co-existence between B and C, E, F, G, etc., entirely agrees with the relation of co-existence which A previously had with those bodies, supposing there has been no cause of change in C, E, F, G, etc., . . .".[53] "For the rest, I have acted rather like Euclid, who, when he could not make it absolutely understood what is meant by *ratio*, in the geometricians' sense, defined properly what is meant by *the same ratios*. In the same way, in order to explain what *place* is, I have tried to define *the same place*."[54]

In other words, since Leibniz is unable to give any significance to 'place' defined in an absolute sense, he defines it instead in terms of the notion of the *same place*—in the sense of objects having the same relationship to other objects. Thus in two similar series, A, C, D, E, F, G, etc.; B, C, D, E, F, G, etc., if A and B stand in the same relation to the rest of the series, or are substitutable for each other, they may be said to occupy the same place. This account bears some resemblance to the 'similarity of position in a relation' of MC, where the related elements are substitutable for each other. In the former case, however, we deal with the substitutability of a term in a series, in the latter with the substitutability of terms within a serial relation.

Another way of defining points is considered in the Theory of Dimensions, in which Whitehead constructs a three-dimensional

---

[52] The resultant points are thus always taken as occurring on a linear real at a time t.
[53] *Philosophical Writings: Leibniz.* Ed. Morris (Everyman's Library), p. 221.
[54] *Ibid.*, p. 223.

geometry applicable to the physical world. He defines the dimensions of a space as well as the property ϕ or 'flatness' of a space. This property deals with the straightness of lines not based on measurement, and plays an important part in establishing the equality of spaces.[55]

ϕ points which cannot have less than three dimensions are defined on the lines of ideal projective points. As Whitehead puts it, "A ϕ-point now becomes simply that class of straight lines concurrent at a point". And he goes on, "The analogy with Klein's 'ideal', or 'projective', points is obvious. Only when the present theory is applied, it will be found that the original 'descriptive' point has entirely vanished."[56] Starting then from such a class of straight lines, he proceeds to define other 'flat' geometrical elements. In this way, with the aid of appropriate definitions and axioms, he is enabled to construct the three-dimensional geometry necessary for Concept V.[57]

X

The Relation of the Memoir to Whitehead's later Philosophy

Though it has been stated that this memoir has a relevance for Whitehead's later philosophy, precisely what this relevance is has not always been made clear. Quine, for example, tells us that Whitehead was occupied in analysing the logical structure of natural science, and the constructions foreshadow to some degree the projected *Principia Mathematica* volume on geometry. A study of the memoir makes one wonder if it did foreshadow this volume to any very marked extent. As we have seen, it is largely an account of different models of the physical world (i.e. of alternative possible worlds), and of how in each case Euclidean Geometry may be constructed by means of purely logical notions. Quine is, however, nearer the truth when he says that the constructions go far outside geometry, "this was the beginning of a quest for the broadest, most basic concepts and principles of nature, and in the decades since *Principia* the quest has issued in a metaphysics".[58]

---

[55] Definitions of 'flatness' are given in MC, 45 and 61, and PR 432.

[56] MC 48.

[57] It is interesting to note that the sections on the Theory of Interpoints and the Theory of Extension in MC bear some resemblance to the chapters on "Extensive Connection" and "Flat Loci" in *Process and Reality*.

[58] *The Philosophy of Alfred North Whitehead*, ed. P. A. Schilpp, p. 163.

One thing is clear. If MC had been discussed in any detail before *Process and Reality* had been published, it might have been noted that there was some connection between the method of speculative philosophy in *Process and Reality* and the axiomatic method used to construct the various concepts of the material world in MC. Those commentators who recognize there is a link between his nature philosophy and *Process and Reality* have tended to start with *Principles of Natural Knowledge*, where we seem to be given a form of phenomenalism, and where the notion of alternative systems of the world is not very evident. It might indeed be argued that Whitehead's philosophy of nature with its emphasis on the 'principle of relativity', is largely a development of Concept V of MC, to which an experiential dimension has been added.

Students of Whitehead's later metaphysical writings have pointed out that there has been a progression in these writings beyond his down-to-earth nature philosophy. They have argued, quite rightly, that *Process and Reality* stresses something which seems absent in the latter. In this earlier work the part played by imaginative generalization and speculation in philosophical thinking does not seem to be broached at all. No doubt it was this down-to-earthness which gave Whitehead's earlier philosophy its appeal to the more positivistically minded philosophers, and also explains their consternation when *Process and Reality* appeared. From one point of view, the nature philosophy period might indeed be regarded as something of an interlude in Whitehead's philosophical development.

In his later philosophy, however, when he advocates the use of the working hypothesis, he could in a sense be said to be returning to his MC position, since the axiomatic method is hypothetico-deductive in character. "Thus", he says, "speculative philosophy embodies the method of the 'working hypothesis'."[59] Some of the criteria which speculative philosophy has to fulfil are satisfied by an axiom system, which might be described as a coherent, logical, necessary system. The setting up of such a system seems also to involve a "play of a free imagination, controlled by the requirements of coherence and logic".[60]

In *Process and Reality* the proper objective of philosophy is conceived as the gradual elaboration of categoreal schemes,

[59] AI 286.   [60] PR 5 [7].

I

definitely stated at each stage of progress. Metaphysical categories, we are told, "are tentative formulations of the ultimate generalities".[61] When we have constructed such a scheme, we need to put it into use by arguing from it boldly and with rigid logic. For this reason the "scheme should therefore be stated with the utmost precision and definiteness, to allow of such argumentation".[62] A categoreal scheme, at least in its ideal form, would appear to have some of the features of a *hypothetico-deductive* system in which, starting from a set of axioms and definitions, theorems may be derived by the application of logical rules alone.

In MC Whitehead tells us that he discusses the general problem involved in the construction of concepts of the material world, purely from its logical (i.e. mathematical) interest. It has an indirect bearing on philosophy "by disentangling the essentials of the idea of a material world from the accidents of one particular concept".[63] A somewhat similar approach is to be found in a more philosophical setting when he says, "These principles of algebraic symbolism express the concurrence of mathematical formal principles with accidental factors".[64]

There would then seem to be a family resemblance between his account of philosophical method in *Process and Reality* and the axiomatic method as described in MC. His whole account in *Process and Reality* has, however, a much looser texture. With the possible exception of Part IV—"The Theory of Extension"—there is no rigorous formulation of an axiom system on the MC lines. Further, in *Process and Reality*, unlike MC, Whitehead is concerned with the relation of the physical world to a perceiving mind as well as with the nature of existence.

In his preface to *Science and the Modern World* Whitehead has said that "Philosophy, in one of its functions, is the critic of cosmologies". Now although only one cosmology is developed in *Process and Reality*, Whitehead does, however, discuss alternative cosmologies. He compares the cosmology of Newton as it appears in the *Scholium* with that of Plato as expressed in the *Timaeus*.[65] The former is, of course, the classical concept of MC, whilst the latter is a monistic concept resembling Concept V.

He points out that in the *Scholium* space and time are ready-

[61] PR 11 [12].   [62] PR 11 [13].   [63] MC 11–12.
[64] "Analysis of Meaning", in *Essays in Science and Philosophy*, New York: Philosophical Library, 1947, p. 128.   [65] PR, cf. p. 129 [142–3].

made for the 'forces' which constitute their action and reaction.[66] But there is, he tells us, a side in the *Timaeus* which finds no analogy in the *Scholium*, which may be termed its metaphysical character. This shows itself in "its endeavour to connect the *behaviour* of things with the *formal nature* of things".[67] Or, as he states elsewhere, geometry is derivative from the physical societies constituting our epoch. The *Timaeus* type of cosmology resembles that of Concept V, where geometry is derivative from quasi-physical notions and where the behaviour of things is connected with the formal nature of things.

If we are correct in our interpretation, we ought not to conceive the development of Whitehead's philosophy as proceeding in a linear manner from his mathematical period to that of his nature philosophy, and then on to his metaphysics. We need rather to picture this development as a spiral. Whitehead's metaphysics may be said in some ways to be a return to the position of MC, from which his nature writings developed, though of course his whole account is on a higher experiential level. In his later philosophy we deal, among other things, with questions relating to sense-perception, consciousness, judgment, etc., which are not touched upon in MC. The 'spiral' interpretation of Whitehead's philosophical development meets to some extent the objections of those interpreters who reject the 'linear' interpretation on the grounds that his metaphysics seems to deal with radically new kinds of problem.[68]

APPENDIX

SUMMARY OF THE MEMOIR

Preface. The object of this memoir is to initiate the mathematical investigation of various possible ways of conceiving the nature of the material world. Five main concepts and four variants are described.

[66] PR, cf. p. 130 [143].   [67] PR 131 [144].

[68] Even in *Process and Reality* (cf. pp. 126–7 [139–140], Whitehead conceives cosmology as having a somewhat arbitrary character. In this epoch, he tells us, Maxwell's equations of the electromagnetic field hold sway. However, the arbitrary factors in the order of nature are not confined to the electromagnetic laws. There are the four dimensions of the spatio-temporal continuum, the geometrical axioms, even the mere dimensional character of the continuum—which are additional to the more basic facts of extensiveness. Even extensiveness allows of arbitrary grades.

Part I (i) General Considerations. Whitehead discusses the nature of the problem and the method of procedure. He defines what is meant by a *Concept of the Material World.* In each case it is made up of a set of fundamental relations and the entities which form the fields of these relations. These relations are of two sorts: (*a*) a multi-termed essential relation from which Euclidean geometry is derived; (*b*) extraneous relations superposed on the derived geometrical entities, and in terms of which the laws of dynamics are defined. The logical steps to be followed in constructing an axiom system are also set out.

(ii) Explanation of Symbolism. An introduction is given to the PM symbolism. Whitehead explains some of the basic concepts of symbolic logic, e.g. class-membership, propositional functions, relations, etc.

Part II. The Punctual Concepts. Three main concepts and two variants are considered. These are based on the Newtonian classical concept of the material world, which is regarded as dualistic, since it assumes an absolute space and particles of matter moving therein. The classical concept is contrasted with Leibniz's theory that space is nothing but a relation of co-existence between things. Concepts of the material world based on this theory are described as monistic.

Part III (i) General Explanations of Linear Concepts. Linear concepts are usually monistic in character. Points in these concepts are derivative from linear entities which correspond empirically to physical 'lines of force'.

(ii) The Theory of Interpoints. This theory demonstrates how points may be constructed from linear entities by means of the notion of 'similarity of position' in a pentadic essential relation.

(iii) Concept IV. This concept has two variants. In each case, points are defined in terms of the theory of interpoints. Geometrical elements—lines, planes, etc.—are constructed from points, which are now complex and have a time reference. The permanence of matter is identified with the continuity of a type of motion.

Part IV (i) The Theory of Dimensions. The number of dimensions possessed by points and other geometrical elements—in this case, three—are defined. The conception of 'flat loci' or straightness of lines is introduced, and points are defined in the manner of ideal projective points.

(ii) Concept V. Both the theory of interpoints and the theory of dimensions are used in this concept to define points and dimensions. As in Concept IV, geometrical elements are constructed from points which are complex and have a time-reference. The permanence of matter is also identified with a continuity of a type of motion.

EVA SCHAPER

AESTHETIC PERCEPTION

X

EVA SCHAPER

AESTHETIC PERCEPTION

I

Whitehead's thought on aesthetics manages to be both profound and vague at the same time. He conveys to his readers the feeling of great urgency and importance attached to the asking of aesthetic questions, and he often disappoints by the sweeping suggestiveness of his answers. There can be no doubt that Whitehead considered the study of aesthetics as still being in its infancy. Perhaps that is why his own contributions are often baffling; we seem to be asked to run before we can properly walk. Sometimes Whitehead's claims appear truly extravagant. "Indeed, when the topic of aesthetics has been sufficiently explored, it is doubtful whether there will be anything left over for discussion." He qualifies this: "But this doubt is unjustified. For the essence of great experience is penetration into the unknown, the unexperienced."[1] The qualification fails to limit the extravagance of the first statement; it merely refers us to the further extravagance of boundless experience.

A detailed and careful collation and interpretation of Whitehead's scattered remarks on aesthetic topics is badly needed. Only then will his thought on the matter be open to assessment, and possibly to criticism.

Meanwhile we can perhaps pursue some very limited and preliminary aesthetic questions in the light of Whitehead's general approach. This involves proceeding on the assumption that Whitehead would not have protested against his thought being used as a backcloth to the exploration of problems which were not formulated by him in this way. If, as Whitehead once remarked, "Philosophy asks the simple question, What is it all about?",[2] philosophical aesthetics has enough questions immediately on hand. Not only

[1] MT 86.
[2] "Analysis of Meaning", *Essays in Science and Philosophy*, New York: Philosophical Library, 1947, p. 122.

Whitehead, but many other philosophers in the Western tradition have persistently referred to the 'aesthetic mode of experience' and 'aesthetic perception'. What follows is strictly limited to an exploration of some basic questions concerning such a mode of experience. The adoption of Whiteheadian lines of thought will provide the general frame of reference; for the conclusions, however, Whitehead can not in detail be held responsible.

The phenomenology of aesthetics has always been better developed than its analysis. Thus when it comes to descriptions of the experience in question, we can draw on a fairly wide area of agreement among philosophers. I shall select and summarize what seem to me to be the most important points.

Aesthetic experience heightens the sense of subjective individuality through the intensity of enjoyment; and it evokes the awareness of compelling entities other than ourselves which lay their grip on us in such experiences. This dual aspect of deepened subjectivity and undoubted compulsion from without is often said to constitute the uniqueness of the experience. We indicate this uniqueness by speaking of the aspect of tension, of balance, of poised equilibrium, of arrested attention in moments of aesthetic concern. From the time of Plato and Aristotle, one or the other pole of this duality has come to the fore. Plato knew of the dangers of subjective ecstasy in aesthetic transport, and condemned it because it lacked the clear light of reason. Aristotle was aware of the structural qualities and formal features most likely to sustain the experience here in question, and the analysis of kinds of 'unity in variety' assumed great prominence in later Aristotelian thought. Whilst classicism throughout the ages has tried to fix on the canons and rules for objective order, harmony, beauty, and unity, romanticism throughout the ages has with equal persistence demanded concentration on the privacy of feeling and emotion, joy and delight, and the ineffable residue of subjectivity in aesthetic moments. Only a few thinkers in aesthetics have not succumbed to the temptation of reducing the experience to one or other of these extremes. Kant insisted with deep seriousness on the peculiar 'in-between' status of the aesthetic experience; his highly complex philosophical system was needed to account for it. But formulations like 'disinterested enjoyment', and 'purposiveness without purpose', have never again dropped out of the general aesthetic vocabulary; they embody Kant's recognition of the ambivalence and ambiguity, or the bi-polarity, of the aesthetic experience. Friedrich Schiller in his *Letters on the Aesthetic Education of Man* sustained the Kantian insight, and elaborated and refined its application. 'Living form' is his conceptual welding together of subjective, living, felt experience with the formal unity in the experience of aesthetic balance. The aesthetic, for Schiller, is no static moment; he saw it as the dynamics of play, involving the deepest resources of activated imagination. "Man plays only when he is in the fullest sense of the word man; and he is only wholly man when he is playing."[3] In our own time, Susanne K. Langer has made a notable contribution to aesthetic thought with the doctrine of the correlation of feeling and form, resulting in the aesthetic concept of 'felt form'; she speaks of the 'logical congruence' of feelings with objective patterns or structures. Important thinkers such as these three, and a number of others of the same order, share the conviction that in an adequate description of aesthetic experience, the privacy and ineffability of feeling must be respected as well as the formal nature of its content.

This is not the only frequently mentioned dual aspect in the aesthetic mode of experience. Two other clusters of characteristics which the aesthetic attitude is commonly supposed to possess, lend themselves to a similar presentation.

'Experiencing aesthetically' usually implies a negative assertion: we are confronting something without the wish to appropriate or possess, or to make use of it for anything but its enjoyment. This is the aspect of the experience which Kant described as its 'disinterestedness'—an attitude which is not directed towards any practical ends or moral evaluations. Nevertheless, it is not an attitude without objective content; 'disinterestedness' indicates the refusal to use the experienced object for further ends, but it clearly implies that there must be an object towards which such an attitude is taken up. 'Aesthetic distance' is a more modern concept designed to express the peculiar detachment in aesthetically arrested attention, which isolates its object, contemplates it for its own sake, not for the sake of extrinsic ends. Here again we have the factor of balance and equipoise, of sustained tension between involvement and detached contemplation. Such poised concentration is often said to reveal the object or situation which is so experienced, in its uniqueness and particularity, as against its

3 Fifteenth Letter.

generality, its similarity to others, or its implications in schemes of action. Whatever is so experienced 'for its own sake' is said to be 'fully apparent' in its concrete individuality. Aesthetic awareness, considered under this aspect, is the moment of arrested attention to the full appearance of things, situations or configurations, for no sake other than their own.

'Experiencing aesthetically' is not adequately described without reference to it as involving the sense-perception of the experiencer. Perceptual awareness appears to be a *sine qua non* of aesthetic concern. The 'here and now' of arrested attention, its peculiar presentness, is that of direct vision ('vision' is here used in the widest meaning, in which the sense of sight usually does duty for any perceptual awareness). Yet reference to mere sensory perception does not seem sufficient, and a distinction between 'ordinary perception' and 'aesthetic perception' cannot easily be dismissed. The question is how this distinction can meaningfully be made. Whilst 'ordinary perception' is not usually considered to be an end in itself, 'aesthetic perception' is best characterized by just this peculiar trait of self-sufficiency. Aesthetic perception is perception for its own sake, for no ulterior ends. Its self-sufficiency, however, is based on an amplification of sensory perception by imagination—imagination here understood in the widest sense as the power somehow to represent to consciousness what is actually absent. It is usually recognized that the imaginative activity is based on, and is even cumulative of, perceptual content. What is 'ordinarily' perceived is this or that sensory surface. But what is perceived 'aesthetically' has depth, meaning, evocative power, and a background of suggestions. Thus we acknowledge the amplifying of perception through imagination, and the suspension of activities normally following upon 'ordinary' perception, such as acting upon perceiving, judging what is perceived, or theorizing about it. Here again we have a dual aspect: the aesthetic experience is inconceivable without present perception, yet imagination, which is involved with equal necessity, transforms it into an experience endowed with dimensions which both enlarge and negate this character of pure presence; we often speak of the 'unreality' of moments of deep aesthetic experience.

To sum up so far. We are looking for an adequate account of the aesthetic mode of experience in which the following sets of features find an explanation:

(1) The dual aspect of subjective feeling and objective, formal unity or structure felt in such experiences.

(2) The dual aspect of disinterestedness, which implies that the object is experienced for its own sake, and detachment, which stresses emotional distance.

(3) The dual aspect of perceptual presentation to the senses and imaginative amplification, counterbalancing this presentness by a dimension of illusion.

II

It is here proposed that Whitehead's general theory of experience is a doctrine in terms of which these descriptions of the aesthetic experience can make sense—more sense, in fact, than in terms of alternative theories in the philosophical tradition. Perhaps the best way of introducing the Whiteheadian position is to contrast it with the alternative theory of experience which he himself explicitly rejected, namely subjectivist sensationalism, based, in the last resort, on Cartesian dualism.

Subjectivist sensationalism, in any of its variants, is patently unsuitable for the purposes of aesthetic exploration. The view that experience begins with clear-cut sensory impressions and ends with a mental synthesis of them, does not encourage any further probing for the explanation of the aesthetic experience. On such assumptions, the experiences here described as 'aesthetic' remain so incurably private that the old dictum *de gustibus non disputandum est* seems to be all that can ever be firmly asserted. Historically speaking, sensationalist doctrines from Hume onwards have not shown any conspicuous success in the field of aesthetics. This is not surprising. If one wants an explanation of experiential modes in which feelings and emotions are objectively centered, and formal structures intensively felt, the last quarter to get it from is that of a doctrine which postulates an unbridgeable gap between feelings or emotions and that which is objectively correlated with them. The disadvantage shows up not only when we are concerned with the status of feelings and emotions. Values—of whatever kind and in whatever field—are, on sensationalist grounds, derivative from subjective states, and explicable at best in terms of needs, wants, and desires, or in terms of large-scale generalizations of private subjectivity into sociological constructs. Aesthetics, which is, among other things, a study in value theory, has received harsh treatment on such grounds. The approach to it via subjectivist sensationalism has historically failed to provide satisfactory results, and must systematically fail to do so because of the dualistic assumptions to which it is committed. These assumptions postulate the separation of the subjectivity of felt experience from the objectivity of description in quantitative terms; they postulate the separation of value and matter of fact.

Whitehead's philosophy of experience is one of the great constructive alternatives of our time. Whitehead once said: " 'Value' is the word I use for the intrinsic reality of an event",[4] thereby summarizing a totally different approach to general value theory than that possible along the lines of traditional dualistic philosophy. In Whitehead's alternative, fact is not devoid of value, nor is feeling just a subjective reaction to emotionally neutral fact. Contrary to theories which regard what is felt as a private construction upon that which is simply and clearly given in sense-awareness, Whitehead considered the feeling of actual things by actual things to be absolutely basic to more high-grade and specialized experience. Here the clue to a better understanding of the aesthetic phenomena seems to suggest itself.

Whitehead's general theory of experience is a protest against philosophical dualism. For Whitehead, feeling components and emotional tones are of the essence of our contact with real things. The felt elements do not belong to the world of private subjectivity; they are as 'real' as any objectively verifiable components in an experiential situation. Whitehead's theory, to put it in very general terms, accepts two fundamental presuppositions: (1) the basic presupposition of all realism, that there is something real to be experienced, that there is a real world to be encountered in experience; and (2) the basic presupposition of all unconscious trust in the intelligibility of things, that what can be experienced at all is, in the last analysis, not totally different from the experiencing agent.

Whitehead explicitly sets out to avoid the pitfalls of the traditional subjective-objective dichotomy. The latter, whether in its radical or a more moderate form, allows the felt and enjoyed item in experience at best the status of being derivative from sensation, at worst that of being an arbitrary and purely personal idiosyn-

4 SMW 116.

crasy. It is then impossible to conceive what is 'merely' felt as in any way constituting elements of a real, common world. Whitehead aims at avoiding such a disjunction. His 'realism' considers felt experience as information about the world 'as it really is', and about the world which includes the feeling agent as an integral part. It should be noted, however, that Whitehead does not deny the legitimacy of the traditional distinction between subject and object; he only considers it a mistake if such a distinction be taken to imply an absolute distinction between different kinds of actuality. On his theory of actuality, subject and object, experiencing self and thing experienced, are not so fundamentally different as not to allow of a still further metaphysical analysis into the same generic features: active, experiencing, feeling agency—'actual entities'. 'Subject' and 'object' are useful terms on certain levels of analysis; we remember that, for Whitehead, what is subject in one situation or experiential relation will become 'objectified', i.e. object for another such situation. Seen thus, the experienced externality is not on a completely different level from that of the feeling about it.

This, considered from a slightly different angle, constitutes Whitehead's break also with the material-mental dichotomy of traditional empiricism. Whitehead does not deny the validity of speaking in terms of material particles and mechanistic relations, any more than he would reject talking about mental happenings and spiritual events. But this, he maintains, is talk on a very high level of abstraction. What is concretely there, however, is, on Whitehead's theory, basic actuality in the process of becoming. Distinctions such as 'living and dead' do not apply here. The differentiation into such special forms of existence is due to the grouping together of concretely existing entities into more complex routes and societies, so that group features can be read off. Of course, what is capable of being abstracted must in some sense be contributed by the concrete actualities. Whitehead realized this when he submitted that every basic actuality comprises in its individuality both a physical and a mental pole. Every actual thing is dual in many ways, according to contrasting features being selected for abstraction; but the whole of actuality is not split into two (or more) different kinds of entities. "Whenever a vicious dualism appears, it is by reason of mistaking an abstraction for a final concrete fact."[5]

5 AI 245.

More important for the present context are Whitehead's proposals for a general theory of perceptual experience which rejects and overcomes traditional sensationalism. Here again, Whitehead does not abandon the valid insights of the empiricist view. These had been in the main concerned with the recognition of the importance of sense-perception for manageable clarity and practical reliability. Whitehead does not deny this; but on his theory, it becomes an only partial truth. In his own doctrine of the two perceptual modes, he makes a genuinely novel and far-reaching contribution. The instances of sense-perception, upon which a person relies for all precise information, are interpreted by Whitehead as fairly high-grade occurrences in a total experiential relation. Sense-perception already presupposes omission of a great deal of experienced content; it involves selection, differentiation, rejection of irrelevance for the sake of accuracy. Sense-perception, on Whitehead's theory, is essentially an abstraction, eliciting into clarity some features of an encountered complexity to the neglect of others. Sensory details "add definition. . . . They are interpretative and not originative. What is original is the vague totality."[6] 'Vague totality' here stands for the initial contact of the experiencing agent with something other than himself. Such contact, according to Whitehead, is of the nature of active beings feeling the activities of others. Primary experience, presupposed by sensory discrimination, is the entertained feeling towards other actualities, and the entertained feeling of the definiteness of other actualities, as yet only dimly discerned. This 'confused togetherness' is the basis for conscious illumination. As against sensationalism, which regards what is felt as a private construction upon what is sense-given, Whitehead regards the feeling by actual beings of actual things as underlying and making possible the more high-grade and specialized phases of experience. "The basis of experience is emotional. Stated more generally, the basic fact is the rise of an affective tone originating from things whose relevance is given."[7]

This last passage provides a concise summary of Whitehead's groundwork for a new interpretation of the structure of experience. It can also serve as the basis for a new analysis of the structure of aesthetic experience. To remain within Whitehead's terminology, 'the rise of an affective tone' can, more technically and on a different level of analysis, be described as a 'prehension', that is to

[6] MT 149.   [7] AI 226.

say, a feeling of an entity in conformity with a datum or object in an act of experience. 'Originating from things' stresses that such prehension, though active from within, is always provoked by something else, by a real thing or situation; 'whose relevance is given' sums up the intricate interconnections between individual occasions of experience, in which the perspectives are determined as much by individual achievements in the past of the experiencing agents as by the state of the whole active environment at that particular moment. Despite the emphasis on interconnection, togetherness, and interdependence in Whitehead's analysis, it remains true to say that the 'basic fact' which is completely real, is the individual 'rise of an affective tone'. The occasion of feeling, in which the entity in question becomes itself through prehending others, is, in Whitehead's own words, a "moment of absolute self-attainment as emotional unity".[8] On Whitehead's epochal theory— which is here not considered in any detail, but presupposed—the achievement of emotional unity, however, is an attainment which cannot last. Once fully become, the entity as *this* subject is no more; its creativity has become absorbed into the becoming of future occasions. Such 'perishing'—to use a favourite term of Whitehead's —is not an annihilation, but only a transformation of subjective feeling into what can now be objectively felt. "The occasion arises from relevant objects, and perishes into the status of an object for other occasions."[9] But in between there lies the moment of sheer immediacy. It is this individual moment to which Whitehead refers not only as 'feeling' or 'prehension', but also as 'self-enjoyment'.

Let us consider the implications of a theory in which sense-perception is a secondary and derivative mode of experience, based on and dependent upon a primary mode of direct contact with things. Whitehead calls the primary mode 'causal efficacy', and the higher, derivative mode, corresponding to traditional sense-perception, he calls 'presentational immediacy'.[10] Both, however, are 'perceptual' modes—an indication that Whitehead does not wish to restrict the connotation of 'perception' to 'sense-perception'; this point will be of interest later.

To get an idea of what is meant by this 'mode of direct contact with things', it helps to think, if only for the purposes of illustra-

<hr/>

[8] AI 227.   [9] AI 227.
[10] Cf. Symb, Chap. I, § 8 and *passim*; PR Part II, Chap. II, § I; Chap. IV; Chap. VIII.

tion, of such intimate though vague experiences as the awareness of a presence in a dark room, the immediate reaction for or against a strange person, the apprehension of the atmosphere of a place as 'enchanted', 'homely', or 'haunted', the drive of sympathy towards persons or realized values in human action, etc. None of these experiences can be coherently explained as derivative from sensation and synthesis upon it. Whitehead maintains that they could fruitfully be regarded as prior to sensory recognition, vaguer in outline, but more inevitable and compelling. The instances of sense-perception are then secondary in the sense of being abstracted from concrete, direct experience in the primary mode. Such abstraction involves omission from what is originally felt, omission for the sake of clarity and manageable simplicity.

The traditional view of sense-perception as primary and feeling-tones as derivative is here inverted. Sense-perception is seen as presupposing omission. It highlights by selection from more complex experiences, making them handy and manageable. It elicits into comparative clarity some features to the neglect of others. It places the emphasis on details which can claim attention for the sake of further use and abstraction; it introduces possible perspectives for action. What is clear and simple is regarded as primary in the sensationalist tradition, with all complexity being synthetic upon it. On Whitehead's theory, this is inverted: the primitive is more complex and comprehensive, though confused, whilst clarity and simplicity are always the sophisticated result of later abstraction.

The basic mode of experience, along Whiteheadian lines, must be seen as constituting an initial phase of encounter, in which the experiencing agent is concerned with real entities whose features and structures are capable of being felt and re-enacted in experience. Whitehead proposes that feelings should be considered as re-enactions, under subjective perspectives, of the forms of definiteness of encountered or inherited actualities. Thus he avoids the pitfalls of both naïve subjectivism and naïve realism.

One more important point in summary of Whitehead's position. This basic mode of experience from which sense-perception elicits and selects, is understood as unconscious or pre-conscious. It is a mode of experience which underlies and makes possible a selection from it. Consciousness, according to Whitehead, is not itself a mode or level of experience, but an activity of attending upon something experienced. That to which it attends and from which it selects is therefore itself pre-conscious. Such an initial mode can thus never be demonstrated directly; it is postulated as that which conscious attention necessarily presupposes, as that which is required for the activity of selecting and attending to operate upon.

"What is our primary experience which lies below and gives its meaning to our conscious analysis of qualitative detail? In our analysis of detail we are presupposing a background which supplies a meaning. These vivid accidents accentuate something which is already there. We require to describe that factor in our experience which, being a matter of course, does not enter prominently into conversation. There is no need to mention it. For this reason language is very ineffective for the exposition of metaphysics.

"Our enjoyment of actuality is a realization of worth, good or bad. It is a value experience. Its basic expression is—Have a care, here is something that matters!"[11]

III

We can now return to the quest for an explanation of the features of the aesthetic experience as described earlier on. The obvious question is: What can this Whiteheadian scheme of the two perceptual modes contribute to our understanding of the 'aesthetic' experience?

Whitehead's primary mode of experience, the mode of 'causal efficacy' ('causal' stresses the element of real connection with real forces, i.e. the element of impact) certainly brings to mind a number of aspects previously described as characterizing the aesthetic experience: such as the felt contact with things, or the initial richness and suggestiveness of a background of undiscriminated experience. Yet this element of lack of definiteness and discrimination stands in the way of recognizing Whitehead's primary mode as an 'aesthetic' mode. An essentially unconscious and precognitive experience can hardly be identified with the aesthetic experience. Being a highly complex and yet conscious mode of experience on any account, it will not fit the simple role of constituting the basic phase of experience. An identification of the 'aesthetic' with 'primary' experience would leave us in no better

[11] MT 158–9.

position than that of Croce's or of other doctrines operating with the notion of 'levels of experience', and equating the aesthetic with the basic level upon which others, such as the cognitive, moral, or economic, are superimposed. The difficulties and shortcomings of such views have often enough been exposed to criticism. Theories regarding aesthetic experience as primary and primitive, as underlying all other kinds of experience, fail to explain a feature which figures prominently and necessarily in every adequate account of this mode of experience: its character of wakeful attention to experienced things, situations, or configurations, and its high degree of sophistication.

Aesthetic experience clearly involves selection, concentration, highlighting and emphasis. This brings to mind Whitehead's secondary mode of 'presentational immediacy', which is just such a mode of selection and abstraction. But it is fairly obvious that, despite the conscious, selective, and presentational character of aesthetic experience, it can no more be equated with sense-awareness than it could with basic experience. For aesthetic experience lacks the clear-cut simplicity and emotional neutrality of such a phase. An identification of the 'aesthetic' with this mode of sense-experience would hardly be able to avoid the shortcomings of a sensationalist aesthetics.

Thus Whitehead's distinction of the two perceptual modes—'causal efficacy' and 'presentational immediacy'—does not as such provide us with a ready explanation of aesthetic experience. It would certainly be detrimental to aesthetic thought to equate what we normally call 'aesthetic experience' with either Whitehead's primary experience, or with the more abstract mode of sense-awareness. Yet the Whiteheadian scheme with its distinction of perceptual modes is not therefore useless for this particular inquiry. I shall now attempt to develop some of its implications.

The secondary mode of perception has been described as a mode of abstracting from the primary concrete encounter. It will be helpful to consider the ends towards which such abstractions can be effected. This is to say that high-grade modes of experience involving abstractive phases are to be seen under the aspect of ends towards which the abstractions are aimed. In general one might say that a 'mode' of experience, when seen under this functional aspect, is the way or manner in which experience is aimed at the achievement of certain ends or purposes. For instance, the 'cognitive mode' is the mode of experiencing for cognitive ends; the 'practical mode' is the mode governed by practical purposes; 'experiencing aesthetically', then, is experiencing for aesthetic ends. Different theoretical schemes will naturally differentiate different modes. The point here is only that the analysis into modes of experience is incomplete without considering the different functions of experience, or the different purposes and ends towards which experiences can be directed.

On the theory here adopted, sense-perception is a mode of abstracting from initial complexity and basic, unconscious awareness of real things encountered and impinging. Such a mode is indispensable for purposes of everyday living and biological survival. We are familiar with this kind of selecting and abstracting in our various ordinary actions. Selection and abstraction, therefore, can take place for a variety of purposes. Through sense-perception we select for different ends and purposes—we look in order to recognize, in order to understand, in order to act upon it, in order to enjoy. Strictly speaking, the mode of sense-perception is not as such an end in itself, but always a means towards achieving certain ends. It plays an essentially mediating role, and is defined by the context in which it operates, and in which it normally goes well beyond the mere presentation of bare, abstract sensa.

All theories of perception except radical sense-data theories would agree that when we perceive something, we do not perceive a mere sensum, like a patch of colour. We perceive a coloured thing. According to Whitehead's theory of experience, this is so because the 'sensum' is a sensory feature abstracted from the initial contact with things and elicited into consciousness. The features prominently selected from the total and complex character of the encountered thing or situation are those which most readily serve the purposes of clear definition and orientation. Our attention is directed to a selection from the totality, and yet we experience this selection as a 'thing'. This amounts to saying that in the total perceptual process, we go beyond the abstracted sensum; we use the sensum for reference beyond itself. Only on rare and exceptional occasions is this process of referring arrested and perception confined, by a special effort, to the coloured patch or any other bare sensum.

On sensationalist theories, such a process of referring the sensa is usually interpreted as an inferential construction, i.e. as an act of drawing an inference from sensed items to constructed and postulated things. It is here maintained with Whitehead that there would be no basis for valid inference from the occurrence of bare sensa to objects sensed unless something real had been encountered in an initial, preceding phase. The 'inference' then becomes a 'reference' in the full sense of the word, for, on this doctrine, the sensa are abstractions from the directly experienced totality to which they subsequently refer. Only when we assume a common ground between that from which reference starts, and that to which it refers, will such occurrences as 'associations' and 'conjunctions' through and in sensory experience become explicable.

It should be noted that on the theory of experience here maintained, reference through sensa need not be confined to immediately preceding phases of initial contact and encounter. On Whitehead's doctrine of inheritance through routes of epochal agents, reference by sensa can elicit into consciousness previously encountered things or similar things encountered and felt previously. In fact, Whitehead would stress that high-grade experience draws heavily on past experience and its re-enaction under new perspectives.

When some factors in experience elicit reference to other factors, we can speak of 'symbolism', for such a process of reference, a functioning by reference, is basic to all symbolic action. Symbolization occurs in any relation in which present components elicit a reference to something else. An item in experience becomes a symbol when it functions in a specific way, namely when it elicits, by reference, some other item—such as a concept, an image, an emotion, a feeling—as its meaning.[12] This covers 'natural' as well as all kinds of 'artificial' and 'conventional' symbolism. The 'symbol' is any item from which a reference starts; whatever item, or set of items, is elicited in the process of reference is the 'meaning' of that symbol. With this very general conception of symbolization, 'items' may be components of experience, and elicited factors may be derived from antecedent experience, often embodying, in a complex way, the results of earlier symbolic references. This provides the ground for, though it does not, of course, give an account of, the complexity of high-grade symbolisms such as, for example, that

---

[12] Cf. Symb 9: "The human mind is functioning symbolically when some components of its experience elicit consciousness, beliefs, emotions, and usages respecting other components of its experience."

occurring in language—into the discussion of which I shall, however, not enter. Here I am only concerned with what can be gained by the application of this conception of symbolism to the analysis of experiential modes and functions as so far considered.[13]

Since, on Whitehead's doctrine, the items experienced in sense-perception are not sterile sensa, but are capable of eliciting other components, i.e. capable of referring beyond themselves, we can now think of sensory reference as a kind of symbolization. Indeed, it may well be that this is the most primitive instance of symbolization. Sensa in the mode of 'presentational immediacy' are abstractions from the basic, confused, encountered contact, selected and brought to consciousness. In ordinary perception, the sensa do not remain thus abstract, but function by reference to the things or complex situations from which they have been abstracted. As Whitehead says, "when human experience is in question, 'perception' almost always means 'perception in the mixed mode of symbolic reference' ".[14] "Symbolic reference between the two perceptive modes afford the main example of the principles which govern all symbolism."[15] It should be noted that with this account of symbolic functioning, the possibility of error is admitted. In general it means that the information gained in complex experience, when it involves phases of symbolic reference, may be mistaken. There is no guarantee for correct referring. Thus Whitehead's stark epistemological realism is tempered by his doctrine of symbolism, and yet remains 'objective'.

Symbolic reference through sensory items is by no means always of the same kind. We recall what has been said earlier about different ends and purposes of high-grade experiences, constituting the modal differences. Also, we recall that sensory perception has already been specified as an intermediate mode. Thus we can say

[13] Whitehead's main concern in *Symbolism: Its Meaning and Effect* is with high-grade social symbolisms, including those of language and the arts. His account of the symbolism of sense-perception, as well as the account of the two perceptual modes, is very brief and compressed, although important references to it are scattered through the whole book. Also the discussion in *Process and Reality* (Part II, Chap. VIII), though more detailed, does not carry us much further in this respect. However, Whitehead clearly indicates that he regards the perceptual symbolism as basic to the more sophisticated kinds. Cf. Symb 3: "There is still another symbolism more fundamental than any of the foregoing types [language, mathematics, art] . . ." and Symb 5: "Symbolism from sense-presentation to physical bodies is the most natural and widespread of all symbolic modes."

[14] PR 236 [255–6].   [15] PR 254 [274].

that the symbolic operation of sense-perception differs as to ends and purposes, and accordingly forms part of different high-grade experiential modes. Sensory symbols can elicit as their meanings different aspects of the original felt totality, depending upon the ends and purposes towards which they abstract. Aesthetic ends and purposes constitute one among other possibilities, for not only in aesthetic experience does the intermediate mode of sense-perception fulfil a symbolic function. We can distinguish a number of modes which have the symbolic operation of sense-perception in common, but which nevertheless differ profoundly in what they achieve via this symbolic stage. The most common purpose towards which normal human sense-perception operates—so common that it is often mistaken for the only end and purpose of sense-perception—is that of recognition and understanding. This mode can be described as the conceptual or cognitive mode. No more than an outline of its analysis is here attempted. But such an outline is helpful. For it is by comparison and contrast with this more common function that we can best appreciate the distinctive character of the aesthetic experience.

In both the cognitive and the aesthetic modes, the items perceived in sensory awareness are abstracted from initially felt contact. These abstractions function symbolically, that is to say, sensory details, when experienced as symbols, refer to, or elicit, something else or something more. This is where the difference between cognitive and aesthetic purpose of experience becomes obvious; it is the difference in the features elicited as meanings from the initial contact, depending upon the ends governing the symbolic reference.

Let us first consider the symbolic operation for cognitive ends. Knowledge, cognition, recognition—whether for further practical purposes or for the further purposes of purely theoretical understanding—is based upon the discerning of the general features of things, i.e. the features by virtue of which we can compare and differentiate, establish relationships and differences. In experiences directed towards cognitive ends, therefore, the role of sensory symbols is that of eliciting to consciousness the general features of things or situations. That is to say, if the end of an experience via the mediation of sense-perception be that of orientation, understanding, conceptual grasp, etc., then the sensory symbols direct attention towards what the experienced things or situations mean in their generality, in their general form.

By contrast, sense-perception plays a very different role in experiences directed towards aesthetic ends. Sensory abstractions, i.e. abstracted details, are, as in the cognitive mode, experienced for their symbolic reference. But in the aesthetic mode, sensory symbols refer not to general formal features, but to the formal features as felt in the primary phase of contact. They elicit to consciousness not the bare generality of things, but the forms of things as initially and unconsciously felt. What was basically felt does not, and cannot, rise into consciousness as a total complex; for what is wholly concrete is not as such recognizable, since recognition involves discrimination which presupposes at least some abstraction.

Aesthetic experience is thus no less abstract than conceptual understanding; both involve sensory abstractions from the concrete act of encounter. The difference lies in the kind of features they elicit to consciousness as meanings: formal features in their generality in the case of cognitive experience, and formal features as felt in the case of aesthetic experience. When sensed items are entertained aesthetically—or entertained in the aesthetic mode—we can therefore with equal correctness say that they are entertained as aesthetic symbols. Aesthetic symbols bring to consciousness those formal features in the past contact with things which embody the relation between experiencing agent and experienced world—not, as in cognitive abstraction, only the generalized features of the objects. In cognitively directed experience, what matters are those formal features which can be stated and repeated in more or less complete independence of the initial situation of encounter. What matters in aesthetic experience are those formal features as they were previously felt in their uniqueness. Both these modes of experience must abstract, both can only focus on abstractions from the concrete togetherness. But whilst the cognitive mode uses sensory symbols exclusively to highlight what can be known in dissociation from the particular preceding act of primary experience, the aesthetic mode uses sensory symbols to highlight, and thus to bring into dispassionate consciousness, the form of feeling, i.e. that which can be symbolized of the concrete and confused encounter which would otherwise remain an ineffable and inarticulately private background of involvement.

In both these complex modes, sense-perception is instrumental towards something else: either towards recognition of general features, or towards eliciting the 'feel of' forms. In both cases, sense-perception functions symbolically, directing attention to meanings. The difference in functioning is the difference of the ends and purposes of the two modes.

IV

We are now in a position to return to the three sets of characteristics of the aesthetic mode which were listed earlier on as being in need of an explanation. The theoretical framework provided so far is admittedly very sketchy, and the problematic character of a large number of issues raised has hardly been touched upon. Application of the foregoing general theory of experience to a few assorted questions concerning the 'aesthetic mode' of experience should therefore be taken as more in the nature of confirming the promise of the theory than of establishing its detailed validity.

(1) We mentioned in the first place one dual aspect of such experiences: aesthetic experiences are emotionally charged and yet, far from being private day-dreams, they are experiences of something compelling and definite. In the history of aesthetic thought, this combination has been recognized in theories which treat 'unity in variety' or 'felt harmony' as key-concepts. Deeply felt and yet objectively centred, concerned in equal measure with individual attitudes towards things and with formal structures discerned—this should now make sense in the light of the foregoing considerations.

If we hold with Whitehead that feeling is basic experience, feeling of actualities by actualities, and if we further bear in mind that the primary phase of felt contact is as such unconscious, we see the importance of regarding the aesthetic as a complex, high-grade mode. Whilst involving abstraction in sensation, the sensory symbols refer, as it were, back to the feeling-relation from which they were initially abstracted. At the same time, the sensory details emphasize and highlight some of the formal features of the things encountered, through which alone the felt relation can be symbolized: the sensible features of things. The joint awareness of feeling and form in conscious discrimination is thus one of the basic traits of the aesthetic mode. Absolute concreteness, as well as sheer individuality, though the basis for all further discrimination, can never be incorporated *in toto* in a higher conscious mode. Aesthetic experience, through aesthetically directed symbolic functioning of sense-perception, comes nearer than any other mode to re-capturing the initial encounter with things, the 'feel of' things. This is why we so easily speak of the aesthetic mode as being more concrete, more concerned with unique particularity, than other modes. But it is not therefore identical with primitive, primary experience. For of equal importance is its highly wakeful character, its concentration on the forms of things encountered. The aesthetic attitude can be described as conscious attention to the given definiteness of felt things. 'Conscious' attention, because it involves sense-perception which always is abstractive and selective; 'given' definiteness of things, because without present data, there could be no symbolic function; 'definiteness' of 'felt' things, because the symbolic reference is to structural features, albeit as felt.

Thus the description of the aesthetic experience as an emotion-ally charged experience is on this analysis not only compatible with, but directly required by, its being an experience of the formal features of experienced things.

(2) In the second place, another related duality of characteristics was listed in the descriptive account of the aesthetic experience. 'Disinterestedness', i.e. absence of any extrinsic purpose, and 'detachment', i.e. isolation from merely personal involvement in the felt experience—these are among the attributes of the aesthetic experience which no description can afford to leave out. Tradi-tionally, the aspect of disinterestedness figures in all theories which insist on the autonomy of the aesthetic experience, on the factor of freedom, of non-commitment, and even of play. And the aspect of detachment as here understood figures in all those theories which speak of 'psychic distance', or of balance and equipoise, and of the contemplative factor in the aesthetic attitude.

Both disinterestedness and detachment are explicable on the theory here advanced. Sensory symbols can function in various ways, for instance, as signposts for action, as generalizing aids for cognition, or as pointers to previously established contact. But the same item cannot function in two different ways at once. Function-ing symbolically in two different ways would entail duplication of the symbol. This is not to exclude multiple reference of a symbol, but only multiplication of the kind of function a symbol can have at one and the same time. Thus whilst a symbol functions aestheti-cally, it cannot, at the same time, be used as a symbol facilitating practical action or theoretical recognition. When an item or a set of items refers symbolically to the felt background, it cannot simultaneously function as a symbol pointing, as it were, in the opposite direction, to further abstraction towards practical or conceptual ends. This means that attention is arrested by the sensory details and directed not onwards, but inwards, into the felt background of experience. Such a symbolic reference does not allow of any other kind of reference at the same time, although, of course, other references starting from the same sensory details are perfectly possible at other times. A thing may be experienced aesthetically now, and cognitively, i.e. as an instance of this or that kind, later.

Here the 'fully apparent' character of an object in aesthetic awareness also finds its explanation. Sensory symbols, when functioning aesthetically, remain present to the senses, thus ruling out any other reference through the same sensory features, which would allow the intrusion of concern for the future, of speculation or utilization—all destructive of the total absorption in the full present.

'Detachment' concerns the isolation from emotional upheaval, and it is thus the counterpart to 'disinterestedness', which refers to the disconnection from all engagement in the future. 'Detachment' stresses the distance from the primary impact, from the direct involvement with things—just as 'disinterestedness' stresses the other kind of distancing, that from concern with further and future ends. On our theory, the primary mode of contact was seen to be basic to all high-grade experience. 'Detachment' emphasizes that the aesthetic mode is no mere relapse into this primitive, emotional phase. If there cannot be any aesthetic awareness without sensory awareness, then the element of consciousness is already admitted as essential; consciousness, we recall, means selection, selection from mere unconscious feeling. When attention in the aesthetic attitude becomes arrested by sensory items functioning symbolically, the focusing upon these more or less clear-cut features detaches the experiencer from mere entanglement and strong personal involvement such as it must be felt in the confusion of direct contact. The initial contact is now symbolically evoked, not re-enacted *in toto*. This means that the agent is now aware of *what* it is he feels—he no longer merely feels it. Symbolization through conscious discrimination of features in the aesthetic mode means distancing from the closeness of mere impact, without, however, losing that aspect of the felt relation which can be symbolically elicited.

(3) The interplay of sense-perception and imagination in the aesthetic mode was the last of the three topics mentioned in the beginning as posing problems for explanation. On the theory here given along Whiteheadian lines, this should now also fall into place. In order to have aesthetic experience at all, it is absolutely essential that something should be present to the senses. What is present and fully apparent are the sensory items, the sensed qualities, clear and manageable, and, on the theory here adopted, abstract. In order to function as symbols, they have to be present and apparent. During the process of reference, they remain important as pure sensory items. The meanings they elicit are not themselves further abstractions, but part of the fuller, felt relations of the initial contact. Aesthetic symbols, unlike other symbols, are therefore not just important for what they mean; they are not simply replaceable by their meanings, for they must themselves remain present for the reference to be effected. But not all symbols needed for the cumulative reference can be actually present at the same time. One has to allow for symbols which are not actually there, but present only in imagination. Imagination is here understood as achieving the gathering of previous sensory symbols into cumulative presentation over a stretch of time. The actually present sensory data are thus supplemented by the introduction of imagined, i.e. non-actual, presences.

In traditional aesthetic discourse, the term 'sensory surfaces' is often used to refer to this presentational aspect of aesthetic experiences. Such a term, however, also suggests that sensory surfaces are not all that matters, for 'surfaces' are usually surfaces of something (the visual metaphor must, of course, be understood as covering all sensory aspects). Nothing but these sensory 'surfaces' are 'given' in the full sense of being present. The symbolic reference elicits, in the aesthetic mode, as meanings of these sensory symbols the felt relations from the immediate past. The retention or recalling of past events in the widest sense belongs to what is traditionally called 'imagination'. Whitehead is at one with David Hume in conceiving imagination as a retentive, reflexive activity. On Whitehead's theory, however, with the inversion of the empiricist account of the primacy of sense-data, sensory perception must needs be abstraction from the full contact, and imaginative retention then becomes explicable as symbolic reference to past, felt relations. When perception functions for aesthetic ends, it is directed towards re-capturing as much of the previously felt contact as can be symbolized by sensory symbols. In the aesthetic mode, perception is thus amplified by imagination.

Such amplified perception is what we have earlier on called 'aesthetic perception'. We are now in a position to make sense of the apparently puzzling assertion that aesthetic perception is 'perception for its own sake', 'for no ulterior ends or purposes'. Seen strictly etymologically, 'aesthetic perception' comes close to being a tautology, $\alpha \math"iota\sigma\theta\eta\sigma\iota s$ being the Greek word for 'perception'. But etymology is here not decisive; nor is it, however, completely irrelevant. 'Aesthetic' is not—and never was—a synonym for 'perceptual'; but the etymological derivation points to an important connection, recognized in every worth-while analysis of the experience here in question, namely the connection between sensory awareness, actual or imagined, and aesthetic awareness. In its full Greek sense, $\alpha \math"iota\sigma\theta\eta\sigma\iota s$ was not restricted to sense-perception. Plato's use of it in the *Theaetetus*,[16] rather than Kant's use in "Transcendental Aesthetic" in the *Critique of Pure Reason* is relevant here. On the basis of Whitehead's theory of experience for which I have argued, it becomes both terminologically useful and philosophically tenable to resurrect the wider meaning of 'perception'. 'Perception' in this wider sense then covers all experiential contact with things, whether conscious or unconscious; whilst 'sense-perception' covers only the restricted field of conscious attention to sensory abstractions. Whitehead, as I have already pointed out, refers to both the initial phase of direct, but indiscriminate contact—the mode of 'causal efficacy'—and the derivative, clear and conscious sense-perception—the mode of 'presentational immediacy'—as 'perceptual' modes. Thus we have yet another way of describing the difference of the aesthetic from other complex modes of experience. For we can distinguish between perceptual and non-perceptual ends of the symbolic functioning of sense-perception. In aesthetic experience, sense-perception symbolically brings to consciousness some important factors of the initial and primary perceptual basis; i.e. sense-perception functions for 'perceptual' ends. The aesthetic mode can be contrasted in this respect too with other high-grade modes—cognitive understanding,

[16] Cf. F. M. Cornford, *Plato's Theory of Knowledge*, London, 1935, p. 30.

r example. In the latter, sense-perception can also function
ymbolically—not, however, as referring back to the earlier percep-
ual basis of felt contact, but as facilitating yet further abstractions;
e. sense-perception here functions for 'non-perceptual' ends. On
his theory it makes sense to say that 'aesthetic perception' is
perception for its own sake', or 'for no ulterior ends'. In a way, the
Platonic sense of αἴσθησις is here restored: when sense-perception
unctions *aesthetically*, 'perception' in the fullest sense is achieved.

HERMANN WEIN

IN DEFENCE OF THE HUMANISM OF SCIENCE: KANT AND WHITEHEAD

XI

HERMANN WEIN

IN DEFENCE OF THE HUMANISM OF SCIENCE: KANT AND WHITEHEAD [1]

I

Some remarks about the present-day decline in the relationship between Philosophy and Science

(*a*) At the height of a scientific one-world civilization such as ours at this historical stage, paradoxically enough the question arises whether science has anything to do with humanism. The purpose of science is regarded as the technical exploitation of the world in the ideology of Karl Marx on the one hand, and in Martin Heidegger's doctrine of the 'technical appropriation of the world' (*'technische Weltbemächtigung'*) on the other.

Few thinkers still defend the humanism of scientific procedure. Among the few who do, the connection with Kant is noticeable in the work of Charles Sanders Peirce, Nicolai Hartmann, and Karl Jaspers. As regards Alfred North Whithead, the following remarks are designed to show the relevance of his philosophy to a humanistic interpretation of science.

(*b*) At the present time, Whitehead's characteristic conception of the achievements of rational thought as 'adventures of ideas' represents a bridgehead. In the tradition, Kant represents a bridgehead for the endeavour to incorporate science into the structure of humanistic modes of realization. I am thinking of his deeply serious conception of the knowledge of nature as a questioning of nature by the 'judicial' reason of man. Both these formulae of Whitehead and Kant controvert clearly enough the utilitarian and instrumentalist conception of science, and the identification of 'science' and 'technology'. They make clear that the search for truth is deeply rooted in human nature. What this means can best be seen by confronting it with opposing, non-humanistic conceptions of science, which, at least in Germany at the present time, have largely pushed into the background the influence of Kantian critical thinking.

[1] Translated from the German by Eva Schaper.

"Science is enclosed in its own procedure, and closed against metaphysical speculation. It is enclosed in the absolute light and clarity of the vision which is sure of itself. Its knowledge is certain knowledge, valid for everybody; but it moves in ignorance of what it is, whence it comes, and what that is with which it deals. Not only is it thus ignorant on three scores; but the kind of knowledge it has even debars it from recognizing this ignorance. By fully unfolding itself, it completely forgets its own nature and origin. This forgetting, however, is not due to any lack of clarity and light, but rather to the dazzling of thought by the light of self-certainty. This dazzling results in presumptuousness, for modern science claims to possess the basic kind of knowledge and of what is knowable. It is this light, so sure of itself, which obscures what *is*. This infinitely extending clarity obscures being. But is not then the light of the self-certainty of modern knowledge, enclosed in itself, really a kind of darkness with regard to, and from the standpoint of, being? The light which hinders the seeing of that which is, is darkness even if it deludes itself into believing that it is the purest light. If this be the case, no difference will be made by enlarging and supplementing the knowledge of contemporary science, or by substituting another kind of knowledge, such as the Greek ἐπιστήμη or the medieval *scientia*, or even a kind of knowledge still to be invented. All enlarging and supplementing, all positing and substituting remain within the domain of a reason which is based on its own legislation."[2]

Here science is to be excluded from the 'real'. Behind such a conception stands Heidegger's philosophy. "Some thinkers nowadays appear to be struggling with the need to find for the workings of modern technology, and of modern science which is identical with it [*sic!*], a conception of history in which the state of the world produced by these workings can be accommodated and made intelligible. But even if this were successful, modern technology and the science assigned to it would still remain unknown in its essential nature."[3] Here and in other statements of existentialist philosophy, 'science' is the name for a catastrophe of mankind; for Heidegger science is '*Seinsvergessenheit*', 'forgetfulness of being'.

[2] Karl Heinz Volkmann-Schluck, *Die Wandlung des Wissens in sein neuzeitliches Wesen, Vortrag im Rahmen des Studium Generale an der Universität Köln*, 27 January 1953, p. 12.

[3] Martin Heidegger, "Aufzeichnungen aus der Werkstatt", in *Neue Züricher Zeitung*, No. 264.

Philosophy in particular has nothing to expect and nothing to hope for from science.[4]

(c) This assessment is destructive (in the full sense of the word) of the rational conception of philosophy in the Graeco-European tradition. In this conception, "its sole preoccupation is wisdom; and it seeks it by the path of science, which, once it has been trodden, can never be overgrown, and permits of no wandering. Mathematics, natural science, even our empirical knowledge, have a high value as means, for the most part, to contingent ends, but also, in the ultimate outcome, to ends that are necessary and essential to humanity."[5] According to the opposite, the existentialist assessment, the co-operation of philosophy and science, with its tradition in ancient Greece, in the Western Europe of the modern era, and in the Germany of the age of Enlightenment, is rejected *a priori*. With it is also rejected the life-work of two great thinkers of science and philosophy of the present age: Nicolai Hartmann's and A. N. Whitehead's conception of a philosophical cosmology.

(d) Today the problem is how neither to ignore the fundamental relation between science and the modern world, nor, at the other extreme, to allow philosophy to be wholly dominated and guided by science—to which the office of 'censorship' is then conceded. This second extreme is demonstrated on the one hand by the so-called 'progressive' materialistic world-view, and on the other hand by what lies between the *philosophie positive* of Auguste Comte and the 'physicalism' of Rudolf Carnap during the twenties and thirties in this century.

Heidegger is right in this: science, when excluded from the structure and balance of humanistic modes of realization, *is* a catastrophe.

(e) In what follows, such a conception of science will be confronted with, first, the 'open system' of Kant's *Critiques*, where the centre of gravity lies in human reason; and secondly, with A. N. Whitehead's basic aim "to construct a system of ideas which bring the aesthetic, moral, and religious interests into relation with those concepts of the world which have their origin in natural science",[6]

---

[4] Cf. Martin Heidegger, *Platons Lehre von der Wahrheit. Mit einem Brief über den 'Humanismus'*, Bern, 1947.

[5] Kant, *Critique of Pure Reason*, B 878. All quotations from the *Critique of Pure Reason* (hereafter KRV) are in the translation by Norman Kemp Smith (London: Macmillan & Co., 1933).

[6] PR vi [vi].

an aim expressed in *Process and Reality*, in *Science and the Modern World*, and in *Adventures of Ideas*.[7]

(*f*) There remains a profound difference between Kant and Whitehead. But under the aspect of opposition against isolating science and making it absolute, or degrading and de-humanizing science, we can name Kant and Whitehead together in this crisis of the present age. They both exhibit as men and as philosophers—or, to use a fashionable term, they exhibit 'existentially'—the synthesis of science and philosophical humanism; their 'being philosophers' culminates in the striving for just this synthesis.

(*g*) In German post-Kantian thought, Fichte's *Wissenschaftslehre* and Hegel's and Schelling's philosophy of nature destroyed the incorporation of science in philosophy which had been unquestioned throughout the ages. They divorced and contrasted philosophical pretension and scientific sobriety. Afterwards the later nineteenth century produced a number of philosophical 'isms' in the wake of the sciences which had by then become self-righteous, and been enlarged into *Weltanschauungen*: materialism, positivism, historicism, logical empiricism.

The small band of present-day thinkers who are seeking to re-establish the proper relation between science and the humanities are thus engaged in a renaissance of a 'cosmos' of civilization, such as Kant, Goethe, Alexander and Wilhelm von Humboldt—to give German examples—once stood for.

(*h*) There is a peculiar kinship, transcending the boundaries of countries and languages, between those thinkers who make the ages of synthesis of science and philosophy their point of departure. Thus there are remarkable and far-reaching convergences between A. N. Whitehead and Nicolai Hartmann—contemporaries who knew each other by name, but not through their work.[8] The

---

[7] Despite the estrangement between Whitehead and Bertrand Russell in later life, there remains something in common between the two. Russell says, "philosophy has always been important to him as an instrument for the rational defence and justification of some extra-philosophical body of beliefs: first religion, then mathematics, finally science". Anthony Quinton, "Russell's Philosophical Development", *Philosophy*, XXXV (1960), p. 2.

[8] Cf. Hermann Wein, *Zugang zu philosophischer Kosmologie, Überlegungen zum philosophischen Thema der Ordnung in nach-kantischer Sicht*, München, 1954; "The Categories and a Logic of Structure", *The Journal of Philosophy*, XLIX/20 (1952); "Nicolai Hartmann's 'Kategorialanalyse' und die Idee eine 'Strukturlogik', in *Nicolai Hartmann, Der Denker und Sein Werk*, ed. H. Heimsoeth und R. Heiss, Göttingen, 1952. Also Jitendra Nath Mohanty, *Nicolai Hartmann and Alfred North Whitehead*, Calcutta, 1957.

relevance of the philosophies of Kant, Hartmann, and Whitehead to our present age consists, among other things, in their being able to form a counterweight to (1) the isolation of philosophy and science from each other, (2) dogmatic rationalism, and (3) dogmatic empiricism.[9] Nicolai Hartmann and A. N. Whitehead explicitly opposed the wholesale dismissal of problems (*Problemkehraus*, in Hartmann's words) by the positivistic and logistic movements in our century,[10] in the course of which the so-called 'scientific philosophy' became an *ancilla scientiarum*, and all other philosophy was declared to be 'verbal magic'. Whitehead's *Process and Reality, An Essay in Cosmology*, and Nicolai Hartmann's *Der Aufbau der Realen Welt* and *Philosophie der Natur* may well stand in something like a 'splendid isolation' among the philosophical literature of our time. But these works which draw on science are, in the life-work of both thinkers, harmoniously integrated with the philosophical treatment of value questions, of aesthetics, and of philosophy of civilization. In their opposition to the fashionable philosophical style which furthers the isolation of science under one or other aspect, both Hartmann and Whitehead take their orientation from the great landmarks in the history of thought.

(*i*) Hartmann's 'critical ontology' continues from Kant, the critic of dogmatic ontology. To take up the pre-Kantian tradition of unified philosophy and science is one of the leading ideas of Whitehead's *Essay in Cosmology*. Whitehead's general "reliance on the positive value of the philosophical tradition"[11] encourages us to look for the positive side in his otherwise not too close relation to Kant, the destroyer of an uncritical *cosmologia rationalis* as a closed deductive system.[12]

(*j*) The contemporary fashion of denying any relevance whatever to *philosophical* cosmology can be met by a polemical reference to what lies behind it. Today we sometimes do not see the wood for the trees, that is to say, we do not see physics for nuclear

[9] Cf. Hermann Wein, "Heutiges Verhältnis und Missverhältnis von Philosophie und Naturwissenschaft", *Philosophia Naturalis*, Vol. 1, 1/2, Meisenheim am Glan, 1950.

[10] Cf. Morton White, *The Age of Analysis*, A Mentor Book, New York, 1955, p. 17: ". . . most philosophers in the logico-analytic tradition shy away from the issues of public and personal life, from the problems of culture and practice, as though they are of no importance to philosophers."

[11] PR ix [ix].

[12] Cf. Christian Wolff, *Philosophia prima sive ontologia*, 1729; and *Cosmologia generalis*, 1731.

physics, we do not see *natura naturans* for atomic power, and we do
not see the genuine scholar of nature in the fashion of a Spinoza
or a Newton or an Alexander von Humboldt for all the politicizing
and philosophizing nuclear physicists.

(*k*) Immanuel Kant was, in the first place, a philosopher who
was productively engaged in mathematics and natural science, as
the last in the line of the classics. He was in this respect not of the
stature of the very great, such as Descartes, Newton, or Leibniz.
But his geometrical and cosmogonical grasp was up to the best of
his time. In the second place, he was one of the absolutely sincere
and pure thinkers, like Galileo, Pascal, or Spinoza.

In both these respects Whitehead continues in the Kantian
tradition as it has grown out of Western thought at the age of
Enlightenment; but he also gave it new directions. That Whitehead
does not continue the 'idealism' which neo-Kantians later found in
Kant, is obvious. We shall return to this point later. The formulation used by Kant to characterize his own philosophy, 'empirical
realism *and* transcendental idealism', does apply in its relational
mechanics to the most difficult part of Whitehead's philosophy,
namely, to the relation of 'actual entities' and 'eternal objects'.[13]
The relata in this relation, it is true, are of a different nature from
those in Kant's relation. Whitehead's 'actual entities' and 'eternal
objects' were developed from a deep penetration into post-
Einsteinian natural science. The relata of the Kantian formula,
'appearances' and 'things-in-themselves', are the result of the
epistemology—or better, of the philosophical theory—of 'classical'
natural science under the fused influence of Newton and Leibniz
on the one hand, and Locke and Hume on the other.

II

The Philosophical Office of 'Censorship' according to Kant

Kant's doctrine of nature as the totality of appearances aims at
something which, even today, we have not sufficiently thought
out. One of his most profound, most compressed, and to us most
relevant remarks about the concept of 'appearance' runs as follows:
"For in an appearance the objects, nay even the properties that we
ascribe to them, are always regarded as something actually given.
Since, however, in the relation of the given object to the subject,

[13] Cf. J. N. Mohanty, *op. cit.*, p. 45 f.

such properties depend upon the mode of intuition of the subject, this object as *appearance* is to be distinguished from itself as object *in itself*. Thus when I maintain that the quality of space and of time, in conformity with which, as a condition of their existence, I posit both bodies and my own soul, lies in my mode of intuition and not in those objects in themselves, I am not saying that bodies merely *seem* to be outside me, or that my soul only *seems* to be given in my self-consciousness. It would be my own fault, if out of that which I ought to reckon as appearance, I made mere illusion."[14] Kant's doctrine of appearance is directed towards a third term besides 'subject' and 'object', namely towards the relation between the two, in which subjective and objective traits are interwoven. This, among other aspects, is expressed by the formula, 'empirical realism—transcendental idealism'.

Here it is not a question of a compromise between realism and idealism. The point lies elsewhere. Kant's proudest word is: "What the things-in-themselves may be I do not know, nor do I need to know...."[15] When we here emphasize the word 'know', we see that this sentence in its critical recognition of the extent and limitations of the sphere of human activity goes far beyond the central phenomenon of modern Europe—the age of Enlightenment; it even goes beyond the whole Graeco-European optimism *and* pessimism as to the possibility of ontology—that is to say, metaphysics *and* anti-metaphysics—since the time of Plato and Aristotle, or the Sophists and the Sceptics respectively. I refer to the belief in the knowability of 'being as such', ὄντως ὄν, on the one hand, and, on the other hand, the despair at not being able to gain any knowledge of this superhuman sphere.

With the sentence quoted above, Kant makes room for science. That is to say, science is autonomous in its own sphere. Only the 'censorship' of philosophy is above it—but not of a philosophy which insists on either radical knowledge or radical ignorance, and on subjecting science to this claim. This is the position into which Kant puts natural science. Beyond it he sees—but only in respect of the practical activities of man—a place left free, and with this his controversial word is concerned: "I have therefore found it necessary to deny *knowledge*, in order to make room for *faith*."[16] Here 'knowledge' refers to dogmatic rationalism, and 'faith' refers to the possibility and duty of going beyond the sphere of the

14 KRV, B 69.   15 KRV, B 333.   16 KRV, B xxx.

science of appearances in our practical, moral self-realization. These distinctions represent a consequence and a transcending of the thought of the Enlightenment.

In critically adjusting the ontological optimism so characteristic of the great philosophers and scientists who initiated the modern era, Kant stands at the threshold of the historical consciousness of the present. He does not actually make the point that the relation between subject and object of knowledge varies as between epochs, civilizations, and linguistic structures. But Kant prepared the way for the recognition of the historicity of all human knowledge; he undoubtedly belongs to the line leading from Luther to Hegel and after. Such a relation between what is subjective and what is objective is an entirely dynamic relation. In analysing knowledge Kant starts from action, or better, from the interplay of 'spontaneity' and 'receptivity'. What is not affected by human understanding in this sense, and by the progress of human knowledge in general, i.e. what is static and 'being as such', remains outside the human sphere, and need not concern active man. This holds in the widest sense. The human sphere of knowledge is that of action. Achievement in this sphere happens through step-by-step progress and regress. Kant's famous chapter on the antinomies of human reason is opposed to all views which ignore the historicity of human action. It is opposed to the view that human knowledge can have anything to say about the beginning and the end of the world, about the ultimate elements, about the totality of being, as it had been presumed in the systems of the rationalists (Kant calls them 'dogmatists'); and it is equally opposed to the view that human knowledge could make final statements about the physical observation of the world—a view which Kant summarizes as 'empiricism'. The present tendencies towards a 'physicalism', towards construction of the 'logical structure of the world', etc., also remain 'restricted' by the active nature of man. Under the aspect of 'adventures of ideas', philosophy even today must seek the mean between metaphysical dogmatism and anti-metaphysical dogmatism. If we nowadays wish to avoid the extremes which ignore the connection of all human activities—including the pursuit of science and rational thinking—with man's fallibility and historicity, we would do well to remember Whitehead's works: "Rationalism never shakes off its status of an experimental adventure. The combined influences of mathematics and religion, which have so greatly contributed to the rise of philosophy, have also had the unfortunate effect of yoking it with static dogmatism. Rationalism is an adventure in the clarification of thought, progressive and never final. But it is an adventure in which even partial success has importance."[17]

Philosophy must make a 'transcendental' distinction between science as it is possible for human beings, and total knowledge of 'being as such' (Kant spoke of the *Ding an sich*, translating *ens a se* into German) as it is not possible for human beings. Whitehead detests the 'transcendentalists'.[18] He does not speak of 'things-in-themselves'; but he restricts his statements to 'our cosmic epoch'. Thus he agrees in at least one important respect with Kant's criticism of dogmatic rationalism.

'Reason' in opposition against all 'dogmatism' serves 'practical' humanity and the 'whole vocation' of man in the world. One must, of course, understand these terms first in their specifically Kantian sense. The spirit of the age of Goethe and Schiller is alive in them. But the ascetic severity of Kantian morality can also be found in them: "Such, then, in general, is the idea of metaphysics. At first more was expected from metaphysics than could reasonably be demanded, and for some time it diverted itself with pleasant anticipations. But these hopes having proved deceptive, it has now fallen into general disrepute. . . . We can therefore be sure that however cold or contemptuously critical may be the attitude of those who judge a science not by its nature but by its accidental effects, we shall always return to metaphysics as to a beloved one with whom we have had a quarrel. For here we are concerned with essential ends—ends with which metaphysics[19] must ceaselessly occupy itself, either in striving for genuine insight into them, or in refuting those who profess already to have attained it. . . . That, as a mere speculation, it serves rather to prevent errors than to extend knowledge, does not detract from its value. On the contrary this gives it dignity and authority, through that censorship which secures general order and harmony, and indeed the well-being of the scientific commonwealth. . . ."[20]

These sentences from the end of Kant's *Critique of Pure Reason* point to the real 'interest' of human reason. Reason exercises the 'censorship' for the sake of essential 'ends'. But these culminate in

---

[17] PR 12 [14].   [18] Cf., e.g., PR 9 [11].
[19] Kant is here speaking of *critical* metaphysics.   [20] KRV, B 877–9.
K*

the human positing of ends,[21] in the autonomous legislation of man who is morally free. The autonomy of man alone thus stands above the autonomy of science.

With this Kant reached a *tertium* as against the most stirring philosophical disjunction in modern Europe. The antinomy in the modern post-Galilean epoch had been this: methodical, measuring and calculating science which was rapidly advancing towards the leading intellectual position, raised doubts as to whether the concepts of God and the soul in Christian metaphysics had really been refuted by the scientific cosmology, or whether they could not rather be proved by a strictly scientific metaphysics. Hobbes and later the fathers of classical materialism and positivism in France inclined to the first view. The creators of the great rationalist systems, mathematicians and philosophers such as Descartes, Newton, Leibniz, Christian Wolff, believed that they had achieved the second.

Kant's doctrine of appearances, as opposed to both these alternatives, maintains that the existence of something beyond nature can theoretically be neither proved nor refuted, and that, practically, neither proof nor refutation are necessary to man. From here we can throw a bridge to Whitehead's progammatic sentence: ". . . there is an essence to the universe which forbids relationships beyond itself, as a violation of its rationality. Speculative philosophy seeks that essence."[22]

Science—for Kant mathematics and natural science—is therefor 'possible experience'. "Mathematics is only concerned with appearances", says Kant in the *Prolegomena*. The objects of possible experience whose ordered 'field' is called 'nature', are the appearances, and as such they are always bound up with the relation to the active and receptive subject.[23] On the other hand, this field of objects is indefinitely open for genuine experience of novelty and variety within the inexhaustible history of human knowledge and penetration into nature. Only the field of Practical Reason (Kant's name for ethics) and the religious postulates developed from it are realms of the supernatural which are accessible to man.

Critical philosophy is analysis of the conditions of the possibility of experience, analysis of the *a priori* 'forms' of experience, and of the limitations of such experience. Kant calls the philosophical method which is committed to such an undertaking 'transcendental'. Behind it and above it there is nevertheless the peculiar conception of the 'tribunal' of reason, to which we shall have to return later.

Kant approaches religion by way of the practical aim and supreme end of man. Man's real vocation lies in the practical realm, in the moral conduct of a 'rational' being who is more than a mere animal. The "whole vocation of man"[24] transcends his vocation as a rational being who is merely active in science and thereby contained within critical limitation and the bounds of nature.

Kant's ethics rests on the self-legislation of practical reason. In the *Critique of Pure Reason* Kant mentions the Platonic model of the philosopher as the 'legislator in accordance with the ideas'. The latter are, in Kant's opinion, not realizable in possible experience. However, it is man's vocation to realize them outside the realm of nature, for "it is quite otherwise with us. With all the exertion of our reason we have only a very obscure and ambiguous view into the future; the Governor of the world allows us only to conjecture His existence and majesty, not to behold or clearly prove them; the moral law in us, without promising or threatening us with anything certain, demands of us a disinterested respect; finally, only when this respect has become active and dominating, it allows us a view into the realm of the supersensuous, though only a glimpse. Thus only can there be a truly moral character dedicated directly to the law. . . ."[25] In this way we transcend the limitations of the realm of appearances. But this contributes nothing to a closed system of the supernatural, nothing to a 'metaphysics' of the dogmatic kind as we have it in the rationalistic systems. It leads to no philosophical 'isms' whatever; it has nothing to do with the "monopoly of the schools", as Kant put it.[26] From practical reason alone can man derive his meaning and purpose. This practical, humanistic purpose is binding also for natural science. For science grows from human activity, albeit as a definite, distinctive field.

The Kantian *Critiques* thus (a) limit science, assign to it its position by delineating positively and negatively the field of appearances, i.e. Kantian 'nature'; (b) they subordinate science to a central *humanum* over which 'reason' watches as 'censor'.

---

[24] KRV, B 868.
[25] *Critique of Practical Reason*, V, 147 (Academy Edition). From the translation by L. W. Beck.   [26] KRV, B xxxii.

Whitehead, in his co-ordination of science, aesthetics, ethics, religion, and philosophical cosmology (as presented in *Science in the Modern World*, *Process and Reality*, *Adventures of Ideas*), proceeds in a manner different from that of Kant. But he shares with the Kantian philosophy the conviction that such a co-ordination of the humanistic spheres of realization in an 'open' system is necessary.

In the strongest contrast to the closed systems of Leibnizians, such as Christian Wolff and Alexander Gottlieb Baumgarten (to whom Kant especially applies the term 'dogmatists'), philosophy in Kant's hands becomes criticism of pseudo-science, of scientific and unscientific dogmatism. In this capacity the critique of reason becomes the 'tribunal' over the various 'rational' activities of man. The "higher judicial reason"[27] is not to be mistaken for *scientia* or *theologia*—but neither is it *ontologia sive philosophia prima*. With this we are outside the antinomy of rationalism and irrationalism, which so predominates in the history of German thought. Reason becomes critique—but critique of reason itself. On the other hand, we are far remote from the disastrous radicalism of Luther who regarded reason as 'foolish madness' and 'the devil's playmate', deserving to have its neck wrung. Kant's position prepares the way for Hegel's dialectically mediating chapter in his *Phenomenology of Mind*, the chapter "The Struggle of Enlightenment with Superstition". As is well known, Hegel here proceeds differently from what the title might lead us to expect. For this chapter was written in 1807, that is to say, not at the time of Luther or Hutten, nor at that of Voltaire and Rousseau, but in the age of Schiller and Goethe, the intellectual climate of which cannot be conceived without Kant and Spinoza. At that time, for a little while at least, neither reason nor faith were charged with heresy. It was the last epoch in which philosophy was not an academic subject or a museum, but an intellectual centre.

According to the conception of the age of Kant and Schiller, philosophy follows its old mission of making man aware of himself and free. Since the undatable Delphic inscription, "Know Thyself", since Socrates, since Plato's simile of the cave, since Descartes' *Meditationes* and Hume's *Enquiry*, this has constituted the European nature of philosophy and the essentially 'philo-

[27] KRV, B 767.

sophical' character of philosophy—as distinct from other interests of the mind, such as science and religion. Kant's image of the 'censorship of philosophical reason' is impressive enough. As in so many important passages, Kant here makes use of a legal metaphor.[28] The explication of what Kant, in the light of his conception of the supreme human task of philosophy, condensed into his idea of the function of 'judicial' reason, will occupy us later in connection with Kant's theory of natural science.

Kant's critical work as a whole gives an outline of the constellation of science, religion, and philosophy. The *Critique of Pure Reason* and the *Prolegomena to Any Future Metaphysics Which Will Be Able to Come Forth as Science* determine the extent and limitations of science, and sketch the relation between theoretical and practical reason. The *Critique of Practical Reason* and the *Groundwork of the Metaphysic of Morals* determine the extent and limitations of the realm in which morality and religion find their place. But religion remains for Kant "within the limits of reason alone" (see Kant's essay of 1793 bearing this title, for which he was severely reprimanded by the Prussian ministry). The *Critique of Judgement* gives Kant's aesthetics, and the self-legislation and self-articulation of philosophy. 'Reason' remains the title of the jurisdiction spanning all these separate realms, ordering the republic of all the sciences, i.e. "the scientific commonwealth".

What is 'objective' is that which is constant and constitutive in the relation to the subject. Nature as the totality of appearances is the *tertium* between the merely subjective (illusion) and 'being as such' (things-in-themselves). In this way Kant redefined the physical realm, and this definition has a revolutionary significance. For it is not the case that 'behind' the physical there is simply the metaphysical—about the latter, no theoretical truth can be attained; in this respect Kant remained in complete agreement with the scepticism of David Hume who 'awakened him from his dogmatic slumber'. Nor are force and matter, atoms and electrons 'behind' nature. A materialistic extension of physics, seeing matter as 'being as such', is therefore equally incompatible with Kant's analysis of our knowledge of nature. This follows not from Kant's controversial idealistic metaphysics, but from his critical analysis of physical knowledge. Kant's achievement is the breaking down of the alternatives presented in the following scheme:

[28] Cf. Hans Barth, *Die Idee der Ordnung*, Zürich, 1958.

A *subjective*	*B* *objective*
(1) in the psychological (Kant's 'empirical') sense: 'Schein'	in the ontological sense (i.e. the sense of *ontologia* of the tradition): 'Ding an sich'
(2) John Locke: secondary qualities (ideas in the mind)	primary qualities (in the bodies)

Kant's novel concept of objectivity results in the overcoming of this dualism: what is really (i.e. objectively, scientifically) knowable to man belongs neither to the field of *A* nor to that of *B*. This is worked out in detail in Kant's doctrine of appearances and categories.

The Kantian table of categories must surely be divested of its pedantry. It must be supplemented in the direction indicated by the much wider modern categoreal schemes of A. N. Whitehead and Nicolai Hartmann. Nowadays there are not many orthodox Kantians left who would defend the deducibility of the categories. In any case, the extravagant overstraining of the category of causation in the 'scientistic' nineteenth century—culminating in the fiction of Laplace's formula for the calculation of all future events —cannot be blamed on Kant. Kant's treatment of the category of causation and the category of interaction in strict parity destroys the monopoly of the causal determination in the sense of the mechanistic and materialistic conception of nature.

III

Philosophy as 'Self-connection of Subjectivity' according to Whitehead

Alfred North Whitehead in his basic scheme of natural knowledge —especially since he cannot be called pro-Kantian[29]—bears out Kant in his steering a course which avoids 'dogmatism' as well as 'empiricism'.

The main theses in what follows can be summarized thus: Whitehead, whether positively or negatively, is related to the theme of the Kantian *Critiques*, (1) as the only great philosopher of the present age who, after Hegel and Schelling, confesses to 'speculative philosophy'; (2) as the only philosopher who—post-

[29] Cf. PR vi [vi], viii [viii], *et al.*

Hegel and yet independent of Hegel (whom he never studied directly but knew only via McTaggart and Bradley)—attempted to reunite science and religion through philosophy. "Philosophy frees itself from the taint of ineffectiveness by its close relations with religion and with science, natural and sociological. It attains its chief importance by fusing the two, namely, religion and science, into one rational scheme of thought."[30]

In the midst of the contemporary spectacle of philosophy as, on the one hand, *ancilla scientiarum*, philosophy of science, the theory of language-construction, analysis of ordinary language, or as, on the other hand, philosophy of existence, an edifying decoration of age of denominations and ideologies, Whitehead salvaged a central Kantian idea without which philosophy might as well give up the ghost. What Whitehead calls the 'criticism of principles' which he considers the function of philosophy, is no longer couched in terms of the 'tribunal of reason' or the 'censorship' of philosophy. But the material similarity with Kant's 'judicial reason' cannot be overlooked: "Thus one aim of philosophy is to challenge the half-truths constituting the scientific first principles."[31] "In its use of this method natural science has shown a curious mixture of rationalism and irrationalism. Its prevalent tone of thought has been ardently rationalistic within its own borders, and dogmatically irrational beyond those borders. In practice such an attitude tends to become a dogmatic denial that there are any factors in the world not fully expressible in terms of its own primary notions devoid of further generalization. Such a denial is a self-denial of thought."[32]

The basic scheme of natural knowledge according to Kant has at least one point of contact with the new orientation in the present-day post-Einsteinian and post-Planckian conception of nature, of which Whitehead is one of the interpreters.[33] In the famous simile from the preface to the second edition of the *Critique of Pure Reason*, Kant conceives natural knowledge as the testimony of witnesses who are compelled to answer definite questions. The testimony of witnesses has a mediating function. As is well known, in legal procedure such testimony stands 'between' the objective facts which are to be cognized, but which do not themselves speak, and the cognizing subject—the judge in our simile. According to a

[30] PR 21 [23].   [31] PR 13 [15].
[32] PR 7 [8].   [33] Cf. CN, PRel, PNK, *et al.*

tradition going back to classical antiquity, Kant uses the 'judge' as a symbol for the epistemological subject seeking the truth (see also his phrases 'judicial reason', 'censorship of reason', 'tribunal of reason', etc.). Let us suppose that the cognizing of the truth by the judge involves the scrutinizing and utilizing of the testimony of the witnesses. But the witnesses will not say anything to the point without proper questioning, that is to say, without a specific relation to the judge. If, however, the judge suggests the desired answer to the witness by insinuating his own opinion, then the finding of the truth is also inhibited. All this is what is meant by assigning to the testimony of witnesses a 'mediating function'. In non-metaphorical language, it means that the mediating role is played by the 'appearances'. For Kant 'synthetic' knowledge means primarily natural science; the latter is penetration into nature, and 'nature' is the totality of appearances.

It is in remarkable agreement with this view that according to the conception of many contemporary scientists, knowledge of nature proceeds via a mediating stage. Niels Bohr calls it the 'phenomenon', defined in a novel fashion; Werner Heisenberg calls it the "web of relations between man and nature", into which the old concept of natural science is dissolved. A. N. Whitehead has 'interplay' between 'interpretation' and 'fact', defining these terms in a very fruitful way.

The following quotations are given in support of this general assertion. Niels Bohr thinks that the concept of the 'phenomenon' is inseparable from the concept of the 'observational situation'. This agrees with the Kantian definition of appearance as the "relation of the given object to the subject".[34] In Bohr's essay "On the Notions of Causality and Complementarity"[35] we read: ". . . one may strongly advocate limitation of the use of the word phenomenon to refer exclusively to observations obtained under specific circumstances, including an account of the whole experiment." "Altogether, the approach towards the problem of explanation that is embodied in the notion of complementarity suggests itself in our position as conscious beings and recalls forcefully the teaching of ancient thinkers that, in search for a harmonious attitude towards life, it must never be forgotten that we ourselves are both actors and spectators in the drama of existence."

[34] KRV, B 69, and footnote B 70.
[35] *Dialectica*, Vol. 2, No. 2/3, Neuchâtel, 1948, p. 317 and 318.

According to Werner Heisenberg, "natural science no longer stands over against nature as a spectator, but recognizes itself as part of the interplay between man and nature". "If we can at all speak of an idea of nature in the exact natural sciences of our time, it is not really an idea of nature, but rather an idea of our relations with nature." "Above all we have the web of relations between man and nature, the web of those relations by which we as bodily living beings are dependent parts of nature, and at the same time as men make her the object of our thought and action. . . ."[36]

These pronouncements by men who have made modern natural science what it is, do anything but confirm logical empiricism. Nor, however, do they promote ontology. There then remains only a philosophy of 'appearances' (not in the idealistic sense), or of 'actual entities'.

The measure of agreement of the preceding quotations from Bohr and Heisenberg with some of Whitehead's philosophical formulae is undoubtedly remarkable. "Every scrap of our knowledge derives its meaning from the fact that we are factors in the universe."[37] "Our datum is the actual world, including ourselves; and this actual world spreads itself for observation in the guise of the topic of our immediate experience. The elucidation of immediate experience is the sole justification for any thought; and the starting point for thought is the analytic observation of components of this experience."[38] "The technical phrase 'subject-object' is a bad term for the fundamental situation disclosed in experience."[39]

All these are formulae of non-Kantians about the interplay of the subjective and the objective. With their aid we can more clearly understand the profundity of Kant's concept of appearance. One can hardly deny that these views correspond to the basic Kantian scheme of natural knowledge, or that here the doctrine of active and receptive man, as it underlies the Kantian epistemology, has found its translation into modern language.

Kant's anthropological point of view,[40] it is true, remained under

---

[36] "Das Naturbild der heutigen Physik", *Die Künste im technischen Zeitalter*, München, 1956, pp. 45–6.

[37] MG § IV.   [38] PR 5 [6].   [39] SMW 188.

[40] This point of view becomes explicit in the *Critique of Pure Reason* only at the end of the Transcendental Aesthetic (B 72). The late work of 1798, *Anthropologie in pragmatischer Hinsicht*, has had hardly more effect than to suggest a programme, as for instance to C. S. Peirce.

the surface. It did not go well with the classical science of nature of Kant's time, nor did it find favour with the religious orthodoxy of his Prussian environment. Philosophical self-government, based on 'judicial reason'—reason thinking itself (*Selbstdenken*)—culminates in moral autonomy. Here the difference from heteronomous ethics is clear, i.e. from the view that the good is good because God has so decreed it. This anthropocentric gravitation of Kant's *Critiques* must be properly understood.

Heinz Heimsoeth, in the following, quotes two remarkable, little-known Kant passages: "God knows everything by himself and *a priori*; 'but finite beings cannot by themselves know other things, since they are not their creators, except only in so far as they are mere appearances which they can know *a priori*'.[41] Man is '*cosmotheoros* who himself creates *a priori* the elements for his knowledge of the world, the elements from which he as an inhabitant of the world constructs his vision of the world in the idea'[42]—thus the opus posthumous".[43]

In a classical sentence from the preface to the second edition of the *Critique of Pure Reason* Kant describes the interaction of man and nature thus: "When Galileo caused balls, the weights of which he had himself previously determined, to roll down an inclined plane; when Torricelli made the air carry a weight which he had calculated beforehand to be equal to that of a definite column of water; or in more recent times, when Stahl changed metal into lime, and lime back into metal, by withdrawing something and then restoring it, a light broke upon all students of nature. They learned that reason has insight only into that which it produces after a plan of its own, and that it must not allow itself to be kept, as it were, in nature's leading-strings, but must itself show the way with principles of judgment based upon fixed laws, constraining nature to give answer to questions of reason's own determining. Accidental observations, made in obedience to no previously thought-out plan, can never be made to yield a necessary law, which alone reason is concerned to discover."[44] For Kant's 'previously thought-out plan'—'*Entwurf*', a term thus not introduced into philosophical language by Heidegger or Sartre ('*projet*')—Whitehead has a

[41] XVIII, 6048 (Academy Edition).   [42] XX, 31 (Academy Edition).
[43] Heinz Heimsoeth, *Studien zur Philosophie Immanuel Kants*, in *Kant-Studien Ergänzungshefte* 71, Köln, 1956, p. 199.
[44] KRV, B xii–xiii.

number of specific concepts, such as 'conceptual scheme', 'categoreal scheme', 'scheme of ideas': ". . . the true method of philosophical construction is to frame a scheme of ideas, the best that one can, and unflinchingly to explore the interpretation of experience in terms of that scheme . . . all constructive thought, on the various special topics of scientific interest, is dominated by some such scheme, unacknowledged, but no less influential in guiding the imagination. The importance of philosophy lies in its sustained effort to make such schemes explicit, and thereby capable of criticism and improvement."[45]

To quote Kant again: "Reason, holding in one hand its principles, according to which alone concordant appearances can be admitted as equivalent to laws, and in the other hand the experiment which it has devised in conformity with these principles, must approach nature in order to be taught by it. It must not, however, do so in the character of a pupil who listens to everything that the teacher chooses to say, but of an appointed judge who compels the witnesses to answer questions which he has himself formulated. Even physics, therefore, owes the beneficent revolution in its point of view entirely to the happy thought, that while reason must seek in nature, not fictitiously ascribe to it, whatever as not being knowable through reason's own resources has to be learnt, if learnt at all, only from nature, it must adopt as its guide, in so seeking, that which it has itself put into nature. It is thus that the study of nature has entered on the secure path of a science, after having for so many centuries been nothing but a process of merely random groping."[46] Here Kant—who is not always fortunate in his stylistic formulations—shows himself gifted with an exceptional power of words. And here something important about the real, historical events constituting the making of European science is captured. But this many-levelled analogy captures also something fundamental about *all* scientific practice, which has not changed after Einstein and Planck. The conception of natural science expressed in terms of this model is that of a harmonious synthesis. The extremes of speaking of either the 'kernel' or the 'shell' of nature, or the extremes of either extending natural science to a science of being-as-such, or of seeing it as an idealistic or operationalistic construction of reality, are overcome in this synthesis. When compared with the actual procedure of the scientist questioning nature, and with

[45] PR x [x].   [46] KRV, B xiii–xiv.

the interplay of all factors involved, all such extremes exhibit their deficiency. Kant's analogy must be understood as stating clearly that the antinomy of rationalism and empiricism is capable of being dissolved.

Here again we have a point of material connection with the general position of Whitehead's 'philosophy of organism'. The latter presents itself as a synthesis of Plato and Locke. It further claims to harmonize Spinozistic and Heracleitian motifs. The beginning of *Process and Reality* shows clearly that this was Whitehead's fundamental starting point.

Must we regard Kant's picture of the interplay of human spontaneity and receptivity in scientific practice, published in 1787, as now out of date, as superseded, perhaps by the work done in nuclear physics? Werner Heisenberg, in a congress speech in 1950, refers to the "old conception, deeply rooted since Descartes, of the division of the world into an objective world happening in space and time, and a separate soul mirroring this world, now being in conflict with new conceptions in the light of which this separation can no longer be effected in the old, primitive manner".[47] Kant's conception—a century and a half before Quantum Mechanics—of principles of reason in the subject, and of the ordering of the given into appearances under the forms of subjectivity, was already directed against Descartes. In the quoted analogy from the preface to the second edition of the *Critique of Pure Reason*, and in the centre of his difficult epistemology, Kant emphasizes the interplay of subjective and objective factors. The 'primitive separation' of *cogitatio* and *extensio* according to the Cartesian scheme is frequently criticized by Kant. Kant's counter-formula, 'empirical realism, but transcendental idealism', can hardly be called 'primitive'. It is a linguistically clumsy expression for the conjunction which is to take the place of the separation.[48]

Kant's impressive metaphor for the procedure of the natural scientist stands the test even in the pragmatist and operationalist

[47] Heimo Dolch, "Werner Heisenberg", in *Forscher und Wissenschaftler im heutigen Europa—Weltall und Erde*, Oldenburg, p. 97.

[48] It is curious that the identity with Kant's standpoint is not explicitly mentioned when nuclear physicists nowadays make statements such as these: "In natural science too the object of research is no longer nature as such, but nature as exposed to human questioning." (W. Heisenberg) Or: "We compel the atom to communicate its qualities to us in an adequate language." (C. F. von Weizsäcker.)

camp, and of a modern theory of information. In a recent publication, *Communication, Organization, and Science*,[49] the American cyberneticist Jerome Rothstein writes: "In a sense which is deeper than mere simile, the scientist 'speaks' with the universe. He asks questions with his experiments. The reply (consisting of the result of observation) is information. . . ."

The essential point of the Kantian simile for the questioning of nature is this: nature does not speak by herself. Human consciousness is not like a photographic plate. There is nothing that is merely 'given'. This can be read off from Kant's simile, and from his entire theory of the interdependence of spontaneity and receptivity in human knowledge. In modern language, A. N. Whitehead elaborates the same point: "Our co-ordinated knowledge, which in the general sense of the term is Science, is formed by the meeting of two orders of experience. One order is constituted by the direct, immediate discriminations of particular observations. The other order is constituted by our general way of conceiving the Universe. They will be called, the Observational Order and the Conceptual Order. The first point to remember is that the observational order is invariably interpreted in terms of the concepts supplied by the conceptual order. The question as to the priority of one or the other is, for the purpose of this discussion, academic . . . Observational discrimination is not dictated by the impartial facts. It selects and discards, and what it retains is rearranged in a subjective order of prominence. This order of prominence in observation is in fact a distortion of the facts. Thus we have to rescue the facts as they are from the facts as they appear. We have to rescue the facts in the discard, and we have to discard the subjective order of prominence which is itself a fact of observation."[50] The concept of 'interpretation' is very fruitful. Only that 'statement' by nature which is induced by the inquirer and interpreted in his categories, is knowledge: ". . . there are no brute, self-contained matters of fact, capable of being understood apart from interpretation as an element in a system. Whenever we attempt to express the matter of immediate experience, we find that its understanding leads us beyond itself, to its contemporaries, to its past, to its future, and to the universals in terms of which its definiteness is exhibited. . . . Thus the understanding of the immediate brute fact requires its

[49] The Falcons Wing Press, Indian Hills, Colorado, 1958, cf. pp. 27–30.
[50] AI 198–9.

metaphysical interpretation as an item in a world with some systematic relation to it."[51]

Here we clearly see the connection with (1) Kant's Analogies of Experience: "All appearances are, as regards their existence, subject *a priori* to rules determining their relation to one another in one time";[52] (2) Kant's extraordinarily modern terms, such as 'field', or 'context of possible experience', in which the 'analogies of experience' are the 'guiding threads'; and (3) Kant's conception of truth: "All our knowledge falls within the bounds of possible experience, and just in this universal relation to possible experience consists that transcendental truth which precedes all empirical truth and makes it possible."[53]

A valuable supplementation of this approach is provided by the following highly original sentences by Whitehead: "When thought comes upon the scene, it finds the interpretations as matters of practice. Philosophy does not initiate interpretations. Its search for a rationalistic scheme is the search for more adequate criticism, and for more adequate justification, of the interpretations which we perforce employ. Our habitual experience is a complex of failure and success in the enterprise of interpretations. If we desire a record of uninterpreted experience, we must ask a stone to record its autobiography. Every scientific memoir in its record of the 'facts' is shot through and through with interpretation."[54]

Yet another note to the same topic. The Kantian metaphor of the judge who, in his search for truth, brings about and judges upon the testimony of witnesses, does not only hold for the questioning of nature. According to the anthropocentric structure of the Kantian *Critiques*, it is ultimately directed to the critical self-examination and self-guidance of man, and only thus, according to Kant, to the supreme human task.

Kant again and again compares the essential procedure of the critique of reason with the workings of a court of law, where 'rational' man judges over man. In metaphysics, "reason is indeed meant to be its own pupil",[55] not, however, in traditional metaphysics as criticized by Kant, but in future metaphysics which Kant, through his critique of reason, had supplied with a method and a secure foundation.

Here the simile of the judge takes on an even wider significance.

[51] PR 19 [21–2].   [52] KRV, A 177.   [53] KRV, B 185.
[54] PR 19–20 [22].   [55] KRV, B xiv.

Philosophy is legislation by the higher judicial reason for human reason as a whole. And by 'reason' Kant means that which makes man human.[56] Kant's humanistic conception of philosophy as man's "exodus from his self-incurred tutelage" on the one hand, and his critical co-ordination of science, ethics, and religion on the other hand, coincide in the essentially judicial office of philosophy. Whitehead brought these two aspects to one formula: "Philosophy is the self-correction by consciousness of its own initial excess of subjectivity."[57]

Kant's simile, elicited from scientific procedure, of the questioning of nature as a lawsuit, is a very precise picture. The judge, through his own planned and compelling questions, reconstructs from the witness—who is both independent and yet 'put before him'—the objective state of affairs. The judge, as subject of the procedure, is himself dependent upon the witness, listening to him ('receptive'), not fictitiously ascribing anything to him; at the same time, in comparison with the witness, he is the spontaneously determining partner. For the conversation with the witness proceeds according to his, i.e. the judge's, categories or principles, according to his 'preconceived plan'. The whole procedure, however, serves only the search for truth and its values.

This is a true picture of the procedure of genuine science. Nowadays, in the shadow of the factual operationalism of our technocracy on the one side, and the theoretical identification of science and technology in Heidegger's sense on the other side, some philosophers tend to forget that there would never have been any science but for that selfless striving after truth.

The outcome is: (*a*) What Kant really says in this story of the judge who questions the witness, is not a consequence of his 'idealistic' standpoint. The 'isms' of metaphysics and anti-metaphysics alike fail to take account of the interplay of human power and impotence. Only if Kant's doctrine be treated as an 'ism', can it be ignored. But it is strictly neutral with regard to epistemological trimmings, constructions, and destructions, from Plato to Wittgenstein.

(*b*) The history of thought in Europe exhibits two basic schemes for the understanding of nature. First, man has tried to understand nature by contrast with the supernatural, that is to say, by means of

[56] Cf. KRV Chapters I and III, "Transcendental Doctrine of Method".
[57] PR 20 [22].

a dualistic scheme, imposing "relationships beyond the universe" (Whitehead). Secondly, man has tried to understand nature by means of a natural science which takes itself literally, i.e. which believes that nature *is* force and matter, atoms and electrons, etc. This second scheme, exemplified for instance by Democritus, is as old as the first scheme.

The notable feature about the concept of nature in both Kant and Whitehead is that it stands against both these schemes. For Kant, this is bound up with his philosophy of appearance; for Whitehead, with his philosophy of organism. 'Organism' does not indicate a metaphysical biologism. Here, as in the case of Kant, what is meant is a definite synthesis of the antithetic features which are admittedly there in our relationship with nature. The call is for the 'censorship' of reason "which secures general order and harmony" of the "scientific commonwealth".[58]

The point of this concept of nature which dissociates itself from the antinomy of the metaphysical as well as of the anti-metaphysical tradition, is akin to that of Goethe's rejoinder to Albrecht von Haller. The latter, a scholar of medicine and natural science, a poet and *homo religiosus*, at Göttingen and elsewhere, had written: "No finite mind can penetrate into nature's innermost sanctum; happy is he to whom she shows her outer shell." To this Goethe replied with the famous lines: "O thou philistine! Everywhere we are within. Nature has neither kernel nor shell; she is everything all at once."[59] And : "Where is the kernel of nature but in man's heart?"[60]

Goethe, as well as the mathematician and physicist Whitehead, is above the suspicion of an idealism of constructs, which assigns nature to merely subjective consciousness.

Kant quite explicitly says that according to his concept of nature, we do penetrate into nature: "Through observation and analysis of appearances we penetrate to nature's inner recesses, and no one can say how far this knowledge may in time extend."[61]

It is important to recognize that in Kant's doctrine of appearances, these terms are used in anything but a naïve sense; on the

---

[58] KRV, B 879.

[59] Both quotations from Goethe's poem *Allerdings* (*Dem Physiker*).

[60] From Goethe's epigram "Wir kennen dich, du Schalk!". Cf. also Goethe's sentence: "When I know the relation to myself and to the external world, I call this 'truth'. Everybody can have his own truth, and yet it is always the same."

[61] KRV, B 334.

contrary, compared with Kant's doctrine, the metaphors of 'kernel' and 'shell', as well as many contemporary materialistic and pheno-menalistic concepts of nature and natural science are naïve.

(c) Kant's simile of the judge who questions, listens to those who are questioned, and is thus in search of the truth, allows, perhaps, of an even more esoteric reading. The rational synthesis of subjectivity and objectivity ultimately concerns man not only in his epistemological and scientific role, but in his total function of self-realization. This subordinates science and knowledge to the practical and humanistic 'vocation' of man. In classical antiquity, this would have been called 'justice'.

Is it plausible that mere 'technical appropriation of the world' (Heidegger's *technische Weltbemächtigung*) is the impulse behind the scientific achievement of Europe? Even if this were applicable to science, it would not apply to the scientists. Is it not precisely when seen under the philosophical aspect of existence that the technical utilizer of science and the scientific precursor of tech-nology have hardly anything in common? The reminder that the one is after use, the other after truth, is not intended *pour épater les bourgeois*. But what if 'truth' be a metaphysical illusion, a 'mystical relation', or 'verbal magic' (F. Mauthner, C. K. Ogden, I. A. Richards, H. Feigl, etc.)? Then it is the due of this illusion that it be given a just critique before the tribunal of human reason. For it was this 'illusion' that led to the 'adventures of ideas' of Graeco-European man over the last three thousand years, forming one of the most obvious impulses towards man's peculiar self-realization—from Socrates and Diogenes to Einstein and Bohr. One must remember that those men who searched not only for know-ledge, but for knowledge about knowledge, all had something to say in criticism of 'technical appropriation of the world'.

European humanism, torn today between flight into the past and flight into the future, seems to be set on depriving itself even of its compass. The men who strive for truth have built this European world in which alone it is possible (1) for truth to be criticized; (2) for critique of science to be science; (3) for reason to remain 'its own pupil'. For, "there remains the final reflection, how shallow, puny, and imperfect are efforts to sound the depths in the nature of things. In philosophical discussion, the merest hint of dogmatic certainty as to finality of statement is an exhibition of folly."[62] It

[62] PR x [x].

would indeed be unreasonable to assert dogmatically that the
self-critical task of man has been completed by Kant, and is
now committed to the results of Kant's *Critiques*, and to the
'*Kritizismus*' of his disciples.[63]

The formula of the 'self-realization' of rational man contains no
idealistic or other unseasonable ambition. This is so not despite, but
because of the fact that what is 'rational' is in continuous need of
philosophical examination.[64] It only needs one realistic look at
those scholars and scientists in the history of thought on whose
achievements we depend, for us to see clearly that the reductions
which are nowadays so favoured—in existentialist or phenomeno-
logist or materialist ways—of the vast phenomenon of Graeco-
European science belong to an 'age of the feuilleton' (Hermann
Hesse); for us to see that they are 'reductive fallacies' and 'fiction
stories', by contrast with which the amusing stories of Herodotus,
for instance, about the origin of geometry in Egyptian land survey-
ing, come out rather well. One cannot with a dictum of Bacon or
Descartes pass judgment on Kepler, Huygens, Newton, Kant, or
Whitehead.

Perhaps this is what the symbol of the judge, and the conception
of the 'philosopher' as understood and lived by Kant and then
again by Whitehead, are meant to convey to us. The living tradition
of the philosopher-judge cannot be overlooked in the span from
Plato, St. Augustine, Thomas Aquinas, Bacon, Hobbes, Spinoza,
Locke and Hume, Vico, Voltaire, Rousseau, Benjamin Franklin
and Thomas Jefferson, Hegel, Kierkegaard, Marx, Wilhelm von
Humboldt, Auguste Comte, John Stuart Mill, and Nietzsche.

Thus Whitehead is right when he says:

"It has been an objection to speculative philosophy that it is
overambitious. Rationalism, it is admitted, is the method by which
advance is made within the limits of particular sciences. It is,
however, held that this limited success must not encourage
attempts to frame ambitious schemes expressive of the general
nature of things.

"One alleged justification of this criticism is ill-success:

[63] Cf. Nicolai Hartmann, "Ziele und Wege der Kategorialanalyse", *Kleinere
Schriften*, Vol. I, Berlin, 1955. Hartmann here demonstrates that categoreal
analysis still continues after Kant.
[64] Cf. Hermann Wein, "Der Streit um Ordnung und Einheit der Realwelt",
Philosophia Naturalis, Vol. V, 2/3, Meisenheim am Glan, 1959.

European thought is represented as littered with metaphysical systems, abandoned and unreconciled.

"Such an assertion tacitly fastens upon philosophy the old dogmatic test. The same criterion would fasten ill-success upon science. We no more retain the physics of the seventeenth century than we do the Cartesian philosophy of that century. Yet within limits, both systems express important truths. Also we are beginning to understand the wider categories which define their limits of correct application. Of course, in that century, dogmatic views held sway; so that the validity both of the physical notions, and of the Cartesian notions, was misconceived. Mankind never quite knows what it is after. When we survey the history of thought, and likewise the history of practice, we find that one idea after another is tried out, its limitations defined, and its core of truth elicited. In application to the instinct for the intellectual adventures demanded by particular epochs, there is much truth in Augustine's rhetorical phrase, *Securus judicat orbis terrarum*."[65]

[65] PR 18–9 [20–1].

PAUL WEISS

HISTORY AND OBJECTIVE
IMMORTALITY

XII

PAUL WEISS

HISTORY AND OBJECTIVE IMMORTALITY

Historians, in somewhat radical contrast with other types of inquirers (e.g. mathematical physicists), never give up the world of common-sense objects and occurrences for any other, no matter how clear or rational this other may be. Believing that one can learn what will be by knowing something about what had happened, historians seek to find what in the past is relevant to what is present. The objects they now confront are for them the termini of processes which began with common-sense items, went through common-sense changes and transformations, and terminated in present common-sense objects.

Like everyone else, the historian finds his evidence in the present. There is no other place to look. The oldest object in the world is, if present, just as completely here and now as any other. To speak of it as having any age at all of course is to imply that it did not come into being in the present, and that it has relevant antecedents; it is not to imply that it is locatable anywhere other than the present.

Whatever came to be out of the past will ground an inference into the past. As a rule, though, the historian focuses on something which is distinctive in being or activity, in value or meaning. But where a scientist would want to reduce those distinctive items, along with others, to formulae, laws and implications, the historian treats them as irreducible bases for a knowledge of the past. Whatever patterns might be discovered he treats as residua of vital activities. The patterns are, for him, not only without power, but are incapable of exhausting the nature of any historic occurrence.

The warrant and validity of an inference does not depend on the direction in which one must go for its conclusion. Inferences to the past can therefore have as much warrant and be as impeccable as inferences to anything else. Those inferences can be grounded in most acceptable premises, and may closely follow along the lines of a well-approved logic. They are of at least five different kinds:

inferences to *stadia*, *predecessors*, *antecedent components*, *unifying grounds*, and *orientation points*.

Inferences to Stadia

The objects we confront are more than surfaces. They resist, persist, make themselves manifest in multiple ways over a stretch of time. They are substances or are sustained by substances. This brown leaf, for example, is a substantial leaf. Its colour is rooted in the leaf, and is there inseparably connected and infected by the texture, shape, size, weight and other features of the leaf. When logicians treat 'This leaf is brown' as a conjunction of two assertions, 'This is brown' and 'This is a leaf', they abstract from the fact that the brown is integral to the leaf. If we wish to stress this fact we should say not 'This leaf is brown' or even 'This is a brown leaf', but 'This is a brown-leaf'. The hyphen emphasizes the fact that the colour and that of which it is the colour are not to be separated as distinct items.

Though the leaf is here and now, just as fully as any other thing, we find that we understand it better when we treat it as having undergone adventures in the past. We may have watched the leaf for a while and noticed that it changed; we may have noticed that other leaves had changed and supposed that it was like them; or we may have noted that the leaf, in contrast with other leaves, is further along in a process of becoming browned. In the first case we rely on memory, in the second on a simple induction, and in the third on an understanding of what it means for a being to have a career of a certain kind. All three provide a ground for inferring from the leaf as it now is to what it had been.

The recognition that the leaf has gone through a process of change, makes it possible to speak of the leaf in two equivalent ways. 'This is a browned-leaf' adds to the brown-leaf the fact that it had come about through an antecedent process of change. 'This browned-leaf was once green' instead refers to the colour or hue the leaf once had. The latter is reached through a process of inference from the present to a pivotal point or stadium. The furthest back we can go in this type of inference is to the colour which the leaf once had—to it as a green-leaf. Any further step would take us to a predecessor, to what was a first stadium for the green-leaf, but not for the brown-leaf.

A stadium is a position in the past from which a relevant stretch of change can be said to have begun. An inference to the green-leaf thus gives us a position from which we can trace the process of browning, until we arrive at the point from which we began, the brown-leaf. We engage in a similar inference when, given the fact that a man is dead, we suppose that he was murdered and infer to the time when the killing occurred.

Inference to Predecessors

The green-leaf to which we inferred by an inference to a stadium, is that which was once substantial and is now recognized to be distinct from the leaf today. That green-leaf itself was the product of adventures in a time preceding its own. The green-leaf can therefore provide us with a new position from which an inference to a prior stadium can be employed. An inference to the predecessor of a present object is thus expressible as a sequence of inferences to stadia. This predecessor may be quite different in being and nature from what is the present. A whole series of inferences to predecessors will take us evidently far from the present object, and many historians, having arrived at some predecessor, are content to spend their days in moving from this, not back to the present, but to some less remote predecessor.

Inference to Antecedent Components

A leaf has *parts* into which it can be subdivided. These are demarcated portions of the leaf, having no independent status. They contrast with the *constituents* of the leaf, which have a being that the parts do not have, with powers and natures distinct from that of the leaf. The right half of the leaf is one part of it, the left another; the cells in the leaf make up one set of constituents, the molecules another. The leaf also has *components*. These, like the parts of the leaf, are on the same level with it; like the constituents of the leaf they can be known through analysis and construction. They are items on which one focuses in order better to articulate and understand what is in fact complex. The stem of the leaf and the sap in the leaf are components of it.

Parts, constituents, and components can be made to ground inferences to their stadia or predecessors. A study of the predecessors of the parts or constituents of a leaf, though, will tell us little or nothing about the leaf, for the leaf had a unitary career to be grasped only by attending to its components and their past. The

L

sap in the leaf had a career which was a component of the process of browning through which the leaf went. The sap changed in consistency and action over the course of time. The inference to antecedent components is thus essentially the product of three acts. We must first isolate components in a present object, then infer along one or more component lines of development, and finally terminate in stadia or predecessors at the end of one or more lines of inference. The products of the interplay of organic beings, particularly when these result in artifacts having an importance for social life, are the primary objects which are subject to this three-fold set of operations. The outcome is a set of distinct stadia or predecessors quite unlike anything to be found actually or analytically in the initial object.

Inference to Unifying Grounds

Instead of beginning with the acknowledgment of some single item, and ending with a plurality of components which may exist at distinct places and times, it is possible to begin with a plurality of present items and from there converge on some single past stadium or predecessor of the plurality. Many brown leaves spread around the tree lead us to the tree itself as their original locus. Documents, books, commentaries, monuments ground a plurality of inferences, all ending with the defeat of Napoleon at Waterloo.

Inference to Orientations

All the above inferences can be carried a step further. The outcome of each can be oriented in something other than itself. Since objects change in constitution, numbers and character over time, the number of orientations possible for inferences to stadia, predecessors, components, and grounds is evidently enormous. Each can be made to have primary reference to some particular object, institution or men as at that time; they can be made to have primary reference to them as at some later time; or they can be oriented in individual men as here and now.

All these inferences can be employed on natural objects, on the objects which constitute civilization, and on the items of a humanistic history. In the largest sense of the term, history comprises all that occurred in the human and subhuman realm. The historic consciousness need not then restrict itself to a consideration of humanistically oriented events, though history as now understood by historians does have this restriction.

II

Our inferences can be made as exact as one likes. But none will ever satisfy entirely. They remind one of an inference to the existence of God. No matter how good this might be no one trusts it. The following little dialogue may perhaps make the point evident:

"I know that God exists."

"How?"

"I infer it."

"Oh!"

"But it is a very good inference."

"I don't care how good it is. It just won't do. If you want to show me that you know that God exists, you must come up with more than an inference."

We don't trust the best possible inference to God. Does the situation change when we turn from such inferences to the inferences to the external world, to mathematical entities, or to the intent of man? Sceptics, constructivistic mathematicians, behaviourists and materialists do not think so. No proof would ever convince them. Is this because they will not listen to reason? Or is it because they sense that something necessary is missing, something without which one can have no confidence in the existence of God, the existence of an external world, the reality of some mathematical entity, or the existence of an intention?

What more is needed? It must either be other inferences, or something outside the realm of inference. It cannot be the former, for it is inference itself, not this or that type, which is here found wanting. The objector in our dialogue points up no flaw in the inference; his is an objection based bluntly and simply on the awareness that an inference alone does not suffice to bring us to the existence of God. And there is justification in his objection. Inferences by themselves can only end, have termini, and cannot possibly reach something outside themselves or outside the area where they are produced. We will be satisfied only when we go outside them, to that at which they terminate. We want to encounter, confront, face data outside the area of inference. Our inferences can lead us to the data, but we must leave our inferences behind if we want to lay hold of them. Only if we actually encounter that at which our inferences terminate, can we have a sufficient warrant for believing in the existence of Gods, immortal souls, external objects, private intents—and past events.

III

But can we encounter the past? It is gone, outside our reach. Any attempt to get into the past must disturb it, make it other than it was, for it was not that which was being reached into from the present. And if we could get to it, we would somehow be able to travel backwards in time, taking an ongoing time all the while in order to engage in this activity. How foolish then it is to suppose that when we look up at the sky we see a star aeons ago. The star as in the past is gone, finished. It cannot be encountered. Perhaps this is because it does not exist at all? No one, to my knowledge, has made this suggestion in connection with the star, but it has been made with respect to historical occurrences. Thus Croce: "History is contemporary history . . . an act of thought . . .", and Ortega y Gasset: "History is . . . a science of the present in the most rigorous and actual sense of the word." Their views have power, but they are essentially views which replace history by historiography, the past that has been by a present thought or by a narrative. If the past does not exist, every inference to it will be unsatisfactory. If it does exist, but in an impenetrable realm, our inferences will be futile, for we will never know that it exists at all. We must affirm that the past, as existing outside the present, cannot be encountered. But unless history is pure fiction, we must be able to encounter it somehow. The past is a realm of data to which our history must answer.

Each of the five inferences to the past allows for encounters. The inference to stadia, since it terminates in some phase of the leaf that is now before us in fact allows for four distinct kinds. The other inferences, referring as they do to pasts which existed before the leaf was in existence, are supported by encounters of quite different sorts.

1. Four Encountered Stadia

An inference to a stadium is an inference to a stage in the career of an object. It goes from the present dark brown-leaf to the leaf when this had a lighter brown or was green. These stadia no longer exist. They cannot be encountered in the present in the guise they had when they were present. But they can be encountered in the guise of a power now manifesting itself through the brown of the leaf.

(*a*) We need not attend to the past to know that the brown is a component of the substantial leaf here and now. But we must attend to it to know why the brown is a distinctive brown, now in the leaf in a distinctive way. The leaf would not now hold on to the brown as it does had the leaf not gone through the career it had. The past through which the leaf has gone is exhibited in the guise of an act of possession making the brown of the leaf substantial and unique.

Psychoanalysts have seen this point quite clearly. A man, let us say, always stumbles at a given spot. There seems to be nothing in the spot which should cause a stumble. Since the event involves a present man and a present action, one can find all one needs to explain this event in the man's movements in that situation. We might therefore try to explain the stumble in terms of physiological disequilibria, of physical disturbances too slight to notice, in terms of deliberate intent, and so on. But what we will not then be able to explain is why the man always stumbles, or even more sharply, why it is that he stumbles in a peculiar way when he comes to that spot. The psychoanalyst tries to account for it by looking for something in the past of the individual—perhaps some traumatic experience suffered at that spot. He provides an explanation which goes beyond the pure description of the stumble as a loss of equilibrium involving such and such tendons and muscles, or beyond the external causal explanation which might find a force being exerted. The physiological account would go beneath the surface but only to analytic components; the external causal explanation would look for antecedents of constituents. The historical explanation would instead look for a present determination of the act of stumbling. It will recognize the stadium through which the individual had gone in the shape of an effective distinctive determination of the stumble.

(*b*) We encounter the past stadium in the guise of powers which make the features, natures, and activities of present objects distinctive. We encounter it also in the guise of an act of self-maintenance, by which it stands over against other things.

The insistence and resistance of the present object, if taken as a brute ultimate fact, as a function of the pressure and influences others exert on it, are left inexplicable. They deserve an explanation. Since they do not vary in simple accordance with the degree and kind of pressures and influences exerted, it is necessary to look elsewhere than to external conditions for an explanation of their occurrence. Beings resist and insist with different stresses on different occasions in ways which require a reference to what they are within.

The leaf is not conscious, nor does it remember, but it responds to what it now interplays with in the light of what it had once been. Any structural alterations in it which we might find will not wholly explain the degree and kind of self-maintenance now being manifested. When it was green its response to sun and wind was other than what it now is; it now acts as it does because of the way it had once responded. For one thing, it is more or less susceptible than it had been to the very influences which operated on it before. An inference to the green-leaf gets warranting support from the way the leaf now maintains itself over against all else; the past stadium is expressed as a present active power of self-maintenance.

The desire or lack of desire on the part of men to continue to struggle and to live evidently has an explanation similar to that of the insistence and resistance of the leaf to external forces. In the very same circumstances undergone before, a man, without reflection, memory, or consciousness, suddenly sinks into despair. The despair is an aspect of his attitude towards the world, an attitude which carries out into the open a stadium through which he had once gone, and which is now being encountered in the guise of a despairing self-maintenance.

(c) Objects are encountered not only as unique or self-maintaining, but as having a directionality, a kind of purposiveness, a disposition, habit, or tendency in some direction. These are not open to observation; one can see only sequences of activities, never the links between them. We acknowledge them so far as we know that things continue to move or function in a certain direction which the structure or features of the things do not explain. There is no gain in giving up the idea of causality for the idea of habit as Hume did, if what one seeks is to reduce what is, to what can be atomistically observed. Causation and habits are equally unobservable.

The potentialities in a thing are realized in a sequence due to the fact that the being had gone through a certain stadium. We encounter that stadium in the guise of an inward disposition. The entire weight of the past of an individual is being made manifest in the shape of the direction which its present nature, features, and activities are being inwardly determined to take.

(*d*) There is a self-containedness, a kind of irreducibility to every object which cannot be accounted for by looking outside it, or by studying its various features. The nature and force of this is constantly changing; its character depends on what the object had undergone. The leaf now has a being, in contrast with every other. Because it had been green, the leaf, without losing a core of identity, has an interior nature unlike what it had before or what it will have at another time. The counterpart of an inferred stadium of the leaf is encountered whenever we face the leaf as 'othering' us in a way which is now distinctive for it.

Our selves are constants, the loci of our self-identity. But they also bear the marks of our guilt and hopes, our defeats and our adventures. We are self-same despite the fact that we change. Our self-same nature is now expressed in a new way, the acknowledgment of which is an acknowledgment of the present role of a past stadium of ourselves.

Every object is unique, self-maintaining, directional, and self-contained. And it is not hard to see why this must be so. At every moment each struggles to continue to be. Each achieves the nature and being it has as a consequence of the fact that it lays hold of some prospect, realizes this, and thereby is related to a further prospect, demanding a new act of unification. Because the stadia to which we infer were in fact produced through this four-fold process, they can be encountered in the guise of an act of possession, self-maintenance, directionality, and self-containedness.

2. *Encountered Predecessors*

Predecessors of the present objects are, like it, distinctive substances. Whatever characterizations are appropriate to the one are appropriate to the other. But we cannot find the predecessors operating in the present object. Caesar does not act in or through the document or monument we have before us in the way the green does in the present brown-leaf, or as my past experience does in my present stumble. Since I have nothing else to encounter but the object as here and now, either I am forced to say that the predecessors of the present object are beyond the reach of any encounter, or I must somehow encounter them here and now.

The predecessors to which I infer are conceptualized by me. They provide barriers through which the nature of the encounter can be filtered, thereby qualifying the nature of that encounter. By intermediating my encounter of the brown-leaf by the inferred predecessor of it, say a conceived bud, the effectiveness of the green-leaf is altered and I thereby undergo the experience of an encounter with the bud. That encounter can now be further modified by being mediated by the predecessor of the bud, the stem, and so on.

But if it be possible to modify the nature of an encounter by filtering it through a conceived idea, what check can we have on our inferences to predecessors? Any idea, it would seem, would provide a qualification of the encounter which a stadium in the present object provides. If we had inferred or merely imagined Brutus or some non-existing man and used this as the intermediary we would have just as effectively qualified the nature of the encounter now being undergone. This is true, but it is to be noted that we inferred to Caesar not in a capricious way, but because the evidence drove us there. We are therefore in a position to distinguish between the value of the qualification which the idea of him provides, in contrast with that which some other conceived figure could. The sequence of inferred predecessors leading up to the present offers an intelligible, ordered set of qualifications, terminating in the present experience.

From the standpoint of the historical consciousness, all objects are to be understood as so many different qualifications of a primary power, that of existence. It knows that we encounter existence as funnelled through present objects. That existence had been qualified by a whole series of objects. Those objects are now encountered in an existence filtered through my ideas of those predecessors.

3. *Encountered Components*

An inference to antecedent components is faced with the same problems as one which moves to predecessors. But in addition it is up against the fact that the components to which it moves are themselves diverse in nature, having no single qualification to impose on the existence we encounter in this present object. Ruins are the outcome of the interplay of cannon and house; they do not have the nature nor the power of the cannon, the house or their interplay. However, since the ruins are the product of aspects of these, not of them in their full concreteness, it is not necessary to refer to the cannon and house in their full concreteness. The component antecedents of the ruins are the house as constructed in such and such a way and out of such and such material, the cannon as impinging at such and such a rate and at such and such a place, and the interplay of their diverse insistencies—it is not the house as a full actuality in the past, not the cannon balls as they hurl through space, nor the interplay of house and cannon with all its noise and explosive force. Our encounter with the present ruins is an encounter that is rich enough to accommodate these abstract antecedent components and to which we infer over a number of divergent lines.

4. *Encountered Grounds*

Present leaves spread around the tree, observed ruins scattered over the hill, available documents narrating one and the same incident, lead to the construction of ideas of single unifying grounds. It is the effects of such unifying grounds that are said to be dispersed over regions at this later time. We construct the idea of such grounds when we want to understand what had contributed components to the single object we now confront. We engage in it too when we want to deal with a number of items all of which seem to have a single cause or source.

Since what we have in the present is dispersed and what we seek is unified, the terminus of an inference to a unifying ground does seem to require an encounter of a kind which is not available now. No encounter with the items in the dispersed collection will yield the kind which would be appropriate to a unity. And we have no way of adding the encounter with one entity here to the encounter of another there. However, it is to be noted that the items which we now confront are not merely external elements in an aggregate, but are all part of a single spatial world. The inference we make has its appropriate encounter not in the various items, taken severally or bunched together by us, but as subtended by the field in which they are embedded. When we infer to the unitary ground of the various items, we encounter the field as a unity for them all.

L*

Our unitary ground finds its proper encounter in the field in which our evidence for that ground is to be found. And this is proper, for what we seek to know in history is not the nature of this or that being but the nature of existence as expressed through various objects. Our encounter with the field is an encounter with the energy which once had filtered through a past reality and now is expressed as the connection that exists between the various present effects of it.

The Caesar I construct on the basis of the available evidence, if it is not to be the construction of a faint image of a man, must envisage him as having features, such as heart and lungs, blood and tendons, and as engaging in activities such as passing through various intermediary points between signal places. To make Caesar most human we must go beyond the facts to what might, so far as the evidence is concerned, be only fiction. This fact, however, need not disturb, and for two reasons. We make our construction plausible by imposing it on a present encounter and thereby see how the encounter is modified by being filtered through the idea. Secondly, though we do bring in details that go beyond the evidence, they are details which make it possible for the evidence and the inferences from it to be integrated in a plausible way. We infer to Caesar, and though he may not have existed in just the shape in which we envisage him, we do thereby learn something of him—if only it be that he qualified the existence we are encountering in the shape of the field of connections among the present dispersed evidences.

5. Encountered Orientation

It is rarely that we are content to remain with any neutral inference to a stadium, predecessor, component or ground. The result has too cold a sense, too detached a meaning to interest us for long. We qualify the outcome of these inferences with a reference to some central or focal object. These are themselves not directly encounterable unless they exist in the present. If they are in the past, something in the present must function as their representative. That representative must be a member of the same class as the represented objects, if it is not to distort the nature of that represented object.

An individual man can represent the rest of us so far as he knows, judges, acts in ways that illustrate rules, conditions and criteria germane to us all. He can therefore orient the past in all of us, thereby making it a humanized past. By relating a past occurrence in a present encountered representative individual, we can see what the past's import is for man. The historian is such a representative man. Sooner or later he turns from the evidence to himself as undergoing and qualifying his encounters. When he merely encountered the evidence he acted as an individual; the recognition that his experience is representative enables him to see what that encounter means for any man. The historian thus escapes solipsism and idiosyncratic reconstructions, not only by attending to the evidence and trying to do justice to all of it, but by making his own encounter with the past, through the body of the present, a representative one. It is the outcome of this representative encounter which he reports.

IV

Whitehead's doctrine of objective immortality maintains that the past is now an active component in the present. His account is closely tied to his thesis that actual occasions perish when and as they become. Held to too tenaciously the view would prevent Whitehead from affirming that there were any beings, other than God, which actually persist. As a consequence he would not be able to explain how a man could be self-identical over the course of an individual life, how any man could ever be guilty for something done by *him* years ago, how there could be an ethics of obligation, political action, artistic production, or an historical process.

The present paper can be treated as a tangential commentary, as a partial independent confirmation, or as a translation into a philosophy which acknowledges substances persisting through historical time, of such passages as the following:

"But the 'perishing' of absoluteness is the attainment of 'objective immortality'. This last conception expresses the further element in the doctrine of organism—that the process of generation is to be described in terms of actual entities."[1]

"The doctrine of objectification is an endeavour to express how what is settled in actuality is repeated under limitations, so as to be 'given' for immediacy. Later, in discussing 'time', this doctrine will be termed the doctrine of 'objective immortality'."[2]

[1] PR 83 [94].   [2] PR 191 [208].

". . . the attainment of a peculiar definiteness . . . passes into its objective immortality as a new objective condition added to the riches of definiteness attainable, the 'real potentiality' of the universe."[3]

"A simple physical feeling has the dual character of being the cause's feeling re-enacted for the effect as subject. . . . Simple physical feelings embody . . . the objective immortality of the past."[4]

"It belongs to the essence of this subject that it pass into objective immortality. Thus its own constitution involves that its own activity in *self*-formation passes into its activity of *other*-formation . . . the future will embody the present subject and will re-enact its patterns of activity . . . objective immortality is a stubborn fact for the future, involving its pattern of perspective re-enaction."[5]

"A pure physical prehension is how an occasion in its immediacy of being absorbs another occasion which has passed into the objective immortality of its non-being. It is how the past lives in the present. . . . How the past perishes is how the future becomes."[6]

[3] PR 314 [340].   [4] PR 336 [363–4].   [5] AI 248.   [6] AI 305.

WILLIAM P. D. WIGHTMAN

WHITEHEAD'S EMPIRICISM

XIII

WILLIAM P. D. WIGHTMAN

WHITEHEAD'S EMPIRICISM

"The unempirical character of the philosophical school derived from Hume cannot be too often insisted upon. The true empirical doctrine is that physical feelings are in their origin vectors, and that the genetic process of concrescence introduces the elements which emphasize privacy."[1]

This somewhat shocking pronouncement of Whitehead's has hardly been given the serious consideration it deserves. In this essay, without entering into the detailed exegesis which Whitehead himself provides, I wish to give prominence to what seem to me to be the most important of its implications, with special but not exclusive reference to the philosophy of science.

Whitehead began his academic career as a pure mathematician. In his investigations of the structure of mathematical thought embodied in the great *Treatise of Universal Algebra* (1898) and later in works on *The Axioms of Projective Geometry* (1906) and *The Axioms of Descriptive Geometry* (1907) he found himself faced with an inquiry into the relation of mathematics to the canons of necessary inference. In this enterprise he was joined by his former pupil, Bertrand Russell, the result of their joint labours being *Principia Mathematica*, which altered the whole face of mathematics and logic. But while Russell went on to apply this new instrument of analysis to the paradoxes and sources of confusions in ordinary language, Whitehead recoiled from what, so one of his pupils told me, he came to regard as a dead end. The next period, whose continuity with that of the *Universal Algebra* is revealed by a study of his long memoir on *Mathematical Concepts of the Material World* (1906), was that of the philosophy of science, *sensu strictu*, marked by *Enquiry into the Principles of Natural Knowledge* (1919) and *The Concept of Nature* (1920). Both these works are of course well known. Less well known is his *Organisation of Thought*

[1] PR 447 [481].

(1917), which was reprinted rather inconspicuously in *The Aims of Education* (1929). In the *Organisation of Thought* Whitehead is uncompromising in his attempt to keep the philosophy of science unpolluted from metaphysics. He does not deny that metaphysics has an important function, but "the basis of science does not depend on the assumption of any of the conclusions of metaphysics; . . . both science and metaphysics start from the same given groundwork of immediate experience and in the main proceed in opposite directions on their diverse tasks".[2] His subsequent anatomizing of some scientific ideas in the same work is almost positivistic, though there are reservations to be made to this. This early analysis and some of the *obiter dicta* in the *Principles of Natural Knowledge* and the *Concept of Nature* have misled many of those who have studied his works, and among them the most sympathetic, to miss the point of the revolution in thought which he ultimately brought about. A typical example of this is the late Sir Edmund Whittaker's statement in his Eddington Memorial Lecture of 1951. "The philosophical system of my old friend and teacher Alfred North Whitehead is justly regarded as the most important metaphysical achievement of the present century. Whitehead accepts the principle, that in the endeavour to arrive at a philosophy, it is well to begin by first forming a natural philosophy, that is, a philosophy which is concerned with the physical world, and is based on the discoveries of theoretical and experimental science: in a further stage its scope can be enlarged so as to cover the whole of experience, and to investigate the general notions of Being and Reality. The completed system is thus a philosophical generalization of the concepts of science. The development of Whitehead's own thought had this character, from its first communication in his memoir of 1905, *On Mathematical Concepts of the Material World*, to its consummation as set forth in his Gifford Lectures of 1927 on *Process and Reality*."[3] Now Whittaker had one of the most acute minds of this century; also he had a command of language, whose lucidity and persuasiveness might go far to disseminate and perpetuate what I believe to be a serious misunderstanding. He appears to have confused the actual course of the development of Whitehead's philosophy with the structure embodied in its final formulation. A possible hint as to the movement of Whitehead's thought occurs in the Preface to the

[2] AE 161.   [3] Cambridge, 1951, pp. 31–2.

Principles of Natural Knowledge, where he says that "The discussion of the deduction of scientific concepts from the simplest elements of our perceptual knowledge at once brings us to philosophical theory".[4] In other words any assessment of the nature and validity of science is a philosophical enterprise. But at this stage of his thought he expressly denies that it need be a metaphysical enterprise. Metaphysical, that is, in the traditional sense of ontological. It must however be what we should perhaps call meta-scientific; for Whitehead never suffered under the delusion that science can pull itself up by its own bootstraps.[5] Thus, although Whitehead in all his earlier works shows himself convinced of the necessity for the re-examination of the foundations of science, he expressly denied any concern with what may be the relation of scientific ideas to the ultimate realities. In the *Principle of Relativity* he quotes with approval the remark of the Cambridge physicist, Poynting, "I have no doubt whatever that our ultimate aim must be to describe the sensible in terms of the sensible". "Adherence", Whitehead says, "to this aphorism, sanctioned by the authority of two great English physicists [the other was J. J. Thomson], is the keynote of everything in the following chapters."[6] In the remainder of this paragraph Whitehead comes as near as he ever did to the 'bootstrap' theory: "The philosophy of science is the endeavour to formulate the most general characters of things observed. Nature is what is observed, and the ether is an observed character of things observed. Thus the philosophy of science only differs from any of the special natural sciences by the fact that it is natural science at the stage before it is convenient to split it up into its various branches. This philosophy exists because there is something to be said before we commence the process of differentiation. It is true that in human thought the particular precedes the general. Accordingly the philosophy will not advance until the branches of science have made independent progress. Philosophy then appears as a criticism and a corrective, and—what is now to the purpose—as an

---

[4] PNK vii.

[5] A hope expressed with touching *naïveté* in the preamble to the constitution of the B.S.P.S. "The main emphasis", this says, "is upon an approach through the various special sciences to the philosophy of science."

There is no passage *through* science to philosophy. There is passage *from* science to philosophy; and there is or ought to be frequent return from philosophy to science; that is, unless you want such philosophical abortions as Hegel's dialectical deduction of the number of the planets.   [6] PRel 5.

additional source of evidence in times of fundamental reorganisation."[7] Transcended—almost completely inverted—as it was in Whitehead's later works this passage nevertheless contains the shadows of the ideas that are to be found in all his subsequent thought, the central idea being, as he puts it over the page, "When once you tamper with your basic concepts, philosophy is merely the marshalling of one main source of evidence, and cannot be neglected".[8] But here they are literally shadows; the realities will appear only in the light of the deeper analysis of *Science and the Modern World*. They are shadows because they are set in the mist of a *dogmatic* empiricism, which as I shall hope to show, Whitehead later recognized to be ultimately the negation of empiricism. It is for this reason that I believe that Whitehead's empiricism deserves much more serious consideration than it has so far received from philosophers of science.

Whitehead signed the Preface of the *Principle of Relativity* in September 1922. For three years there was silence, during which period he ceased to be Professor of Applied Mathematics at the Imperial College and became Professor of Philosophy at Harvard. This appointment was an imaginative and courageous act, such as was hardly to be expected from such a venerable body. Whitehead was over sixty and had passed through no university school of philosophy. This latter fact probably accounts for the extraordinarily untidy character of the gradual unfolding of his ideas. It is full of glaring inconsistencies, marchings and counter-marchings, as the attainment of each new eminence renders necessary a reappraisement of what from a previous position had been but imperfectly envisaged. But this inconsistency is not to be confused with the appalling opacity of some of his thought, or the alleged obscurity of his language. If these result from his lack of academic discipline in philosophic dialectic it is in quite a different sense from that in which it may be true of the former characteristic. Since he owed allegiance to no school he was able to see, as perhaps none since those great amateurs, Berkeley and Hume, have seen, the overpowering influence of fashion and unconscious presuppositions in the appraisements of even those aspects of experience which appear to be the simplest of its deliverances; indeed of these pre-eminently. It was therefore true, perhaps in a sense rather different from what he had in mind, that his final philosophy was

[7] PRel 5.   [8] *Ibid.* 6.

based upon a "recurrence to that phase of philosophic thought which began with Descartes and ended with Hume".[9] Like Descartes he realized that the time had come for a complete reconstruction from the foundations; but it was both his advantage and his burden to see what a hopeless train of error and confusion followed from the simple-minded dichotomy which Descartes had been willing to build on. As Gilson has shown, there was far less really new in Descartes' system than appears on the surface. Whitehead's approach embodies, I believe, a much more subtle revolution than that of Descartes. Whitehead was therefore faced with the task of deploying a scheme of ideas for which no appropriate language lay ready to hand. That the result is frequently tortuous, obscure, and ambiguous is not to be wondered at. The same accusation was levelled by the contemporary chemists against Avogadro. Fifty years later it was realized that Avogadro's ideas of the structure of matter were far more accurate and fertile than those of Dalton, although to judge from some references to the atomic theory that one still hears, this fact does not yet seem to have been universally appreciated. With this historical precedent in mind one might even go so far as to say that any philosophical work which is both crystal clear and free from internal inconsistencies is so, either because it is merely restating in a clearer form what has already been laboured by more creative minds, or because it is dodging the real difficulties.

I said that after *The Principle of Relativity* there were three years of silence. This is strictly true only in relation to the world that relies solely on printed books. His Presidential Address to the Aristotelian Society in 1922, called "Uniformity and Contingency", contains a passage which clearly foreshadows the coming reorientation of his thought; but even here there is no explicit affirmation of his belief in the insufficiency of natural science and mathematics to form the basis of a philosophy of experience. In *Science and the Modern World* (1925), however, the opening paragraph of the Preface betrays the intellectual somersault which the author had turned in the interval: ". . . each age has its dominant preoccupation; and, during the three centuries in question, the cosmology derived from science has been asserting itself at the expense of older points of view with their origins elsewhere. Men can be provincial in time, as well as in place. We may ask ourselves whether the

9 PR v [v].

scientific mentality of the modern world in the immediate past is not a successful example of such provincial limitation. Philosophy, in one of its functions, is the critic of cosmologies. It is its function to harmonise, refashion, and justify divergent intuitions as to the nature of things. It has to insist on the scrutiny of the ultimate ideas, and on the retention of the whole of the evidence in shaping our cosmological scheme. Its business is to render explicit and—so far as may be—efficient, a process which otherwise is unconsciously performed without rational tests. . . . "Philosophy . . . is the most effective of all the intellectual pursuits. It builds cathedrals before the workmen have moved a stone and it destroys them before the elements have worn down their arches. It is the architect of the buildings of the spirit, and it is also their solvent:—and the spiritual precedes the material. Philosophy works slowly. Thoughts lie dormant for ages; and then, almost suddenly as it were, mankind finds that they have embodied themselves in institutions."

Whitehead's 'somersault' was perhaps more apparent than real. Hardly any of the results arrived at by means of the analysis of the earlier years are jettisoned; but the emphasis is completely reversed. Before this time it might have been possible, as Whittaker thought, for Whitehead to "enlarge the scope" of the philosophy of science to cover the whole of experience; in *Science and the Modern World* this is expressly repudiated. And whereas Whittaker reported that "the completed system is thus a philosophical generalization of the concepts of science", the position that Whitehead will maintain from now onwards is the precise opposite, namely, that science with all its triumphs, and more particularly with all its failures, is a brilliant but one-sided abstraction from the concrete experience of mankind on which it claims to be based: "Clear-sighted men of the sort who are so clearly wrong, now proclaim that the secrets of the physical universe were finally disclosed. If only you ignored everything which refused to come into line, your powers of explanation were unlimited."[10] This reorientation of Whitehead's thought is so vital to his subsequent analysis of experience that at the risk of labouring the point I must quote again: "The historical revolt has thus been exaggerated into the exclusion of philosophy from its proper role of harmonising the various abstractions of methodological thought. Thought is abstract; and the intolerant use of abstractions is the

[10] SMW 147.

major vice of the intellect. This vice is not wholly corrected by the recurrence to concrete experience. For after all, you need only attend to those aspects of your concrete experience which lie within some limited scheme. There are two methods for the purification of ideas. One of them is dispassionate observation by means of the bodily senses. But observation is selection. Accordingly, it is difficult to transcend a scheme of abstraction whose success is sufficiently wide. The other method is by comparing the various schemes of abstraction which are well founded in our various types of experience. . . . Faith in reason is the trust that the ultimate natures of things lie together in a harmony which excludes mere arbitrariness. . . . The faith in the order of nature which has made possible the growth of science is a particular example of a deeper faith. This faith cannot be justified by any inductive generalization. . . . To experience this faith is to know that in being ourselves we are more than ourselves."[11] Faith. Faith . . . Faith . . . Faith especially in the "sense of things far more deeply interfused". Faith born not in the solitude of the hermit's cell, but as for Wordsworth, from the "direct inspection of the nature of things as disclosed in our own immediate present experience".[12] This faith in the existence of an already existing order in nature coupled with the denial that anything can be *merely* itself is the core of what Whitehead called the philosophy of organism. It is the result of retaining the *whole* of the evidence in shaping our cosmological scheme; for we have no warrant, *in experience*, for asserting that experience starts with green patches, smooth surfaces and agreeable smells, which are thereafter synthesized into apples. Experience in general is at least of an apple in its concrete immediacy: it may be a delusive apple painted by a consummate artist, but that is not the point. It may be merely what Whitehead calls failure of symbolic reference. It may be that an element of judgment enters into all perceptions; but this again is not in general given in experience any more than isolated smells and colours. I have twice qualified my statement by 'in general'; this might be thought to have given away the whole position like Descartes' appeal to the pineal body. But it leaves the vast majority of perceptions untouched, and is inserted to forestall objections based on the experience that perception has to be learned. Thus it would be as absurd to state that a baby perceives a presented apple as an apple, as to suggest that it

[11] SMW 26-7.   [12] *Ibid.*

perceives isolated colours, smells and feels. Nothing in Whitehead's account is at variance with William James's view that all the baby is at first aware of is a booming buzzing confusion: there is at first nothing that could be dignified by the name perception. The same applies to the case of a person blind from birth and subsequently achieving sight—he also, as is well known, has to learn, almost painfully, to see. I also qualified my statement by 'at least'— "Experience in general is *at least* of an apple in its concrete immediacy". The further qualification of experience which is thereby implied is hardly touched upon in *Science and the Modern World*, in which, as Whitehead says, all epistemological questions are expressly excluded. Whitehead's main assault on the problem of knowledge was made in his Barbour-Page Lectures to the University of Virginia in 1927 and published in a book of a hundred small pages called *Symbolism*. Of all Whitehead's works this might turn out to be the most valuable short-range contribution; for it is an attempt to analyse the modes of experience in terms as close as possible to the data of experience; also it is almost entirely free from that terminological apparatus which is accounted a stumbling block to all but the most persistent of his readers. I should be surprised if any psychologist, who was concerned with anything more than the passage of pointer-readings through the statistical mill, or who was not completely bemused by cybernetics, could fail to find illumination in it. Its contents were absorbed into the ultimate cosmological structure which Whitehead expounded in his Gifford Lectures of 1927-8 called *Process and Reality*; and since the latter displays the relation of the former to the traditional problems of philosophy I shall make use of both these sources in what follows. I shall however avoid as far as possible the purely metaphysical issues raised in *Process and Reality*.

Whitehead warns us that the word 'experience' is one of the most deceitful in philosophy. A false step in the analysis of the simplest type of experience involves the whole of the subsequent philosophical construction. The origin of the confusion in modern accounts of experience is the failure to redesign the categories of explanation to conform to enlargement of the knowledge of the *mechanism* of perception. "The Greeks", Whitehead notes, "looked at a stone and perceived that it was grey. The Greeks were ignorant of modern physics; but modern philosophers discuss perception in terms of categories derived from the Greeks. The Greeks started from perception in its most elaborate and sophisticated form, namely visual perception."[13] This, according to Whitehead, is the wrong foot on which so much modern discussion starts. Our knowledge of physiology shows that the final common form of all perceptions is a wave of action-potential directed by an axis cylinder whose histological structure appears to be independent of the nature of the final response. This does away at the outset with any distinction between primary and secondary qualities. As far as any kind of immediate perception is concerned the perceived apple in the mirror is just as 'real' as the perceived apple on the table. "To call anything unreal", Whitehead notes, "is merely to define 'reality' in such a way as to exclude the thing concerned." But perhaps this is today hardly a matter of dispute. To give an account of the nature of perceptual experience we should avoid the subtleties of sight so ably brought out by Berkeley in his *New Theory of Vision*, and concentrate on the features common to all perception. On this question Whitehead quotes Hume, who wrote: "But my senses convey to me only the impressions of coloured points, disposed in a certain manner. If *the eye is sensible* of anything further I desire it may be pointed out to me."[14] In this and other similar quotations Hume explicitly asserts that *the eye sees*. "The conventional comment", Whitehead observes, "on such a passage is that Hume for the sake of intelligibility is using common forms of expression; that this is only really speaking of impressions on the mind, and that in the dim future some learned scholar will gain reputation by emending 'eye' into 'ego'. The reason for citing the passages is to enforce the thesis that the form of speech is literary and intelligible because it expresses the ultimate truth of animal perception."[15] Whitehead continues: "The ultimate momentary 'ego' has as its datum 'the eye as experiencing such and such sights'."[16] This last sentence is charged with the essence of Whitehead's *empiricism*: this is comprised in the two phrases "momentary ego" and "eye experiencing such and such sights"; but they constitute an organic whole. We have seen that Hume had already as it were intuited the objective aspect of the transaction—"eye sensible of coloured points"—but he betrayed the ideal of empiricism by ignoring it in the subsequent development of his epistemology. It is a cardinal feature of Whitehead's teaching that "the philosophy of organism is apt to emphasize just those ele-

[13] PR 164 [179].   [14] *Ibid.*, 165 [180].   [15] *Ibid.*   [16] *Ibid.*

ments" in the writings of the earlier philosophers "which subse-quent systematizers have put aside".[17] Why have we been taught to forget that we see "with the eye" when not even a philosopher would shy at feeling a stone with the finger? The final common form at the brain terminals is an action-potential—neither a sight, nor a feel of cold smoothness. There are two questions here: first, how do we 'know' that the eye is seeing, the finger merely feeling? How can the sensations be so different if the character of the end of the transmission chain is the same in both cases? The possibility of discrimination is a physiological question. The common mode of transmission and terminal excitation are indeed indistinguish-able; but the skin receptors patently differ from the retinal receptors. Therefore they do not respond to the same stimulus: if you shut your eyes you can not see with your hands. A similar difference occurs at the central termini of the cerebrum. This suffices for the *possibility* of discrimination; but it in no way explains *why* one action-potential is 'felt' as cold and another as red. Note that I have introduced the term 'felt' for both kinds of sensation. This usage of Whitehead's is a recurrence to that of Hume, as empiricist, to whom all experiences were either primary impres-sions or recalled impressions differing from the former only in 'force and vivacity'. For Whitehead *feelings* (thus avoiding the abstract mechanical associations of 'impression') constitute what he calls the subjective pole of every realized occasion in the universe. The point which Whitehead wishes to emphasize is that in normal unsophisticated experience every perception has a feeling-tone. Again Hume points the way in recognizing that cold, taste, anger and joy are all alike impressions, though the former are held to originate in the outside world, the latter—at any rate at the sophisticated level—in the bodily organs. To this it may be objected that in the psychological laboratory when we are studying the nature of visual perception we are devoid of any feeling-tone in respect of the colour patches displayed to us. To which Whitehead would reply that we do not, except for a few eccentrics, pass our days in psychological laboratories. The situation created for us when we are there is an artificial one, in which the immediacy of the stimulus is heightened to such a degree that feeling-tone is virtually abolished. Professor A. D. Ritchie was, I imagine, thinking along the same lines when he wrote of the celebrated

[17] PR v [v].

Pavlovian experiments on conditioned reflexes: "It was a model of experimental technique from the point of view of eliminating uncontrolled variables; unfortunately the dog was one of the variables eliminated."[18] I have just spoken of the immediacy of the stimulus. When this is heightened we may feel justified in saying that we are experiencing a red patch—just that. This experience, because it can be expressed in simple *terms* with all the normal variables controlled, has been thought by philosophers to be a simple *experience*. Whitehead urges that on the contrary it is one possible only in the last stages of sophistication, and could happen, as a recognized experience, only at that level. For the purposes of living—even high-grade living—it is vacuous. It is vacuous, because *in itself* it can refer to nothing else whatsoever. It can lead to nothing except what Santayana has called the 'solipsism of the present moment'. And yet, in experience, every perception *does* refer to something else; that is, it has a meaning. How is this possible? Because, according to Whitehead, every perceptual occasion has a two-fold character, of which this presentational immediacy, as he calls it, is the less fundamental, though in its abstract potentiality, none the less important. Before we consider the other aspect, let us return to a phrase mentioned some time ago—the momentary ego.

One of the reasons for the sterility of the traditional epistemology is the neglect of the durational aspect of experience. Almost every philosopher has recognized it before pushing it into the background as an inconvenient intrusion. But no analysis of perception can have any ultimate validity which ignores duration as an integral part of it. There is no experience whatever without temporal thickness, as Whitehead calls it. Much play has in the past been made of instantaneous experiences and of nature at an instant. But there are no instants in nature. Now if this be granted, it follows that every perceptual occasion involves an element of non-sensuous perception—the 'knowledge' (I think Whitehead's term here might be improved) of our own immediate past. Doubtless there are innumerable other non-sensuous perceptions—the *petites perceptions* which Leibniz recognized as going to build up any unit of perceptual experience. But this particular unconscious 'knowledge' clearly provides the basis for the continuity of our actions, and in Whitehead's hands the basis of his metaphysic. For if it

[18] *The Natural History of Mind*, London: Longmans, 1936, p. 105.

provides the basis for subjective continuity it does no less for the particularity of perceptual occasions. Every specious present inherits from the immediate past and has significance by virtue of its immediate future—what Whitehead calls its subjective aim. The first hint of this Whitehead found in Locke—again an example of a stone which former builders rejected. Locke's essay, as Whitehead observed, is more remarkable for its adequacy than for its consistency. Locke's only objection to the existence of ideas of particular things is that no mind could be big enough to contain them. For Whitehead, the receiving of an idea of a particular thing is precisely what takes place in perception—sensuous and non-sensuous alike. But in order to avoid the hopelessly confused (and completely non-empirical) notion of a 'mind' full of 'ideas' he called the process 'prehension' of an actual entity by the percipient actual entity. With remarkable sagacity Locke illustrated this by reference to the formation by children of 'pictures' of the nurse and mother; ideas of individual things are primary; afterwards, as he says, they "become general by separating from them the circumstances of time and place and any other ideas that may determine them to this or that particular existent". But for Locke the pressure of the subject-predicate expression of the relation of ideas, and the powerful influence of Galileo and Descartes, were too strong; elsewhere in his *Essay* he expounds his doctrine in terms of atomic sensa representing the actualities contemplated. Logical simplicity has been mistaken for priority in the process of constituting an experient occasion. This false identification has, Whitehead thinks, vitiated thought and procedure from the first discovery of mathematics and logic by the Greeks, and accounts for some of the worst defects in educational practice.

The above hint from Locke provides as it were the material for Whitehead's account of perceptual occasions, but is vitiated by the limited conception of the mind as a storehouse. Yet elsewhere Locke's description of time as a "perpetual perishing" goes half-way to form Whitehead's account of subjective continuity. But time, *pace* Newton, is not a flowing river, refreshing or otherwise; rather, as Lucretius and Berkeley knew well enough, an abstraction from the contemplation of change. "Whenever I attempt", wrote Berkeley, "to frame a simple idea of time, abstracted from the succession of ideas in my mind . . . I am lost and embrangled in inextricable difficulties."[19] Time is no simple essence; it is not *time* that perishes but the actual entities. This is a hard saying, and had better be left over until we have dealt with the last aspect of perceptual experience which I intend to refer to.

I return now to the other aspect recognized by Whitehead in every perceptual occasion—that which he calls *causal efficacy*. Granted the adequacy of the theory that perception is primarily nothing but the contemplation of sensa, which of course Whitehead flatly denies, then causation is and must remain a baseless mystery. As an empiricist Hume was honest enough to admit that in this connection we have a feeling of necessitation; as an eighteenth-century philosopher he was honest enough to admit that there is no *reason* in the atomic sensa to account for this; so he wisely went to his dinner and backgammon board. Whitehead not only admits the feeling of necessitation in the causal situation but draws attention to other aspects of experience generally overlooked by philosophers, but not so often by psychologists. More important still he asks how *could* there be a reason in an occasion analysed purely in terms of presentational immediacy? It can point to nothing except the 'solipsism of the present moment'. I have already referred to Whitehead's claim that an analysis in these terms is not an analysis of *normal* experience at all; but of experience at its most sophisticated level under exceptional controls. It is therefore not an empirical analysis. In the transaction of ordinary life the essence of perception is the recognition of significance, and we have seen that a red patch *qua* red patch can be significant of nothing but itself. Only when it has been as it were incorporated in a routine of significance is it normally perceived. Consider the innumerable sensa waiting in vain to be perceived. The sources of stimulation are there; the physical energy is pouring out and entering the appropriate sense organs; but the sensa are simply not perceived. 'Sensed' they must be if by 'sensed' we mean evocation of some physical response in the nervous system; but that is a matter of physiological psychology and not part of the experience of the percipient subject, with which alone we are concerned. To drag in events in the body of the percipient which can be observed only by another observer is to introduce phenomenological confusion.

On this question of significance Whitehead wrote an illuminating passage in the last of his major works, *Modes of Thought*. "During

[19] Berkeley, *The Principles of Human Knowledge*, § 98.

many generations there has been an attempt to explain our ultimate insights as merely interpretative of sense-impression. I
suggest to you that this basis for philosophic understanding is
analogous to an endeavour to elucidate the sociology of modern
civilization as wholly derivative from the traffic-signals on the main
roads. The motions of the cars are conditioned by these signals. But
the signals are not the reasons for the traffic."[20] I mentioned the
annihilation of feeling tone in the visual-psychology laboratory:
Whitehead points to the complementary experience when sensory
stimulation is reduced to a minimum; instead of external reference
being reduced to a minimum, as it should be on the basis of the
usual theory of 'interpretation of sense data', the opposite is the
case—the *experience* of vague presences devoid of any sensory
concomitants. Try walking blindfold across a large smooth field
devoid of any objects: even moderate speed becomes impossible;
the *feeling* of lurking obstacles or even opposition becomes more
and more oppressive. Of course if there are virtually *no* sensa,
unconsciousness ensues; but in the type of experiences just
referred to, when the high-grade sensa of sight and sound are
absent, the fundamental animal characteristic of perception—
causal efficacy—is heightened. The same is true of strong emotion
—it is a causal efficacious man we hate, not a collection of sense
data, which in the extreme of passion may become vague to the
point of vanishing: then we 'hit out blindly'. The relation between
the perceptual modes in normal experience is revealed most clearly
in the experience of the cricketer or the fencer. If the ball or the
sword-point be well placed the feeling actually (that is, in respect
of causal efficacy) *experienced* is that of the ball on the bat or that
of the opponent's body at the sword-point. Those philosophers
who have insisted that the feeling is 'really' at the touch receptors
of the hands or in the brain and is 'referred' to the bat or sword-
point have done so because the analysis of perception, misled by
abstractions legitimate in physiology, has been solely in respect of
presentational immediacy. A misdirected blow or thrust conversely can so enhance the mode of presentational immediacy that
it is in my hand that I feel the pain. But the two sets of receptors
are almost contiguous.

The full impact of Whitehead's analysis of experience can not of
course be realized without a consideration of his metaphysic, which
both arises out of the analysis and gives it its coherence. I propose

[20] MT 43–4.

to deal with only one aspect of this, since it seems to violate the conservation principles of science.

The most striking novelty in Whitehead's metaphysical grounding of experience is his statement that it is not time that perishes but the actual entities—the 'really real' constituents of the universe which he postulates as the sufficient reason for every concrete experience. His justification of this apparent paradox is twofold. Negatively, time can not perish; since, apart from the actual entities and their perceived relations which we call events, it does not exist; and that which has no real existence can not cease to be. But to maintain the *experienced* distinction of past and present, in the sense that the experienced present has a being categorically different from that of the experienced past, *something* must perish. So long as the ultimate category of scientific explanation (the 'classical' equivalent of the 'actual entities') was the "hard, massy, movable particles" of Newton, Whitehead's attempt at the analysis of temporal experience would have been untenable; 'perishing' and 'conservation' are mutually exclusive attributes. But the conservation principles of modern physics have nothing to do with bits of timeless matter moving about in timeless space. What is held to be conserved is mass-energy; that is, some fundamental entity in the precise formulation of whose nature *time* enters as an essential constituent. For the inseparability of the 'conserved' entity from the notion of 'frequency' implies a minimum time-lapse in which it can express its nature. Nor is this merely a qualitative fact, but can be given quantitative expression in terms of the relation $e = hv$. The fundamental entities of physics—electron, photon, etc.—are not of course to be *identified* with the 'actual entities' of Whitehead; rather are they the 'forms of definiteness' in which certain characteristics of the latter achieve expression in certain conditions of the extensive continuum. Hence the above discussion is in no sense a 'proof' of the correctness of Whitehead's (in part metaphysical) account of the function of time in experience. It merely shows how the independent reformulation of physical principles has removed a barrier to the acceptance of a theory of time and change in which "in every act of becoming there is the becoming of something with temporal extension; but . . . the act itself is not extensive".[21]

Yet a metaphysical doubt still lingers: how can the 'really real'

[21] PR 96 [107]. In regard to the physical aspects of this question I have been greatly helped by discussion with my colleague, Dr C. McCombie.

constituents of the universe perish? To answer this would necessarily demand a metaphysical discussion which would here be out of place. Part of the answer is, however, of special significance to biology: it is summed up by Whitehead in the phrase, "*How* an actual entity *becomes* constitutes *what* that actual entity is";[22] as it 'perishes' it is 'prehended' into other 'actual entities', thereby attaining 'objective immortality'. If a sequence of such actual entities retains a larger measure of the pattern and modes of objectification of the former we may call it an individual. But its persistence is in part an illusion: "After a few years we recognise the same cat, but we are thereby related to different molecules." Similarly the 'person' studied by the psychologist is to some extent an abstraction: he is the historic route of a society of actual entities, every one of which continually perishes but is objectified in the satisfaction of the succeeding ones—or not, if the historic route intersects that of a motor-bus.

[22] PR 31 [34].

DANIEL D. WILLIAMS

DEITY, MONARCHY, AND METAPHYSICS:
WHITEHEAD'S CRITIQUE OF THE
THEOLOGICAL TRADITION

XIV

DANIEL D. WILLIAMS

DEITY, MONARCHY, AND METAPHYSICS: WHITEHEAD'S CRITIQUE OF THE THEOLOGICAL TRADITION

Whitehead believed that the Christian tradition needs a purification of its doctrine, especially of its doctrine of God. This purification, he held, can be accomplished in part through metaphysical speculation which is the work of reason seeking for the notions of widest generality. Yet Whitehead has a complex view of the origin and nature of metaphysical knowledge, and an acute sense of the limitations of all human understanding. He warns, "The speculative methods of metaphysics are dangerous, easily perverted. So is all Adventure; but Adventure belongs to the essence of civilization."[1]

In this paper I propose to examine Whitehead's critique of certain doctrines in Christian theology. He makes specific criticisms of the traditional doctrine of God which he regards as having been determined by the conception of the Divine Monarch or Despot. There is a wider problem underlying Whitehead's consideration of the doctrine of God, since he makes the claim that metaphysical thought can arrive at knowledge of God, and can correct religious doctrines. The problem of the relation of theology to philosophy has become increasingly acute in the twentieth century, and Whitehead's thought offers an important occasion for analysing the problems involved. In this paper we shall consider what Whitehead says about the significance of philosophy for religious knowledge, and raise further questions which are implied by his position.

Out of the many aspects of Whitehead's doctrine of God I have selected one for special emphasis, that is the question of how God acts in or upon the world and the creatures. This is of fundamental importance in Whitehead's proposal of an alternative to the doctrines he criticizes, and furthermore it is a topic of crucial importance for contemporary Christian theology with its emphasis in the biblical perspective upon the action of God in history.

[1] AI 380.

I

There is no idea to which Whitehead returns more frequently in his writings than that Christian thought has fastened upon religious thinking a conception of God which had its barbaric origin in the despotism of early monarchical social organization. From the earlier Hebrew prophets to the Augustinian synthesis, Whitehead says, the decisive period "begins in barbarism and ends in failure. The failure consisted in the fact that barbaric elements and the defects in intellectual comprehension had not been discarded, but remained as essential elements in the various formulations of Christian theology, orthodox and heretical alike. Also, the later Protestant Reformation was, in this respect, an even more complete failure, in no way improving Catholic theology. The Quakers perhaps form a minor exception to this statement."[2]

'Barbarism', I believe, is never defined by Whitehead; but there is no question as to what he identifies with the barbaric in religion. It is the conceiving of God in the image of the arbitrary ruler with no checks upon his power. It is "the fashioning of God in the image of the Egyptian, Persian, and Roman imperial rulers".[3] The Semitic concept of God as a definite, personal, individual entity, "is the rationalization of the tribal gods of the earlier communal religions".[4]

We come then to the specific content of the Christian conception of God. Whitehead finds three strains of thought in the developed Christian doctrine: the imperial ruler, God in the image of the personification of moral energy, and God in the image of an ultimate metaphysical principle. The last is derived from the fusion of Aristotle's Unmoved Mover with the doctrine of God as the Eminently Real which has been favoured in Christian theology.[5]

Since Whitehead is going to argue that metaphysical thought can criticize this doctrine, what is to be said about the metaphysical element which it already contains? One of his criticisms of the traditional doctrine is that "it leaves God completely outside metaphysical rationalization".[6] Whitehead acknowledges that the Alexandrine theologians made a metaphysical discovery in their doctrine of immanence, as applied both in Christology and in the

---

[2] AI 212.   [3] PR 485 [520].   [4] RM [68].
[5] PR 484–5 [519–20].   [6] RM [70].

general notion of God's relation to the world; but "their general concept of the Deity stopped all further generalization. They made no effort to conceive the World in terms of the metaphysical categories by means of which they interpreted God, and they made no effort to conceive God in terms of the metaphysical categories which they applied to the World. For them God was eminently real, and the World was derivatively real." He goes on to object that with this gulf between God and the world there is no way of knowing God, and that unqualified omnipotence must be responsible "for every detail of every happening".[7]

Whitehead's position concerning the function of metaphysics in the religious doctrine he is criticizing is the following: the conception of God as the eminently real exercising an absolute fiat over the world is a "metaphysical sublimation of the doctrine of God as the supreme agency of compulsion" whereby "he is transformed into the one supreme reality, omnipotently disposing a wholly derivative world".[8] Whitehead at least twice uses the term 'sublimation' in this connection. What happened was that the Semitic concept, which is "clear, terrifying and unprovable was supported by an unquestioned religious tradition. . . . It was also supported by the conservative instinct of society, and by a history and a metaphysic, both constructed expressly for that purpose. Moreover to dissent was death." While affirming that the metaphysic was constructed *ad hoc* to support the Semitic concept, Whitehead observes that "to some extent this was justifiable, because both history and metaphysics must presuppose some canons by which to guide themselves".[9]

We are faced then with the question whether there is such a thing as an independent metaphysics. Some observations about this issue may be pertinent here. There are two points which I think Whitehead does not quite sufficiently underline as essential to his argument. Both points are related to his evolutionary perspective and to certain assumptions he makes about the progress of civilization.

First, Whitehead assumes the possibility of progress in metaphysical understanding. He sees in the life of reason an instrument by which man can free himself from false conceptions. In contrast to Bergson, Whitehead sees reason as the supreme instrument of

<hr/>

[7] AI 217.   [8] AI 213; cf. AI 216–7.
[9] RM [75, 79].

creative advance in the universe, at least in that region of it where man lives.

The point to be noted is that while Whitehead acknowledges that every metaphysical doctrine has its origin in some particular human situation and is guided by some specific interests, he avoids complete relativism through the evolutionary assumption that there is a movement in man and in the universe itself toward a more spiritual, valid, and adequate expression of the good and the true. Whitehead clearly holds that there is such a tendency. He sees a factor in the Universe which constitutes a "general drive towards the conformation of Appearance to Reality". He asserts this against the Kantian doctrine that the conformation of appearance to understanding is derived from the structure of the mind without direct knowledge of the ultimately real. Such conformation Whitehead says is not 'necessary'. If it were necessary then "Morality would vanish . . . Art would also be a meaningless term. For it presupposes the efficacy of purpose."[10] The mind may fail in its grasp of the truth, but it has partial successes and these are supported by a function of the universe itself.

It is by this same evolutionary-metaphysical doctrine that Whitehead supports the appeal in metaphysics to the exceptional aspects of experience. He asks us to remember that "the present level of average waking human experience was at one time exceptional among the ancestors of mankind. We are justified therefore in appealing to those modes of experience which in our direct judgment stand above the average level."[11] These include Art and its gradual sublimation into Truth and Beauty, the sense of tragedy, the sense of evil and the persuasion towards Adventure beyond achieved perfection, the sense of Peace.[12]

The second important point to be noted here is that while Whitehead stresses the aesthetic categories, implicit within them is his appeal to moral intuition. It is here that the most important element in his protest against the divine Monarch appears. Whitehead's argument is that theological doctrine has lagged behind the fundamental ethical intuition both of Plato and of the Gospel itself. Plato came to the final conviction "that the divine element in the world is to be conceived as a persuasive agency and not as a a coercive agency". " . . . the power of Christianity lies in its revelation in act, of that which Plato divined in theory".[13]

[10] AI 378.   [11] AI 379–80.   [12] AI 380.   [13] AI 213, 214.

There are several aspects to this moral critique of the divine Monarch. One is that the traditional God as Whitehead sees the matter must be the direct cause of every happening in the world. Therefore he is as responsible for the evil as for the good. He is the direct cause of both. Whitehead accepts Hume's argument here and sees no answer to it in the tradition.

Again, if persuasion, as opposed to coercion, which Whitehead generally identifies with 'brute force', or sheer compulsion, is seen to be the mode of achievement of all high values then God must leave the creatures free in his action upon them or through them. It is not only that God must not be the cause of evil; but he must be conceived as exercising his metaphysical function in such a way that the higher goods are realized only through persuasion. In Whitehead's view the traditional Deity becomes a bulwark of tyranny, for he himself is a tyrant, and he subjugates his people by fear. "The Christian world (in the early period) was composed of terrified populations."[14] He quotes II Thessalonians here, with its announcement of the time when the Lord "in flaming fire will take vengeance on them that know not God, punishing them with everlasting destruction".[15]

It is not only the divine sanction of coercion which calls forth Whitehead's ethical protest, but he believes that it has been the source of the absolutizing of particular moral systems. "Moral codes have suffered from the exaggerated claims made for them. The dogmatic fallacy has here done its worst. Each such code has been put out by a God on a mountain top, or by a Saint in a cave, or by a divine Despot on a throne, or, at the lowest, by ancestors with a wisdom later beyond question. . . . The result is that the world is shocked or amused, by the sight of saintly old people hindering in the name of morality the removal of obvious brutalities from a legal system. Some *Acta Sanctorum* go ill with civilization."[16]

Whitehead extends his criticism not only to the specific content of moral codes but to legalistic religion itself which he believes is exposed by "keener ethical intuitions". "Every great religious teacher has revolted against the presentation of religion as a mere sanction of rules of conduct."[17]

He recognizes that judgment about a particular moral rule for

14 RM [75].   15 II Thessalonians i: 8–9.
16 AI 374.   17 SMW [274].

conduct varies from situation to situation and age to age.[18] But there is no question of the upward line of religion. "Gradually, slowly, steadily the vision recurs in history under nobler form and with clearer expression. It is the one element in human experience which persistently shows an upward trend. It fades and then recurs. . . ." The religious vision "claims nothing but worship".[19]

Whitehead nowhere seems to have taken the position that only persuasion is ever ethically justified. Writing in 1939, he said that "war, even if successful, can only increase the malignant excitement. The remedy is peace, fostering the slow growth of civilized feelings. War may be necessary to guard world civilization. But for Central Europe the effective remedy is peace." In the same essay he gives a realistic appraisal of the motives in modern nationalism none of which he says "is completely evil or completely good".[20] He expressed in 1931 his enthusiasm for the achievement of Lord Irwin and Gandhi in avoiding strife in India. In that year, he wrote: "We stand at a moment when the course of history depends upon the calm reasonableness arising from a religious public opinion." And he asks, "must religion always remain a synonym for hatred?"[21]

We might from one point of view say that Whitehead has declared for an 'ethical theism', resting upon the deepest intuitions both of Christianity and of certain major philosophical figures, especially Plato. We might accept this as a conclusion drawn from the general development of moral insight through the rise of civilization. Or we could regard it as one reflection of the impact of the Christian revelation upon the form of the human conscience, and agree that Whitehead here makes a protest against certain elements in the traditional doctrine of God which can be brought under the judgment of the Gospel itself.

But Whitehead does not leave the matter here. He argues that in metaphysical thought itself the corrective can be found for the errors in the tradition. Reason operating at the level of speculative metaphysics can demonstrate what is wrong with the traditional doctrine, reconstruct the conception of God so as to avoid these errors, and thus throw light on the questions with which Whitehead is left after he has exposed the monarchical Deity. How then is God

---

[18] AI 375.   [19] SMW [275].
[20] "An Appeal to Sanity", in *Essays in Science and Philosophy*, New York: Philosophical Library, 1947, p. 56.   [21] AI 221.

related to the actions of his creatures, and especially, how does he act effectively as the persuasive agency amidst the clash of brute force? Such questions must be answered if Whitehead is to justify his position, and they must be answered metaphysically. At least, the general metaphysical position must make the religious answers intelligible. It is this radical and superior role which Whitehead assigns to metaphysics which constitutes the method for his positive critique of the tradition. If Whitehead is right then metaphysics has a religious function which reaches to the centre of the Christian faith. Reason becomes the primary resource for the purification of inherited doctrine.

It is necessary therefore that we examine what Whitehead means by metaphysics, how he asserts his rational critique of the divine Monarch, and what he proposes to put in place of this conception of God.

II

Whitehead's definition of speculative philosophy identifies it with metaphysics. It is the "endeavour to frame a coherent, logical, necessary system of general ideas in terms of which every element of our experience can be interpreted".[22] This definition and its implications could be analysed at length, but for our purpose we may point to four aspects which bear directly on the significance of metaphysics for religious thought.

First, the validity of metaphysical generalization is tested by its adequacy to account for the wide range of evidence. "The chief danger to philosophy", Whitehead says, "is narrowness in the selection of evidence".[23] "The main sources of evidence ... are language, social institutions, and action, including thereby the fusion of the three which is language interpreting action and social institutions."[24]

The second aspect of metaphysical method is the search for rational coherence. The validity of a system is to be found in its general usefulness not in the peculiar clarity of its first principles, an important point where Whitehead reverses Descartes. Incoherence is "the arbitrary disconnection of first principles".[25] The coherence of the scheme is not simply its lack of logical inconsistency; but the interrelatedness of its concepts displaying the

[22] PR 3 [4].   [23] PR 477 [512].   [24] AI 291.   [25] PR 8 [9].

interfusion of the various modes or aspects of existence, with the eternal structures which are exemplified in them.

Third, the metaphysician seeking interpretation of the width of experience, should not neglect the special significance of the higher experiences, including those of religion. "Rational religion must have recourse to metaphysics for a scrutiny of its terms. At the same time it contributes its own independent evidence which metaphysics must take account of in framing its description."[26] When Whitehead elaborates his doctrine of God in *Process and Reality*, he says frankly that here thought depends upon "the elucidation of somewhat exceptional elements in our conscious experience", "those elements which may roughly be classed together as religious and moral intuitions".[27]

This point needs to be underlined as it bears on our main query in this paper. Whitehead is arguing for the possibility of a metaphysical critique of theology, but he does not argue for a metaphysical position which is constructed apart from the special intuitions of religious experience. We ask, Does this not give the whole scheme away to the historical variety of religious experiences? He concedes that all the versions of Christian thought could equally appeal to history. "The conclusion to be drawn from the appeal entirely depends upon the value-judgments guiding your selection, and upon the metaphysical presuppositions dictating your notions of a coherent theology."[28]

I have pointed earlier to the importance of Whitehead's conception of an evolutionary development integral to the nature of the universe as a defence against a purely relativistic answer to the question of the status of metaphysics. There are to be sure different value-judgments, and there may be different metaphysical presuppositions brought into the definition of the nature of coherence. But because we define coherence in a certain way there is no guarantee that we have achieved it. It is precisely the business of reason to raise the questions which necessarily must be raised about any doctrine, and to challenge it to exhibit its capacity to interpret coherently the wide ranges of experience. What persists through every doctrine about the nature of the world or God is the demand that it hold together in the light of all we know. It is the demand for an organically unifying interpretation of experience. If we ask where this demand comes from, and how it is justified, I

[26] RM [79].   [27] PR 486 [521].   [28] AI 211.

think Whitehead must agree that here we are at the faith of rationalism, a faith supported both by religious experience and by the nature of the world, but still a faith which cannot be absolutely justified by any amount of argument.

Once we grant, however, the necessity for coherent interpretation, we are involved in the discussion of what constitutes coherence and evidence, and we are open to the examination of the nature and results of metaphysical thinking.

We come then to the fourth point about metaphysics. Implicit in its search for coherent interpretation there is the requirement that God is not to be treated as an exception to all metaphysical principles; "he is their chief exemplification".[29]

This is a fundamental link in Whitehead's argument. If metaphysical principles are discoverable at all, they are descriptive of the constituent structures in all being. That is what it means to say they are metaphysical. But if they are genuinely so, then God's being cannot be exempt from them, else there is not being which he shares with the creatures, and hence no *analogia entis*, making rational discourse about God possible.

If coherent metaphysical doctrine can be derived at all, it can be shown what is required in a doctrine of God—and shown on the basis of metaphysical reason. This is Whitehead's claim. And it is his charge against the tradition that precisely here, while it had a metaphysical dimension in its doctrine of God, and indeed trembled on the edge of a major revision of the classical *ens realissimum* doctrine, it failed, and thereby fell into incoherence both in its own rational principles and in relation to its deepest religious intuitions.

I have deliberately used the term *analogia entis* here, for it raises the question of whether metaphysical principles are univocally applicable both to God and to creatures. This is a decisive question for Whitehead's thought because it can be shown without serious question that his doctrine of God does allow exceptions in the mode of God's being as distinct from the requirements laid upon the creatures. William Christian has shown this quite clearly with respect to God's experience of time in Whitehead's system.[30] We have therefore the question whether Whitehead can really

---

[29] PR 486 [521].
[30] William A. Christian, *An Interpretation of Whitehead's Metaphysics*, Yale University Press, 1959, pp. 292–4.

M*

escape some doctrine of *analogia entis*, some way, that is, of qualifying the application of metaphysical principles as applied to God. I will not dwell further on this point here; but reiterate the main thesis that however he qualifies his principle Whitehead intends to find community of being between God and the creatures. They share the ineluctable elements of the metaphysical situation. It is within this intention and its carrying out that he finds his primary means of criticism of the tradition and his clues as to its reconstruction.

There are three fundamental elements in what Whitehead finds in metaphysics to correct the tradition. Two of them are stated in the following quotation from *Adventures of Ideas*:

"What metaphysics requires is a solution exhibiting the plurality of individuals as consistent with the unity of the Universe, and a solution which exhibits the World as requiring its union with God, and God as requiring his union with the World. Sound doctrine also requires an understanding how the Ideals in God's nature, by reason of their status in his nature, are thereby persuasive elements in the creative advance. Plato grounded these derivations from God upon his will; whereas metaphysics requires that the relationships of God to the World should lie beyond the accidents of will, and that they be founded upon the necessities of the nature of God and the nature of the World."[31]

What grips our attention here is that twice Whitehead affirms that metaphysics requires such a solution, and once that "sound doctrine" requires it. That is, metaphysical reason, set free from the need to sublimate or defend the Divine Monarch, and attending strictly to the evidence in its width and depth leads us to a doctrine of God which does two things. First, it reconciles the unity and diversity of beings without denying either aspect.

It is not often observed how strictly Whitehead's metaphysical analysis is concerned with the traditional formulation of the problem of the One and the Many. Both are ineluctably given for metaphysical reason, and any solution which does not preserve and reconcile unity and diversity is false.

Hence, Whitehead is led to the somewhat startling conclusion that both God and the World are One and Many. He finds a reconciliation of unity and diversity in actual occasions which

[31] AI 215.

synthesize many prehensions into one definite unity of feeling. And he finds both unity and diversity in God who experiences the diversity of the world as a unity through his primordial aim, but whose unity of vision requires the absorption of the multiplicity of the world's effort.[32]

The second part of the argument has to do with the doctrine that process is metaphysically inescapable. Conceivably there could be a unity and diversity which was purely static, but Whitehead appeals to the experience of change. "If all things can be together, Why should there be process? ... How can the unchanging unity of fact generate the delusion of change? Surely, the satisfactory answer must embody an understanding of the interweaving of change and permanence, each required by the other. This interweaving is a primary fact of experience."[33] Here Whitehead appeals beyond diversity and unity as general concepts to an aspect of experience which he finds in all the diversity and unity we encounter.

When it is said then that metaphysics *requires* a certain solution, in what sense are we to take this? I think we have to say that Whitehead is appealing not to metaphysics as a pure and independent discipline which can completely and adequately correct every false notion, but rather to an enlargement of rational insight made possible by the freeing of the mind in certain cultural epochs to take a further look at experience. This freedom involves its escape from the necessity of protecting an inherited doctrine, and its willingness to re-examine experience.

The critical question is whether alternative metaphysical positions are possible. Whitehead, of course, does not deny that there have been alternative constructions. He makes the suggestion in *Modes of Thought* that the wavering of the metaphysical tradition on the reality of change is related to the fact that orthodox philosophic thought expressed the exhaustion following upon the first three thousand years of civilization, and he warns against philosophies which "express the dominant emotions of periods of slow social decay".[34]

There are some difficulties here for Whitehead's view of the purification of religion and ethics through metaphysics, for how does one judge what is a period of social decay and one of advance? Presumably this judgment itself requires a metaphysical insight. How is one to know then which philosophy one should be wary of? Is there not a circle here? Perhaps Whitehead's remark about 'exhaustion' is somewhat incidental to his main argument. He does believe in the gradual freeing of metaphysical intuition from origins which stamp it with the necessity of sublimating special and peculiar circumstances.

Anyone reading Whitehead's rational defence of democracy—"the basis of democracy is the common fact of value-experience, as constituting the essential nature of each pulsation of actuality"[35]—may well raise the question of whether the metaphysical requirement is the foundation of democracy or whether in this case the metaphysician's commitment to democracy is the key to his conclusions. I think it is clear that Whitehead must rely upon his more general assumption of an advance of creative reason, freeing itself from the distortions of its barbaric origin, and achieving a purification of insight through rational reflection upon wider and wider ranges of experience. Within this broad faith his argument has cogency. It is hard to deny that reason can expose rationalizations of particular social systems, through an appeal to wider experience. Scientific knowledge has demonstrated its capacity to check the world views in which religious feeling expresses itself, and the metaphysician has scientific knowledge as part of his data. Whitehead's polemic against the tradition then is not based upon an appeal to pure reason, but it is a perspective upon the meaning of experience developed within a particular cultural and historical situation, and appealing beyond this to considerations which are overlooked, concealed, or confused by certain elements in the traditional positions. At the very least one could say he shows the function of reason in opening up alternative ways of construing the world, ways which may have been closed off for centuries by the dogmas either of religion or of philosophy. Often the first step in the advance of insight is the demonstration that possible alternatives have been overlooked. Charles Hartshorne has expanded this thesis significantly.[36]

III

We turn then to the question of what Whitehead proposes in place of the traditional Monarch or Despot. Is a consistent meta-

35 MT 151.
36 Charles Hartshorne, *Man's Vision of God*, Chicago, 1941, Chap. 1.

physical doctrine of God possible which avoids the difficulties in these conceptions?

Without seeking here to expound Whitehead's full doctrine of God, I raise two questions about it which must be asked in the light of our major theme. Does Whitehead himself avoid the problem of the divine Despot? Is his God too arbitrary? And second, if he avoids the Despot, is his God too weak? It is necessary to ask both questions partly because of the complexity of Whitehead's doctrine, and partly because of the development of his position from God as the principle of concretion in *Science and the Modern World* to the later position in *Process and Reality*.

In the interpretation of God as the principle of concretion Whitehead proposes a doctrine of how God acts upon the world. There must be a limitation upon creativity antecedent to the course of events which involves conditions, particularization and standards of value. God is that limitation. No reason can be given for his nature, but as the principle of limitation he is the determining factor not only of the *how* of actualization but in regard to the *what* of fact.37

In *Process and Reality*, Whitehead keeps the principle of concretion, for God is "that actual entity from which each temporal concrescence receives that initial aim from which its self-causation starts".38 He is "the principle whereby there is initiated a definite outcome from a situation otherwise riddled with ambiguity".39

It is fair to ask whether the Monarch has not reappeared here in another guise. For if God by himself as an ultimate metaphysical fact contributes the initial aim to every creature, and is himself the sole principle by which a definite outcome is achieved in every occasion of experience, then it is possible to construe this as saying that God is another name for the fact that everything happens exactly as it happens. Whitehead, of course, throughout disavows the doctrine that God is the author of evil, but we have still to ask how evil gets into this universe if the sole principle of *whatness* is God's own nature.

Perhaps Whitehead anticipates this objection when he goes on in *Process and Reality* immediately after discussing the principle of concretion to say: "If we prefer the phraseology, we can say that God and the actual world jointly constitute the character of the creativity for the initial phase of the novel concrescence."40 To

37 SMW [256].   38 PR 345 [374].   39 PR 488 [523].   40 PR 346 [374].

which we must say, if we are to avoid the monarchical Deity we certainly must prefer this phraseology, for only in this way can that increment of freedom and self-decision for the creature in its relation to God be preserved.

I am not certain that Whitehead ever intended the doctrine of the principle of concretion to mean any more than that God is the ultimate structure which makes the unity of the world and of each creature possible at all. He offers only an ultimate adjustment of harmony as a lure for the creature, without finally determining the precise way in which the creature will respond. God as the principle of concretion is "never force", he says.[41]

We turn then to the developed doctrine of God in *Process and Reality* as having two polar aspects, the primordial nature and the consequent nature. And, we ask, how does this God act upon his world so as to be at once the redemptive agency and yet never the coercive monarch? And further, is this conception of God too weak to allow for the vital redemptive function?

God's primordial nature is his conceptual valuation of the entire realm of possibility with its eternal objects, its gradations of relevance, and its logical coherence.

God's consequent nature "results from his physical prehensions of the derivative actual entities".[42]

If we ask how God acts upon the world the answer is complex because it involves both poles of his being. The primordial nature acts as the lure for feeling. Every creature knows itself and its world through its grasp of the primordial nature of God. It participates in the realm of possibility with its order, and its grades of relevance. In his primordial nature God moves the world without being moved. He is experienced as the wealth of conceptual valuation, as he holds before each occasion its possible fulfilment in relation to all other occasions including that nontemporal actual occasion which is God himself.

So far the aspect of persuasion is carried to the limit by Whitehead, if our interpretation is correct that we allow for freedom in the creature in its concrete response to the initial aim which it derives wholly from God.

The consequent nature might at first view appear to be wholly passive. God derives his physical feeling, that is, his concrete feelings, initially "from the temporal world". In the static

41 SMW [276].   42 PR 42 [46].

majesty of his vision God absorbs the "World's multiplicity of effort".[43]

But it would be too simple to say that the consequent nature is constituted wholly by the world's action upon God, for it is, according to Whitehead, the "weaving of God's physical feelings upon his primordial concepts".[44] This means that in God the world's action receives its final unity, its immediacy is retained, and it is transformed by his wisdom.

There is something puzzling in Whitehead's doctrine here. What is it in God that functions to achieve this retention of the past and the transmutation of diversity into unity? Surely it cannot be merely his unconscious conceptual valuation of the realm of possibility, for this in itself has no transforming power except as it is responded to by concrete beings. And no creature in the world or the world as a whole has the power to achieve this retention in full. There must be a concreteness in God's nature which is his own actual feeling prehending the creatures, and lending his subjective and transforming aim to the way in which he experiences the world.

Leaving this objection for the moment, we can answer the question as to how the consequent nature of God is effective in the world. It is effective as it is experienced by the creatures. This occurs in two ways, I take it. First, through the mutual immanence of all occasions the creatures have an experience, however dim, of God's consequent nature as the felt union of immediacy of the world without loss or obstruction.[45] Here the widsom which uses the wreckage in the temporal world, which saves everything which can be saved, and which passes a judgment upon the world is known directly. Thereby the creature's feelings are transformed through participation in the transformation which takes place initially in God.

Second, there is the love of God for the world which passes back into the world, again through our experience of him. It is the particular providence for particular occasions. Here Whitehead's use of the term 'providence' suggests specific divine action. God's love "floods back again into the world".[46] But the divine activity is interpreted by Whitehead as the holding before the creature of the ultimate possibility of transmutation of present evil into some real good. In *Religion in the Making*, Whitehead says: "This

43 PR 489 [524], 494 [530]; cf. 491–2 [527]. 44 PR 488 [524].
45 PR 489 [524]. 46 PR 497 [532].

transmutation of evil into good enters into the actual world by reason of the inclusion of the nature of God, which includes the ideal vision of each actual evil so met with a novel consequent as to issue in the restoration of goodness."[47] We must insist that for Whitehead this "restoration of goodness" is not without its tragic aspect. God is "the fellow-sufferer who understands".[48] He does not deny the reality of evil, but only its finality as resisting all transformation into good.

The question to be raised here is whether Whitehead's account of the divine causality leaves God without concrete power in the world. Put in another way, is whatever power God has exercised only through the creature's experience of the divine wisdom and compassion which are in themselves passive to the world's effort? If this view be held strictly, Whitehead has solved the difficult problem of keeping from assigning some specific effect in nature to the direct causality of God by asserting that God acts only as a lure for feeling, as object of experience, not as one efficient cause among others. But if this be the doctrine, the result is that God acts only by persuasive disclosure of a vision of the transformation in himself of the happenings in the world. He sets certain limits to the creatures and absorbs the world's activities in a certain way. But does he act with power to transform the world beyond presenting it with an ideal aim?

We may ask if Whitehead has replaced the Arbitrary Monarch with a Constitutional Monarch, who to be sure is unlimited in his power to establish the general constitutional conditions for the world's action; but who after having made the initial address to the cosmic parliament, only waits to receive reports as to what his subjects do, and who then is able to see all the concrete acts of the subjects as having an ultimate unity in his divine perspective. My question concerns the divine initiative in history and the way in which it is exercised. Does God only listen or does he speak?

As one thinks of the alternatives in Christian theology, Whitehead's doctrine here seems to me most at home in spirit if not in detail in certain strands of modern Russian theology and in Berdyaev's thought, in which the action of God is seen in the divine humility on the Cross. This is taken as the standard and criterion of all divine action. Persuasion is finally identified as the key to the meaning of love, and the solitary route to redemption. I

[47] RM [155].   [48] PR 497 [532].

mention this as an indication that similar theological outlooks can be developed from rather different metaphysical premises. This is not an argument against the use of metaphysical analysis, but a caution that in any metaphysical system there may be at work a fundamental religious orientation which can achieve articulation in more than one way.

IV

Any simple judgment either on Whitehead's method or his conclusions ought to be immediately suspect. It is a philosophy woven of many strands. He is highly self-conscious as to its sources and criteria, and is disarmingly candid as to the openness of its conclusions. His critique of the Christian doctrine of God is so forthright and so radical that it cannot be ignored by any contemporary theology or religious philosophy which seeks the relevance of religious faith to contemporary culture. I have shown that Whitehead raises very sharply the issue for every theism of how God's action in and upon the world is intelligible.

Two points deserve further comment in conclusion. The first concerns the extent to which Whitehead's critique of the tradition rests upon metaphysics, and the second involves two aspects of the doctrine of God which he proposes as an advance beyond the tradition.

First, Whitehead's method affords opportunity for an important case study in the possibility and the limits of speculative metaphysics as a means of criticism of religious doctrine. It is clear that there is no presuppositionless search for the categories of being, nor is there any purely rational standard to which particular religious doctrines must be brought for judgment. Whitehead seems to acknowledge this in his descriptions of metaphysical method, but he sometimes puts it in such a rationalistic way that the real status of metaphysical reflection is obscured. Is it really clear for example that both the advance of reason and the development of religion show a persistent upward trend? And is not the judgment as to what is *advance* the central problem?

Further, it is possible in judging any metaphysical system to analyse its special presuppositions. Whitehead always calls for this. But we may ask if he has fully applied it to this ethical preference for persuasion which he sees not only as a high value but as the definition of the true nature of all existential striving toward a higher good? It may be that his preference for persuasion as an ethical value led him to an analysis of the nature of God and of his relationship to the world which projects this value as metaphysically ultimate. What does the evidence say about this so far as we can see?

The coercive aspects of being seem as necessary to a real universe as the persuasive aspects if we are to speak accurately about the mode of existence, the relationships, the functioning and the fulfilment of actual occasions. To say this is not to argue for brute force and coercion as ethical norms, but to recognize a fact of experience. Granted all the 'tendernesses' in life (Whitehead's term), no organism would survive five seconds on the exercise of tenderness alone. Whitehead's doctrine, moreover, leads him to ignore the wide ranges of types of force, of coercion, and of mutual interaction. These would seem to have their place in the necessities of being, and therefore require us to find their place in God's being.

The conclusion is warranted then that every metaphysical system is a function of the perspective in which the data are seen as well as of the data themselves. This is not to deny the necessity or relevance of metaphysical doctrines. I would defend the view that there is no reflective interpretation of man's life which does not involve metaphysical structure. But the point is that a metaphysical system has the status of a partially tested hypothesis. In the judgment of its adequacy there come into play elements in the human apprehension of the world which are not derived from metaphysical reflection or a wide survey of experience, but from specific faiths, decisions, and orientations which have within them elements both of historical fate and of personal evaluation.

When we turn to the question of how God acts upon the world we see that Whitehead has thrown important light upon some aspects of this perplexing problem. He has shown how abstract structure can be causally efficacious, and with his doctrine of the mutual immanence of God and the creatures he has developed a conception of how God's way of having his world may in turn enter into the way in which the creatures experience both the world and God.

But it still may be that Whitehead has underestimated the disclosure of the divine initiative in religious experience. I believe it can be shown that he has not carried through with his metaphysical method fully in his interpretation of the being of God. It is precisely in that aspect of God which makes him a fully actual, effective subject where Whitehead seems not to make clearly the affirmations which he needs to complete his doctrine. I suggest that it is because Whitehead has reacted so justifiably against the divine Monarch that he has given a partially inadequate account of the relation between God and the world.

This means that a doctrine of God on Whitehead's own standard will have to analyse the problem of the means of action, and the forms of causal efficacy. A way must be found to deal with the uniqueness and the analogical character of the divine causality. Most modern theology seems to have agreed that Calvin's assignment of efficient causality to God in every detail of existence is impossible.[49] But we still have to interpret that aspect of the total religious problem which Calvin saw clearly, the priority, the initiative, and the efficacy of the divine power. It is not surprising that the difficulties of this problem drive many to the assertion that God's action is not in any way subject to metaphysical analysis. But how then can we call it 'act'?

Finally, there is an aspect of Whitehead's critique which does appear convincing against the divine Monarch, when he affirms the suffering of God. Here is Whitehead's primary objection to the traditional God who has no way of reacting to the world for reaction would mean change. Whitehead's God is not in this difficulty, for every phase of his experience invokes a specific response to the concrete activities of the creatures.

There remains a question as to whether Whitehead's God may fail to find anything less than complete satisfaction in every moment of the world's course. Stephen Ely interprets him as saying that God sees every evil as completely contributory to ultimate good and declares that "it is not likely to give anyone much comfort to know that, no matter what happens in this world, God can see it in an ideal setting that makes it an enjoyable sight".[50]

This criticism must be taken seriously by any Whiteheadian. William Christian holds that for Whitehead no actual occasion can alter the intensity of God's satisfaction.[51] Does this mean that for God the world is a fully realized value at every moment? Satisfac-

[49] John Calvin, *Institutes of the Christian Religion*, Philadelphia, 1936, Book II, Ch. 4; Book III, Ch. 21, 5.
[50] S. L. Ely, *The Religious Availability of Whitehead's God*, Madison: University of Wisconsin Press, 1942, p. 41.   [51] Christian, *op. cit.*, p. 360.

tion, we must note, is a technical term in Whitehead's philosophy. It means the definite outcome of a particular concrescence. Does the measure of intensity of satisfaction then mean that every happening in the world simply confirms an absolute quantum of desire in the divine reality? If this were the real meaning of Whitehead's doctrine, one might charge that he has turned the divine Despot into the divine Aesthete who lacks an adequate principle of discrimination and distils a complete satisfaction out of every spectacle no matter how terrible. William Christian is suggesting an alternative explanation, I think, when he says that the *qualitative pattern* of God's satisfaction varies with the advance of nature while the intensity of his satisfaction is invariant.[52]

The consideration which really corrects Ely's interpretation seems to be this, that while intensity of satisfaction is in the aim of God as in that of every creature, God's aim includes in an absolute love the good of the creatures. His aim for each creature is "depth of satisfaction as an intermediate step toward the fulfilment of his own being".[53] Now it is clear enough that the creatures' satisfactions vary in depth. Any creature may fail to realize a creative harmony within itself, with the other creatures, and with God. It may, tragically, end in self-destruction of various kinds. In some sense, all creatures thus fail. This must mean a genuine loss for God. That which the divine wills absolutely has not come to pass, whatever further good he may bring out of the wreckage. This is to say that Whitehead keeps the tragic element in the divine nature: "Peace is the understanding of tragedy, and at the same time its preservation."[54]

At a critical point therefore Whitehead has transformed the unfeeling and unmoved Monarch into "the fellow-sufferer who understands". That this can be done in a coherent, intelligible metaphysical structure is a great gain for Christian theology which has been burdened for centuries with the Platonic doctrine of the divine impassibility. Whitehead's philosophy is highly relevant to the quest for a theology in which biblical faith will have intelligible expression.

Whitehead once remarked that Christianity is a religion in search of a metaphysic.[55] One may judge from his work that the search must continue, but it is not fruitless.

---

[52] Christian, *op. cit.*, p. 359. (Italics mine.)   [53] PR 147 [161].
[54] AI 368.   [55] RM [50].

NOTES ON CONTRIBUTORS

WILLIAM A. CHRISTIAN is Associate Professor of Religion in Yale University.

Author of *An Interpretation of Whitehead's Metaphysics* (1959), and of *Meaning and Truth in Religion* (forthcoming). Articles in various philosophical and theological journals.

Contributor to *A Companion to the Study of St. Augustine* (1955).

FREDERIC B. FITCH is Professor of Philosophy in Yale University. Guggenheim Fellowship 1945-6; Chairman of the Committee on the Communication Sciences; President of the Association for Symbolic Logic (1959-   ).

Author of *Mathematico-Deductive Theory of Rote Learning* (with others, 1940), *Symbolic Logic: An Introduction* (1950). Articles in various philosophical journals.

Consulting Editor, *Journal of Symbolic Logic*.

CHARLES HARTSHORNE is Professor of Philosophy in Emory University. He was Terry Lecturer, Yale University, 1947; Visiting Professor at Goethe University, Frankfurt, 1948-9; Fulbright Lecturer, University of Melbourne, 1952; Fulbright Lecturer, Kyoto University, 1958.

Editor (with Paul Weiss) of *The Collected Papers of Charles Sanders Peirce* (Vols. I-VI). Editor (with Gottfried Martin and Ivor Leclerc) of a forthcoming German Edition of the philosophical writings of A. N. Whitehead.

Author of *The Philosophy and Psychology of Sensation* (1934), *Beyond Humanism* (1937), *Man's Vision of God* (1941), *The Divine Relativity* (1948), *Whitehead and the Modern World* (with Victor Lowe and A. H. Johnson, 1950), *Reality as Social Process* (1953), *Philosophers Speak of God* (with W. L. Reese, 1953).

Contributor to *Philosophical Essays for Alfred North Whitehead* (1936), *Philosophical Essays in Memory of Edmund Husserl* (1940), *The Philosophy of George Santayana* (1940), *The Philosophy of Alfred North Whitehead* (1941), *Science, Philosophy, and Religion* (2nd Symposium, 1942), *History of Philosophical Systems* (1950), *Structure, Method, and Meaning: Studies in Honor of Henry M. Sheffer* (1951), *Studies in the Philosophy of Charles Sanders Peirce* (1952), *The Philosophy of Sarvepalli Radhakrishnan* (1952), *The Theology of Paul Tillich* (1952), *American Philosophers at Work* (1956), *Religion and Culture: Essays in Honor of Paul Tillich* (1959).

Many articles in philosophical, religious, and scientific journals.

A. H. JOHNSON is Professor of Philosophy and Head of the Department of Philosophy in the University of Western Ontario.

Author of *Whitehead's Theory of Reality* (1952), *Whitehead's Philosophy of Civilization* (1958), and many articles on Whitehead's philosophy in various journals.

Editor and co-author (with Charles Hartshorne and Victor Lowe) of *Whitehead and the Modern World* (1950).

Editor of *The Wit and Wisdom of Whitehead* (1947), *The Wit and Wisdom of Dewey* (1949), *Whitehead's American Essays in Social Philosophy* (1960), *Whitehead's Interpretation of Science* (forthcoming).

NATHANIEL LAWRENCE is Professor of Philosophy and Chairman of the Department of Philosophy in Williams College, Mass.

Author of *Whitehead's Philosophical Development* (1956), and of articles in various philosophical journals.

IVOR LECLERC is Lecturer in Logic and Metaphysics in the University of Glasgow. Visiting Professor in the University of Bonn, 1961.

Editor (with Gottfried Martin and Charles Hartshorne) of a forthcoming German Edition of the philosophical writings of A. N. Whitehead.

Author of *Whitehead's Metaphysics: An Introductory Exposition* (1958), and of articles in various philosophical journals.

Translator (with Eva Schaper) of Gottfried Martin's *Einleitung in die Allgemeine Metaphysik*, forthcoming as *An Introduction to General Metaphysics*.

VICTOR LOWE is Associate Professor of Philosophy at the Johns Hopkins University.

Co-author (with Charles Hartshorne and A. H. Johnson) of *Whitehead and the Modern World* (1950).

Author of the Whitehead section in *Classic American Philosophers* (1951), of the essay on "Whitehead's Philosophical Development" in *The Philosophy of Alfred North Whitehead* (1941), and of many articles on Whitehead's philosophy.

Contributor to *The Philosophy of C. I. Lewis* (forthcoming).

GOTTFRIED MARTIN is Professor of Philosophy in the University of Bonn.

Editor of *Kant-Studien*; Chairman of the *Kant-Gesellschaft* (Landesgruppe Rheinland-Westfalen). Editor (with Ivor Leclerc and Charles Hartshorne) of a forthcoming German Edition of the philosophical writings of A. N. Whitehead.

Author of *Wilhelm von Ockham* (1949), *Immanuel Kant: Ontologie und Wissenschaftstheorie* (1951; English translation *Kant's Metaphysics and Theory of Science*, 1955) *Klassische Ontologie der Zahl* (1954),

Einleitung in die Allgemeine Metaphysik (1957; forthcoming English translation, *An Introduction to General Metaphysics*), *Leibniz: Logik und Metaphysik* (1960). Articles in various philosophical journals.

W. MAYS is Senior Lecturer in Philosophy in the University of Manchester.

Author of *The Philosophy of Whitehead* (1959), and of articles in various philosophical and scientific journals. He is at present preparing a work on *The Epistemology of Piaget*.

EVA SCHAPER is Lecturer in Philosophy in the University of Glasgow.

Assistant Editor of a forthcoming German Edition of the philosophical writings of A. N. Whitehead; has translated Whitehead's *Religion in the Making*, *Function of Reason*, and *Symbolism*, as Volume VII of this Edition.

Translator (with Ivor Leclerc) of Gottfried Martin's *Einleitung in die Allgemeine Metaphysik*, forthcoming as *An Introduction to General Metaphysics*.

Articles in various philosophical journals.

HERMANN WEIN is Professor of Philosophy and 'Lehrbeauftragter für Philosophische Anthropologie' in the University of Göttingen. He was Rockefeller Foundation and Harvard University Research Fellow (1951-2); Visiting Professor in Istanbul, 1957; and has been invited to be Visiting Professor in Andhra University, India.

Author of *Das Problem des Relativismus* (1950), *Zugang zu philosophischer Kosmologie* (1954), *Realdialektik* (1957), and of articles in various philosophical journals.

PAUL WEISS is Professor of Philosophy in Yale University. He was Mahlon Powell Lecturer in the University of Indiana, 1958.

Editor of *The Review of Metaphysics*, and Editor (with Charles Hartshorne) of *The Collected Papers of Charles Sanders Peirce* (Vols. I-VI).

Author of *Reality* (1938), *Nature and Man* (1947), *Man's Freedom* (1950), *Modes of Being* (1958), *Our Public Life* (1959), *The World of Art* (forthcoming), *Nine Basic Arts* (forthcoming).

Contributor to *American Philosophy Today and Tomorrow* (1935), *Philosophical Essays for Alfred North Whitehead* (1936), *Science, Philosophy, and Religion* (1st and 2nd Vols. 1941, 1942), *Moral Principles of Action* (1952), *Studies in the Philosophy of Charles Sanders Peirce* (1952), *A. R. Wadia: Essays in Philosophy presented in his Honor* (1954), *American Philosophers at Work* (1956), *Determinism and Freedom* (1958). Many articles in philosophical journals.

WILLIAM P. D. WIGHTMAN is Reader in the History and Philosophy of Science in the University of Aberdeen.

Author of *Science and Monism* (1934), *The Growth of Scientific Ideas* (1950), *Science and the Renaissance* (forthcoming), and of articles and reviews in various philosophical, scientific and other journals.

DANIEL DAY WILLIAMS is Roosevelt Professor of Systematic Theology in the Union Theological Seminary, New York. He is American Editor, Library of Constructive Theology, and Chairman of the Committee on Research and Counsel of the American Association of Theological Schools.

Editor of *The Ministry in Historical Perspectives* (1956).

Author of *The Andover Liberals* (1941), *God's Grace and Man's Hope* (1949), *What Present Day Theologians are Thinking* (1952, revised 1959; English title *Interpreting Theology*), and of articles in various theological journals.

Co-author of *The Advancement of Theological Education* (1957).

Contributor to *A Companion to the Study of St. Augustine* (1955), and *Reinhold Niebuhr, His Religious, Social, and Political Thought* (1956).

INDEX

GEORGE ALLEN & UNWIN LTD.
London: 40 Museum Street, W.C.1

Auckland: 24 Wyndham Street
Sydney, N.S.W.: Bradbury House, 55 York Street
Cape Town: 109 Long Street
Bombay: 15 Graham Road, Ballard Estate, Bombay 1
Calcutta: 17 Chittaranjan Avenue, Calcutta 13
New Delhi: 13–14 Ajmeri Gate Extension, New Delhi 1
Karachi: Karachi Chambers, McLeod Road
Mexico: Villalongin 32-10, Piso, Mexico 5, D.F.
Toronto: 91 Wellington Street West
São Paulo: Avenida 9 de Julho 1138–Ap. 51
Buenos Aires: Escritorio 454-459, Florida 165
Singapore: 36c Princep Street, Singapore
Hong Kong: 1/12 Mirador Mansions, Kowloon